ENGLISH COMPLEX SENTE
An introduction to systemic gr

NORTH-HOLLAND
LINGUISTIC SERIES

4

Edited by S. C. DIK and J. G. KOOIJ

ENGLISH
COMPLEX SENTENCES

An introduction to systemic grammar

R. A. HUDSON

Department of Phonetics and Linguistics
University College London

NORTH-HOLLAND PUBLISHING COMPANY
AMSTERDAM • NEW YORK • OXFORD

425
H886e

Library of Congress Catalog Card Number 74-157031

ISBN 0 7204 6183 9

1st Edition 1972
2nd Printing 1973
3rd Printing 1978

PRINTED IN THE NETHERLANDS

To Gay

PREFACE

In this book I have tried to explain both what systemic grammar is, and why it should be considered as a serious rival to the transformational-generative kind of grammar.

For some ten years a number of linguists in Britain have been developing this model (once called the 'Scale and category' model), and have been writing grammars in terms of it; the published articles and books describing this work include: Catford, 1965; Dixon, 1964; Halliday, 1961, 1963, 1964, 1966a, 1966b, 1969a; Halliday et al., 1964; Huddleston, 1965; Huddleston and Uren, 1969; Hudson, 1967, 1970; Leech, 1966; Scott et al., 1968; Sinclair, 1965. However, since Halliday's 1961 article, 'Categories of the theory of grammar', there has been no comprehensive description of the theory, attempting to explain and justify its underlying assumptions and principles. I have tried to provide such a description in this book.

Moreover, the field of linguistics as a whole has changed a lot in the past ten years, and a number of us in University College London have tried to take account of the major changes — and in particular, of the reorientation of linguistics towards the goal of generativeness. In the summer of 1967 there was a series of discussions involving Michael Halliday, Rodney Huddleston, Kenneth Albrow, Alick Henrici and myself, in which we tried to develop the theory, as we then saw it, so that we could use it as the basis for generative grammars. The results of these discussions have been reported only rather briefly, in Halliday, 1969a; and this book can be seen as a belated attempt to make the more recent developments in systemic theory available.

I owe a lot to these and other discussions which I had with my colleagues, particularly Rodney Huddleston and Michael Halliday. Nevertheless I should like to make it clear that I have found it necessary to make several major changes to the model, and that none of my colleagues would accept all that

I say in this book. So the fact that they contributed in one way or another to this theory of grammar does not necessarily mean that they would wish to be associated with this or, for that matter, any other version of systemic theory. However, I believe that in most respects this version of systemic theory represents the current views of Michael Halliday, and will give a clear idea of the theoretical background to his more recent writings on the functions of language (e.g. 1967a, b, 1968, 1969b, 1971).

It is fair to expect of any new theory of grammar that we should be able to use it in writing generative grammars for natural languages. In order to show that this is indeed possible with this systemic theory, I have included a detailed and comprehensive grammar for English sentences that contain noun-clauses. This area of grammar includes a fair number of the complexities that we can expect in natural languages — discontinuity and 'understood' elements, for instance; so if I have succeeded in writing a generative grammar for it, then systemic theory will have passed a fairly stiff test. I leave it to the reader to decide whether I have succeeded or not.

Finally I should like to explain how this book came to be written. In 1967 I helped to write a research report (Huddleston et al., 1968), by writing the section dealing with constructions involving clauses coòrdinated or subordinated to each other. Rodney Huddleston has since rewritten the section for which he was responsible (Huddleston, forthcoming), and in 1968 I wrote most of the first draft of a book covering the topics that I had dealt with in the report, but in a more generative way. This book was to have included an introductory chapter on systemic theory, and in 1969 I rewrote this chapter, but it turned into a monograph, 'Grammar in use', which was read and criticised by the following: Dwight Bolinger, Fred Castro, Simon Dik, Sidney Greenbaum, Michael Halliday, Alick Henrici, Rodney Huddleston, Felicien Planchon and Randolph Quirk. To all these people I am very grateful, but it became clear from their comments that I ought to show that systemic theory was capable of handling large and complex areas of grammar, so I added grammars for English complex sentences and non-finite clauses. These grammars made some major theoretical changes necessary, and these in turn demanded changes in the theoretical chapters, so the result is once again a different book. I hope that those who gave me their comments will not feel that their time was wasted.

And last but not least I should like to express my admiration to Miss Sally Averill for turning a decidedly tricky manuscript into a presentable typescript, and to thank my wife Gay for encouraging me to finish it during the last few hectic months.

R.A.Hudson   Bloomsbury, 1970

CONTENTS

1. INTRODUCTION

1.1. The aims of systemic grammar

There seems to be a large measure of agreement among linguists on the aims of a linguistic theory, but it is rather easy for common ground to be forgotten in the dispute over methods for achieving these aims. In what follows there will probably be points at which the reader will disagree with the methods that I have to offer, and if the reader is accustomed to the transformational-generative (TG) way of doing things his tolerance is likely to be severely tested — for one thing, both transformations and the distinction between deep structure and surface structure will be dispensed with. This being so, it is a good thing to start by stressing the common aims of this version of systemic theory and of the various current versions of TG theory. It goes without saying that as far as many of these aims are concerned I am indebted to Chomsky for their formulation, to much the same extent as any practitioners of TG grammar are.

The universality of the theory

In the most general terms, the aim of systemic grammar is to provide a framework within which the grammar of any natural language can be described. In the first place the framework must of necessity be very general and unspecific, and will simply specify the *kinds* of information that a grammar will include, and how the various kinds of information will be related. For TG theory, the 'framework' consists inter alia of a number of 'components' and a definition of the kinds of relations that are found within and between these components; for systemic theory the content of the framework is comparable, although in detail it is not the same. The first two chapters of this book are intended to describe this general framework that systemic theory defines, so there is no need to say more about it here.

1

This general model of grammar should be empirically based, in the sense that it should arise out of attempts to describe natural languages: each version of the model is provisional and will be modified, or abandoned entirely, if we find an area of grammar in some language which it cannot handle satisfactorily. Needless to say, this applies to the version of the model which is described here just as much as to any of the earlier versions which it has superseded: it seems to be able to accommodate the facts that we have to describe in relation to English complex sentences better than any of the earlier models which I have tried, but it is more than likely that it will need modification when we come to apply it to some other area of English grammar or to the grammar of another language.

One way of making sure that one's theory fits the facts that it has to accommodate is to develop a different theory for each body of facts — to have one model for English and another for Eskimo, or even one for English complex sentences and another for English compound sentences. In the long run it may prove necessary to do just this, but it is too early to be certain that there is no way of avoiding it, and in the absence of convincing evidence to the contrary it is more satisfying to try to develop a single theoretical model which will work equally well for all languages and all areas of grammar within each language. One very good reason for seeing the present version of systemic theory as only provisional and open to improvement is that it has been developed mainly out of work on English syntax. Work on other languages, or on English morphology (for instance) may bring serious shortcomings to light. Nevertheless, what follows should be seen as an attempt to provide a model which is equally suitable for all aspects of grammar in all languages.

I said above that the framework provided by systemic theory must in the first place be very general and non-specific. That is, it defines the overall structure that grammars must have, by defining the kinds of categories that must appear in them and the way in which these are related to each other in the grammar; for instance, according to systemic theory a grammar will define a large number of 'features' and a large number of 'functions', and these must be related to each other in the ways defined by the theory. Again, it is possible that in the course of time we shall be able to make the framework more specific, so that it specifies not only what *kinds* of category must occur in any grammar, but also some of the particular categories that must occur. This might mean that a term such as 'noun' or 'clause' would be as much a part of the theory as is 'feature'. It might also mean that the theory would define a certain number of broad 'functional components', such as those referred to as 'interpersonal', 'ideational' and 'textual' by Halliday (1971, et passim), which would correspond to major self-defining areas of the grammar. Both of these possibilities look promising and attractive, but it seems to me still too early to do much more than speculate about them.

In Chomskyan terms, then, I shall be postulating certain *formal* universals of grammar, but I shall avoid making any claims about *substantive* universals. We can make the same distinction in Halliday's terms: what is universal are the *theoretical* categories, whilst the *descriptive* categories, including those like 'noun' and 'clause', are to be thought of as language-specific.

We can assume that the more successful a model of grammar of this kind is, the closer will be its relation to the way in which language is stored in the human brain; and that the more successful a particular grammar is, the nearer it will come to representing, in some abstract sense, some part of the native speaker's knowledge of his language. Clearly it is only one part that is represented by the grammar: other parts will be represented by the description of the language's semantic structure and by the description of the ways in which language forms are related to socially defined situations. But the part represented by the grammar is a very important — and interesting — part and we can expect to learn something about the human mind from a study of grammar in general and of particular grammars.

The evaluation of grammars

What the word 'successful' means in the last paragraph is, of course, one of the big questions of linguistic theory, and one for which systemic theory cannot give any easy answer. Certainly a grammar's success does not depend on the procedures by which the linguist brought it to its final state — in other words, 'discovery procedures' are of no more interest to those using systemic theory than for transformationalists. Given then, that one's approach to the evaluation of grammars has to be 'synchronic' rather than 'diachronic', there are a number of other criteria that one might take into account.

On the one hand one might assume that each grammar is constructed for some particular practical purpose, and evaluate it according to the results it produced: thus a particular grammar could be relatively successful as the basis for a foreign language teaching programme, but unsuccessful when applied in the diagnosis of aphasia. On the other hand, however, one might believe that one was in some sense aspiring to capture 'the truth' about a language, so that each grammar should be measured against the same absolute yardstick: how true is it?

In choosing between these two approaches the linguist is presumably bound to be guided by general aesthetic and philosophical considerations that are not specific to the study of language. I myself tend to favour the second approach, and to believe – or at least to hope – that the 'truth' to which our grammars approximate has to do with the way in which the native speaker's knowledge of his language's grammar is stored in his brain. This is at least the assumption underlying the various bits of grammar offered in this book, although there are some aspects of these which I know to be untrue, and had to include for the sake of brevity or because the truth would have taken many more years of research to find. However, it is possible that the more we investigate language the further we shall move from the idea of grammar as a single structure waiting to be discovered and described; so adopting the second, 'God's truth', hypothesis is simply a convenient starting point for the study of grammar, pending the discovery of conclusive evidence one way or the other.

However, even if we assume that there is one thing which every grammar of a particular language is trying to describe, it is not easy to decide which of two grammars is the more successful in doing so. Clearly there are certain general characteristics that we can expect of a grammar: generality, comprehensiveness, elegance, simplicity, economy, and so on. These are the kinds of qualities which I have tried to achieve for the grammar in chapters 3 and 5, but it is not always easy to see how to balance one quality against another when they conflict.

The data of grammar

A grammar is intended to describe some of the 'facts' of some language, so we can expect that it should in some sense be empirically testable. The question is, how do we test it? Or, to put the problem from the point of view of the *constructer* of the grammar, what kinds of data do we take into account? If one takes a corpus as one's only source of data, there are problems: how to generalise from the corpus, how to distinguish slips of the tongue, anacolutha and so on from the 'good' parts of the corpus. But if one uses 'informants' then a lot of data will be indeterminate: some sentences are marginally grammatical, others may or may not be taken as grammatically ambiguous according to taste, and so on. Taking account of the views of large numbers of informants does not make the indeterminacy less than if one used oneself as informant, as the investigations of Quirk and his colleagues have shown (Greenbaum and Quirk, 1970 and references therein).

Moreover, acceptibility varies according to situation. For instance, the *having been -en* form of 'reduced relative' clause occurs in 'officialese':

> Those having been vaccinated more than five years ago
> should apply for a further vaccination,

whereas in other contexts the relative clause would simply have an -en form verb:

> People vaccinated more than five years ago really ought to
> go and get themselves done again.

One might restrict oneself to taking account of the informant's views on grammaticality and ambiguity, and try to ignore everything else that he 'knows' about utterances (though this is difficult in practice when one is acting as one's own informant). In fact, however, one tends to take far more than this into account. To take a simple example, the informant can tell us that the 'factuality' of the italicized clause is the same in both the following:

> He realised *that he'd missed the turning,*
> He didn't realise *that he'd missed the turning.*

Similarly the informant can distinguish between the grammatical form that smacks of 'officialese' and the other one, in the previous example. What conclusions one should draw from such information is a separate question; but there is no obvious reason for ignoring it, or pretending to ignore it, as a matter of principle.

If we are trying in some way to reflect the native speaker's knowledge of his language's grammar in our grammatical description, then our problem is not only how to *discover* what he 'knows', but also how to *formalise* it. All formalised linguistic theories that we have at present, including the systemic one, face the same problem here: human beings can cope with 'messiness' in their language, but linguists cannot. The problems of distinguishing between utterances that are grammatical or acceptable and those that are not are too well known to discuss here. We shall come up against this problem in a big way, for instance, in deciding which lexical verbs and adjectives can occur in which constructions (see 4.2.15 and appendix), but I shall do no more than acknowledge it and act as though it did not exist. To the extent that a grammatical theory is more rigid than the human mind, it must be inadequate. Systemic theory seems to suffer from this shortcoming as other theories do.

Deep and surface

It goes without saying that we are concerned to just the same extent with 'deep' and with 'surface' phenomena, since these are equally a part of the native speaker's knowledge of his language. For instance, if we set out to describe the constructions involved in sentences like

What did he say had happened?

we must show that *what* is the subject of the subordinate clause, and we
might consider this fact relatively 'deep'; and also that the conjunction *that*
is impossible in constructions of this kind, although it would have been possible if *what* had been object of the subordinate clause, a relatively 'surface'
phenomenon:

> * What did he say that had happened?
> What did he say that he wanted?

This raises a terminological point, however: the meaning of 'grammar'. In
systemic terminology, 'grammar' is the name of the level of language which
includes syntax and morphology, but it does not include either phonology
on the one hand, nor lexis or semantics on the other. So the deepest facts
about language, and also the most surface, are outside the province of
grammar as such, and the task of grammar is to provide a satisfactory account
of the relation between them; this means that the grammatical account must
be deep enough to make contact with the semantics, and surface enough to
make contact with the phonology, and both deep and surface enough to make
contact with the lexis.

Where the dividing line between semantic, lexical or phonological phenomena and grammatical phenomena should be drawn is a separate question;
indeed, it is still an open question whether there should be a clear division
between grammar and semantics or lexis at all. Until the actual content of a
semantic description becomes clearer, it is premature to try to formulate any
general principles for deciding what kinds of phenomena to assign to it and
what kinds to put in the grammatical description — and similarly for phonological descriptions. All that I can say is that I have assumed that grammar *is*
separate from lexis, semantics and phonology, and have used what I consider
linguistic 'common sense' to decide what should be included in grammar. The
reader is of course entitled to disagree with my decisions.

If we take the narrower definition of grammar, where it includes just
syntax and morphology, then there is still a sense in which the aim of the
grammar is to generate pairings of semantic and phonetic representations
(Chomsky, 1967: 398, et passim): the semantic and phonetic representations
are themselves generated by other levels of the description, and the grammar,
together with the phonology and the lexical description, pairs the semantic
and phonetic representations with each other. One could quibble about the
nature of phonetic and semantic representations — whether they are in fact

quantisable, for instance, and if they are not, whether they can strictly speaking be paired with each other — but the basic principle is fairly clear and well established.

Generativeness

Last but not least, this version of systemic theory tries — and, I believe, manages — to be generative in the usual sense of this term in linguistics: a grammar should consist of rules that can be used in a completely mechanical way to decide whether or not any given object is well-formed (the word 'object' is vague, but intentionally so — see below). As the rest of this book will show, the rules are of a different kind from the rewrite rules used in TG grammars, but, as far as I can see, they are no less explicit and therefore no less generative. (Indeed, to the extent that they do not lead to the problem of indeterminate derived constituent-structure, they are more explicit.)

The reason for wanting a grammatical description of a language to be generative, in the sense of explicit, is that this is the only way of finding out precisely what one has to know in order to be a native speaker of that language — we must take none of this knowledge for granted, so we must spell everything out in a completely explicit way. This is a commonplace of modern linguistics, and it is also a commonplace that we cannot write a satisfactory explicit grammar without a formalised framework to make it unnecessary to define the place of each category in the overall language-system separately — in other words, so that we can avoid 'ad-hoc-ery'. So we define a number of very general categories, such as 'function', and define the ways in which different instances of a given category can be related to each other or to other categories. It is such a model for grammatical description that systemic grammar tries to provide.

However, as I have already suggested, it seems to me a genuinely open question whether any kind of formalism can ever encompass *all* that we should want to include in a complete description of what a native speaker must know. There can be few linguists who have grappled with the 'raw data' of language who would confidently answer that such a formalism will inevitably be found in the course of time. For any grammar we have to delimit the area that it covers so that it only has to cover facts that it *can* cover, leaving out all kinds of important phenomena. And this is not simply a question of competence versus performance, since our 'competence', by any reasonable definition of the term, includes a lot of 'messy' areas of language — the use of quotations from foreign languages, and of 'odd' accents and voice qualities, for instance.

If, then, there *are* aspects of language that are inherently beyond any for-

malism that will handle the more 'canonical' areas, then we should perhaps
see our models as models of linguistic *description* (the framework which
allows the linguist to write a good grammar), rather than as models of
language as such (the framework that we must be born with in order to
acquire the grammar of a natural language). Even if we take this more
'agnostic' view of formal models, however, they are still absolutely indis-
pensible to the progress of the study of language and languages, and they
must inevitably have *something* to do with the native speaker's knowledge
of his language, even if the relationship is an indirect one.

The objects generated by a grammar

Let us return to the question of the 'objects' that a grammar generates:
what are they? It is clear first of all that they are *not* particular utterances,
but rather utterance-types — that is, the objects that a grammar generates are
abstractions rather than particular events. Thus, deciding whether a particular
utterance-event is generated by a grammar means in effect deciding whether
there is any abstract 'utterance-type' with which it can be matched; so there
are in fact two steps in applying a grammar to a particular utterance-event:
assigning the utterance-token to an utterance-type, and finding whether the
utterance-type is generated by the grammar.

What then are 'utterance-types'? Again there will presumably be general
agreement that they can be represented by configurations of abstract categories of one kind or another — in other words, by linguistic representations,
each of which identifies a particular combination of semantic, grammatical,
lexical, phonological and (perhaps) phonetic categories.

A partial and rather primitive kind of linguistic representation is the
orthographic representation, but this is only a very partial one, as witness the
fact that it does not distinguish the two utterance-types exemplified in stock
examples of ambiguity such as 'Flying planes can be dangerous'. It is perhaps
a pity, though inevitable, that linguistics is practised so much through the
medium of writing, since it is impossible to quote an utterance-token — the
nearest one can get is to give an orthographic representation of an utterance-
type.

Summary of aims

The reader will probably have agreed with at least most of this subsection,
even if he would have put some points in a different way. The theory of systemic grammar is intended to be a general model equally suitable for describing the grammar of any language, where 'grammar' is taken to include just
syntax and morphology, to the exclusion of semantics, lexis and phonology.

If it is a satisfactory model for the description of this area of languages, then we can hope to learn from it something about the way in which the native speaker's linguistic knowledge is organised in his mind, although there seem likely to be important areas of this knowledge that we cannot characterise in this – or perhaps any other – formal framework.

The theory which is to be applied in this way consists of a number of rather general kinds of categories and relations, such as 'function' and 'sequence' respectively. This framework allows us to write fully explicit, and therefore generative, descriptions of the grammar of particular languages, and it has been developed to its present form because this seems to be the best able to accommodate certain complicated areas of grammar. In this book one such area is discussed in detail: complex sentences in English. The theory thus aims to have a strong empirical basis, and it will certainly have to be changed as more systemic descriptions are produced.

1.2. The content of a grammatical description

In the next chapter we shall be concerned with the theoretical apparatus that systemic theory offers as the basis for grammars of languages – in other words, the systemic means for achieving the aims outlined above. However, we first have to specify our aims in a little more detail, deciding what kinds of information a grammatical description should convey, rather than simply saying that we want to generate grammatical descriptions of utterance-types. Again there may be relatively little that most readers will object to in what follows, since on the whole I shall not be talking about the form of a grammatical description, but about its content.

1.2.1. *General*
Grammar and the other levels of language

I have already discussed some aspects of this question of the relation between grammar and other levels of language. Firstly, I have said that we distinguish grammatical statements from statements on other levels of language – from phonological, lexical or semantic statements. This means that 'grammar' as used in systemic theory has a more restricted meaning than in TG theory, and covers just facts of syntax and morphology. Exactly which kinds of statement should be covered in the grammar, and which in the phonology, lexis and semantics, is hard to discuss in terms of general principles, but it does seem clear that we need to generate at least three kinds of structure, a phonological one, a grammatical one and a lexical one.

There are a number of reasons why we cannot expect to be able to combine all these kinds of information into a single all-embracing structure, but perhaps the most straightforward reason is that the elements that we isolate on the different levels can cut across each other. It is generally agreed (see for instance Hockett, 1961) that grammatical and phonological elements can conflict: it is not the case that every morpheme consists of an integral number of syllables — or even of phonemes — since the relation between morphological (i.e. grammatical) elements and phonological elements is one of 'realisation' rather than of constituency. Similarly, grammatical and lexical units need not match each other neatly: a lexeme presumably consists of an integral number of morphemes, but it can consist of morphemes which do not exhaust a single grammatical element.

An example will make this point clearer. Consider the sentence

They're pulling your leg.

There are a number of problems in analysing this grammatically, but it is at least conceivable that we should want to show, firstly, that *they're* is in most respects grammatically the same as *they are* — i.e. subject noun-phrase followed by auxiliary verb — and secondly that *pulling your leg* is grammatically indistinguishable from *pulling your arm*. However, the former analysis will conflict with the phonological analysis of *they're*, which is likely to show it as consisting of one syllable with one long vowel phoneme belonging equally to the subject noun-phrase and to the auxiliary verb. (We could avoid this 'portmanteau morph' if we had a morphophonological level, but this would still leave a discrepancy between the grammatical elements and the phonological elements.) As for the grammatical analysis of *pulling your leg*, it will conflict with the lexical analysis, since we shall presumably want to enter *pull -'s leg* as a single lexeme in the lexical description of English, although *pull -'s leg* has no status at all as a grammatical element.

As for the semantic level, I shall assume that it is separate from the other three levels, although it is far too early to be very sure about this. Once again, the most obvious reason for separating semantic representations from grammatical representations is that there can be discrepancies between them, but we cannot adduce discrepancies in constituency since we do not know much about the role of constituency in a semantic representation. Other examples are easy to find, however. For instance, various 'deictic' categories will be distinguished in the grammar, including one for *this* or *here* and another for *that* or *there*; but the details of how these categories are *used* will presumably all be put in the semantic level. Again, in the grammatical analysis of complex sentences in chapter 5, I shall assume that it is up to the semantic description, and not the grammatical one, to identify the 'understood subject' in non-finite clauses like

> He promised her *to wash the car*,
> He asked her *to wash the car*,

Gramatically the italicized clauses are not distinguished — though their environments are — and it is only in the semantic representation that the differences come out.

The difference between semantic and lexical representations is harder to illustrate, because the definition of a lexeme is unclear and tends to involve semantic factors which reduce the discrepancies between the two levels. However, it is easy to find examples of sentences which, in some sence of 'meaning', mean roughly the same although they have very different lexical (and grammatical) structures. To take some obvious examples, 'I'm very grateful to you' means much the same as 'Thank you', and 'He may well have finished' means something like 'There's a good chance that he's finished'. How we are to show these semantic similarities is of course a separate question.

What I shall be assuming, then, is that the linguistic description of an utterance-type will consist of four separate representations, each corresponding to a different level of language: phonological, grammatical, lexical and semantic. These representations will be related to each other in ways that the description of the language will have to specify, and it is likely that there will be direct connections of one kind or another between each pair of the four levels, although the direct connection between semantics and phonology is perhaps open to dispute. Thus a comprehensive description of a language will have the following structure:

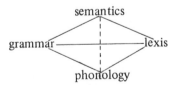

Descriptions will be generated on each of these four levels, and these descriptions will all be abstract and symbolic, just like the grammatical descriptions that we shall be discussing in the rest of this book. However, it seems to me at least that the linguist's task has still not finished when he has related the four levels to each other, and he should also be able to relate the semantic and phonological levels to phenomena outside language. He has to say how his phonological abstractions are manifested phonetically, in terms of sounds, but he also ought to be able to relate semantic categories to the situations in which they are used, in a very general sense of 'situation'. The uncertainty of how this is to be done for semantics makes it questionable whether semantics can in fact be treated as an autonomous level of language, but it will make no difference to what follows in this book whether we keep semantic representation separate from situational correlations or merge them.

The overall structure of the description of a language that I am proposing clearly has a lot in common with Hjelmslev's three-way distinction between 'form', 'substance' and 'purport' (1943/1961) and this similarity is not coincidental. Adding these terms to the diagram above, we get the following:

purport   situation

substance   semantics

form   grammar   lexis

substance   phonology

purport   sounds

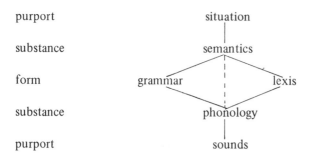

In this book I shall be expounding a systemic theory of grammar in this relatively restricted sense of 'grammar'. It seems likely that some parts of the theoretical apparatus of system-networks, realisation rules and structure-building rules that I shall describe will be relevant for other levels of language as well as to grammar, but this cannot be taken for granted. What follows, then, applies only to the level of grammar, to the exclusion of semantics, lexis and phonology.

Deep and surface phenomena

A second point that I have already made is that a grammatical description has to reflect both deep and surface phenomena, since it has to be possible to relate the grammatical description both to the semantic description and to the phonological one. Where there is a *direct* connection between semantic and phonological descriptions — as there may be with some kinds of interjection — then there is no difference between deep and surface, and indeed it may not be necessary to give any grammatical description to such utterances at all. But with the more 'ordinary' kinds of utterance that linguists tend to concentrate on there is no such simple relationship between semantics and phonology, and the grammatical (or lexical) description has to accommodate all the discrepancies between the two. This is the main role of transformational rules in TG grammars, and in systemic theory we achieve the same effect mainly by means of 'realisation' rules, to which we shall return in the next chapter.

The preceding paragraph could be taken to imply that in grammar all 'phenomena' (to use a deliberately vague term) can be classified as either deep or surface; this impression must now be dispelled. As in TG theory, we have a progression from *relatively* deep to *relatively* surface, rather than a clear line between deep and surface. That is, 'depth' is relative rather than absolute, so that one and the same phenomenon can be deep relative to one other phenomenon, but surface relative to another.

For instance, consider the italicized clauses in the following sentences

(1) I'll ask her *whether he had already left*,
(2) *Had he already left?*
(3) *Had he already left* we'd never have found him.

There is a deep similarity between the clauses in (1) and (2) — they are both 'polar' (or 'yes/no') interrogatives — but there is a surface difference between them, due to the fact that one is an independent (or 'main') clause whilst the other is a dependent ('subordinate') one. This difference is in their respective structures: in (1) but not in (2) there is a conjunction (*whether*), and in (1) the finite verb follows the subject whereas in (2) this order is reversed. This situation we can represent as follows

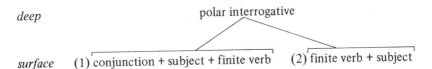

deep polar interrogative

surface (1) conjunction + subject + finite verb (2) finite verb + subject

From the point of view of this comparison, then, the fact that the finite verb precedes the subject in (2) is a surface phenomenon, and the corresponding deep phenomena is the fact that the clause concerned is a polar interrogative, just like (1). However, we ought to describe the former difference in rather more abstract terms, in order to be able to make a further comparison, in the next paragraph. Instead of describing *had* simply as 'the finite verb' in both (1) and (2), we can show that it is the 'focus' of the question, in just the same way as the wh-item in a wh-interrogative: in polar questions, the uncertainty involves the polarity (positive or negative) of the clause, whilst in wh-questions it involves the referent of the wh-item. Thus we can call both the wh-item in a wh-question and the finite verb in a polar question the 'mood-focus', which is a more abstract way of describing *had* than simply calling it the finite verb. It is the 'mood-focus' that comes first in independent clauses, but for a number of reasons (which are not relevant here) it is best not to use the term 'mood-focus' in describing the structures of dependent clauses, so that *had* is question focus in (2) but not in (1). We can now revise the diagram above

deep   polar interrogative

surface (1) conjunction + subject + finite verb   (2) finite verb/question-focus
                                                          + subject

We can now bring sentence (3) into the discussion. The italicized clause consists of just the same words, in the same order, as the one in (2); and in particular, the finite verb precedes the subject. However, in (3) the finite verb cannot be described as the 'mood-focus', for two reasons: firstly, the clause is not a question, so it is meaningless to ask where the question 'focuses'; and secondly, there is a restriction which suggests that *had* is less similar to ordinary question-words like *who, how* and so on, and more similar to subordinating conjunctions like *whether* and *since* — or *if*, as we might expect from the meaning of the construction.

The restriction in question is that the finite verb must be the first element of its clause; so for instance we cannot add an adverbial like *when she arrived* before *had*, as an adjunct of the subordinate clause:

* *when she arrived had he already left* we'd never have found him.

A similar restriction applies to subordinating conjunctions, including *whether*:

* I'll ask her *when she arrived whether he had already left,*

but not to a finite verb in an independent interrogative clause:

when she arrived had he already left?

The conclusion to which this discussion leads us is that *had* in (3) is in

some way different from *had* in (2); and whereas in (2) we called it 'mood-
focus', in (3) we can call it 'binder', on the understanding that we shall also
call conjunctions like *whether* 'binder'. However, in spite of this difference
between the two instances of *had* there is clearly a big similarity between
them as well: they are both finite verbs — indeed, they are instances of the
same finite verb.

To return to our discussion of deep and surface phenomena, the difference
between the two instances of *had* is deeper than what they have in common,
so once again we can produce a diagram showing a discrepancy between deep
and surface phenomena:

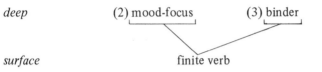

But the deep phenomena here also figured among the surface phenomena in
the earlier diagram, so we have now illustrated the general point, that the difference between deep and surface phenomena is a relative rather than an absolute matter. We can show this by merging the last two diagrams:

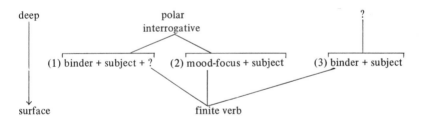

1.2.2. *Sequence*

One thing that a grammatical description clearly has to contain is information about the temporal sequence in which the elements occur, since otherwise it is impossible to relate the grammatical description to the phonological
one. The obvious way to achieve this in the grammatical representation is to
let the progression from left to right across the page represent the move from
earlier to later, and as far as possible we shall want to keep this correspondence a simple one. Thus in the simplest cases there will be no conflict between the left-to-right ordering of the grammatical elements and that of the
corresponding phonological elements, nor between the latter and the earlier-
to-later ordering of the sounds making up the corresponding utterances.

In some cases, there may be conflict at one of these points — for instance, in the classic example of French *au*, represented as a series of two morphemes on the grammatical level, but as a single phoneme on the phonological level. But in general the order of elements in the grammatical representation will be made to match the order of elements in the phonological representation, and similarly the latter will be constructed in such a way that it corresponds to the order in which the corresponding 'segments' of sound occur.

Deep and surface sequence

This much would probably be accepted by all linguists: that a complete grammatical description should at least reflect the 'surface' order of the elements. However, it is tempting to go further than this, to expect the grammatical description to reflect a deeper, 'underlying' sequence of the elements.

An example of this is the standard treatment of English auxiliary verbs, in which the order of suffixes and stems in the deep structure is different from that in the surface structure:

deep structure:

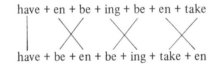

surface structure:

The advantage of this analysis is that it shows each auxiliary as being next to the suffix that it takes on the immediately following verb, so that we can introduce the two together by a single phrase-structure rule. In this way we can show the dependency between the auxiliary and the following verb's suffix (between *have* and *-en*, for instance), because neither can be present in the deep structure without the other.

This example illustrates perhaps the commonest reason for making 'deep' sequence different from 'surface' sequence: if two elements have some kind of dependency relation between them, then it is easier, if we are using phrase-structure rules, to introduce them together, which means that they should be next to each other in the deep structure even if they are not in the surface structure. However, it is important to stress that this argument holds only if we are using phrase-structure rules to introduce the elements: within a systemic framework, there are no phrase-structure rules, nor does it seem necessary to have a deep sequence different from the surface one.

We shall see below how a systemic grammar can show interdependencies, such as that between *have* and *-en*, but briefly it is done as follows: the *syntagmatic* interdependencies between the ICs of an item are left implicit, since they can be deduced from the way in which the ICs help to manifest the *paradigmatic* characteristics of the larger item, the constitute. In the case of *have* and *-en*, the interdependency is implicit in the fact that they both are needed in the manifestation of the paradigmatic feature [perfect].

Given a theoretical framework not based on phrase-structure rules, then, it is *possible* to avoid setting up a deep sequence of elements different from the surface one. Moreover, it seems *desirable* to avoid doing this, for three reasons. We can discuss these with reference to the rules for using *each*, as set out in Hudson (1970).

Let us start by showing why we might want to postulate a deep structure in which *each* is in a different place from its position in surface structure. Consider the following sentences:

> The neighbours have given him three presents *each*,
> The neighbours have *each* given him three presents.

In both of these sentences, *each* depends in some sense on *the neighbours*, although it is not next to *the neighbours* in either case; so it would be tempting to attach *each* directly to *the neighbours* in the deep structure, and to introduce them both by the same rule. Moreover, *each* can be attached directly to this noun-phrase in the surface structure itself, as a modifier:

> *Each* neighbour has given him three presents.

This seems to support a deep analysis for the first two sentences in which *each* is closely attached to the subject noun-phrase: if we generate a single deep structure which is near to the surface structure of the third sentence, we can let the same structure underlie the first two sentences as well.

The semantic relevance of surface sequence

The first disadvantage of this kind of analysis is that it raises the problem of the semantic interpretation of surface structure, because the position of *each* in the surface structure can make a difference to the meaning of the sentence. This is not so in the examples above, but it is in the following:

> The neighbours have given one child three presents *each*.
> The neighbours have *each* given one child three presents.

The reader will probably agree that the first sentence refers to a single child, whereas in the second sentence the number of children is unknown, but there could be as many children involved as neighbours. If we give both these sentences the same deep structure, then we shall have to relate the difference in meaning directly to the difference in surface structure, so that we shall have two kinds of relation between semantics and grammar: one between semantics and deep structure, and another between semantics and surface structure.

This is the conclusion to which Chomsky and others have come, and within the TG framework it seems an inescapable conclusion, although it is still unclear precisely how the existing models will be adapted to take account of it. However, it seems more satisfactory to avoid the problem entirely, as we can in a systemic framework, since there is then no need for two different kinds of rule relating semantics to grammar.

Moreover, by not trying to set up a more abstract deep structure, we avoid the problem of deciding what factors we are to take into account in setting it up — should it by definition be relatable directly to semantics, so that our sentences containing *each* would by definition have to be given different deep structures, or should it be made to reflect grammatical dependency first and foremost, as we were assuming above? The first assumption would be nearer to the 'generative semantics' approach, and the second would be the more conservative Chomskyan approach. It is hard to see how to reconcile these two approaches, but systemic theory prevents the conflict from arising.

The first advantage of having only one sequence for the elements in a grammatical description, then, is that all sequence relations are equally 'near' to semantics, so that we need only one set of rules for relating grammatical sequence to semantics.

The theoretical demands made by deep sequence

The second advantage is similar to the first: the discrepancy between deep and surface sequence in TG description is one of the main reasons why transformational rules are needed, so if we remove this discrepancy, it will be easier to do away with transformational rules, thereby simplifying our model of grammar. This is clearly not a very strong argument, since there are so many other factors involved: there might be other reasons why transformational rules are needed, or we might need to enrich the model so much in other directions that it would be simpler to keep the transformational rules. However, other things being equal a model which does not require the grammatical description of any sentence to include several different and conflicting structures, is presumably preferable to one which does; and by removing conflicts of sequence we reduce the need for conflicting structures.

The indeterminacy of deep sequence

The third reason is that it can be hard to decide what the deep sequence should be: in other words, if we have decided that two elements are closely interdependent and must therefore be next to each other in the deep structure, which of them should be on the left of the other?

For instance, if we attach the node representing *each* directly to the one representing the noun-phrase on which it depends, should we attach it on the left or on the right? If we are to make the deep sequence match the surface sequence found in the third kind of sentence, where *each* is a modifier, then *each* must be represented on the left; then we should have to have a transformation to move it to the right for the other kinds of sentence. There are quite good reasons for adopting such an analysis. However, there are also reasons for not adopting it. In particular, where the *each* is on the right of the noun-phrase, there may be no corresponding surface structure where it is in the modifier position, so that the only relevant surface structure is one in which the position of *each* is *not* the same as in the deep structure. For instance, if *each* depends on an indefinite noun-phrase, or on a conjunction of noun-phrases, the modifier position is not possible:

> Some neighbours of ours/Sam and Liz have each
> given him three presents,
> * Each some neighbours of ours /Sam and Liz have
> given him three presents.

If we give most weight to constructions like these, we shall probably decide to have *each* on the right of the noun-phrase in the deep structure, but if we give most weight to the other kinds of construction, where *each* can occur in the modifier position, we shall probably put it on the left. Balancing criteria against each other in this way is not an easy task, and in many cases we seem to be seeking the answer to a rather meaningless question.

A similar problem arises in the morphology of the Beja verb (Hudson, 1964): there are two classes of verb-stems, which we can refer to as 'strong' and 'weak', and these differ only in that grammatical categories that are manifested by prefixes with strong verb stems are manifested by suffixes with weak stems. For instance, /r-b/ ('refuse') is a strong stem, while /tam/ ('eat') is a weak one, so their corresponding past tense paradigms are as follows:

	/r-b/('refuse')	/tam/('eat')
1st singular	a-rib	tam-an
2nd singular masculine	ti-rib-a	tam-ta-:

2nd singular feminine	ti-rib-i	tam-ta-i
3rd singular masculine	i-rib	tam-ia
3rd singular feminine	ti-rib	tam-ta
1st plural	ni-rib	tam-na
2nd plural	ti-rib-na	tam-ta:-na
3rd plural	i-rib-na	tam-ia:-na

Should the underlying deep structures of these verbs be *tense + stem* (+ *gender/number*), to fit the strong paradigm, or *stem + tense* (+ *gender/number*) to match the weak paradigm? Or should the parallel between the two paradigms be shown in a more abstract way, as in traditional word-and-paradigm grammars or in a systemic grammar, without trying to set up an underlying structure common to both sets of words?

The conclusion to which these arguments lead us is that surface sequence is a characteristic of a sentence which the grammatical description must reflect, but that if we are inclined to postulate any kind of 'sequence' other than this, it will be because of the assumptions that we make about the way in which grammatical dependency should be shown in the description, rather than because of genuine properties of the sentences being described. Since it seems advantageous not to set up deep sequences of elements which will conflict with surface ones, if we can avoid it, and since in systemic grammar it is possible to avoid this conflict, there is only one sequence of elements in a systemic grammatical description, and that is 'surface' sequence.

1.2.3. *Constituency*

So far in this discussion I have deliberately used the rather vague term 'element', saying that a grammatical description must specify the sequence in which the 'elements' in a sentence occur. It would not matter much if we equated these elements with morphemes, as far as the specification of sequence is concerned: once we have specified the sequence of the morphemes, there is nothing left to specify as far as sequence is concerned. However, we would not be satisfied with a grammar which generated just strings of morphemes in the right sequence, even if it were possible to write such a grammar: the structures generated must also show the constituency relations among the morphemes. We shall adopt the usual notational conventions for showing constituency, by means of a kind of tree structure in which the relation of left to right represents the relation of earlier to later, and the relation of higher to lower represents that of constitute to constituent.

There is no difficulty in reaching agreement on the principle that a grammatical description should show constituency; for instance, linguists would

presumably all agree that the following sentences are different in their grammatical constituency:

> She'll probably say *that she slept at her sister's* tomorrow evening,
> She'll probably say *that she slept at her sister's last night.*

In each case the italicized will be treated as a single constituent, to show that
tomorrow morning and *last night* stand in different relationships to the rest
of the sentence: in the second sentence it is a part of the reported clause, but
not in the first sentence. It is hard to see how this difference could be shown
otherwise than by means of constituency.

Similarly, but less simply, there are cases where it will be generally agreed
that a constituent is discontinuous. For instance, we can adapt our last two
examples to show this by moving the time adverbials to the front of the sentence:

> Tomorrow morning she'll probably say *that she slept*
> *at her sister's,*
> *Last night* she'll probably say *that she slept at her sister's.*

If *last night* is a constituent of the reported clause when it comes at the end
of the sentence, then so is it when it is at the beginning. We shall have to be
able to show this kind of discontinuity in our grammatical descriptions, but
it is hard to do so just by means of the normal kind of tree-diagram, so we
shall have to use other means. We shall return to this problem in 2.5 and
5.1.3 below.

The criteria for determining constituency

Most linguists would probably accept what I have said so far about constituency – that a syntactic analysis of a sentence must show constituency
relations, and that some constituents may be discontinuous – but there is a
surprising amount of disagreement among linguists when it comes to deciding
how to identify constituents.

To take an obvious example, some linguists treat the direct object as an
immediate constituent of the clause on a par with the subject, whilst others
group the direct object and the lexical verb together as a single element, to
the exclusion of the subject; the former analysis is exemplified by Jespersen's
S-V-O analysis, and the latter by the traditional subject-predicate analysis.
For the first kind of linguist, the natural way to analyse

Snoopy stalked the sparrow.

would be as follows:

Snoopy   *stalked*   *the sparrow*

For the second kind, it seems equally natural to analyse it as follows:

Snoopy   *stalked*   *the sparrow*

   There are clearly a lot of questions begged by these trees, notably whethei they are meant to represent deep or surface structure, but nevertheless they illustrate the difference between the two ways of analysing English clauses into their constituents. Moreover, differences of this kind arise between linguists in many other areas of English grammar, with some linguists preferring analyses with more layers of structure and less ICs per layer, and other linguists preferring the converse (I suggested the terms 'few-ICs approach' and 'many-ICs approach' for these two approaches to constituency in Hudson, 1967). On the whole, linguists working within a TG framework tend to prefer the few-ICs kind of analysis, including the subject – (auxiliary) – predicate analysis, while those working within either a tagmemic or a systemic framework prefer the other kind, so that they favour the S-V-O analysis.

   How can we explain the inability of linguists to agree among themselves about the way in which a sentence should be divided into constituents? Clearly it is at least to some extent due to the different assumptions they make about the part that constituency should play in a grammar: in other words, different linguists are liable to be applying different criteria when they try to decide between two conflicting constituency analyses. This means that constituency reflects the linguist's theoretical assumptions more than was the case with sequence: in the case of sequence, it is easy at least to decide what the correct surface analysis should be, whereas even this is a difficult operation as far as constituency is concerned, involving considerations almost as abstract as those involved in 'deep' constituency.

   This difference between sequence and constituency is a consequence of the relation between grammatical and phonological patterns: the phonological elements appear in a clear sequence, and the order in which the elements appear in the grammatical description can simply follow this, but the constituency patterns on the phonological level — i.e. the hierarchical organisation into 'phonemes', syllables, etc. — need have little or no direct relevance to the constituency on the grammatical level. Examples of the discrepancy between phonological units and grammatical units are too obvious and well known to need quoting — suffice it to point out that it would be reasonable to analyse the sentence *'They're off!'* in such a way that no grammatical unit would correspond to an integral phonological unit (at least for Southern British English, in which /r/ cannot be syllable-final).

It will be recalled that one of the main arguments in favour of separating the various levels of language from each other was that the units needed on one level need not coincide with those needed on other levels. What I have just said about the relation between grammatical and phonological constituents is a particular instance of this principle, which means more generally that there is no point in trying to establish grammatical constituency primarily on the basis of constituency on some other level. Therefore we must look for some other basis for it, within the level of grammar itself.

The most general principle that most linguists would probably accept is that we group elements together as a single larger element if we thereby make it easier to write the grammar (in some undefined sense of 'easier'). For instance, we obviously gain by treating nouns and their modifiers as single elements (noun-phrases), since this allows us to give one set of rules defining the arrangements of modifiers and nouns within the noun-phrase, and another, more or less independent, set of rules for the use of noun-phrases in larger constructions.

A particularly clear instance of the advantage of setting up intermediate constituents is where embedding recursion is possible — as is the case with indirect speech:

John said that he thought that she had told him that ...

If we do not treat the reported clauses as grammatical constituents, then we cannot even say that this is a case of recursion, since there would be no kind of pattern to recur. Less still could we allow for this recursion in our grammar, since this is possible only if we identify both the reporting structure and the reported structure as in some sense instances of some construction — i.e. both as clauses or sentences.

In a systemic description, we follow this general principle, so that the constituents that we identify are just those that we need in order to write the most efficient possible grammar of the language; and it is (regrettably perhaps) hard to define more precisely than this the criteria that we take into account in deciding between different constituency analyses. However, it is clear that the model we presuppose in writing a grammar will make a big difference to the constituency analysis that we prefer, and this is why different linguists advocate different analyses, as we recognized above. It is perhaps worth showing how one particularly important difference between the systemic model and the TG model leads to a difference of this kind.

The difference in question concerns the different ways in which the two models allow us to show syntagmatic dependencies between constituents: in a systemic description they are implied by the dependencies among more abstract, paradigmatic, categories to which the constituents are indirectly related, so there is no point in making the constituency reflect them as well; whereas in a TG description it is an advantage if the constituency reflects the dependencies between the elements quite closely. For instance, there is a kind of dependency between the direct object and the main verb, because the class of the latter determines whether or not the former is possible; and the question is how the grammar should show this.

In a systemic description, both the class of the latter and the presence or absence of the former would be related to the same set of paradigmatic categories, specifying the clause's 'transitivity', and this fact would show the special connection between the main verb and the direct object. Consequently there is nothing to be gained by treating the main verb and the direct object as a single constituent within the clause's structure; indeed, there is much to be lost by so doing, because this analysis would conflict with the analyses that we should need for other reasons, and we should have to start giving more than one structure to each sentence.

On the other hand, in a TG framework it does seem to be easier to write a grammar of English if the object and main verb are isolated as a single unit, so that we can then concentrate on the relations between them. Of course, if we follow Fillmore in putting the 'direct object' on the same footing, vis à vis the main verb, as the 'actor', then we no longer require to treat the direct object and main verb as a single constituent, either in the deep structure or in the surface structure, unless we find some other reason for doing so.

What I have tried to argue, in connection with constituency, is this: that the way in which we decide to analyse a sentence into constituents depends as much on our theoretical assumptions as it does on the characteristics of the sentence itself, and that where we need to group elements together if we are using a TG model this is often unnecessary if we are working within a systemic framework. In particular, constituency does not need to reflect syntagmatic inter-dependencies in a systemic description, whereas in a TG description it does. The reader will remember that we came to precisely the same conclusion with regard to sequence, so it should be becoming clearer why systemic grammatical descriptions need not involve more than one structure per sentence: the actual shape of the structural tree does not have to carry nearly as much information as it does in a TG description.

The constituency analysis of auxiliary verbs

Let us consider what difference these general principles regarding constituency make when it comes to analysing a particular area of English grammar, constructions involving auxiliary verbs. There are two main issues, which we can illustrate with reference to the sentence

Our dog has been biting the postman again.

Firstly, how do we show the special relationship between *has* and the participle suffix in *been*, and between *been* and the suffix in *biting*? And secondly, how do we show the special relationship which binds the three verbs *has*, *been* and *biting* together?

We have already discussed the first issue, in connection with the difference between the TG and the systemic treatments of sequence (p. 16). One way of showing that some form of *have* and the *en* suffix are interdependent is by introducing them together in a phrase-structure rule, such as the now outdated one of Chomsky (1957):

$$\text{Aux} \rightarrow \text{T(M) (have + en) (be + ing)}.$$

In this formulation, either we can have both *have* and *en* in the deep structure, or we can have neither of them, and without this reconstructed sequence we could not formulate such a rule. From the present point of view, what is significant is that in this deep structure there is no constituent consisting just of *be* and *en*, to the exclusion of *have*. This we find only in the surface structure. This analysis illustrates the general principle that in a TG grammar it is best for two elements to be 'sisters' in constituency (i.e. ICs of the same larger element) if they depend on each other.

Another way of achieving much the same effect is to introduce just one of the elements concerned in the phrase-structure rules, and to introduce the other by means of a transformation. It seems reasonable to assume that we should introduce *have* (or perhaps *past*, which then gets converted into *have* — see McCawley, 1969) in the first way, and then introduce *en* transformationally. For this analysis it would not be necessary at any point to treat *have*

and *en* as sister constituents, because the dependency would already have
been shown by the fact that the introduction of *en* depends on the presence
of *have*.

As it happens, this very dependency raises a problem, because it is in fact
not at all certain that this is the right direction for the dependency. Indeed,
I shall argue in 3.2.3 (p. 145) below that the dependency works in exactly the
opposite direction: *have* is introduced in the environment of *en* (informally
speaking). But whichever way the dependency works, we can show it in a TG
analysis in the way just described, or in a systemic analysis in the way that I
shall describe below, without treating *have* and *en* at any point as sister constituents.

The disadvantages of grouping the verbs together

The second question is how we are to show the special relationship among
the verbs, both auxiliary and main. The assumption is for instance that in our
sentence

Our dog has been biting the postman again.

the connection between *has* and *been* is closer than that between *has* and *our
dog*, because, e.g., *has* and *been* are both verbs, involved in selections of tense
aspect, polarity, etc. whilst *our dog* is not. Similarly we may (or may not) decide that *biting* is more closely related to *been* than it is to *the postman*. If
we do decide this, then we may conclude that the constituents of this sentence are as follows:

Our dog   has been biting   the postman   again

In this analysis, there is a constituent *has been biting*, which we might call a
verbal group (Halliday et al., 1964). However, if we decide that *biting* is not
as closely related to *been* as it is to *the postman*, then we shall prefer an analysis like one of the following, which are more similar to TG deep structure:

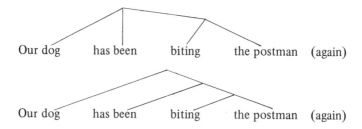

Our dog   has been   biting   the postman   (again)

Our dog   has been   biting   the postman   (again)

Rather than trying to choose between the first analysis and that resulting in the last pair of trees, I believe we should question the assumption upon which they are both based, and reject them both. The assumption, as I suggested above, is that we ought to group together the auxiliary verb, with or without the main verb, because the kinds of rules that apply to them are different from those that apply to other constituents of the clause.

One of the main things that unites the verbs is that it is to them, but not (say) to the subject noun-phrase, that we have to refer in discussing tense and aspect. However, this in itself is not a sufficient reason for setting up a constituent to contain just the verbs, as far as systemic theory is concerned, since the grammar will be able to show that only the verbs are related to tense and aspect whether the verbs are grouped together as a single constituent or not. Moreover, it is not only verbs that are involved in tense and aspect in English: time adverbials are also involved, so it would be inconsistent in a sentence like

Our dog has been biting the postman since Christmas,

to group together *has*, *been* and (possibly) *biting* as one constituent and not to include *since Christmas* with them.

As far as I can see there is nothing to be gained by postulating a constituent (which we can refer to as the 'verbal group') exclusively for the auxiliary verbs, with or without the main verb, provided we are working within a systemic framework. Moreover, there are a number of arguments in favour of *not* setting up the verbal group as a constituent — whereas, by way of contrast, there are parallel arguments in favour of treating the noun phrase as a constituent:

(a) There are three sets of circumstances under which the verbal group would be regularly separated into two or more parts by other items not belonging to it — whereas the noun-phrase is discontinuous only under rather exceptional conditions. Firstly, the verbal group would be interrupted by the subject whenever the subject and the finite verb are inverted:

Has our dog *been biting* the postman again?

Secondly, some adverbials are regularly located among the auxiliary verbs:

He *may* well really *have* just *been* almost *hitting* the target.

Thirdly, in coordination one or more auxiliaries can be 'shared' by all the coordinated clauses:

He *has* (*bought* a book and *been reading* it during
the last few evenings).

If we grouped all the verbs together as one constituent, then these constructions would be relatively difficult to handle because they would involve discontinuity, so we should have to have quite strong reasons for grouping the
verbs together in the first place.
(b) Another difference between the noun-phrase and our hypothetical verbal
group is that the former can be embedded in itself, but the latter cannot (at
least as far as the analysis that I shall be suggesting is concerned). Thus there
is no construction involving verbal groups which parallels

the gate by the bridge over the stream in the valley ...

or

the little girl's big sister's best friend.

The possibility of recursive constructions of this type is very strong evidence
that the noun-phrase is a constituent, supporting a lot of other evidence all
pointing in the same direction; but no such evidence supports the 'verbal
group' type of analysis.
    The conclusion to which I have come, then, is that there is no justification,
in a systemic framework, for postulating a constituent containing the clause's
verbs but none of its other constituents. Instead of such an analysis, I shall
assume one, throughout this book, in which each verb is an *immediate* constituent of the clause, just like the subject (for instance); so the constituency
of our original sentence will not be as shown in any of the trees quoted above,
but rather:

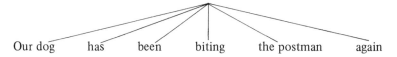

Our dog   has   been   biting   the postman   again

    This analysis is typical of systemic analyses, in that relatively little of the
information in the syntactic description is shown by the shape of the tree,
compared with other analyses, since more information is located in the
labelling of the nodes in the tree. In this particular case, we show that only
has, *been* and *biting* are related to tense and aspect selections not by grouping
them into a single constituent, but by giving only these three words function-
labels which relate them to tense and aspect. It should become clearer in the
following chapters how this is achieved.

1.2.4. *Syntagmatic relations*

I have deliberately put constituency and sequence first in this discussion of the kinds of information that we can expect a grammar to allow us to give about a sentence. The reason for this was that the systemic treatment of these two aspects of grammatical structure makes a systemic description fundamentally different from a TG description: a systemic grammatical description consists of a *single* tree with various kinds of information specified for each node in the tree, whereas a TG grammatical (or syntactic/semantic) description consists of a number of different trees, each covering different aspects of the information conveyed by the total description. Admittedly, my first aim in this chapter is to summarise the kinds of information that a grammar has to be able to give, rather than the ways in which the information is included in a systemic grammar; but as far as both sequence and constituency are concerned it is hard to keep the two areas of discussion separate.

The preceding discussion has centred round the identification of constituents in a sentence. We can now move on to discuss the relations among these constituents, since these ought to be reflected by a grammatical description. Relations between constituents of a sentence, or between the constituents and the sentence as a whole, are by definition *syntagmatic* relations — in contrast with paradigmatic relations, which we shall discuss below.

Let us take as an example the sentence

These plates have all been dried.

If we base our analysis on the systemic grammar I shall be outlining in this book, we shall identify the following constituents:

these plates
have
all
been
dried
these
plates
plate
s
be
en
drie
d

(The analysis into morphemes is tentative.) In addition to these thirteen constituents, we have the sentence as a whole, so there are altogether fourteen grammatical items that are syntagmatically related to one another.

The first kinds of syntagmatic relations that we can identify are those of constituency and sequence, which we have already discussed. For instance, *these* is an immediate constituent of *these plates*, and the latter in turn is an IC of *these plates have all been dried*; and *these* precedes *plates*, and *these plates* precedes all its sister ICs. These claims all involve syntagmatic relations within the sentence, and they are clearly shown by means of a tree such as the following:

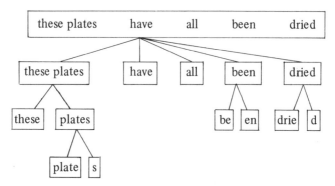

In addition to these two kinds of syntagmatic relations, there are a number of others involving some kind of grammatical dependency:

(a) *all* presupposes *these plates*, in that the former can occur only because the latter is plural;

(b) *have* presupposes the participial suffix in *been*, marking the 'perfect' aspect, and similarly *been* presupposes the participial suffix in *dried*, which signals passive voice (this apparently back-to-front way of describing the relations was mentioned above (1.2.3), and will be justified in 3.2.3 below);

(c) *have* is in concord with *these plates*, in that *has* would have been used if the latter had been singular;

(d) *these* is in concord with *plates*.

Low-level and high-level syntagmatic relations

These three kinds of syntagmatic relation — constituency, sequence and dependency — are certainly part of the information that a grammatical description should convey (although the dependency relations need not be seen in quite the way in which I formulated them above; for instance, is *these* plural because the noun-head, *plates*, is plural or because the noun-phrase as a whole is plural?). However, there are two questions that we have to answer about them: first, what is their relation to grammatical functions, such as subject or actor? and secondly, how are we to incorporate them into the grammatical description? These questions are closely connected, as we shall see.

To start with their relation to grammatical functions, it is clear that these too identify syntagmatic relations: saying that *these plates* is the grammatical subject tells us a lot about its syntagmatic relations to its sister ICs or to the whole sentence (according to how we formulate the relation, as 'subject of the verb X' or as 'subject of the clause X'). So in effect we can distinguish not three but four kinds of syntagmatic relations: constituency, sequence, dependency, and functional relations.

However, these four kinds of syntagmatic relation are not really on the same footing, since the first three enter into the definition of the last kind. For instance, when we attempt to define the function 'subject', we are likely to invoke constituency, in that the subject is an IC of a clause (or sentence, according to terminology); sequence, in that the subject precedes the main verb and either immediately precedes or immediately follows the finite verb; and dependency, in that it is the subject with which the finite verbs shows concord. Thus, the function of subject brings together three kinds of syntagmatic relation under a single more complex category. Similarly, for most or all of the other established grammatical functions, such as 'modifier' and 'head', or 'relator' and 'axis', their definition involves one or more of the first three kinds of syntagmatic relation. Even a term as abstract as 'actor' can be defined in terms of constituency, sequence (in active clauses, the actor occurs in the place identified as subject) and possibly dependency (the selection relations between actor and verb are different from those between, say, goal and verb).

Given this difference between functional relations (subject—main verb or subject—clause; modifier—head; and so on) and the other kinds of syntagmatic relation, we can refer to the former as 'high-level' relations and the latter as 'low-level' ones. The high-level relations are defined in terms of the low-level ones, often in quite a complex way, so each high-level relation *implies* a number of low-level relations. For instance, if we define the subject as I did in the last paragraph, then saying that *these plates* is subject is tantamount to saying that it is an IC of a clause, that it occurs either immediately before or immediately after the finite verb, and that the finite verb is in concord with it.

We can now turn to the second question: how should we incorporate the information about low-level syntagmatic relations into a grammatical description? As far as the first two kinds of low-level relation (constituency and sequence) are concerned, we have already given the answer: they are shown by means of a tree-diagram. For the third kind of information, grammatical dependency, we can also give an easy answer: since dependency relations are implied by functional relations, we need not specify both, but can just mark the latter explicitly and allow the former to remain implicit. So for instance we can add a label to the tree-diagram for our sentence showing that *these plates* is subject, and this will in turn imply that there is a concord relation between *these plates* and the finite verb.

The last paragraph strictly speaking goes beyond the scope of this chapter, since it is concerned explicitly with the *way* in which information is shown, rather than with *what* information is to be shown. Moreover, a TG linguist would probably want to disagree with my conclusions, objecting that we could push the argument further and leave functional relations implicit, as well as dependency relations, so that we are left with just constituency and sequence as explicitly indicated syntagmatic relations. However, my general thesis will be easily accepted, and is worth making here, that *some* of the information we must give in a grammatical description can be left implicit. So even if we agree that some particular grammatical fact about a sentence should be reflected in its grammatical analysis, it does not necessarily follow that this fact must be shown explicitly.

There are a number of points to be made about functional relations, but before making them I should note two kinds of relation that are syntagmatic but do not seem to me to be on the level of grammar. The first is the 'selection' relation found between lexical items — whereby for instance *drive* collocates with *car* but not with *bicycle* and *ride* with *bicycle* but not with *car*. This kind of relationship seems to belong to the level of lexis rather than to that of grammar. And the second is one that I prefer to locate in semantics rather than in grammar: anaphoric (or 'cataphoric') relations, such as those between a third-person personal pronoun and the noun-phrase to which it 'refers'. The main reason for excluding these relations from grammar is that there need not be any definable grammatical relation between the pronoun and the noun-phrase to which it 'phors' (by anaphora or cataphora).

Functional relations

Linguists would probably all agree that an adequate grammar of a language must take account of functional relations, though they would not agree on how best to do this. For instance, any linguist faced with the following two sentences:

>   Everyone enjoyed last night,
>   Everyone slept last night,

would want his grammar to assign different analyses to them, showing that the functional relations between *last night* and the rest of the sentence are different in the two cases.

However, it is easier to agree that functional relations should be reflected in a grammar than to agree on how to recognise functional relations, or even on what a functional relation is. For instance, most discussions of grammatical functions centre round those that are semantically significant — actor, goal, etc.; subject; topic, comment — but are functions by definition semantically significant? If so, we must make sure that we take semantic factors into account in identifying functions, and we shall be able to assign no functions at all to words that have no direct connection with meaning (like the *to* in the infinitive, or *the* in *the Sudan*); but some linguists — among them those in the systemic and tagmemic schools — would claim that *every* grammatical constituent can be given a function, so for them having semantic significance cannot be part of the definition of grammatical functions.

Functions (or 'function') are often distinguished from 'form', and this distinction gives us at least the beginnings of a definition of grammatical functions: an item's function has to do with the way in which it is being used in a particular sentence, whereas its form has to do with its own 'shape'. A limiting instance of the difference between function and form is that one and the same word (phrase, etc.) can be used in different ways in different sentences; this was the case with *last night* in the pair of examples just quoted, but it also arises where the same noun-phrase is used as subject in one sentence and as direct object in another:

>   *These plates* are going to fall over,
>   I've dried *these plates*.

Furthermore, I have just suggested that functional relations reflect the lower-level syntagmatic relations of constituency, sequence and dependence. For those who accept this, it should follow that there need not be a connection between grammatical functions and meaning — or at least not a direct one — and that every grammatical constituent can be assigned a function, since every constituent contracts relations of constituency, sequence and dependence with its grammatical environment.

The identification of grammatical functions

However, if these suggestions are correct, then we are very far from being able to say exactly what factors should be taken into account when we are identifying grammatical functions — for instance, if we want to decide whether any of the italicized items in the following sentences have the same functions:

(1) *These plates* have been dried,
(2) I haven't dried *these plates*,
(3) *These plates* I haven't dried,
(4) *These plates* are dry,
(5) *Which plates* have been dried?
(6) *Which plates* have you dried?

Firstly, function is different from form, so we cannot draw any conclusions either from the fact that the italicized items in 1–4 are identical in form or from the fact that they are different in form from those in 5 and 6. Secondly functional relations reflect three low-level syntagmatic relations, but there is no general principle for deciding *which* of these low-level relations a function should reflect. For instance, a difference of sequence need not always be reflected in a difference of function, so we do not know whether *these plates* has the same function in 2 as it does in 3; nor need identity of sequence mean that the same function is involved, so the initial items in 3–6 may or may not have the same functions. And thirdly, functional relations need not have any direct connection with semantic relations, so the fact that in 2 and 3 *these plates* is in roughly the same semantic relation to the rest of the sentence is of no more significance than the fact that this semantic relation is different from the one in 4.

How do we resolve this dilemma? Clearly the details of the answer depend very much on the model of grammatical description that we are presupposing, but irrespective of the model we can perhaps agree on two general principles.

Firstly, grammatical functions should reflect *all* the factors we listed above, rather than just one kind of factor, and we shall justify functions with reference to their effect on the grammar of the language as a whole. This means that we shall assign different functions to the italicized items in the above sentence if this improves the grammar, but not if it does not.

Secondly, many of the questions we asked about these sentences were unreal questions, in that they forced us to make an unnecessary choice. For instance, if we have to compare (1) and (5):

(1) *These plates* have been dried,
(2) *Which plates* have been dried?

why should we have to say either that *these plates* and *which plates* have the same function or that they have different functions? Why cannot we have it both ways and say that they have one function in common, but that there is also one function that *which plates* has but that *these plates* does not (or vice versa)?

In the TG model, which allows more than one grammatical structure per sentence, *these plates* can be given one function in one structure and a different one in another (and similarly for *which plates*), which would achieve the effect we are aiming for. The disadvantage of this approach is that it forces one to treat some functions as deeper than others, since the different structures that a sentence has are ranged in a series between its deep structure and its surface structure.

However, in a systemic description we achieve the same end by combining functions into bundles, so that the description of a sentence could show more than one function for each constituent. Thus, in the descriptions of sentences (1), (5) and (6) we could show both similarities and differences between them:

(1) *These plates* have been dried,
(5) *Which plates* have been dried?
(6) *Which plates* have you dried?

We could give the function 'goal' to the italicized in all three sentences, to show that they all identify the object of the process (drying); we could give the function subject to the italicized in (1) and (5) but not (6); and we could give the function 'mood-focus' to the italicized in (5) and (6) but not in (1).

As far as systemic theory is concerned, grammatical functions play an extremely important part, since the effect of the grammatical environment on a constituent is always mediated by the latter's function. Thus if an item's place in constituency or sequence is determined by its environment, it will have one or more functions which require it to be in precisely these particular low-level relations to the rest of the sentence. Similarly, if it is in some kind of dependency relation to its environment, it will contract this relation because it has some particular function.

One consequence of this characteristic of systemic theory is that functions are far more numerous in a systemic grammar than they would be in a grammar based on a different theory. This need not worry us, however, since the large number of functions that we recognise simply reflects the fact that a grammar contains a very large number of different rules relating constituents to their environments, and that each rule tends to apply to a different range of functions.

A second consequence of the way in which functions are defined in systemic grammars is that the terms of a functional relation are not of the same kind, one term being the function – such as 'subject' – and the other being the environment as a whole. In some cases the relevant aspect of the environment will be the presence of some 'sister'-function, while in others it may be some characteristic of the constitute, such as the fact that it is an interrogative clause. This being so, functions do not go in pairs as they would if the terms of a functional relation were both functions.

Functions in independent interrogative clause structures

To illustrate the way in which functions are used in systemic grammar we can take a fairly straightforward area of English grammar, the structure of the independent (i.e. not subordinate or reported) interrogative clause. Let us try to capture the general patterns underlying the following:

> How do you like mushrooms?
> Do you like mushrooms?
> Who likes mushrooms?

Informally, the rule is that if there is a 'wh-item' (*how, which way, who*, etc.) this comes first, and that the finite auxiliary verb comes before the subject unless the latter is a wh-item. In other words, there may be a conflict between the rule which requires the wh-item to come first and the rule which requires the subject to come after the finite auxiliary, and in such cases the former rule takes precedence over the latter.

Let us start by considering the first sentence:

> How do you like mushrooms?

Here there are three items of interest, *how, do* and *you*. *How* has the function MOOD-FOCUS (p. 14), which means that it has to be initial in the clause (except for certain kinds of adverbial that can precede it). *Do* has the function PRE-SUBJECT, which means that it must come before the subject, and also that it must be a finite auxiliary, and must not be the main verb. *You* has the function SUBJECT, which means that it must follow PRE-SUBJECT (but must not follow the main verb).

Only two items, *do* and *you*, are of interest, in the second sentence: Do you like mushrooms? *You* is SUBJECT, as in the first sentence, and this again means that it must come after PRE-SUBJECT but before the main verb. *Do* on the other hand combines the functions of both *how* and *do* in the first sentence. It is initial in the clause, like *how*, because it has the function MOOD-SUBJECT, but it also has the function PRE-SUBJECT, with the same implications as before.

On the basis of these first two sentences, we can formulate a simple general rule for the structure of independent interrogative clauses: they always contain items that have the functions MOOD-FOCUS, PRE-SUBJECT and SUBJECT, and the relation between these functions is that MOOD-FOCUS is always initial and PRE-SUBJECT always precedes SUBJECT, but may be combined with MOOD-FOCUS. By implication, this means that SUBJECT can never be initial. The diagrams below show these relations.

How	*do*	*you*	like mushrooms?
MOOD-FOCUS	PRE-SUBJECT	SUBJECT	

Do	*you*	like mushrooms?
PRE-SUBJECT	SUBJECT	
MOOD-FOCUS		

In informal terms, these rules say that if there is a wh-item it must come first (since it will have the function MOOD-FOCUS) and that there must be inversion of the finite auxiliary (with the function PRE-SUBJECT) and the subject. When there is no wh-item, the finite auxiliary takes over the initial position, so it too has the function MOOD-FOCUS.

The problem that we have to solve is how to reconcile these rules with the third sentence, which breaks them:

Who likes mushrooms?

Here there is no inversion of subject and finite auxiliary, and indeed no finite auxiliary, because the subject has to be initial, being the wh-item. What we are looking for is some way of taking account of this exception which will reveal the underlying reason for it.

This we can easily do by allowing SUBJECT to combine with MOOD-FOCUS, but excluding PRE-SUBJECT if it does. This kills two birds with one stone: it makes a finite auxiliary verb necessary only where the subject is not a wh-item, since the auxiliary is introduced in the first two sentences simply as a bearer of the function PRE-SUBJECT; and it makes inversion of subject and auxiliary necessary only under the same circumstances. Thus the rule putting the wh-item at the beginning of the clause is given priority over the rule demanding subject-verb inversion in interrogative clauses. The structure of the third sentence, then, will include the functions MOOD-FOCUS and SUBJECT, but not PRE-SUBJECT, which explains why there is no inverted auxiliary.

> *Who*   likes mushrooms?
> MOOD-FOCUS
> SUBJECT

These rules cover the facts that we set out to cover, and do so in quite a revealing way. But what do we gain by saying that MOOD-FOCUS is always present, being the function of the finite auxiliary if there is no wh-item for it to be assigned to? Surely it would be simpler to introduce it only into wh-interrogatives, avoiding the need to combine it with PRE-SUBJECT in polar interrogatives? There are two advantages of our analysis.

First, we can state the rule for the presence of PRE-SUBJECT with reference to MOOD-FOCUS, so that the former is always present when the latter is, except when MOOD-FOCUS is combined with SUBJECT. This automatically explains why there is no inversion of subject and finite auxiliary in *dependent* interrogatives, since MOOD-FOCUS does not occur in these, and therefore PRE-SUBJECT does not either. Thus we cover all the differences in the order of subject and verb between independent and dependent interrogative clauses in one simple statement: independent clauses contain MOOD-FOCUS, dependent ones do not. The extent of this simplification can be judged by comparing the following lists:

independent		*dependent*
How do you like mushrooms?	—	how you like mushrooms.
Do you like mushrooms?	—	whether you like mushrooms.
Who likes mushrooms?	—	who likes mushrooms.

The second advantage is that our analysis explains the similarity between a wh-item and a finite auxiliary in an independent interrogative clause as far as their positions are concerned: as I have already noted in 1.2.1 (p. 14), they both allow certain kinds of adverbial to precede them, although they are otherwise initial in the clause.

  Tomorrow evening when are you setting out?
  Tomorrow evening are you going to be home at the usual time?

By way of contrast, the finite auxiliary must be absolutely initial in the clause when it is inverted with the subject to mean 'if':

  * Yesterday morning had he posted the letter we'd have
   received it by now.

And if a wh-item is in a dependent interrogative clause, it too must be absolutely initial (ignoring the possibility of discontinuities):

  * She wants to know yesterday why you ignored her.

In neither of these two cases is the function MOOD-FOCUS involved at all, so we need not be surprised that different sequence-rules apply.

  This discussion of interrogative clauses has illustrated the way in which functions are used in a systemic grammar. The functions that are set up are often rather unusual, if for no other reason because they have little or no direct connection with meaning; and there are far more of them, both in the grammar itself and in the description of any item, than is usual in other kinds of grammar. Functions have a very important part to play in the grammar, as the mediators of environmental conditioning of all kinds, often bringing together under one category a number of different and rather complex environmental influences. Without using functions in this way, it would be much harder to write a systemic grammar, and I hope that it will be with reference to their effect on the grammar that they will be judged, rather than against some pre-existing notion of the nature and number of the functions that a grammar should define.

1.2.5. *Paradigmatic relations*
The difference between paradigmatic and syntagmatic relations

  The distinction between paradigmatic and syntagmatic relations is a very well established one, especially in the European and British traditions, so there should be no need to justify it here. It is self-evident that there are two very different kinds of relation that an item can contract: with other items because they occur in the same sentence, and with other items because they are part of the same language. It is hard to exaggerate the importance of the distinction, and there are probably few linguists who would deny the need to recognise it in constructing a grammatical model.

However, it is not so easy to give a precise definition of the two kinds of relation. We might follow Hjelmslev in describing syntagmatic relations as relations 'in praesentia', in contrast with paradigmatic relations which are 'in absentia'; but this would imply that there can be no paradigmatic relation between two items if they both occur in the same sentence. For instance, we should probably want to treat *this* as paradigmatically related to *that* in

This is bigger than the other,

but we should have to see this relation as a syntagmatic one, rather than a paradigmatic one, in

This is bigger than that.

This is obviously not what any linguist would accept, so a paradigmatic relation cannot depend on one or more terms being absent.

But on the other hand we cannot say that a paradigmatic relation exists in the language system whereas a syntagmatic relation exists within a particular sentence, because the latter relations are also defined within the language system: the relation between the subject and the verb is defined by the language system just as much as is that between *this* and *that*.

We might equate the distinction between syntagmatic and paradigmatic relations with the logical one between conjunction and disjunction, saying that a syntagmatic relation is an 'and' relation, whilst a paradigmatic relation is an 'or' relation. To be a little more precise, this could mean that if a relation depends on its terms both being present in the same construction, it is a syntagmatic relation, whereas it is a paradigmatic relation if it depends on the terms being alternatives under some defined set of conditions. By this definition, in

This is bigger than that,

there is a syntagmatic relation (of some kind) between *this* and *that*, but there is presumably a paradigmatic relation between them as well. This way of drawing the distinction between the two kinds of relation seems more satisfactory than the other ways, but there remain two major problems.

The environment of a paradigmatic relation

The first problem is that of deciding what the set of conditions could be under which a paradigmatic relation holds. It is often suggested that a paradigmatic relation must be between items that are in direct contrast, in that either can be substituted for the other without the environment varying. On these terms, there is a paradigmatic relation between *this boy* and *these boys* in

> This boy came late,
> These boys came late,

since we can substitute one for the other without altering the environments. But this is not possible if the verb is present tense, since the verb must then be changed along with the noun-phrase:

> This boy comes late,
> These boys come late.

Consequently we should have to conclude that there is no paradigmatic relation between *this boy* and *these boys* in the environment of a present-tense verb, whereas there is such a relation if the verb is past-tense.

It is hard to see what use such a conception of paradigmatic relations would be in a grammar, since there is no way of deciding how precisely the environment of a paradigmatic relation should be defined. For instance, should we make the above environment *more* specific, by making special statements about the past tense of *be* (which would exclude the paradigmatic relation, contrary to the earlier rule) and the present tenses of the modal auxiliaries like *can* (which would allow the relation, again contrary to the earlier rule)? If we take this approach, the grammar will become hopelessly fragmented and un-general, so should we perhaps make the environment *less* specific, and define it simply as the environment of the subject, so that *this boy* and *these boys* would be paradigmatically related if they are subject, whether the verb is past or present? Clearly the less specifically we define the environment for the relation, the more general will be the part of the grammar in which paradigmatic relations are defined, and this will be a gain; but if we follow this principle, the question arises why we have to impose any environmental restrictions at all. I shall return briefly to this problem below, after redefining paradigmatic relations.

A revised definition of paradigmatic relations

The second problem with the definition of paradigmatic relations that we offered above is that according to it all paradigmatic relations are relations of *contrast*, which raises question what the *terms* of the contrast are. Take the four items *this*, *that*, *these* and *those*. We shall clearly want to be able to show that there are in fact two separate contrasts, one related to 'distance' and the other to number:

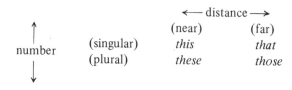

In order to be able to show these relations, we must be able to show not only that *this* and *that* are different from each other, but also that in one respect they are the *same*, both being 'near' on the dimension of 'distance'. This we cannot show as a paradigmatic relation if paradigmatic relations are by definition relations of *contrast*.

One way of overcoming this difficulty would be to revise the definition of paradigmatic relations, and another would be to revise our assumptions about the terms of paradigmatic relations. In fact, as I shall try to show below, we shall need to make *both* kinds of revision.

Let us start by looking at our assumptions about the terms of a paradigmatic relation. In our discussion so far all our examples have involved individual items, such as *this boy* as opposed to *these boys*, or *this* as opposed to *that*. However, we should avoid the problem of showing similarities as well as contrasts if we were to consider the terms of a paradigmatic relation to be *classes* of items rather than individual items. For instance, the relation of number would be between the class of singular items and the class of plural items rather than between, say, the item *this* and the item *these*. The similarity between *this* and *that* would then lie in that they both belong to the same class and therefore both stand in the same paradigmatic relation to the same other class.

There are two consequences of taking this rather obvious step. One is that the paradigmatic relation of number between *this* and *these* is no different at all from the relation between the former and *those*. In other words, as far as the number contrast is concerned, *this* and *that* are both singular and *these* and *those* both plural, and there is no special relationship at all between *this* and *these*. (In this respect, a paradigmatic relationship as we have defined it is not at all the same thing as a traditional paradigm.)

The second consequence of our redefinition of the terms of a paradigmatic relation is similar to the first: lexical differences are not at all relevant to grammatical paradigmatic relations. For instance, both *apples* and *pears* can occur in the environment '– grow in England', so by any definition of para-digamtic relations we can say that there is one between *apples* and *pears* here, but this is a lexical relation, and not a grammatical one, and it is unlikely that we should ever be able to identify a grammatical contrast between them. Moreover, what we said above about the relation between *this* and *these* applies to *apple* and *apples* as well: there is no special grammatical relation-ship between *apple* and *apples*, but only a relation between singular nouns as a whole, including *apple* and *pear*, and plural nouns as a whole, including *apples* and *pears*.

Having revised our assumptions about the terms of a grammatical paradig-matic relation, let us look again at our definition of paradigmatic relations as relations specifically of contrast. The revision we have already made might allow us to keep this definition as it is, as far as the relations among *this*, *that*, *these* and *those* are concerned: the similarity between *this* and *that* lies in that they are both related in the same way to *these* and *those*. However, there is another problem: what kind of relationship is there between classes and sub-classes? For instance, the classes that we named 'near' and 'distant' are sub-classes of a larger class, the class of 'demonstrative adjectives': is the rela-tion between the latter and its two sub-classes paradigmatic or syntagmatic or of some third kind?

This will of course depend on how we define the terms paradigmatic and syntagmatic, but it is certainly easier to make a case for treating such relations as paradigmatic relations than to argue that they are syntagmatic, so it seems reasonable to extend the definition of paradigmatic relations to include sub-classification relations. From there it is a short step to defining paradigmatic relations as classification relations of any kind: relations between classes that are subclasses of the same larger class as well as between those in contrast with each other.

This is how the term paradigmatic relation will be used in this book, and it has the advantage, among others, of allowing us to speak of 'paradigmatic en-vironments' in contrast with syntagmatic environments: the paradigmatic environment of 'near' being 'demonstrative adjective', for instance (see be-low). However, what is involved is mainly a question of terminology, and of how we sharpen the definition of a term which elsewhere tends to be used somewhat imprecisely. If the reader objects to this redefinition, his objection need not go beyond this particular point of terminology.

The environment of paradigmatic relations as redefined

However, there is one consequence of the redefinition which it is best to make explicit, since it appears to involve a break with an important Firthian tradition. In British linguistics it has for long been an agreed principle that 'systems' are tied to 'places in structure' — that is, a paradigmatic relation must be tied to a particular syntagmatic environment, since a contrast which is operative in one environment may be inoperative in another. This is part of what is known as the 'polysystemic' approach.

However, if we accept the redefinition of paradigmatic relations, they will no longer be tied in this way: for instance, there will be a paradigmatic relation between singular and plural noun-phrases even in environments where only one of the classes can occur. I gave reasons above why we should not want to tie paradigmatic relations to particular syntagmatic environments; and now we have a positive alternative: paradigmatic relations are restricted in their environments, but the environments to which they are restricted are not syntagmatic but paradigmatic. So for instance the contrast between singular and plural noun-phrases is just restricted to the paradigmatic environment of the class 'noun-phrase'. The fact that in certain syntagmatic environments one of the contrasted classes is not possible can be shown simply by excluding that class in the environment concerned, rather than by suppressing the paradigmatic relation itself.

Paradigmatic relations as redefined contrasted with syntagmatic relations

I started this discussion of paradigmatic relations by contrasting some definitions of the difference between paradigmatic and syntagmatic relations, so it will be appropriate to show how the two kinds of relation differ, now that we have redefined paradigmatic relations. I shall concentrate on what seem to me to be the two most important differences.

Firstly, grammatical classes by definition show paradigmatic relations, whilst grammatical functions by definition show syntagmatic relations. So in systemic theory we can have completely separate sets of categories for handling the two kinds of relation, as seems appropriate considering how important the difference between them is.

As we would expect, there is a close connection between the two kinds of categories, and there may even be a one-to-one match in some cases: for instance, we shall use a function FINITE as well as a class 'finite verb', although these two are inseparable: every word that belongs to the class 'finite verb' will have the function FINITE, and vice versa. However, this apparent redundancy is not vicious, since the function reflects the word's syntagmatic relations – for instance, that it must be the first verb in the clause – whereas the class reflects its paradigmatic relations to other classes of verbs (non-finite, past, etc.). To try to avoid one-to-one matches between functions and classes would be as wrong as to try to avoid one-to-one correspondences between grammatical and phonological patterns: since they reflect different kinds of information, they are *both* needed.

The second main difference between syntagmatic and paradigmatic relations is that the first are environment-bound whereas the latter are environment-independent. To take an obvious example, the paradigmatic relations into which *our friends* enters are exactly the same in both the following sentences, since it belongs to the same classes in both of them.

> *Our friends* have all met each other,
> Shall we invite *our friends*?

It is true that its membership of the class 'plural noun-phrase' is relevant to its syntagmatic environment in the first sentence (since it is in an environment which requires a plural noun-phrase) but not in the second sentence; nevertheless it belongs to this class in both cases. The difference between its use in the one sentence and its use in the other is located, then, not in the *classes* to which it belongs but in the *functions* that it has – in its syntagmatic relations, not in its paradigmatic relations.

Grammatical classes

The reorientation of linguistics towards the writing of generative grammars has made classification into a tool that we use in writing a grammar, rather than a more or less self-justifying activity. This means that any principles we may formulate with regard to grammatical classes – how we decide what criteria to base them on, how we represent them, how they are related to one another, and so on – stand or fall according to how useful the classes they yield will be in a grammar.

For instance, there will be relatively little use for a class which contains all the items that can occur in a particular environment, if the items we group together in this way have nothing else in common; all we can do with such a class is to list its members, and this means that by bringing all the items concerned under a single head we have not improved the grammar in any sense.

By way of contrast, the class of relative clauses is one that brings together a number of different characteristics, of both distribution and internal structure, and thereby benefits the grammar. The members of this class are found in several different environments, illustrated by the following:

> The man *who built this shed* lives in Nottingham,
> My older brother, *who built this shed*, lives in Nottingham,
> It was my older brother *who built this shed*.

The fact that (with exceptions) the items that can occur in one of these environments can also occur in the other two would already justify setting up the class, since we could then define its membership just once (even if this meant listing them separately) whilst referring to the class in three different sets of distributional statements. However, it is further justified in that it allows us to make certain generalisations about structures: that the members of the class either contain a finite verb, and a relative pronoun (except under certain conditions when the latter is optional) or contain a participial verb, without either a relative pronoun or a subject:

> The man *who built this shed* ...
> The shed *that my brother built* ...
> The shed *my brother built* ...
> The shed *standing at the bottom of the garden* ...
> The shed *built by my brother* ...

   What we gain by setting up a class of relative clauses is the possibility of making generalisations about the distribution of this class and about the structures that its members have, and of keeping these two kinds of generalisation relatively independent of each other. (It is true that the two kinds of statement cannot be entirely independent of each other, since there are some structural patterns that cannot occur in some environments, but these exceptional restrictions can easily be handled by means of special statements about the relevant subclasses of relative clauses.)
   This example illustrates a very general phenomenon in grammar: the discrepancy between distributional groupings of items and groupings based on internal structure. If we were to take account just of the patterns that we can identify in the structures of clauses, we should not bring all the clauses listed above together into one class; for instance we should have been more likely to give priority to the difference between those with finite verbs and those without, or between those with a relative pronoun and those without. As it is, we have distributional reasons for wanting to group them all together in spite of this diversity of structures.

This claim, that there can be a discrepancy between distributional and structural groupings, would be accepted by most linguists. Where they would disagree is on the way of reconciling the differences between the two kinds of grouping. The TG approach is generally to introduce the structural differences that distinguish distributional classes by means of transformational rules, and to do the same for structural differences *within* distributional classes. The systemic approach, on the other hand, is to treat the discrepancy as part of the definition of a grammatical class, so that the class of relative clauses for instance is defined in such a way that it covers the relevant range of structures as well as the relevant range of distributions.

In this respect, systemic theory is representative of the British and European linguistic tradition, with its emphasis on 'WP' (word-and-paradigm, see Robins, 1959); whilst TG is more typical of the American preference for item-based models, whether 'IA' (item-and-arrangement) or 'IP' (item-and-process), described by Hockett (1954).

The size of items being classified

One of the characteristics of systemic grammar that distinguishes it from most other current theories is that we tend to apply a relatively detailed classification to items that are relatively large — whereas in most versions of TG theory the only really detailed classification is by means of features attached specifically to the smallest grammatical items. This difference follows automatically from the different ways in which the models handle the discrepancy between distribution and structure mentioned in the last subsection: in order to group relative clauses together, we have to set up a class of *clauses* in a systemic grammar, where in a TG grammar we might simply postulate a 'relative' morpheme which is transformationally introduced into the structure of any clause which is in an environment that requires a relative clause.

An example of this characteristic of systemic grammar is the treatment of *tense*, which is dealt with not only by means of a classification of verbs, but also by a classification of clauses. Even if we simply have two classes of verbs and two corresponding classes of clauses, according to whether the verb was 'past' or not, the classes yielded by these two contrasts will obviously have completely different members, since in one case the population being divided are all verbs, and in the other they are all clauses; and accordingly we need different names for the classes: 'past-verb' versus 'non-past verb' and 'past-clause' versus 'non-past clause'. It is clear that we both should and can classify verbs as either 'past' or 'non-past'; but why should we try to classify clauses as well?

The main advantage of classifying clauses according to tense is that the relation between the classification of clauses and the classification of verbs is not simple. If it had been the case that every clause that was 'past-clause' contained a verb that was 'past-verb', and that every such verb occurs in a clause that is 'past-clause', then there might have been no need to have both classes. However, there are discrepancies between them; for instance, some clauses that are 'past-clause' do not contain a verb that is 'past-verb', but instead have the tense marked by *have*:

He must have died a long time ago.'

There is no special difficulty in grouping this clause together with

He died a long time ago,

and calling them both 'past-clause'; the difference between them simply involves conditioned alternative manifestations of their common class-membership, similar to the differences among relative clauses.

In order to decide how 'big' the items should be to which a particular contrast applies — whether they should be morphemes, words, phrases or clauses, for instance — we simply apply the general principle of grammatical classification that we have already considered: the items concerned should be the right size for the classification to bring together the discrepancies between distribution and structure. If they are too small, the relevant structural patterns will fall outside them; for instance, if we try to make the tense classification apply only to morphemes, then we may be able to classify *have* as a conditional alternative to *-ed*, but we shall not be able to bring in the *-en* that always goes with *have*. On the other hand, if the items concerned are too big, the structural patterns to which we shall have to refer will be too deeply embedded in them, and therefore relatively hard to characterise.

In a systemic description, then, it is not only the smallest grammatical items that are classified in detail. Because of this, we find nothing in systemic theory corresponding to the distinction between 'features' — such as [+ past] — and 'categories' — such as NP and S — in TG theory: all classification in systemic theory is comparable to that effected by means of features in TG theory. At present features are generally assigned only to morphemes in TG theory, but it has been suggested (e.g. Chomsky, 1970) that they could be assigned to larger items too, such as noun-phrases; this is already what is done in systemic descriptions.

1.2.6. *Summary of the content of a systemic description*

Let us now bring together the various points that have been made in this section about the kinds of information which a systemic grammar ought to enable us to give in a grammatical description.

First of all, what does a grammatical description describe? By definition, the objects of description are *grammatical items*, and these may be as big as sentences or as small as morphemes. In one example sentence (*These plates have all been dried*) we identified fourteen grammatical items, including the sentence as a whole, and each of these can therefore be the object of a separate grammatical description. If we want a complete description of the utterance, which includes all the grammatical information we can muster, then we simply combine the descriptions of all the separate grammatical items contained within it. Thus the sentence as such is only one grammatical item out of the fourteen that can be identified, and its description only includes one fourteenth part of the sum of grammatical information. (In this respect, I have been using the word 'sentence' rather loosely in this chapter, as the reader will have noticed: instead of speaking of the grammatical description of a sentence, it would have been more accurate, but more clumsy, to speak of the grammatical description of a sentence and its constituent parts.)

One of the characteristics of this version of systemic theory is that it requires only one analysis of each utterance-type into its grammatical constituents, so that it is meaningful to ask 'What are the grammatical items in this utterance-type?' In this respect systemic grammars are different from TG grammars, since for the latter each structure, from the deep structure to the surface structure defines a different set of grammatical items. Indeed, the only item which can be guaranteed to be represented in all structures of a TG description is the sentence itself, so there is a very important sense in which TG grammars are grammars for sentences, whereas systemic grammars are grammars for grammatical items in general.

Secondly, what kinds of information should a grammatical description give about each item? Briefly, it must give information about the grammatical relations into which an item enters, namely its syntagmatic relations to other items in the same sentence and its paradigmatic relations to other elements in the same language. These two kinds of relations reflect completely different kinds of factors, so they ought to be kept clearly separate in the grammatical description.

Taking syntagmatic relations first, there are three kinds of relation which will be shown explicitly by the description: constituency, sequence and functional relations. Except where there is discontinuity, the first two kinds of relation can be shown by means of a simple configuration: we ensure that the description (in the sense of the remaining parts of the description) of an earlier item appears on the left of the description of a later one, and that the description of any item is below the description of the item containing it, and connected to the latter by a line. These conventions could produce the normal kind of tree-structure, in which the nodes would be descriptions of items:

However, we shall follow a slightly different convention, whereby each item is represented by a horizontal line, under the description of the item concerned, and constituency relations are always represented by a vertical line:

Where an item is discontinuous, we cannot use these conventions alone to show its constituency relations to other items, but have to include this information among the functional relations.

The third type of syntagmatic relation is the functional relations, and these are represented by means of the names of grammatical functions. Items tend to fulfil more than one function – for instance, a relative pronoun not only marks the clause containing it as a relative clause, but also acts as subject, etc., within the structure of the relative clause; therefore items tend to enter into more than one functional relation, and accordingly their grammatical description will include the names of a number of functions, rather than of just one.

Functional relations are relatively abstract syntagmatic relations, since they bring together all the influences which the grammatical environment exerts on the item, and which determine its other syntagmatic relations (constituency or sequence) or its paradigmatic relations. The function 'subject' is a good example of this principle: when an item has this function, it must be open to a variety of environmental influences which help to determine its place in constituency (it must be an IC of a clause), its place in sequence (it must be in a specified relation to the finite verb), its dependency relations (it and the finite verb must be in concord) and some of its paradigmatic characteristics (it must be 'nominal').

Syntagmatic relations are one part of what an item's grammatical description should reveal, the other part being its paradigmatic relations. As we have defined them, paradigmatic relations are relations between grammatical classes, so we define an item's paradigmatic relations to other items by saying what grammatical classes it belongs to. By so doing, we shall show how it compares with other items in respect of a number of dimensions of classification: for instance, *takes* is the same as all other items that belong to the class 'present-verb', and contrasts with all the members of the contrasting class 'past-verb', but is incomparable, in this respect, with any item (such as *boy* or *if*) which belongs to neither class.

In conclusion, we can revise the diagram given above, showing what the word 'description' stands for: a collection of function-names and a collection of class-names, giving syntagmatic and paradigmatic information respectively.

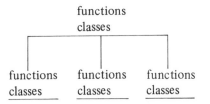

This is a schematic representation of a systemic grammatical description of a number of related items. In the next chapter I shall show how descriptions of this kind can be generated.

2. HOW SYSTEMIC DESCRIPTIONS ARE GENERATED

In chapter 1, I outlined what seem to be to be the kinds of information that a grammatical description ought to enable us to give about any grammatical item; in this chapter I shall show how a systemic grammar generates descriptions that satisfy these requirements. By way of illustration, I shall gradually build up a rather primitive grammar of English which will generate descriptions for a wide range of clausal constructions. In the following chapters I shall improve this grammar, and in particular I shall extend it to cover some kinds of complex sentences in some detail.

2.1. Classification by system-network

One thing that the grammar must enable us to do is to classify grammatical items; this by definition will reveal their paradigmatic relations to each other (1.2.5). Grammatical classes figure in any model of grammatical description, and systemic theory is no exception. In particular, it is normal to assume that we shall have to set up classes of morphemes (in more recent theories) or classes of words (in more traditional theories): so a good point to start discussing systemic theory is with the classification of small items, namely verbs.

Classifying verbs in English: sub-classification and cross-classification

It is useful to classify verbs in English as either *lexical* or *grammatical*; the main verb in a clause is a lexical verb, while the auxiliaries are grammatical. Thus in

He must have been being examined for three hours by now,

there is one lexical verb (*examined*) and four grammatical verbs (*must, have, been* and *being*), two of which are instances of the same verb, *be*. By this initial classification, then, we shall divide the verbs of English into two unequal classes:

(a) grammatical verbs: *must, may, can, could*, etc.; *have; be; do;*
(b) lexical verbs: all others, plus *do* and *have*.

This analysis, like many of the suggestions I shall make, raises a number of questions; for instance, why are *have* and *do* included in both classes, while *be* figures only as a grammatical verb? Why do we use the names 'grammatical' and 'lexical' when the basis for the distinction is primarily a grammatical one? However, I must with regret leave most of these questions unanswered in order to keep the balance between linguistic theory and English grammar, given that this chapter is primarily concerned with linguistic theory rather than with English grammar.

Returning to the two-way classification of verbs into lexical verbs and grammatical verbs, this is obviously not the only grammatical distinction that we shall want to make, since we shall want both to *sub-classify* verbs in these two classes, by dividing these classes into smaller classes, and also to *cross-classify* them, by re-classifying verbs according to criteria that cut across the distinction between 'lexical' and 'grammatical'.

For instance, we can sub-divide the class of grammatical verbs into two classes, 'modal' (*must, can*, etc.) and 'non-modal' (*have, be, do*), and we migh also divide the class of lexical verbs into three classes, named 'copular' (*seem, become*, etc.), 'intransitive' (*walk, glow*, etc.) and 'transitive' (*take, make*, etc.). Moreover, we can further sub-divide the class of 'non-modal' verbs, to yield three classes, each containing one verb: *be, have* and *do*. We can represent successive sub-divisions of this kind by a tree diagram:

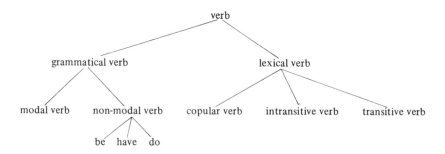

Given this classification, then, the verb *must* belongs to not one class but three: 'modal verb', 'grammatical verb' and 'verb'; and *have* belongs to four classes: 'have', 'non-modal verb', 'grammatical verb' and 'verb'.

However, as Chomsky recognised by 1965, it is not enough for a grammar to allow sub-classification: it must also allow cross-classification. For instance, the classification just given was entirely a question of the verb's stem, so when we classify verbs in a way which reflects just their inflexions we shall have a classification that is independent of the above one. Such a classification will distinguish between 'finite' and 'non-finite' verbs, the former being either 'past' or 'present', the latter being infinitives, ing-forms or en-forms. This classification too can be represented by a tree-diagram, but this also has 'verb' at the top, showing that the classification of verbs requires two trees, and to classify a verb we must locate it on *both* trees:

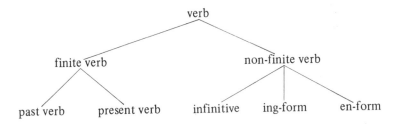

A comparison with word-and-paradigm grammars

The classical verb-paradigm was used precisely for showing the effect of cross-classifying verbs: for instance, it might show tense-distinctions in one dimension and person-number distinction in another. The advantage of this approach is that it allows the same classification for different kinds of verbs even if the differences are manifested in different ways. To take an obvious example from Latin, the tenses of ordinary verbs (like *amo*) and of deponent verbs (like *conor*) could be described in just the same framework in spite of the lack of morphological parallelism between them, which is especially marked in the perfect tenses.

In this respect, it will be seen that systemic grammars are close to the spirit of word-and-paradigm grammars (Robins, 1959) rather than to the item-based grammars developed by the neo-Bloomfieldians: in order to show that *took* and *baked* are both past tense verbs, it is enough to put them both in the class 'past verb'. The question of how we should describe the manifestations of 'past verb' is then a separate one, and does not have to involve assigning a morpheme 'past' to both verbs — unless we define morphemes as 'units of distribution' (Bazell, 1962; Lyons, 1968). In the latter interpretation, there is no difference between 'morphemes' and 'classes' — or rather, between morphemes and 'features' which we shall introduce below.

Another similarity between systemic grammars and word-and-paradigm grammars is that they consist of *statements* about the relations between elements rather than of *instructions* for producing combinations of elements: they describe the various forms that past-tense verbs take, without giving rules for converting the category 'past' into some phonological or graphological shape by rewriting the former as the latter. This means that the rules we use in systemic grammars are like McCawley's 'node admissibility conditions' (McCawley, 1968), which specify the configurations of nodes that are permitted rather than the way in which such configurations could be built up; and they are very different in principle from the 'rewrite' rules normal in TG grammars.

Beside these important similarities between systemic grammars and word-and-paradigm grammars, there are also big differences. For one thing, in order to make the grammar completely explicit it is necessary to go beyond the listing of 'paradigms', in the sense of 'models' from which we generalise in an intuitive way. We shall deal with this aspect of systemic grammar in 2.3 below. Another difference, which is more relevant here, is that we have to be able to make explicit in the grammar precisely what the relations are between the various classes we distinguish: which classes represent sub-divisions of which others, and so on. The relations that we find among classes can be quite complex, so we have had to develop a flexible but explicit way of representing these relations in a generative grammar. It is to this that we now turn.

Systems and system-networks

Whenever we set up a grammatical class, we do so by sub-dividing some larger class with respect to some 'dimension' of classification; so for instance, 'lexical verb' results from a sub-division of the class 'verb' along one dimension, and 'finite verb' results from sub-dividing it along another dimension. This means that each class is contrasted with at least one other class, resulting from the same sub-division, and it is this relation of contrast between the classes corresponding to one dimension of classification which we refer to as a 'system'. There are two systems, in this technical sense, that apply to the class of verbs in English: that which contrasts 'lexical verb' with 'grammatical verb', and that which contrasts 'finite verb' with 'non-finite verb'.

The system is of crucial importance in systemic theory, as the latter's name suggests: for instance, it is to classes in the systems that we relate meanings, rather than to structures, and it is the relations among systems that define syntagmatic relations among constituents. The importance of the system should become clearer in the course of this chapter — and indeed it will be illustrated throughout the book.

A notation has been developed for representing systems and their inter-relations in a diagrammatic way, since this seems to be the easiest way of representing them explicitly. The diagrams are called 'system networks'; it will be seen that they are very different from tree-diagrams, even if we disregard the fact that they tend to get bigger from left to right, whereas trees get bigger from top to bottom.

The notation that we need in order to represent the classification of verbs ·given above is as follows:

(a) The system is represented by a vertical square bracket, indicating an 'or' relation between the classes named on the right of the bracket:

$$\left[\begin{array}{l} \text{lexical verb} \\ \text{grammatical verb} \end{array}\right.$$

(b) The system is related to the larger class which it sub-divides by an arrow, with the larger class at the left-hand end and the system at the right-hand end:

$$\text{verb} \rightarrow \left[\begin{array}{l} \text{lexical verb} \\ \\ \text{grammatical verb} \end{array}\right.$$

In case there is any danger of confusion, it is worth emphasising that this arrow represents a relationship and not an operation, as it would in a TG grammar. Thus the little diagram above means 'Any member of the class 'verb' is also a member either of the class 'lexical verb' or of the class 'grammatical verb', – and not 'Any occurrence of the symbol 'verb' is to be rewritten either as 'lexical verb' or as 'grammatical verb'.' Nor can the arrow be given a psychological interpretation, meaning 'having decided that the item concerned is (or should be) a verb, one decides whether it is (or should be) a lexical verb or a grammatical verb'. In the first instance it reflects a logical relation between classes in the grammar, and whether or not these logical relations have any psychological counterparts is a separate issue.

(c) The terms of one system are themselves classes which can be further subdivided, and we use the same conventions to show these further sub-divisions:

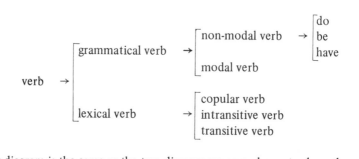

This diagram is the same as the tree-diagram we gave above, to show the relations among the classes concerned, except that it reads from left to right, instead of from top to bottom, and that the diagonal 'branches' of the tree are replaced here by the arrows and square brackets. We start to see the difference between a system network and a tree-diagram only when we move on to the next convention.

(d) A right-facing curly bracket encloses systems that apply to the same class:

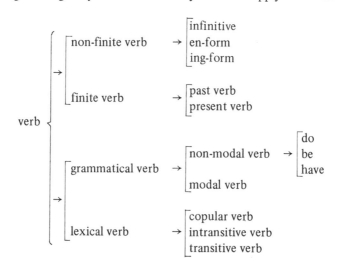

Curly brackets mean 'and' — in contrast with the 'or' of square brackets — and the above diagram means: 'any (member of the class) verb must be either a non-finite verb or a finite verb (etc.) *and* it must be either a grammatical verb or a lexical verb (etc.)'. Like square brackets, curly brackets are used facing in both ways, and we shall see below how they are used facing towards the left.

It is possible to make a factual objection to this system-network: it suggests that modal verbs, like all other kinds of verbs, can be either finite or non-finite, whereas it is one of the defining characteristics of modal verbs that they are always finite (cf. * *has musted*, * *musting*, * *to must*). I shall explain this apparent shortcoming below (p. 64).

Paradigmatic environments of systems

It is easy now to see what I meant in 1.2.5 by saying that the environment for a paradigmatic relation — and more particularly for a system — need not be defined syntagmatically but can be a paradigmatic environment. In the networks I have given so far the environment for each system has been the class to which it applies, each system applying to just one such class. Thus the environment for the system contrasting 'non-finite verb' with 'finite verb' is the class 'verb', and the environment for the system 'past verb' versus 'present verb' is 'finite verb'. The way in which these paradigmatic restrictions work is obvious: for instance, 'past verb' is shown as being compatible with 'finite verb' but not with 'non-finite verb', which means that it is not possible, given this grammar, to classify a word both as 'non-finite verb' and as 'past verb'.

Paradigmatic environments need not be as simple as the ones illustrated so far, where each system had just one class as its environment. Instead of this, the environment may involve a number of different classes, of which all or one must be present for the system to apply — that is, the environment may be either the union or the intersection of the classes concerned.

Restrictions of this kind are hard to illustrate with reference to English verbs, so I shall start by taking abstract examples. Let us assume that there is a system contrasting class x with class y, and that its paradigmatic environment involves two classes, a and b. There are two possibilities: for the system to apply, either we need both a and b, or we need either a or b. To represent relations of these kinds, we use the two kinds of brackets — square and curly — which I have already introduced, but use them facing towards the left instead of towards the right. As before, the square bracket means 'or', so the following diagram means that either a or b must be present:

$$
\left.\begin{matrix} a - \\ \\ b - \end{matrix}\right] \rightarrow \left[\begin{matrix} x \\ \\ y \end{matrix}\right.
$$

The curly bracket means 'and', just as it does when facing right, so we show that both a and b are needed by means of the following diagram:

A typical restriction that would be handled by means of the left-facing curly brackets is the rule that the gender distinction applies to English personal pronouns only if they are both 3rd-person and singular:

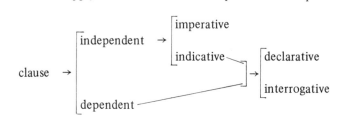

We shall see an example of the use of the left-facing square bracket later in this section when we come to classify clauses (p. 65): the contrast between 'declarative' (statement) and 'interrogative' (question) applies to clauses provided they are *either* independent and 'indicative' (not imperative) *or* dependent — i.e. according to this very crude analysis, the only class of clause to which it does not apply are those which are independent and imperative:

Recursive systems

One special case of the disjunctive kind of complex paradigmatic environment is the recursive system, where one of the alternative environments for the system is one of the system's own terms. Taking an abstract example again, we would represent this as follows:

This diagram would mean that the system 'x' versus 'y' applies either to the class 'b' or to the class 'x', which means that each time the class 'x' is selected the system will apply again, giving the possibility of 'x' being selected yet again (cf. Anderson, 1969).

As it happens, we shall not need to use this facility of systemic theory in this book, but it nevertheless seems worth mentioning it. It will almost certainly be crucially important in a grammar of English coordinative constructions (Hudson, in preparation) where it will be exclusively responsible for the recursive element. Briefly, the grammar is likely to look something like this:

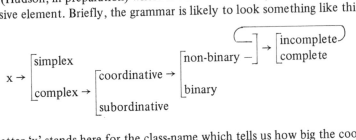

The letter 'x' stands here for the class-name which tells us how big the coordinated items are — clauses, phrases, words, etc. The first system shows members of this class to be either 'simplex' (i.e. single items) or 'complex' (strings of two or more items coordinated or subordinated to each other). The recursive system allows 'incomplete' to be selected any number of times once 'non-binary' has been selected, which is the initial condition for the system.

Take coordinated noun-phrases, for instance. Both *the books* and *the books and the journals* will be classified as members of the class 'noun-phrase', the difference being that the former is 'simplex' while the latter is 'complex' (and 'coordinative'). If we accept for instance that the construction *both ... and ...* should have no more than two terms, then the distinction between two and more than two corresponds to a difference of kind rather than of degree; so we draw a line between constructions with two members ('binary') and those with more than two ('non-binary'). The latter can have any number of coordinates, but for each coordinate above three (or two, for a slightly different interpretation of the 'binary' : 'non-binary' distinction) there would be one occurrence of 'incomplete'; so *the books, the journal, the newspapers and the comics* would be classified as 'incomplete' while *the books, the journals, the newspapers, the comics and the records* would be 'incomplete', 'incomplete'.

It makes relatively little sense to make a distinction according to the number of times that an item belongs to some class, but it will make more sense when we re-interpret classes in terms of features below (p. 73).

The big advantage of allowing direct recursion of this kind in the system-network, rather than in rules that affect the structure directly, is that it does not add unwanted structure. If we use a recursive phrase-structure rule, such as

$$x \rightarrow x + x$$

then we can generate nothing but binary structures, whereas we really want to generate single layers of structure with any number of ICs. In TG theory the way has been found out of this dilemma by the introduction of a new bit of theoretical apparatus, the 'rule-schema', but in systemic theory no special apparatus is needed. We allow 'incomplete' to occur any number of times in the paradigmatic description of an item, by a recursive system, and then we map each occurrence of 'incomplete' onto a separate element in the item's structure.

The possibility of recursive systems is a good example of the versatility of the system network, and of the advantage of separating paradigmatic analysis from the analysis of internal structures: pure linear recursion is easy to handle within this systemic framework, in which syntagmatic relations derive from paradigmatic ones, but it is hard to handle if we try to subsume paradigmatic relations under syntagmatic ones.

Syntagmatic restrictions on systems

A more orthodox Firthian approach to the analysis of English verbs would have looked very different from the one I have just offered, in that it would have identified a number of separate system networks, each applying in a different syntagmatic environment. For instance, if we assume that 'main verb' is the name for one syntagmatic environment in which verbs occur, then there would have been one corresponding network which would allow only for verbs that can actually occur as main verb. It is not obvious what this network would include, but it would presumably not include the systems specifically involving grammatical verbs. Furthermore, we might also identify four other syntagmatic environments, one for each kind of auxiliary verb, and to each of these environments there would correspond a different system-network, reflecting the inflexion found in that position in the chain of auxiliaries.

I have already explained why I have abandoned this approach (1.2.5); it is hard to find a satisfactory basis for deciding what environmental differences are relevant and which are not, and it is hard to generalise from one network to another. However, we still have to show the same basic facts: that the contrast between 'non-modal verb' and 'modal verb' is not relevant in the syntagmatic environment 'main verb', for instance. If we do not do this by excluding the system concerned from that environment we must do it in some other way.

The solution to this problem is simple: we exclude the class which is the system's paradigmatic environment from the syntagmatic environment 'main verb', and this automatically prevents the system from applying. In other words, we stipulate that in the syntagmatic environment 'main verb' it is not permitted to select 'grammatical verb', and therefore all the systems which presuppose 'grammatical verb' are also ruled out. All we need is either a distributional statement about the class 'grammatical verb' which excludes it from that syntagmatic environment — or else one for 'lexical verb' which will make it obligatory in this environment. Of these two approaches it is in fact the second that we shall adopt: we shall cover distributional restrictions by defining the classes which are *required* by a certain environment rather than by defining those that are *excluded* from it.

By allowing both syntagmatic and paradigmatic restrictions on systems, then, we can have much more general system networks than would otherwise be possible: for instance, it would not otherwise be possible to have a single network bringing together all the systems that apply to verbs of one kind or another. However, there is another advantage of allowing both kinds of environmental restriction: we can adduce whichever kind of restriction is the more convenient and this can lead to considerable simplification of the grammar.

A good example of this is the way in which we can show that modal verbs have to be finite. As I pointed out above, the networks I have given so far have all suggested that the distinction between 'finite verb' and 'non-finite verb' applies equally to all verbs, including modal verbs. If we were to correct the grammar by imposing a *paradigmatic* restriction on this system, we should have to change the network into one which was far less symmetrical and generally attractive than the original ones. It might look like this:

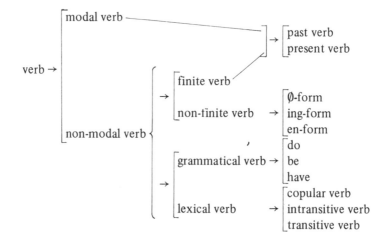

However, there is in fact no need to make this sacrifice, because the syntagmatic restrictions on the distribution of 'modal verb' already cover the desired restrictions: there is only one syntagmatic environment that allows modal verbs (according to the grammar I am gradually introducing, that is), and this environment is one which also requires the verb to be finite. Thus the requirement of finiteness is imposed by the syntagmatic environment, and there is therefore no need to show it in the network as well.

In a systemic grammar, then, we have to define the ways in which the syntagmatic environment restricts the classes that can be chosen from the system-network; this will be the subject of 2.5 below. However, it is worth mentioning here that there are two ways in which we can incorporate syntagmatic environmental restrictions into the grammar. One is by a statement relating a particular kind of environment to a particular class, and saying that in this environment the class concerned is obligatory.

The other is by means of a convention involving 'markedness', whereby some systems have one term which must be selected unless there are environmental reasons for selecting another term. A good example of this is the system contrasting *do*, *be* and *have*: here *do* must be selected wherever there is nothing in the environment indicating that *be* or *have* are required. In one sense of 'markedness', *do* is 'unmarked' and *be* and *have* are 'marked'. Not all systems have unmarked and marked terms, but where there is one, this is shown in the system network by an asterisk against the unmarked term. The system network for verbs has five such systems, as the revised version below shows:

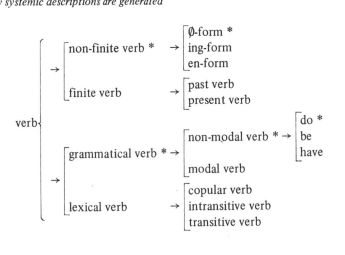

The classification of larger items: dependency and mood

So far nearly all our examples have involved the classification of single words. For those accustomed to word-and-paradigm grammars the idea of classifying words will not seem as odd as that of classifying larger items, such as clauses and phrases, to which we now turn. As I have already mentioned (1.2.5) precisely the same principles of classification are applied in systemic grammars to larger items as to smaller items, so we shall have system networks applying to clauses and to phrases just like the one we have already described.

Let us start by considering a network reflecting mood and dependency:

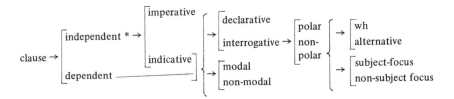

This network provides an example of the left-facing use of the square brackets mentioned above (p. 60); it means 'any clause is either independent or dependent; if it is independent, it is also either imperative or indicative; if it is indicative, *or* if it is dependent, it is also either declarative or interrogative and either modal or non-modal ...'.

This network incorporates two sets of contrasts that are traditionally used as the basis for classifying clauses as such, so there should be relatively little difficulty in accepting at least the principle of doing the same here. The contrast represented by the first system corresponds roughly with the traditional distinction between main and subordinate clauses, but it might be more helpful to identify our 'dependent' clauses with traditional reported ones, since the network then goes on to classify them as either 'declarative' ('reported statements') or 'interrogative' ('reported questions'). This analysis will be replaced by a better one in the later chapters of this book, but the relatively simple one given here will serve to illustrate a number of theoretical points.

First of all, differences of structures need bear no simple relationship to differences of class – unless we deliberately define structures in such a way that they do, in which case there is no need for classes as well. Having rejected this alternative, for reasons given in 1.2.5, we still have to decide how abstract our structures are to be, but even so it is clear that the differences between the structures below do not match the differences of class.

	independent	*dependent*
declarative	It broke	... that it broke
interrogative:		
polar	Did it break?	... whether it broke
non-polar:		
wh, subject-focus	What broke?	... what broke
non-subject focus	Why did it break?	... why it broke
alternative, subject-focus	Did the rope or the pulley brake?	... whether the rope or the pulley broke
non-subject focus	Did it break at the top or the bottom?	... whether it broke at the top or the bottom

Secondly, the decision as to whether a contrast should be identified as a system of the clause or not can be made on the basis of factors purely internal to the grammar. For instance, our network for clauses includes a system contrasting 'modal' with 'non-modal' (e.g. 'You must be crazy' versus 'You are crazy'). One reason for setting up this system (in addition to the system 'modal verb'.versus 'non-modal verb' in the network for verbs) is that it makes the grammar much simpler: it allows us to define a grammatical environment, in the clause's structure, where only verbs that are both modal and finite can occur, and this in turn allows us to keep the system network for verbs relatively simple, as I showed above. For this simplification we pay the price of having an extra system in the clause network, but it fits very neatly into this network. Moreover, we should have to introduce this system in any case, because the manifestation of 'past' varies according to whether the clause is modal or not:

> You must have been crazy,
> You were crazy.

The general point illustrated here is that one of the variables that we have to control in writing a grammar is the place at which we locate a particular contrast: if we embody it in a system that applies to small items, such as morphemes, it may be difficult to define its manifestations — i.e. the structural patterns that reflect it — because these are outside the items being classified. In the last example, 'modal' is manifested outside the modal verb, by the presence of *have*, so the item classified as 'modal' must be big enough to include the *have* as well as the modal verb *must* — i.e. it must be the whole clause.

Transitivity

Another set of contrasts that apply to the clause are those that involve the class of the verb ('copular', 'intransitive', or 'transitive') and the kinds of subjects and complements which the clause contains. Again, we say that these contrasts apply to the clause because they involve not only the verb but also, on the one hand, the subject and complement, and on the other hand the presence or absence of the passive marker *be*. The kinds of contrasts that an adequate analysis of this area of grammar would have to cover are very complex (cf. Halliday, 1968; Fillmore, 1969), but I shall give a very simple analysis:

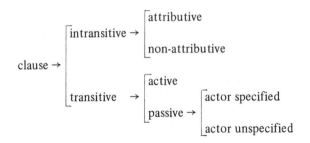

The paradigm below shows the kinds of structural differences that I intend these systems to cover:

intransitive:
  attributive   The wind grew colder
  non-attributive   The wind dropped
transitive:
  active   The wind damaged the crops
  passive:
    actor specified   The crops were damaged by the wind
    actor unspecified   The crops were damaged

This set of contrasts is completely independent of the contrasts included under dependency and mood, so we can simply link them by means of a right-facing curly bracket:

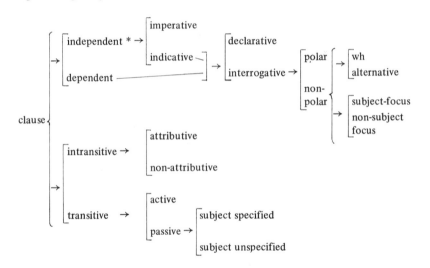

The classification of phrases

I shall have very little to say in this book about phrases as such, so I shall offer an exceedingly crude classification here, making in fact just two contrasts:

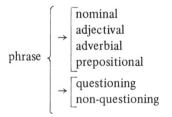

We shall be referring to these contrasts later in the grammar, since we shall have to specify, for instance, that phrases must be nominal if they are to act as subject, and that wh-interrogative clauses are introduced by a 'questioning' phrase, which may be 'nominal' (*which boy, who, how many boys*), 'adjectival' (*how big*), 'adverbial' (*how quickly*) or 'prepositional' (*for who(m), with which axe*).

It is perhaps worth pointing out that one item does not need to have more than one IC in order to count as a phrase; so, for instance, *children* is a phrase in

Children were playing outside his window,

although it only consists of a single word. By treating *children* as a phrase we make it possible to assign it to classes which also include items like *the children*, which means that the rules that cover the use of the latter will also cover it. This makes the grammar much less complex than it would otherwise be.

Rank

We have now looked briefly at some ways in which clauses, phrases and words (or more specifically verbs) can be classified. What then is the relation between these different areas of the grammar? Clearly the answer depends on whether we are talking in paradigmatic or syntagmatic terms.

If we are concerned with syntagmatic relations, then it is possible to make a very rough generalisation to the effect that clauses tend to consist of phrases and phrases tend to consist of words — and words tend to consist of morphemes. In other words, the relation between them is one of constituency, to the extent that our generalisation is correct. In the original 'scale-and-category' theory out of which systemic theory developed, this relation was referred to as the 'scale' of 'rank' — meaning that it was treated as one of three fundamental types of grammatical relation, the other two being 'delicacy' and 'exponence'.

In the present theory however these three fundamental grammatical relations have been replaced by a different triad: syntagmatic, paradigmatic and realisational. (We have already discussed the first two in some detail in 1.2.4 and 1.2.5; realisational relations will come up for discussion in the next section of this chapter.) On the whole, 'delicacy' is subsumed by paradigmatic relations, and 'exponence' by realisational relations. 'Rank' however is harder to map onto the present framework, since it involves both syntagmatic and paradigmatic relations, as I shall show.

As far as syntagmatic relations are concerned, then, clauses phrases and words are related by constituency, which is one of our three main kinds of syntagmatic relation. When we consider their paradigmatic relations, however, we find that 'clause', 'phrase' and 'word' are simply the names of classes of grammatical items, like 'independent clause', 'nominal phrase' and 'verb' except that they are larger classes. As with other classes, they are defined partly in terms of distribution, partly in terms of structure; their only peculiarity being that structure perhaps plays a more important part than in the definition of other classes. Thus the relation between them is simply a system, rather than some other unique kind of grammatical relation.

The scale of rank took account of both kinds of relation among clauses, phrases and words, by making a rough correlation between the two: if we observe the constituency relations between clauses, phrases and words in the simplest kinds of constructions we find that they can be arranged in this order: (1) clauses, (2) phrases, (3) words. However, precisely because rank was an *observation* of this kind, it is unnecessary to treat it as a 'scale' on a par with 'delicacy' and 'exponence', or with 'syntagmatic', 'paradigmatic' and 'realisational'.

If we treat 'clause', 'phrase' and 'word' simply as the names of classes in a system, how does this system relate to the other systems that we have introduced so far? Clearly, its effect is to bring them all together into a single network, which applies to any grammatical item whatever its 'size'. We can now summarise all our earlier systems by showing them as part of an all-embracing system-network. To make it easier to refer to them later, we shall give each system a number.

What a grammar will contain, then, is not a number of different system-networks, each for a different 'rank' (clause, phrase, etc.) or a different environment (subject, main verb, etc.), but a single network which includes all the grammatical systems needed for the language. Treating the relation among 'clause', 'phrase', etc. as a system which binds all the other systems together on the left is simply taking to its logical conclusion the principle that I have already stated: that the syntagmatic environment can predetermine the selection to be made from a system. Thus if some environment allows a word but not a clause or phrase then the only part of the total network which is thereafter available to be chosen from will be the part extending rightwards from 'word'. In this way, it seems to me, we keep the advantages of the Firthian 'polysystemic' approach, but the grammar will be much more integrated than it would be if we left the various systems unconnected.

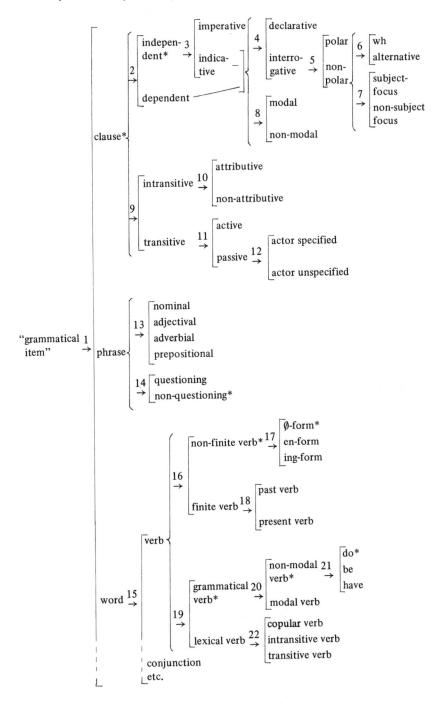

Classes and features

This completes our discussion of classification in systemic grammar, except for two small points, one of which is simply a notational convention.

When we are specifying paradigmatic relations informally, we tend to use an attributive construction, with the 'descriptive' verb *be*; the complement may be a noun-phrase (*'seeing* is a verb'), an adjective (*'seeing* is non-finite'), or a prepositional phrase (*'seeing* is in the ing-form'). However, grammatical descriptions such as these reflect the syntactic resources of English more than they do the properties of any grammatical model; in particular, the difference between a noun-phrase, an adjective and a prepositional phrase is irrelevant as far as the grammatical information conveyed by these statements is concerned. What theoretical categories do these complements correspond to?

From what I have said so far it will be clear that they are simply the names of grammatical classes: 'verb', 'finite', 'ing-form'. Thus, when we say *'seeing* is a verb/non-finite/in the ing-form', what we mean, in more formal terms, is *'seeing* is a member of the class verb/non-finite/ing-form'.

However, there is another way of viewing terms such as 'verb', 'non-finite' and 'ing-form': as the names of *features*. Seen in this way, an item will be said to *have* the category concerned, rather than to *belong* to it: *seeing* has the features 'verb', 'non-finite' and 'ing-form', rather than belonging to classes with these names. Similarly, we can think of the terms of a system as being either classes or features. So for instance the system

$$\text{verb} \rightarrow \begin{bmatrix} \text{finite verb} \\ \\ \text{non-finite verb} \end{bmatrix}$$

can be verbalised either as 'any item which belongs to the class 'verb' must also belong to one of the classes 'finite verb' and 'non-finite verb' '; or as 'any item which has the feature 'verb' must also have one of the features 'finite verb' and 'non-finite verb' '.

In systemic theory, features and classes are in an exact one-to-one correspondence; a different feature is associated with every class, and every class has associated with it just one feature, and the same term is used both as the name for the class and as the name for the feature. This means that every paradigmatic category can be seen both as a class and as a feature, but it does not mean that there is a corresponding redundancy in the grammar, with classes and features expressing separately exactly the same information. As far as the descriptions that are generated are concerned, all they specify is the paradigmatic category as such, and the question of whether this is the name of a class or of a feature does not arise: it is both.

In most cases we can see paradigmatic categories either way, but there are two situations where it is easier to see them as features rather than as classes. One is when we are describing realisation relations between paradigmatic categories and functions or structures, since features are things that items 'have', just like functions and structures, whereas classes represent a different kind of abstraction. For instance, it is easier to say that the feature 'declarative' is realised by the structure pattern 'subject followed by finite verb' than to do this for the *class* 'declarative'. This being so, I shall tend to verbalise realisation rules in terms of features rather than of classes; and more generally I shall refer to paradigmatic categories as features rather than as classes unless there is some advantage in talking in terms of classes.

The second situation where features are more convenient than classes is when we are referring to recursive systems, as I mentioned above (p. 61): it is easier to understand 'x has three instances of the feature 'incomplete' ' than to understand 'x belongs to the class 'incomplete' three times'.

Features in systemic grammars are very much the same as features in TG grammars, except that they are not contrasted with 'categories': in systemic grammar 'noun-phrase' and 'animate' would both be the names of paradigmatic categories with precisely the same theoretical status. Because of the similarity between systemic features and TG features, I have borrowed from TG writers the convention of writing the names of paradigmatic categories between square brackets: [verb], [non-finite verb], etc. Where several features all refer to the same item, they are included in the same brackets: [verb, non-finite verb, ing-form]. This notational convention will help to keep paradigmatic terms separate from syntagmatic ones, which will be written in capital letters without brackets: SUBJECT, HEAD (following Dik, 1968). However, in system networks and realisation rules the brackets would be superfluous, so I shall not include them.

2.2. Structures

It is not enough for a grammar of a language to provide a classification for all the items in the language: it must also deal with the grammatical structures that these items have. For one thing, it has to say what structures are possible and what are not, and for another it has to say what structures are associated with what classes. In this section we shall have to consider the way in which a systemic grammar does these two things, but we shall also have to answer a number of other questions, notably 'What is a structure?'.

Optional and obligatory constituents

It is common to distinguish between optional and obligatory constituents, and to use this distinction as the basis for setting up grammatical functions (cf. Longacre, 1964). It is an interesting distinction, which is worth looking at more closely in this discussion of structures.

This distinction between optional and obligatory (and impossible) constituents is relevant here because it is useful only if we relate it to the class of the constituents. If we say that some kind of constituent A is obligatory, then we mean: in items of such-and-such a class there must be an instance of A. For instance, we might say that a main verb is obligatory in clauses. However, the line between what is obligatory and what is optional or impossible will obviously fall in different places according to how precisely we define the class concerned.

As an example of this connection between the optionality of a constituent and the class of the constituents let us take the subject in the independent clause in English. Let us assume, for the sake of simplicity, that imperative clauses never have a subject, whereas indicative (i.e. non-imperative) clauses always do. Given this assumption, we shall have to say that the subject is (a) impossible, as far as imperative clauses are concerned, (b) obligatory, for indicative clauses and (c) optional, for clauses as a whole.

However, if we allow ourselves to be more accurate, then we shall have to say that the subject is optional for both imperative and non-imperative clauses, since it can be present in imperatives:

You hold this end (and I'll hold the other),

and need not be present in indicatives:

(The rain started at nine and) stopped at ten.

Even with this more accurate picture to describe, though, we still have the choice between saying that the subject is always optional and saying that in one class of imperatives it is obligatory, but in another impossible, and likewise for indicatives.

The second of these two courses seems the better of the two, since the 'optionality' of the subject in indicatives is of quite a different kind from its optionality in imperatives; but if we adopt it, there is no reason why we should *ever* treat constituents as optional, since we can always convert optionality into impossibility or obligatoriness by defining the classes of the constitute more precisely.

Optional and obligatory structural patterns

Given a sufficiently detailed classification, then, no constituent need be treated as optional. This means that in describing the structures that occur in a language either we can describe them without reference to the classes of the items concerned, and show some constituents as optional; or we can take the classes into account and dispense with optional constituents. For a grammar in which classification plays a role as important as it does in systemic grammars, it is clearly better to take classes into account, since we shall sooner or later have to describe the relations between classes and structure in order to be fully explicit.

What this means is that the grammar will enable us to predict what constituents will be present in an item's structure once we know what classes it belongs to. However, the question arises as to what we mean by 'constituent' in this context. Clearly we do not mean a particular constituent-item: the grammatical classification of a clause will never tell us whether the subject is *my friend* or *my enemy*, for instance, and it is not usually a particular item that is described as optional or obligatory in some structure, but some more general category of items. Instead of saying that some particular item is obligatory, we might say either that an item belonging to a particular class is obligatory, or that an item with a particular function is obligatory. Which of these alternatives should we prefer?

In a systemic grammar, it is better to define the obligatory item in terms of its function rather than of its class: to say that an indicative clause requires a subject, rather than to say that it requires a noun-phrase. One reason is that the second description would be insufficient in itself: what is required is not a noun-phrase, but a noun-phrase in a particular syntagmatic relation to its environment. Another reason is that functions are by definition (p. 35) used to sum up environmental restrictions, and the requirements of the constitute's class are just such a restriction. Thus, talking in terms of features rather than classes, what we shall relate to an item's features are the functions that its ICs have, rather than the features that they themselves have.

One aspect of structure that I have not mentioned so far is the sequence of the elements: this too can be treated either as variable or as constant, just like the presence or absence of the constituents. To take the subject in the English clause again, the sequence subject-finite verb could be described as optional if we were trying to cover all indicative clauses, but if we take a more precisely defined class of items it will be either obligatory or, if the obligatory sequence is either finite verb-subject, or main verb-subject, impossible. The arguments used above apply here too, and in a systemic grammar we can predict, from the features that an item has, both what functions will be present in its structure, and in what sequence they will occur.

What is a structure?

There are a number of ways in which 'structure' can be used. Apart from its use to refer to the whole language-system, as in 'the structure of English', there are two ways in which it can be used to refer specifically to the patterns within an item: 'the structure of such-and-such clause is ...'. Firstly, it can be used in a wider sense to include *any* grammatical characteristics of *any* of its constituents; or secondly, it can be used in a narrower sense, including only the syntagmatic characteristics of its own immediate constituents.

In the first sense, the two clauses below have different structures, since the structures of *the book* and *the blue book* are different

> The book fell off the shelf,
> The blue book fell of the shelf.

In the second sense, however, the two clauses as such have exactly the same structure because the difference between *the book* and *the blue book* involves the structures of these noun-phrases but not of the clauses. Similarly, the difference between the pair

> He read the book,
> He read the books,

would make the structures of the clauses different for the first interpretation of structure, but not for the second, since it does not involve the syntagmatic relation of the clauses' ICs.

TG theory and systemic theory are different in the way the word 'structure' is used. In TG theory it is used in the first, more general, sense, whereas in systemic theory it has the more specific meaning. It is important to bear this in mind in the following pages, which otherwise may mislead the reader seriously.

In systemic theory, then, an item's structure is simply the totality of syntagmatic information about its ICs, and it shows firstly the functions of these ICs and secondly the sequence in which they occur. If each item had just one function, a structure would simply be a string of functions, but in fact items tend to have more than one function, so a structure will take the form of a string of *bundles* of functions. For instance, as we saw in 1.2.4, *who* will have at least two functions, SUBJECT and MOOD-FOCUS, in

> Who likes mushrooms?

Therefore the structure of this clause will start with a bundle of functions including SUBJECT and MOOD-FOCUS, followed by a bundle for the next IC *likes* and then one for *mushrooms*.

As I have already mentioned, I shall use capital letters for function names, to keep them clearly distinct from the names of classes or features, which will be written in small letters (and generally between square brackets). This means that a structure, in the systemic sense of the term, will contain nothing that is not written in capital letters.

The generation of structures

In the light of the preceding discussion, what kind of theoretical apparatus do we need for generating structures? There appear to be two different kinds of constraint on structures: those imposed by the features of the constitute, such as we discussed above; and those which are independent of the constitute's features. For the first kind of constraint we need to formulate rules which relate features to structural patterns; these we call *feature-realisation rules*. For the second kind we need rules which relate one structural pattern to another; for want of a better term, we can call these *structure-building rules*.

Feature-realisation rules tend to be concerned with the presence or absence of functions, and can be verbalised as 'If an item has such-and-such a feature (or combination of features), then its structure will contain such-and-such a function'. For instance, in conjunction with the rather crude classification of clauses introduced in 2.1 above, we shall have a realisation rule for the feature [indicative] which says that the clause's structure must contain the function SUBJECT, and also another function, FINITE, reflecting the fact that [indicative] requires a finite verb as well as a subject.

It is rules of this first type that make it unnecessary to show explicitly what the dependency relations are among an item's ICs, since they are implicit in the relation between the latter and the clause's features. In the case just quoted, for instance, there is no need for the structure as such to show that there is a special relation between the subject and the finite verb, in that the latter cannot occur without the former: since SUBJECT and FINITE are both introduced as a reflex of the same feature, this restriction follows automatically. Similarly, we might want to show that all the other ICs in a clause depended on its main verb, on the grounds that this was the only 'obligatory' constituent; but this is already implied by the fact that the main-verb's characteristic function, PROCESS, is introduced by the realisation-rule for the feature [clause], on which depend all the features that are responsible for the presence of all the clause's other ICs.

The second type of rule, structure-building rules, ensure that the functions introduced by the feature-realisation rules appear in the right order, and also add a few new functions to the structure. For instance, the reader will remember that in 1.2.4 (p. 36) I introduced the function MOOD-FOCUS, which occurs as the initial item (barring adverbials) in independent interrogative clauses; this is the function of the wh-item if there is one, and of the finite verb if there is not. This function is present in the structure of any clause that has both the features [interrogative] and [independent], so we introduce it by a realisation rule for [interrogative], in the erfvironment of [independent]. However, we also have to make sure that it occurs in the right place in the clause's structure, and this we do by means of a structure-building rule.

In most cases, then, structure-building rules simply fill out the structure on the basis of the functions introduced by the feature-realisation rules. However, it can happen that the two kinds of rules conflict with each other: the structure-building rules will exclude a structure which is permitted as far as the feature-realisation rules are concerned. We shall meet an example of this in 3.2.4 (p. 131 ff.): the verb-sequence * *being walking* is excluded by a structure-building rule, although it is needed as the realisation of the features [gerundival, progressive, non-perfect]. When this kind of conflict arises between feature-realisation rules and structure-building rules we find a gap in the system — something which we 'cannot mean' because the relatively surface rules of the language do not allow us to.

What we gain by separating the two kinds of rules for generating structures is that on the one hand we make the realisation-rules for features much simpler than they would otherwise be — for instance, they do not need to specify the sequence of functions that they introduce — and on the other by imposing constraints directly on the structures we explain the existence of these structural 'gaps in the system'.

2.3. Specifying structures by means of feature-realisation rules

A systemic grammar comprises a number of different kinds of rules. We have already looked at one kind, without in fact using the word 'rule': the system-network. This is in effect a body of rules, in symbolic form, which specify precisely how features can combine with each other: in other words, which features can appear together in the paradigmatic description of a single item, and which cannot. Each system can be thought of as one rule.

The part of the grammar to which we now turn consists of rules of a different kind: feature-realisation rules. It is easier to see these as separate rules, compared with the systems in a system-network, since they are not interconnected to the extent that systems are. Indeed, the reader will see that the most 'structured' part of the grammar by far is the system-network, since any of the other parts tend to consist of an unordered list of separate rules. It is partly because of this integrating function of the system-network that we consider it to be the 'heart' of the grammar and give the name 'systemic' to the theory of grammar.

The meaning of realisation

Realisation is the name of the relation between grammatical categories of different kinds, where one category is a condition for the presence of the other. It is used here in much the same sense of Lamb's 'realisation' (1964), Halliday's earlier 'exponence' (1961) or Hockett's 'representation' (1961). One example of a realisation relation is that between [indicative] and SUBJECT: the presence of [indicative] among a clause's features is a sufficient condition for the presence of SUBJECT in the clause's structure. The relation is one between a feature and a function, and since these are categories of different kinds, it must be a realisation relation. Another example of a realisation rule also involves a feature and a function: the presence of SUBJECT among an item's functions is a sufficient condition for the presence of [nominal] among its features.

Having cited here these relations as examples of realisation, however, it is clear that there is a difference between them: in the first example it is the feature — [indicative] — that is the condition for the presence of the function — SUBJECT; whereas in the second it is the other way round, SUBJECT being a condition for [nominal]. In other words, realisation is a one-way relation, though in some cases it works from features to functions, and in others from functions to features.

The directionality of realisation relations stems from the fact that they reflect environmental restrictions, which are themselves directional: 'in environment x we always find element y' does not imply that wherever we find element y we must have environment x, nor does it imply that y acts as environment for x just as x does for y. Moreover, the fact that they involve functions as well as features has the same explanation: the role that functions play in the grammar is to mediate the influence of an item's syntagmatic environment.

Thus, to simplify the picture considerably, a function realises the feature-environment that it summarises, and it in turn is realised by the features for which it acts as environment; so the function mediates the environmental restrictions imposed by an item's features on the features of one of its own ICs.

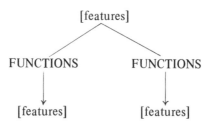

One reason why this picture is unrealistically simple is that there is another set of constraints in addition to those represented by the realisation relations, viz. constraints on the ways in which functions combine into structures (handled by our structure-building rules). Because of these constraints, the set of functions that realise the larger item's features is not the same as the set that are realised by the smaller item's features, so it would be more accurate to represent the relations as follows:

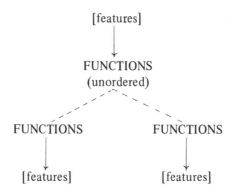

The solid arrows represent realisation relations, while the dotted lines represent the effects of the structure-building rules.

   If a realisation-relation is directional, is there any kind of ordering between its terms? Clearly there is such an ordering if a realisation relation can be interpreted as a causal explanation, where the cause is the 'realisate' and the effect is the realisation. For instance, the realisation-relation between [indicative] and SUBJECT would then mean that the latter is present because the former is, and the relation between SUBJECT and [nominal] means that [nominal] is present because of SUBJECT. However, we can equally well see these restrictions in terms of conditions rather than causation: for instance, SUBJECT can occur provided it occurs with [indicative] — or one of a number of other features. It is often convenient to use the 'causal' interpretation, since this allows us to speak of 'determination' — in particular, of a system being predetermined by its environment — but it is important to remember that any realisation relation can also be interpreted in the other way.

There is one kind of ordering that is *not* implied by the directionality of realisation relations: temporal order. In generating a grammatical description it may be convenient to start by generating the features, and then to apply the realisation-rules to produce a structure, and so on; but this is simply a question of the best way of explaining the interconnections of the rules in the grammar. There is no suggestion that the speaker follows the direction of the realisation relations in constructing his utterances, so that he first decides what features to select, then selects the functions that are demanded by the latter, and so on. This model is completely neutral as between speaker and hearer, and is not intended as a model of performance.

There is one final question about realisation relations: what is their place in the classification of grammatical relations as either syntagmatic or paradigmatic? Of course there is no a priori reason to assume that realisation relations must be either one or the other of these two types, but there seem to be good reasons for subsuming realisation relations under syntagmatic relations. For one thing, the terms of a realisation relation must both be present in the description concerned, which is a characteristic of syntagmatic relations in general. For another, functional relations are one of the main kinds of syntagmatic relation, but one of the main kinds of functional relation is in fact the realisational relation, since realisation relations always involve functions, and serve as part of the definition of these functions.

Types of feature-realisation rules

The rules which reflect realisation relations in which the realisates are features are called feature-realisation rules. In the simplest cases, feature-realisation rules specify just one function as the realisation of one feature. For instance, the feature [clause] is realised in our grammar by the presence of the one function PROCESS, representing the main verb. However, there are more complicated kinds of relation that need to be reflected by more complicated rules.

First of all, the feature may be realised by the presence of several functions occurring together in the same structure. For instance, [indicative], as we have already seen, is realised by both SUBJECT and FINITE (the function of the finite verb — which may, of course, also be the main verb).

Secondly, the feature may be realised by the fact that two functions, whose presence is explained by other factors, are 'conflated' — i.e. are both among the functions of the same item. For example, the feature [subject-

focus] is realised by the fact that SUBJECT is conflated with either QUES-
TION or ALTERNATIVE, whichever is required by the clause's other features: if the clause is a wh-question, then it will contain SUBJECT conflated
with QUESTION, but if it is an alternative question SUBJECT will be conflated with ALTERNATIVE.

> *What*   did the most damage?
> SUBJECT
> QUESTION
> Did *the wind or the rain* do the most damage?
>   SUBJECT
>   ALTERNATIVE

Thirdly, the feature may be realised both by the presence of a function
and also by the fact that it is conflated with some other function. For instance,
[wh] is realised, in [independent] clauses, by the presence of QUESTION
conflated with MOOD-FOCUS; the latter is required by the realisation rules
for [interrogative] but the former would not have been present if it had not
been for [wh]:

> *What*   happened?
> QUESTION
> MOOD-FOCUS

Fourthly, the feature may have the realisation concerned only in the environment of some other feature. We have just met one instance of this: the
realisation of [wh] by the presence of QUESTION conflated with MOOD-
FOCUS only applies to [independent] clauses, so we say that [wh] has this
realisation only in the environment of [independent]. Similarly, [subject-
focus] has two different realisations according to whether it is in the environment of [wh] or of [alternative].

Note that in feature-realisation rules the conditioning environments are
always paradigmatic, expressed in terms of features: in other words, the environment and the realisate are of the same kind – both defined in terms of
features. In contrast, the conditioning environments of function-realisation
rules, as we shall see below, are always syntagmatic, so there too the environment and the realisate are defined in the same kind of terms.

Finally, a feature may have no realisation at all. This is to be taken liter-
ally: it does not mean that a feature is realised by the *absence* of the functions realising the feature with which it contrasts. For instance, [imperative]

has no realisation, whereas [indicative], with which it contrasts, is realised by the presence of SUBJECT and FINITE. This does not however mean that [imperative] is incompatible with both these functions: in a more complete grammar we should still give no realisation to [imperative], but allow certain sub-classes of imperative clauses to have SUBJECT in their structures. If we had treated the absence of SUBJECT as part of the realisation of [imperative], this would have led to conflict between the two rules.

Notational conventions for feature-realisation rules

A realisation rule has two or three parts: the realisate, the realisation, and the conditioning environment (if any). We might use some kind of symbol an arrow or a colon, for instance – to represent the relation itself, but this does not seem necessary, so I shall simply present realisation rules in table-form, with one column for the realisates (features) and another for the realisations (functions) and any environments (features). To help the reader to identify the realisate features, I shall show the number of the relevant system in the network given on p. 71.

Table 1 gives the realisations for all the features from that system network, except for those applying to phrases or words.

The conventions used in feature-realisation rules of this kind are as follows (F stands for any function):

(a) + F   This function must be present, which it otherwise would not be.

(b) F = F   These two functions must be conflated (subject to the condition discussed below).

(c) + F = F   The first function must be present (which otherwise would not be the case), and must be conflated with the second function (again this is subject to the general condition below).

(d) //   The realisation stated on the left of // applies only in the environment of the feature(s) listed on the right of it.

The general condition that applies to (b) and (c) is that the realisation depends on whether or not the second of the two functions is present (as the realisation of other features). If it is, then the realisation is as stated; but if it is not, then the rule applies in a *negative* way: the first function must not be introduced as a result of this realisation rule (case (c)), and any other realisation rule that would otherwise have introduced it (case (b)) must be prevented from doing so. This general condition has an important part to play in systemic grammars since it is one of the means by which we account for 'understood' elements, as I shall now explain.

Table 1

realisate		realisation
system	feature	
1	clause	+ PROCESS
	phrase	+ HEAD
	word	+ STEM
2	independent	−
	dependent	+ BINDER
		+ SUBJECT
		+ FINITE
3	imperative	−
	indicative	+ SUBJECT
		+ FINITE
4	declarative	−
	interrogative	+ MOOD-FOCUS // [independent]
		+ QUESTION = BINDER // [dependent]
5	polar	−
	non-polar	−
6	wh	+ QUESTION = MOOD-FOCUS // [independent]
	alternative	+ ALTERNATIVE
7	subject-focus	QUESTION = SUBJECT // [wh]
		ALTERNATIVE = SUBJECT // [alternative]
	non-subject focus	−
8	modal	+ MODAL
	non-modal	−
9	intransitive	−
	transitive	+ GOAL
		+ ACTOR // *not* [actor unspecified]
		+ TRANSITIVE
10	attributive	+ ATTRIBUANT = SUBJECT
		+ ATTRIBUTE
		+ COPULAR
	non-attributive	+ ACTOR = SUBJECT
		+ INTRANS
11	active	ACTOR = SUBJECT
	passive	GOAL = SUBJECT
		+ PASSIVE
12	actor specified	+ AGENT = ACTOR
	actor unspecified	−

'Understood' elements

One virtue that a TG approach is often said to have is that it explains our informal intuition that there is an 'understood subject' in imperative clauses, and this, it is implied, is something that can only be shown by means of a deep structure in which the subject is represented. However, this intuition (if indeed there is such an intuition for the unsophisticated speaker of English) can be reflected in a systemic grammar without recourse to transformations that delete elements that are in the deep structure.

There are a number of ways in which this can be done in a systemic grammar, but two of them are illustrated in the feature-realisation rules just given. In either case, what we show is not that the 'understood' element *is* present, but rather that it *would have been* present if it had not been prevented by some extraneous factor — which is simply another way of saying that it is 'understood'.

Firstly, a function which otherwise would have been present may be excluded by the operation of a feature-realisation rule of the 'conflation' type. For instance, four of the feature-realisation rules involve the conflation of some function (ATTRIBUANT, ACTOR or GOAL) with SUBJECT; but they are subject to the general condition on conflation-type rules given above, so they will apply positively only if SUBJECT is present. SUBJECT need not be present, though: in particular, it is not present in imperative clauses. Since the structure of an imperative clause has no SUBJECT (which would have been present if the clause had not been [imperative]), these other functions cannot be conflated with it and so they too are absent, although they would have been present if SUBJECT had been present too.

Secondly, the presence of a function may be conditional on the absence of a particular feature. The example of this is to be found in the realisation-rule for [transitive], which includes

+ ACTOR // *not* [actor unspecified].

The conditioning feature is from a relatively 'delicate' system, which contrasts it with [actor specified] and applies to [passive] clauses; it is this system which reflects the optionality of the actor in passive clauses:

The house was sold by an estate agent [actor specified],
The house was sold   [actor unspecified].

As a result of the way in which ACTOR is introduced, there is never any need to delete it: it is introduced only where it will actually appear in the 'surface' structure. This being so there is no problem of deciding how to specify the actor that is deleted. At the same time, however, this analysis shows that the clause is the kind of clause which would have contained an actor if it had not had the feature [actor unspecified].

Conditions for postulating systems

Finally, we can raise a very general question about grammatical systems: how can we decide whether or not a particular contrast should qualify as a grammatical system? For instance, should we postulate a system to cover the contrast between *left* and *right*, which is sufficiently 'closed' to be considered as a possible grammatical system? * We can answer the question by laying down two general conditions that every grammatical system must satisfy; if they are both satisfied, then the contrast concerned can be treated as a system.

Firstly, it must be possible to locate the system in the overall system-network for English, by defining the class of classes which it sub-divides. As far as I know there is no way of defining grammatically a class which includes just *left* and *right*, so there would be no class for a hypothetical system [left] versus [right] to apply to, and therefore the latter cannot be a grammatical system.

Secondly, it must be possible to state the realisations of the terms in the system. If the terms are classes of morphemes, of course, they can be realised by simply listing their members, but if they involve more complex items, then without realisation rules there is no way of relating the systemic contrast to structural differences. If on the other hand there *are* no structural differences, then there is no point in introducing the system in the first place, since any contrast of meaning that it was meant to reflect could be covered simply by giving two alternative meanings for the class it would have sub-divided. For instance, assuming that there are no structural differences between 'genuine present-tense' clauses and 'historic present' clauses, there is no need to have a system contrasting [genuine] with [historic].

This second principle needs to be refined in some respects. For instance, under what conditions do we say that a feature is realised? Does it have to have a realisation of its own or is it enough for its sub-classes to have features that are realised, or for the feature with which it is contrasted to be realised? On this question, it would be too strong a requirement to demand that each feature have its own realisation, and I believe both the alternatives suggested are justifiable, but there remain questions about the nature of feature-

* I am grateful to P.H.Matthews for this example.

realisation that cannot be answered here — for instance, how do we handle phonological realisation of grammatical features? Nevertheless, it seems reasonable to demand that every system should have realisational implications as well as being integrated into the system-network.

2.4. Specifying structures by means of structure-building rules

One of the characteristics of systemic grammars is that structures are entirely predictable from features: given all of an item's features, we can predict exactly what its structure will be. However, this prediction is done in two steps. First, the feature-realisation rules allow us to build up the beginnings of a structure, by specifying certain functions that it must include, and, in some cases, telling us that some of these are conflated with each other. And secondly, the structure-building rules, to which we now turn, fill out this partial structure until it is complete, by adding various functions and getting all the functions in the correct order. Thus we can see the 'output' of the feature-realisation rules as the 'input' to the structure-building rules.

Kinds of structure-building rules

There are four kinds of structure-building rules, which fall into two groups: those that are 'absolute' and those that are 'conditional'. The difference between these two groups is that rules of the first kind apply under all circumstances, provided their explicitly stated conditions are satisfied, whereas the second kind apply only if this will not lead to a conflict with the first group of rules. For instance, if there is an absolute rule which prevents a function F_1 from conflating with F_2, and also a conditional rule which conflates F_1 with a third function F_3, this latter rule will not apply if F_3 is for some other reason already conflated with F_2, since this would mean that F_2 would be conflated, via F_3, with F_1. I shall give a less abstract example of this after introducing the rules for English clauses (p. 92 ff.).

The absolute kind of rules are of two kinds: 'sequence rules' and 'compatibility rules'. As the names suggest, the first kind restrict the sequences in which functions can occur — for instance, there is a rule which ensures that FINITE conflates with whichever of the functions PRE-SUBJECT, MODAL, PASSIVE (representing the passive *be*) and PROCESS (representing the main verb) comes first, and that these three functions come in the order in which they are listed here.

It might be expected that there would be one sequence rule for each 'unit' (clause, phrase, word, etc.), rather like a tagmemic structural formula, but in fact we shall give several different rules just for the structures found in clauses. This is connected with the fact that functions occur in bundles, and not singly. So for instance the finite verb in

Could you see all his mistakes?

has four functions (among others): FINITE, PRE-SUBJECT, MODAL and MOOD-FOCUS. By virtue of the function FINITE, it also has the functions PRE-SUBJECT and MODAL, and because of these two it precedes the item with the function PROCESS; these relations are covered by the rule mentioned in the last paragraph. However, because of PRE-SUBJECT it also has the fourth function, MOOD-FOCUS, which is mentioned in a different sequence rule; this puts it in front of SUBJECT, and it is because of this rule that *could* precedes *you*. Thus two different sequence rules are needed in order to explain the part of this clause's structure that involves *could*: one rule explains why it is modal as well as finite, and why it comes before the main verb; and the other explains why it comes before the subject. To cover all these restrictions in a single rule would have been not just complicated, but impossible.

The other kind of absolute rules are more straightforward than sequence rules. They are called 'compatibility rules', and they simply prevent certain functions from conflating. For instance, there is a rule which prevents POST-SUBJECT from conflating with PRE-SUBJECT, since these are respectively the functions of an auxiliary after the subject and of an auxiliary before it. Although they are 'absolute' in the sense in which I am using this term, they may be subject to conditions: 'functions F_1 and F_2 must not conflate with each other if ...'. None of the rules quoted in this chapter will be conditioned in this way, but there will be examples of such rules in 5.1.3.

The third and fourth kinds of structure-building rules, the 'conditional' ones, are also quite straightforward. One kind are called 'addition rules' and the other kind 'conflation rules'. The former ensure that functions which are not required by the feature-realisation rules are nevertheless present in the structure, given the appropriate structural conditions. For instance, one rule adds PRE-SUBJECT to the structure if MOOD-FOCUS is present and is not conflated with SUBJECT — in other words, this rule adds PRE-SUBJECT if the clause is [interrogative] but not [subject-focus, wh], and thereby ensures that the finite verb will precede the subject (p. 36).

As for the other kind of rules, 'conflation rules', they simply conflate functions that need to be conflated and that would not be conflated by feature-realisation rules. It is such a rule that conflates PRE-SUBJECT with MOOD-FOCUS when the latter is not already conflated with QUESTION.

The environments and ordering of structure-building rules

There are two general points to be made about structure-building rules. The first concerns their environments. All kinds of rules may be subject to environmental conditioning, with the exception of the sequence rules (and it is possible that even these may need to allow environmental conditioning), though none of them have to be conditioned in this way. What is worth pointing out is that the environments are always syntagmatic, rather than paradigmatic — whereas the environments of feature-realisation rules are always paradigmatic. This means that structure-building rules can apply to a structure entirely without regard to the features determining it; and this in turn reflects our claim that there are purely structural restrictions as well as the semantically-oriented restrictions imposed by the system-network.

The second general point about structure-building rules is that they are not extrinsically ordered in any way: it is not even the case that the rules of one type have to apply before the rules of another type do. For instance, an addition rule adds PRE-SUBJECT, a sequence rule conflates it with MODAL (if this is present), but another addition rule adds POST-SUBJECT and conflates it with MODAL, and a compatibility rule prevents POST-SUBJECT from conflating with PRE-SUBJECT (as would be the case if both were conflated with MODAL). Thus the second addition rule will not operate if the first addition rule and the sequence rule have both operated, so the sequence-rule would have to come between the two addition rules if the rules were to be extrinsically ordered. (I shall return to this set of rules again below, in order to make the discussion slightly less abstract.)

Notational conventions for structure-building rules

Structure-building rules are simply descriptions of configurations within structures that are either excluded (by compatibility rules) or required (by the other kinds of rules). Thus there is more variety among these rules than among realisation rules, as the reader will see from the list below, which includes the structure-building rules needed for our grammar. Once again we ignore all parts of the grammar except those dealing with clauses.

Sequence rules

MOOD-FOCUS ⎫ ⪴ (PRE-SUBJECT → SUBJECT) → POST-SUBJECT ⪴
BINDER ⎭ ⪴ PROCESS → POST-VERB
FINITE = (PRE-SUBJECT = (MODAL → PASSIVE) → PROCESS)

Compatibility rules

POST-SUBJECT ≠ PRE-SUBJECT
POST-VERB ≠ QUESTION, BINDER, SUBJECT

Addition rules
  + PRE-SUBJECT // + MOOD-FOCUS ≠ SUBJECT
  + POST-SUBJECT = MODAL, PASSIVE
  + POST-VERB = ATTRIBUTE, ACTOR, GOAL
  + EN = PROCESS // + PASSIVE

Conflation rules
  PRE-SUBJECT = MOOD-FOCUS // MOOD-FOCUS ≠ QUESTION
  PROCESS = COPULAR, TRANSITIVE, INTRANS.

Many of the conventions in these rules are like those for feature-realisation rules:

F = F	The first function must be conflated with the second function, if both are present (structure-building rules are *not* subject to the general condition on feature-realisation rules which leads to the absence of the first function if the second function is absent).
+ F	This function must be present.
+ F = F	The first function must be present if the second is, and the two must be conflated.
//	What is on the right of // is a condition for what is on the left.

There are some, however, which are new:

F → F	The first function must come before the second if both are present.
F ⇌ F	The first function must either precede or be conflated with the second, if both are present.
F | F |	Whichever of the two functions is present will be in the position indicated.
F = (F → F)	The first function must be conflated with whichever of the two functions in the bracket comes first, and the latter must occur in the sequence shown by the arrow.
F ≠ F	These two functions must not be conflated with each other.
// + F ≠ F	(This occurs only in conditioning environments.) ... if the first function is present but is not conflated with the second (which may or may not be present).
(+) F = F, F	If any of the functions separated by commas are present, they must be conflated with the first function (which may have to be added specially to make this possible).

An example

I have mentioned several times that a 'conditional' rule (an addition rule or a conflation rule) may lead to conflict with an 'absolute' rule (a sequence rule or a compatibility rule), and that in these cases the conditional rule is simply waived. Let me give an example of this situation. This will also give me an opportunity to show how the structure-building rules operate on the output of the feature-realisation rules to form complete structures.

Let us start with a combination of features which, according to our system network (p. 71), exhausts the paradigmatic description of some item: [clause, independent, indicative, interrogative, polar, modal, intransitive, attributive]. The reader can easily confirm for himself that this combination of features is permitted by the network, and that no others can be added to it.

By applying the feature-realisation rules (p. 84), we can tell that the item concerned (which we now know to be a clause, of course) has a structure which includes the following functions, though we know nothing at all about the sequence in which they occur (except that ATTRIBUTANT is conflated with SUBJECT): PROCESS, SUBJECT = ATTRIBUANT, FINITE, MOOD-FOCUS, MODAL, ATTRIBUTE, COPULAR. This unordered set of functions is the input to the structure-building rules, which we can start applying in an arbitrary order — the order in which they were listed above.

(1) The first sequence rule is:
$$\left.\begin{array}{l}\text{MOOD-FOCUS}\\\text{BINDER}\end{array}\right\} \gtreqless \text{(PRE-SUBJECT} \to \text{SUBJECT)} \to \text{POST-SUBJECT} \gtreqless\ \gtreqless \text{PROCESS} \to \text{POST-VERB}$$

This tells us that the following functions must be arranged in the way shown:
$$\text{MOOD-FOCUS} \gtreqless \begin{array}{l}\text{SUBJECT}\\\text{ATTRIBUANT}\end{array} \to \text{PROCESS}$$

The remaining functions are still unplaced.

(2) The second sequence rule is:
$$\text{FINITE} = \text{(PRE-SUBJECT} = \text{(MODAL} \to \text{PASSIVE)} \to \text{PROCESS)}$$

According to this, MODAL precedes PROCESS and is conflated with FINITE:

FINITE → PROCESS
MODAL

However, we do not know in what way FINITE and MODAL are related
to MOOD-FOCUS and SUBJECT.

(3) The compatibility rules do not apply (yet) because the relevant functions
are not present.

(4) The first addition rule is:

+ PRE-SUBJECT // + MOOD-FOCUS ≠ SUBJECT

We know that MOOD-FOCUS is present, and until we have evidence to
the contrary we can assume that it is not conflated with SUBJECT. On
this assumption, PRE-SUBJECT must be present.

(5) Returning to (1), we now know that PRE-SUBJECT is present, so it must
precede SUBJECT, and follow (or be conflated with) MOOD-FOCUS:

MOOD-FOCUS ⇄ PRE-SUBJECT → SUBJECT   → PROCESS
                                ATTRIBUANT

(6) Returning to (2), the presence of PRE-SUBJECT allows us to bring the
partial structure of (1) together with the one we have just produced, since
we know that PRE-SUBJECT must be conflated with FINITE and
MODAL:

MOOD-FOCUS ⇄ PRE-SUBJECT → SUBJECT   → PROCESS
                FINITE   ATTRIBUANT
                MODAL

(7) Moving on to the second addition rule, this is

+ POST-SUBJECT = MODAL, PASSIVE

Since MODAL is present, we should have to add POST-SUBJECT, and
conflate it with MODAL, except for

(8) the first compatibility rule (which did not apply when we tried it in (3)):

POST-SUBJECT ≠ PRE-SUBJECT

We know from (6) that MODAL is conflated with PRE-SUBJECT, and from (7) that it should be conflated with POST-SUBJECT, which would mean that POST-SUBJECT would be conflated with PRE-SUBJECT; but this is not allowed by the first compatibility rule, so the rule in (7) does not after all apply, and POST-SUBJECT is not present in the structure.

(9) The third addition rule is:

+ POST-VERB = ATTRIBUTE, ACTOR, GOAL

Since ATTRIBUTE is present, POST-VERB must be conflated with it; and

(10) the first sequence rule (1) tells us that POST-VERB follows PROCESS, so the structure as far as we know so far is

MOOD-FOCUS $\cong$ PRE-SUBJECT $\rightarrow$ SUBJECT $\rightarrow$ PROCESS $\rightarrow$
       FINITE   ATTRIBUANT
       MODAL

              $\rightarrow$ POST-VERB
              ATTRIBUTE

(11) The last addition rule does not apply.
(12) The first conflation rule is:

PRE-SUBJECT = MOOD-FOCUS // MOOD-FOCUS $\neq$ QUESTION

Until we have evidence to the contrary we can assume that MOOD-FOCUS is not conflated with QUESTION, so it must be conflated with PRE-SUBJECT instead:

PRE-SUBJECT $\rightarrow$ SUBJECT $\rightarrow$ PROCESS $\rightarrow$ POST-VERB
MOOD-FOCUS   ATTRIBUANT   ATTRIBUTE
FINITE
MODAL

(13) The second conflation rule is:

PROCESS = COPULAR, TRANSITIVE, INTRANS.

Our original list of functions does include one of these three functions — COPULAR — although we have not yet been able to give it a place in the structure; we now know that it is conflated with PROCESS:

PRE-SUBJECT → SUBJECT   →   PROCESS → POST-VERB
MOOD-FOCUS   ATTRIBUANT   COPULAR   ATTRIBUTE
FINITE
MODAL

There are no more functions from the original list to be placed in the structure, nor are there any structure-building rules that have not yet been obeyed, so this is a complete structure (as far as the present grammar goes). It could be the structure of

> May this cheque prove a bad one?
> Must it grow darker?

2.5. Preselecting features by means of function-realisation rules

After the structure-building rules have applied, all the functions in an item's structure will have been arranged into bundles and the bundles arranged in sequence from left to right. Now each of these bundles comprises the functions of one of the item's ICs (except in the case of discontinuous ICs), and these functions carry the predetermining effects of the larger item's features down to the next layer of items, by helping to determine the features that they have. For instance, the first of the ICs in the structure generated above has the functions FINITE and MODAL because of certain features that the clause itself has, and because it has these functions the first IC itself has to have certain other features.

However, not all functions restrict the features that an item can have. For instance, the function MOOD-FOCUS simply defines the position that its item must occupy, as the initial element in the clause, without in any way restricting its features. Of course, this does not mean that there *are* no restrictions on the kind of item that can have this function: on the contrary, an item can have MOOD-FOCUS as function only if it is either a wh-item or a finite verb. However, these restrictions are imposed by the functions with which MOOD-FOCUS conflates (QUESTION or FINITE), so they need not be attributed also to MOOD-FOCUS.

Discontinuity

Another role that functions can play is to mark an IC as discontinuous. In 1.2.3 I suggested that we should be able to generate an analysis which would show that the underlined items below form a single discontinuous IC of the main clause:

> *Tomorrow* he said *he was going on holiday*.

Similarly we should be able to show that the italicised below are discontinuous ICs:

> *Where* did he say *he was going*?
> *He* is believed *to be very rich*.

In 5.1.3 I shall introduce a pair of functions which will identify discontinuities of the latter two kinds: PRE-CLAUSE and CLAUSE. The former is assigned to the first part of the discontinuous IC (*where*, *he*), and the latter to the second part of it (*he was going*, *to be very rich*). For other kinds of discontinuity, not involving discontinuous 'reported' clauses, we shall need to introduce other pairs of functions, but the same principle will apply.

What the functions do in these cases is to show that two bundles of functions are both part of the description of the same item, although in general different bundles of functions belong to different items. However, they also help to locate functions within the structure of the discontinuous item itself. For instance, in the last sentence quoted the function PRE-CLAUSE would mark the position of the first part of the discontinuous embedded clause; but it also has the function SUBJECT attached *beneath* it, to show that this 'front-shifted' part of the embedded clause must be the IC which has the function SUBJECT. This means, among other things, that the embedded clause must also have features which allow its structure to contain SUBJECT, so in this sense PRE-CLAUSE helps to determine the embedded clause's features. However, in general its role is simply that of marking the discontinuity. The theoretical implications of this kind of analysis, and a new kind of structure-building rule needed to generate it, will be discussed in 5.1.3 when the analysis itself is introduced.

Notational conventions for function-realisation rules

Function-realisation rules are relatively straightforward: like feature-realisation rules, they have either two or three parts, a realisate (a function), a realisation (a feature or features) and possibly a conditioning environment. Once again, we can lay them out in a table, with the realisate in one column, and the realisation (and environment, if any) in another.

Table 2 gives the realisation rules for all the functions that have been

Table 2

functions	realisations
A. Functions of verbs	
COPULAR	[copular verb]
EN	[en-form]
FINITE	[finite verb]
INTRANS	[intransitive verb]
MODAL	[modal verb]
PASSIVE	[be]
PROCESS	[lexical verb]
TRANSITIVE	[transitive verb]
B. Other functions	
AGENT	[prepositional]
ALTERNATIVE	[disjunctive] ?
ATTRIBUTE	[adjectival] *or* [nominal] *or* [prepositional]
BINDER	[conjunction] // *not* = SUBJECT *or* GOAL *or* ATTRIBUTE *or* AGENT
GOAL	[nominal] *or* [dependent]
QUESTION	[questioning]
SUBJECT	[nominal] *or* [dependent]

introduced in this little grammar and that have realisations. All of these are functions of ICs of the clause, but some may be either phrases or dependent clauses, while others must be verbs, so I have divided the rules into two lists: those that must be realised by features or verbs, and the rest.

Except for the queried feature, [disjunctive], all these features will be found in the system-network on p. 71, but that network is very crude, especially for the analysis of clauses and phrases, so this is no guarantee that they are well-founded. As the reader will see, the realisation rules themselves are also rather clumsy, again especially for the second group of functions; but at least some of these infelicities will be removed as the grammar is developed during the remaining chapters.

Only one of these functions has a conditioned realisation, but conditioning is quite common in the more elaborate sets of rules. Moreover, the one conditioned rule quoted above is not a very good example to start with, since the environment is hard to state in terms of the functions available. This is the rule for BINDER, which is the function of the item which introduces a dependent clause and which marks it as dependent. The item in question may be a relative pronoun (or relative phrase, to be more precise), or a wh-item in a reported question, or a subordinating conjunction; and it is when it has none of the functions SUBJECT, GOAL, ATTRIBUTE or AGENT that it is just a conjunction. This is what the rule for BINDER formalises.

As with feature-realisation rules, there is no extrinsic ordering of function-realisation rules. All that is required is that an item's features be compatible with its functions according to the requirements of the realisation rules for the latter; and these demands can be thought of as being imposed simultaneously on the system-network.

Indirectly preselected features

Since the features for verbs are the most satisfactorily worked out, let us see how the function-realisation rules that involve them work. We shall find that the rules preselect not only the features that are mentioned explicitly, but also others that are not mentioned explicitly.

In the structure that we generated as an example in 2.4 (p. 94), there are two bundles of functions that represent verbs. The first contains four functions: PRE-SUBJECT, MOOD-FOCUS, FINITE and MODAL. Only two of these functions have a realisation: FINITE is realised by [finite verb] and MODAL by [modal verb]. Consequently we know that the first IC in the clause, which has these four functions, must have the features [finite verb, modal verb]. In the other bundle of functions there are just two functions: PROCESS and COPULAR; these are realised respectively by [lexical verb] and by [copular verb], so we know that the clause's third IC, which has these two functions, must have the features [lexical verb, copular verb].

However, we can deduce a lot more information about the features of these two ICs just by looking at the system network and following through the implications of its having the features mentioned above.

Firstly, some features logically presuppose other features, so if the former are present, then the latter must be present too. Thus, all the features mentioned presuppose [verb], which in turn presupposes [word]; [modal verb] presupposes [grammatical verb]; and [copular verb] presupposes [lexical verb], which we already know to be present. So we can fill out the features of the two items concerned as follows: the first one has [word, verb, finite verb, grammatical verb, modal verb], and the second has [word, verb, lexical verb, copular verb].

Secondly, we have to take account of the convention for interpreting starred features (p. 64): that they are to be selected in the absence of an environmental pressure towards selecting another feature from the same system. Five of the systems relevant to verbs contain a starred feature: [non-finite verb], [∅-form], [grammatical verb], [non-modal verb] and [do]. As far as our first item is concerned, we know that it has [finite verb], so that excludes [non-finite verb] and [∅-form], and we also know that it has [grammatical verb] and [modal verb], which excludes [non-modal verb] and [do]; so for this item the starring convention adds nothing to its features. But with the second item, the situation is different, since we only know that it has [lexical verb, copular verb], which exclude [grammatical verb, non-modal verb, do], but not [non-finite verb] and [∅-form]. Consequently, the second item must have these two features, simply because there is no good reason for not having them.

Let us take a slightly more extreme example of the way in which the starring convention works: what happens if an item's only realised function is FINITE (as would have been the case with our first item above if the clause had not had [modal] among its features)? The realisation rule for FINITE requires the feature [finite verb], thereby excluding the starred features [non-finite verb] and [∅-form]; but all the other three starred features can, and therefore must, be selected, so the item concerned must have the features [grammatical verb, non-modal verb, do]. This is how the grammar reflects the fact that *do* is just a 'dummy', brought in for lack of any other auxiliary, in

Do they still eat raw steaks there?

Having described these ways in which features may be predetermined, it is worth making it clear that not *all* features of constituent items are preselected in one or another of these ways. For instance, according to the grammar in this chapter there is no way in which the choice between [past verb] and [present verb] can be predetermined, so the only kind of factor which can be responsible for this choice is *meaning*. As far as this particular system is concerned, the grammar appears to be wrong, and is different from the grammar used in the next chapter, but the general principle holds good: that for most constituents, some of their features will be freely selected although there are always some features that are predetermined by the constituent's grammatical environment – which itself, of course, results ultimately from freely made choices.

We can conclude this discussion of the way in which the function-realisation rules interact with the system-network by showing how the system-network's restrictions *conflict* with the function-realisation rules, thereby 'blocking' the generation of a syntactic description which would otherwise have been permitted. Take the functions QUESTION and SUBJECT, for instance. The latter is realised by either [nominal] or [dependent] — i.e. the subject can be either a noun-phrase or a subordinate clause. However, QUESTION is realised by [questioning] , which presupposes [phrase] and therefore is incompatible with [clause] and [dependent] . What happens when QUESTION is conflated with SUBJECT? Clearly, the subject is bound to be a noun-phrase, and cannot be a clause.

In chapter 5, we shall take advantage of this combined 'blocking' effect of the function-realisation rules and the system-network in order to make it unnecessary for the rest of the grammar to show the restriction concerned. We shall also make great use of the same kind of 'blocking device' involving classes of lexical verbs, with the effect of considerably simplifying the grammar, as explained in 5.6.

2.6. Summary of the generative apparatus

We have now discussed all the generative apparatus that is used in a systemic grammar of English or, by hypothesis, of any other language. My claim is that by means of this apparatus we can handle all the complexity of a language, and in the last chapter I shall try to demonstrate this by applying it to the description of a rather intricate area of English grammar, that of embedded noun-clauses. If this claim is true, it is obviously of some significance since it means that we can consider dispensing with the basic elements of the transformational-generative apparatus: the rewrite rule and the transformation. Admittedly the question will still arise as to which of the two approaches is the *better* one: even if we can cover all the complexity within a systemic framework, this may be no simpler or otherwise more efficient than the TG framework. Nevertheless, it will have been worthwhile to call in question the assumption that the TG apparatus is the only one that is at all capable of accommodating the complexities of natural language.

An example

Perhaps the best way to summarise the ways in which the various kinds of rules contribute to the generation of a grammatical description is to give an example of such a description and show how it is generated by the grammar I have introduced in this chapter. The description I shall give is one that would fit, for instance, any of the following clauses:

> Which candidate was chosen?
> What was achieved?

Which of the tents were erected?
How many people were admitted?

The description is given below:

[clause, independent, indicative, interrogative, non-polar, wh, subject-focus,
    non-modal, transitive, passive, actor unspecified]

MOOD-FOCUS	POST-SUBJECT	PROCESS
QUESTION	PASSIVE	TRANSITIVE
SUBJECT	FINITE	EN
GOAL	[word, verb, finite verb,	[word, verb, non-finite
[phrase, questioning,	grammatical verb,	verb, en-form, lexical
nominal]	non-modal verb, be,	verb, transitive verb]
	past]	

This description consists of the names of features (or classes) and the names of functions, all of which are defined in the grammar given above. Since this grammar had nothing to say about the structures of phrases or of words, these are not given in the description, so the latter is within the grammar's generative powers. In other words, the grammar tells us explicitly that this description is permitted. How it does this is what I shall now recapitulate.

Firstly, the *system-network* (p. 71) tells us that the four sets of features, each enclosed by square brackets, are all permitted combinations. This can easily be checked for any combination by locating all the features in the system-network and making sure that they can all be selected without more than one feature being selected from any one system. Moreover the system-network tells us that the feature-combinations are all complete, in the sense that no more features can be added without leading to conflicts.

Secondly, the *feature-realisation rules* (p. 84) tell us that the features combined with clauses need a structure which includes many of the functions shown above, and none which are not shown: PROCESS, FINITE, MOOD-FOCUS, QUESTION, SUBJECT, GOAL, TRANSITIVE, PASSIVE. Moreover, the feature-realisation rules also stipulate that some of these functions must be conflated with each other: MOOD-FOCUS must be conflated with QUESTION and with SUBJECT and with GOAL. Thus from the feature-realisation rules we get a partial specification of what the structure must be, and this does not in any way conflict with the structure given above.

From the third part of the grammar, the *structure-building rules* (p. 89), we have a definition of the remaining characteristics of the structure. In particular, two new functions — EN and POST-SUBJECT — are added to the list, and all the functions are conflated into bundles, including those that were not conflated as far as the feature-realisation rules are concerned: MOOD-FUNCTION, QUESTION, SUBJECT and GOAL comprise one bundle (as we already knew from the feature-realisation rules), FINITE, PASSIVE and POST-SUBJECT form another, and PROCESS, EN and TRANSITIVE form the third.

The fourth part of the grammar, the *function-realisation rules* (p. 96), brings us back to the first part, the system-network. It is true that as far as the latter is concerned, the four sets of features in our description are premitted, but so would many others have been. What the function-realisation rules do is to restrict the choices that can be made from the system-network when an item's functions are known. In some cases the restrictions are nil: where the item has no functions, as is the case with the clause itself. At the other extreme, the restrictions may be total. For instance, the clause's first IC has the functions MOOD-FOCUS, QUESTION, SUBJECT and GOAL, and the realisation-rules for these functions require it to have [questioning] and either [nominal] or [dependent], but since according to the system-network [dependent] is incompatible with [questioning] the first IC's features must be [questioning] and [nominal]. Apart from these two features, only one other — [phrase] — needs to be specified, and this is a feature that automatically follows from the system-network, which shows that it is presupposed by the other two features. However, even when a feature is not explicitly required by the realisation rule for one function, it may still be required because it is starred, and therefore has to be selected unless the environment demands some other feature which would conflict with it.

Predetermination, choice and meaning

One of the characteristics of systemic grammars is that systems have a total monopoly of choice: once all the features are specified, everything else follows automatically, including all aspects of the structure. Since structures are entirely predetermined, there is no need for structural rules which show which elements are optional and which are obligatory. This applies even to such very surface matters as the semantically insignificant choice between having and not having a conjunction *that*: even the difference between pairs like the following

> He thinks that she's wonderful,
> He thinks she's wonderful,

is reflected by a system, just like the difference between [declarative] and [interrogative], for instance. The relevant system is included in the grammar of chapter 5.

However, although all free choice is reflected by systems, it is not the case that all systems always reflect free choice: because of the combined effect of the function-realisation rules and the starring convention an item's environment makes many features obligatory. As I have just said, this may leave no features at all to be freely selected, but for most items at least some features will be freely selected. For instance, the second of our clause's ICs has to have the features [verb, finite verb, grammatical verb, non-modal verb, be] because of its environment, but there is still one feature, [past verb], which represents a freely made choice.

The implications of this discussion for the question of how grammar is related to semantics are obvious. What we shall ultimately want to be able to do is to explain why each element in a description should be as it is and not otherwise, and the factors that we shall adduce will include semantic ones. As far as structures are concerned, they are always determined by features, so they need no further explanation. Similarly, features may be determined by their grammatical environment, and in that case, there is again no need to look for any other kind of explanation. However, for many features their selection cannot be explained as the result of pressures from the grammatical environment, and instead of these we have to find other kinds of explanation, which must be outside grammar.

These may be found in the 'cognitive content' of the utterance — as with [past verb] versus [present verb] — or they may be in the more 'situational' aspects of the utterance, as with the difference between [interrogative] and [declarative]. Some of them, such as the choice between having *that* and not having it, may be hard to relate to anything else, and we may have to say that there are no general patterns at all in the choice of one rather than the other (except where there is grammatical predetermination of the kind dealt with in 5.3.3). However, we might decide to use the term 'semantics' to cover the study of all the factors other than grammatical ones which lead to one feature being preferred to another. The framework which I have outlined seems to offer a particularly convenient basis for the study of the relation between grammar and semantics.

In conclusion, the diagram below summarises the way in which the categories in a grammatical description restrict each other, and how semantic factors make their contribution, as one of the inputs to the system-network.

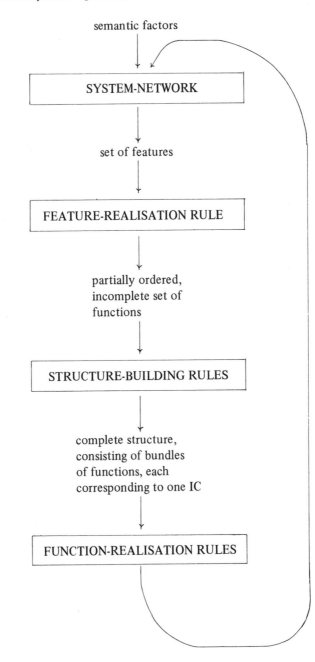

semantic factors

SYSTEM-NETWORK

set of features

FEATURE-REALISATION RULE

partially ordered,
incomplete set of
functions

STRUCTURE-BUILDING RULES

complete structure,
consisting of bundles
of functions, each
corresponding to one IC

FUNCTION-REALISATION RULES

3. NON-FINITE CLAUSES

This chapter will serve a number of purposes. First of all, it will extend the coverage of our grammar of English to show how we can handle a rather more complicated area than we have done so far. This should give the reader an idea of the flexibility which we gain by distinguishing between features (such as [past], [perfect], [passive] and even [gerundival] and [participial], to be introduced below) and their realizations.

Secondly, to the best of my knowledge some of the facts we shall cover in the extended grammar have not been noted before, so to that extent this chapter can be treated as a contribution to the study of English syntax. As might be expected, however, most of them are quite well established in either modern theoretically grounded descriptions or traditional ones.

Thirdly, the discussion of non-finite clauses will act as a bridge between the analysis of simple sentences, in the previous chapter, and that of complex sentences, in the next two chapters. Non-finite clauses will figure very prominently indeed in these chapters, and it will be good to have disposed of a number of problems connected with them before we have to fit them into a more comprehensive analysis. This present chapter covers quite a wide range of constructions involving non-finite clauses, but by no means all the constructions in which they occur; the constructions chosen are on the whole those which we shall refer to again in the following chapters.

3.1. The facts to be covered by the analysis

The scope of this chapter is quite modest: simply to deal with certain aspects of the verb-forms occurring in non-finite clauses. For instance, I shall try to provide generalisations about these verb-forms so that the italicized forms below will be seen as instances of more general patterns:

> Candidates *scoring* over 80% will be accepted,
> I hope *to have been living* in this borough long enough
>   by then to qualify for a grant,
> Do you mind her *having gone* out with him?
> Let me *press* the button,
> Have you ever seen a whale *harpooned*?

That is, I shall not be attempting to account for other aspects of their structures, notably the presence or absence of a subject, the position of the subject
if there is one, and the presence or absence of a conjunction (especially *for*).
All these topics will be taken up in the following chapters.

Perhaps it would be as well to make it clear what I am including under
'non-finite clauses', and why I refer to them as 'clauses' at all. Any item that
includes a non-finite verb among its ICs is a non-finite clause, provided the
'verb' *is* a verb, and is not clearly an adjective (tired, interesting, well-spoken)
or a noun (stuffing, bath). As for constructions like *the shooting of the hunters*,
I agree with Chomsky (1970) in not treating them as clauses, but rather as
noun-phrases — in contrast with *shooting the hunters* or *the hunters being
shot*, which are non-finite clauses. Whether the ing-form word (i.e. *shooting*)
in the former is a verb or a noun (or neither, or even both) is a separate
question that we need not answer here.

Why should we call these constructions clauses, rather than phrases, as in
all traditional grammars? In a sense, the whole of this chapter may be seen as
a justification of this decision, but briefly the answer is that they have a lot
in common with finite clauses (i.e. dependent clauses with finite verbs) — their
structures are built out of roughly the same range of functions, and they can
be classified by drawing on much the same ranges of features — but much less
in common with straightforward phrases such as noun-phrases and prepositional phrases. The main respect in which they are like the latter is in their
distribution, but even here the similarity is often more apparent than real:
alongside the environments where either a phrase or a non-finite construction
can occur, we can range a large number of environments which allow one but
not the other. In particular, extraposition (4.2.2) is possible for finite clauses
but not for phrases, so we can use this as a criterion for separating clauses
from phrases. By this criterion, as by many others that we might use, non-finite
constructions come out as clauses.

3.1.1. *The factors determining the verb-forms*

In order to account for the various verb-forms found in non-finite clauses,
we shall have to take account of three different sets of factors: the clause's
environment, its tense/aspect, and its voice.

For instance, the difference between the clauses in the following two examples are due to their different environments:

    (a) He claims *to be the world expert on their language,*
    (b) He enjoys *being the world expert on their language.*

Exchanging the non-finite clauses leads to straightforward ungrammaticality:

    (a) * He claims *being the world expert on their language,*
    (b) * He enjoys *to be the world expert on their language.*

However, there is no difference of meaning between the two which cannot be traced to the environments of the noun-clauses: in particular, we shall presumably want to assign the latter to the same classes as far as voice and tense/aspect are concerned.

By way of contrast, in the following pair the difference is due to a difference of aspect: non-progressive versus progressive.

    (a) He claimed *to speak Eskimo,*
    (b) He claimed *to be speaking Eskimo.*

And in the next pair, the difference is simply a question of voice: active versus passive.

    (a) He wanted *to drive her home,*
    (b) He wanted *to be driven home.*

Clearly, in neither of these cases can we attribute the difference to the effect of the environment, any more than we can do this for the corresponding differences in main clauses:

    (a) He speaks Eskimo,
    (b) He is speaking Eskimo,
    (a) He will drive her home,
    (b) He will be driven home.

Environmental factors

What categories must we refer to, then, in order to generalize about the occurrence of the various verb-forms? The environmental factors are the hardest to enumerate, so we can start with them.

There are an indefinitely large number of clauses which contain non-finite clauses among their constituents, so in a sense we might say there are an indefinitely large number of environments in which non-finite clauses can occur. Clearly, however, not all differences are relevant, and the number of environments that we shall have to distinguish in order to account for verb-forms will be finite and quite small — maybe somewhere between ten and fifty. We do not yet have a complete list of the relevant environments, and it is likely to be some time before such a list comes into being. So all I can do here is to exemplify the way in which the clause's environment is reflected by its verb-forms, taking as my models environments which I know for certain to be grammatically different in one way or another — environments, moreover, which will for the most part be distinguished in the next chapter.

For our purposes we can take nine environments, which we can refer to by quoting a typical verb found in the 'matrix-clause' (i.e. the clause containing the non-finite clause as constituent clause). They are illustrated below but the notion of 'environment' will be explained in 3.1.3 below. The non-finite clause is italicized, though its delimitation cannot be justified till the next chapter.

1: *seem* —
a. *His newspaper* seems *to be sold mostly outside the Union.*
b. He admitted *his newspaper to be sold mostly outside the Union.*
2: *tend* —
a. *His newspaper* tends *to be sold mostly outside the Union.*
b. He needs *his newspaper to be sold outside all the Unions in the country.*
3: *let NP* —
a. They won't let *his newspaper be sold outside the Union.*
b. Her influence helped him *be accepted as a bona fide newsvendor.*
4: *regret NP* —
a. Nobody ever regrets *his newspaper being sold outside the Union.*
b. *His newspaper being sold outside the Union* impressed all his friends greatly.
5: *keep* —
a. *His newspaper* keeps *being confiscated outside the Union.*
b. So far he's always avoided *his newspaper being confiscated outside the Union.*
6: *need NP* —
a. He really needs *his newspaper banning by the police* — then people would buy it.
b. *His newspaper* needs *banning by the police.*

7: *see NP –*

a. Eventually he saw *his newspaper confiscated by the police.*

b. The police had *his newspaper confiscated.*

8: *need NP –*

He needs *his newspaper banned by the police.*

9: *(Det) N –*

a. Any newspapers *sold outside the Union* are guaranteed scurrilous.

b. *Although sold outside the Union*, this newspaper is not an official union publication.

In one way or another, all nine environments are different in their effects on the non-finite clause's verb-forms, as we shall see below. Where possible, I have quoted two different examples for each environment, in order to show that quite a wide range of different constructions can have the same effect on the noun-clause's verbs.

It is perhaps worth drawing attention to the fact that the effects of the environment are most obviously seen in the *first* verb of the non-finite clause, which according to the environment will have a different one of the four possible non-finite forms of the verb (if we include *to + infin*, inaccurately, as 'a form of the verb'): bare infinitive (*take*), to-infinitive (*to take*), ing-form (*taking*) or en-form (*taken*). Traditionally, we should classify non-finite constructions (i.e. clauses) as infinitives, gerunds or participles in order to reflect these differences, ignoring the form of any later verbs; and this is precisely what we shall do below. That is, we shall classify as 'infinitival' clauses containing clusters of verbs such as *to take, to have taken, to be taking, to be taken, to have been taking, to have been taken* and *to have being taken*: as far as the environments in which they can occur are concerned, they all follow the rules for infinitival clauses.

Tense/aspect and voice

Apart from the clause's environment, the other two factors influencing its verb-forms are tense/aspect and voice. These are easily disposed of, since the contrasts involved are precisely the same as those we need for accounting for the verb-forms in finite clauses (or rather, a sub-set of the latter): [past] versus [non-past], [perfect] versus [non-perfect], [progressive] versus [non-progressive] and [active] versus [passive]. Moreover, in the simplest cases these features have precisely the same realisations in non-finite clauses as in finite ones, with the exception that in non-finite clauses [past] always has the same realisation as [perfect], as far as the verb-forms are concerned. Ignoring the distinction between [past] and [non-past], we can see the degree of similarity between the realisations of the remaining features in finite and non-finite clauses by comparing the forms found (a) in a finite modal clause (involving, say, *must*) and (b) in a to-infinitival clause (after, say, *seem* – but this verb will not be shown):

			active	passive
non-perfect	non-progressive	non-progressive	must take to take	must be taken to be taken
		progressive	must be taking to be taking	must be being taken to be being taken
perfect		non-progressive	must have taken to have taken	must have been taken to have been taken
		progressive	must have been taking to have been taking	must have been being taken to have been being taken

The [past]:[non-past] distinction is made in non-finite clauses in precisely the same way as in modal (finite) clauses, provided the modal verb has its true modal meaning – i.e. a meaning related to the speaker's certainty with regard to the truth of the rest of the clause. That is, [past] is realised by the presence of *have* followed by an en-form (just as [perfect] is), and [non-past] by its absence:

finite, modal: He *must love* her very much.
                  He *must have been born* before the War.

non-finite   :   He seems *to love* her very much.
                  He seems *to have been born* before the War.

However, as we shall see in 3.1.2 and 3.1.3 the relation between non-finite and finite clauses is not always as simple as this: sometimes the range of tense/aspect or voice categories is different, sometimes their realisations are different. Even so, the general point remains true: that the tense/aspect and voice categories needed for finite clauses can also be applied to non-finite clauses, so that there is no need to develop a completely separate set of categories for the latter.

3.1.2. *The realisations of tense/aspect and voice*

I introduced the nine different environments by giving one or two examples of clauses in each environment. These examples were deliberately chosen so that in each case the non-finite clause thad the same tense/aspect and voice features: [non-past, non-perfect, non-progressive, passive]. (There was a reason for choosing this particular combination of features: it is the only combination that occurs in all environments, as I shall show in 3.1.3.) The reader will find, if he looks back at these examples, that no less than five different kinds of verb-cluster occur in the non-finite clause:

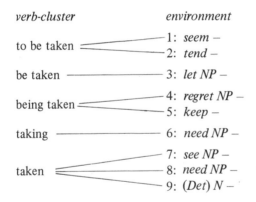

verb-cluster	*environment*
to be taken	1: *seem* – 2: *tend* –
be taken	3: *let NP* –
being taken	4: *regret NP* – 5: *keep* –
taking	6: *need NP* –
taken	7: *see NP* – 8: *need NP* – 9: *(Det) N* –

The same kind of variation can be seen from environment to environment for any of the tense/aspect and voice categories, though not in quite such an extreme form as this; and all these variations are due simply to the influence of the environment. What we have to do in this section is to make explicit whatever pattern there is in this environmental influence. In order to do this, we must first divide non-finite clauses into three classes: infinitival, gerundival and participal. Each of these classes occurs in a different range of environments, and each shows a different pattern of interaction between the environment and the tense/aspect and voice categories.

Infinitival and gerundival clauses

In the infinitival and gerundival classes this pattern is simple (with one complication, which I shall save till after the general pattern has been discussed). In both cases, the realisations of the tense/aspect and voice feature are precisely the same as their realisations in finite clauses (with the usual reservation about [past] having the same realisation as [perfect]):

feature	*realisation*
[past] [perfect]	presence of some form of *have* followed by en-form
[progressive]	presence of some form of *þe* followed by ing-form
[passive]	presence of some form of *be* followed by en-form

The first verb in the series is not in a finite form, as in finite clauses, but in a form determined by the environment – i.e. by whether the clause is infinitival or gerundival. If infinitival, the first form is an infinitive (which may or may not be preceded by *to*, reflecting a further subdivision of the class 'infinitival'); and if gerundival, it is an ing-form.

The complication is presented by the simple ing-form verb found in examples like:

>   This letter needs *signing.*

This is complicated because the verb form is the one we would expect in an active clause, but the clause is in fact passive – as witness, for instance, the possibility of an 'agentive' phrase:

>   This letter needs *signing by the Dean.*

In other words, in these clauses the normal realisation of the passive (*be* followed by an en-form) is simply missing, and the only factor that is overtly reflected in the verb-form is [gerundival], which is realised by the fact that the verb is an ing-form.

Participial clauses
    With this exception, then, the infinitival and gerundival classes present a relatively simple pattern. They occur in environments 1 through 6 (infinitival in 1–3, gerundival in 4–6). When we come to the participial class, on the other hand, the pattern is much more complicated, and it is quite hard to decide which characteristics of the verb-cluster reflect the tense/aspect and voice features, and which the environment. There is also an additional complication in one of the three environments where participial clauses occur (7–9), but we can again ignore this for a few paragraphs.

The reduced-relative analysis of postmodifier participial clauses

In only one of the three environments are all the tense/aspect and voice features represented: where the non-finite clause is used as a postmodifier, i.e. where it might be treated as a 'reduced' relative clause:

> The lecture *going on in there* will soon be over,
> The lecture *that is going on in there* will soon be over.

On the basis of pairs of examples such as these it is tempting, within a TG framework, to say that the two have the same deep structure, to which a transformation has been applied in the first case (but not in the second) deleting the nodes corresponding to the relative pronoun and *is*. However, we shall see below that this analysis would not work in all cases, since (for one thing) the deep structure would not always contain a node corresponding to a form of *be*; for instance, consider

> A parcel *weighing half a ton* has just been delivered.

This non-finite clause does not correspond in meaning to a progressive finite clause (*that is weighing half a ton*) but to a non-progressive one (*that weighs half a ton*). Indeed, since *weigh* is a stative verb some people might even consider the former (... is weighing ...) ungrammatical.

This argument could well be parried by the claim that stative verbs do have a progressive marker in the deep structure, but that this is then obligatorily deleted if it has not already been deleted by the transformation that reduces relative clauses. Even if this analysis were accepted, there would still be cases where the 'reduced relative' analysis would not work — for instance, the following:

> Anyone *providing* information *leading* to the conviction
> of those responsible will receive a reward not
> *exceeding* £1,000.

This sentence contains three non-finite postmodifiers, none of which corresponds in meaning to a finite relative clause containing a form of *be*; and only in the third case is the verb stative:

> Anyone who *provides* information that *leads* to the conviction
> of those responsible will receive a reward that *does*
> (*will?*) *not exceed* £1,000.

Admittedly, examples such as these tend to smack of 'officialese', but they must be covered at least by a grammar that purports to cover officialese, and presumably by any grammar of English as a whole.

Thus it is not the case that for every non-finite postmodifier there is a finite one which differs from it only in containing, either in its deep structure or in its surface structure, a relative pronoun and a form of *be*. This conclusion does not raise any particular problems for a systemic grammar, since there would never be a question of generating the non-finite clauses by in any sense deleting the relative pronoun and *be*. However, it is worth making the relevant facts clear and stressing this aspect of them since the analysis that I shall be giving below may appear excessively complicated. It is true that it is moderately complicated, but this is because the facts are complicated.

The sources of complexity in postmodifier participial clauses

What then are the verb-forms found in participial clauses, as represented by postmodifier clauses? All four contrasts allow both terms, so a postmodifier clause may be past or non-past, perfect or non-perfect, progressive or non-progressive, and active or passive.

		non-progressive		progressive	
		active	passive	active	passive
non-past	non-perfect	taking	taken	taking	being taken
non-past	perfect	having taken?	taken (having been taken?)	having been taking?	having been being taken?
past	non-perfect	having taken?	taken (having been taken?)	having been taking?	having been being taken?
past	perfect	having taken?	taken (having been taken?)	having been taking?	having been being taken?

The forms with a question-mark are generally rejected as unacceptable by native speakers who are sensitive to style; but again they are not unlikely in 'officialese':

> Anyone *having seen this accident* is requested to get in touch
> with their nearest police station,
> Applicants *having been driving* before 1937 should write
> 'not applicable'.

Moreover, the system would be very unsymmetrical if we excluded these doubtful forms. However, the reader will appreciate that it would be very easy to change our grammar so that these forms, and only these, would be excluded (in just the same way that *being taken* is excluded — see 3.2.5).

One of the characteristics of this set of forms is the difference between the non-progressive passive forms, on the one hand. and all other forms on the other: the former are always *taken*, whether their clauses are perfect or non-perfect, past or non-past (though it is possible that it can be replaced by *having been taken* in some cases):

> (a) The British Museum has a right to one copy of any book
>   *published in Britain*,
> (b) This library does not stock books *published since 1900*,
> (c) This library has a particularly good collection of books
>   *published before 1700*,
> (d) The library at Alexandria stocked all the books *published
>   since the Golden Age.*

In example (a) the italicized clause is [non-past, non-perfect] ; in (b) it is [non-past, perfect] ; in (c) it is [past non-perfect] ; and in (d) it is [past, perfect] . These analyses reflect the clauses' meanings, and also the time-adverbials with which they can occur.

It is interesting to compare these four examples with the corresponding sentences containing *appear* instead of *publish* — i.e. with the postmodifier clause active instead of passive. Here we find that we have to either use finite clauses, or use the verb-forms that are doubtfully acceptable, introduced by *having* ... :

> (a) The British Museum has a right to one copy of any book
>   *appearing in Britain*,
> (b)? This library does not stock books *having appeared
>   since 1900*,

> This library does not stock books *that have appeared since 1900,*
>
> (c)?   This library has a particularly good collection of books *having appeared before 1700,*
>
> This library has a particularly good collection of books *that appeared before 1700,*
>
> (d)?   The library at Alexandria stocked all the books *having appeared since the Golden Age,*
>
> The library at Alexandria stocked all the books *that had appeared since the Golden Age.*

This difference between active and passive forms means that we cannot describe the realisations of tense/aspect independently of those of voice, as has been possible hitherto: *taken* can represent a kind of 'portmanteau' realisation, which realises both passive and perfect or past.

However, the situation is even more complicated than this: we cannot even separate the combined realisations of tense/aspect and voice from the realisation of [participial]. This is easily proved by pointing out that all these participial forms have no one common characteristic such as we could identify (in the first verb) for infinitival and gerundival clauses. It is true that in most of the verb-clusters in the table above the first verb is an ing-form: *taking, having taken* (?), *being taken, having been taking* (?), *having been taken* (?) and *having been being taken* (?); but there is one exception (*taken*), which is enough to prove that the realisation of [participial] is not the presence of an ing-form. So we must conclude that *taken* represents the portmanteau realisations of up to three different features: [participial], [passive] and (sometimes) either [perfect] or [past].

There is another instance of [participial] being realised in the same word as another feature: *taking*, which can realise either [participial] and [progressive] or [participial] and [non-progressive] (in either case it realises [active] and [non-perfect]). For instance, the following is ambiguous between [progressive] and [non-progressive]:

> Anyone *sitting down when I turn round* will pay a forfeit.

If it is [non-progressive], it means the same as

> Anyone *who sits down when I turn round* will pay a forfeit.

But if [progressive] it corresponds to

> Anyone *who is sitting down when I turn round* will pay
> a forfeit.

The ambiguity can be resolved in the non-finite clause by adding *still* (making it unambiguously progressive) or changing *when* to *as soon as* (making it non-progressive):

> Anyone *still sitting down when I turn round* will pay a forfeit,
> Anyone *sitting down as soon as I turn round* will pay a forfeit.

The rules for verb-forms in postmodifier participial clauses

What patterns can we discover, then, in the verb-forms of participial clauses? Although there is some complexity and divergence from the simple kinds of pattern we encountered in the infinitival and gerundival clauses, there is also some regularity. The generalisations we can make are as follows:
(a) There are five positively realised features: [participial], [past], [perfect], [progressive], [passive]. Two of these — [past] and [perfect] — always have the same realisation, so we can ignore [past]. The remaining features — [non-past], [non-perfect], [non-progressive], [active] — have no realisation, so we can ignore them too.
(b) Each of the four positively realised features has two different realisations, in complementary distribution:

feature	realisations
[perfect]	a form of *have* followed by an en-form; or just an en-form
[progressive]	a form of *be* followed by an ing-form; or just an ing-form
[passive]	a form of *be* followed by an en-form; or just an en-form
[participial]	an en-form or an ing-form

(c) These features can be numbered as follows: [participial], 1; [perfect], 2; [progressive], 3; [passive], 4. As far as sequence is concerned, the realisation of a lower-numbered feature must not follow that of a higher-numbered one, but they *can* be merged into a single portmanteau realisation.
(d) Of a feature's two realisations, the shorter is chosen whenever possible; otherwise the longer one has to be chosen; and of the two equally short realisations of [participial], the ing-form is chosen unless there is a reason for choosing the en-form.
(e) The shorter realisation will *not* be chosen if it would lead to either of two situations: one word having to appear in two different forms at the same

time, and in particular as both an ing-form and an en-form; or an en-form realising [particpial] but not [passive] (in other words, realising just [perfect]).

(f) Where there is a conflict between the shorter realisations of two features, only *one* of the features has to have its longer realisation, and this is always the one with the higher number.

Let us see how these rules apply. Take the combination of features [participial, non-perfect, non-progressive, active]. None of them have any realisation except for [participial], so there is nothing to prevent this from having its unmarked realisation, an ing-form — hence *taking*, as in

> Anyone *taking more than three hours* will be disqualified.

If we change one of these features, we might expect a change in the realisation; as, for instance, if we were to change [non-progressive] to [progressive]. However, [progressive] can be realised either by a form of *be* followed by an ing-form, or just by an ing-form; and since the latter is one of the permitted realisations of [participial], it can be chosen here. So [participial, non-perfect, *progressive*, active] will also be realised as *taking*:

> He was trying to persuade students *still taking drugs*
> to give them up.

Next consider [participial, non-perfect, non-progressive, *passive*]. Here [participial] and [passive] are the only realised features, but once again there is a realisation that they share — simply an en-form — so they can have a portmanteau realisation, *taken*:

> The time *taken to say 'I'm sorry'* is less than one second.

Changing [non-perfect] to [perfect], we get not two but three features needing to be realised; but the situation is just the same as before, since an en-form is a possible realisation for [perfect] as well as [participial] and [passive], so *taken* can also occur in clauses that are [*participial*, perfect, non-progressive, passive]:

> The number of girls *so far taken out by Sidney* is in excess
> of one hundred.

If, however, we were to change [non-progressive] to [progressive], rather than [non-perfect] to [perfect], we should find a difference of realisation, since [progressive] and [passive] do not share any realisation. This means that the longer realisation of one of them must be used, and since realisations are chosen from right to left, we choose the longer realisation for the one on the right: a form of *be* followed by an en-form, as realisation of [passive] . This produces a 'blank' verb (a form of *be*), for which the shorter realisation of [progressive] can select the form — an [ing-form] : *being taken*.

> The girls *being taken out by Sidney at the moment* are all sisters.

If we now once again change [non-perfect] to [perfect] , we produce another conflict, this time between the realisations of [perfect] and of [progressive] ; so we now have to choose the longer realisation not only of [passive] , but also of [progressive] , giving *having been being taken*. It is hard to contrive a stylistically acceptable examples of this, but the following may be a candidate.

> Any girl *having been being taken out for more than two weeks*
> *by Sidney since last Christmas* is bound to have met
> Gladys.

Participial clauses after 'see NP ...'
These relatively simple and general rules account for the rather odd collection of forms that we find occurring in participial clauses. However, there is yet another complication, which I promised at the beginning of the discussion of participial clauses. This concerns the verb-forms found in participial clauses in environment 7: *see NP* −.

When we consider the following examples, it seems reasonable to treat the italicized as participial clauses, since they exactly follow the rules we have just formulated; moreover, the alternative would presumably be to treat them as gerundival clauses, but this would spoil a generalisation we shall be able to make about gerundival clauses, namely that they cannot be [progressive] unless they are also [perfect] (see 3.1.3).

> (a) I saw *them taking him away in a big black van*,
> (b) I saw *him taken away in a big black van*,
> (c) I saw *him being taken away in a big black van*.

These are all [non-perfect] , and (a) and (c) are [progressive] , with (b) [non-progressive] , while (b) and (c) are [passive] , (a) being [non-passive] .

			infinitival		gerundival		participial	
			with *to*	without *to*	normal	special passive	'bare'	'inflected'
active	non-perfect	non-progressive	to take	take	taking		take	taking
active	non-perfect	progressive	to be taking	be taking			taking	taking
active	perfect	non-progressive	to have taken	have taken	having taken		having taken?	having taken?
active	perfect	progressive	to have been taking	have been taking	having been taking		having been taking?	having been taking?
passive	non-perfect	non-progressive	to be taken	be taken	being taken	taking	taken	taken
passive	non-perfect	progressive	to be being taken	be being taken			being taken	being taken
passive	perfect	non-progressive	to have been taken	have been taken	having been taken		taken (having been taken?)	taken (having been taken?)
passive	perfect	progressive	to have been being taken	have been being taken	having been being taken		having been being taken?	having been being taken?

What about the missing form, [non-progressive, active] ? If it were an ordinary participial clause, like the other three, it would be the same as (a), since *taking* can be either [progressive] or [non-progressive] . It is not the same, however; it contains not *taking* but *take*:

> I saw *them take him away in a big black van.*

One way of explaining the verb form would be to say that this clause is not participial, like the other three, but a bare infinitival clause, like those found after *let*. A much more satisfactory analysis is to divide participial clauses into two kinds (just as we divide infinitival clauses into those with and those without *to*): the kind where [participial] is realised by either an ing-form or an en-form; and the kind where it has no realisation at all. We then have to specify the infinitive (*take*) as the unmarked verb-form, which occurs when there is no reason for any other form to occur. This would explain why *take* occurs only in clauses that are [non-perfect, non-progressive, active] : none of these features have any realisation, so there is nothing at all to determine the form of the verb. As soon as we change any of these features, though, we have a feature with a realisation, and this determines the form of the first verb as an ing-form or an en-form.

Summary of the factors influencing verb-forms in non-finite clauses

The table opposite sums up the relations between verb-forms and the three factors which determine them — the distributional class to which the clause belongs and which reflects the environment, the clause's tense/aspect, and its voice. In this section we are concerned primarily with the forms of verbs, rather than with the possibility or impossibility of a particular category occurring in a particular environment; so we shall concentrate in the table on information that is relevant to this question, by not distinguishing environments, and also not showing [past] forms as well as [perfect] forms, since they are the same. The gaps will come up for discussion in the next section.

3.1.3. *Permitted and excluded categories of tense/aspect and voice*

There are three pairs of contrasting tense/aspect features — [past] : [non-past] , [perfect] : [non-perfect] , [progressive] : [non-progressive] — and one of voice features — [passive] : [active] . These four contrasts yield sixteen possible combinations of features, provided the contrasts are all operative. But in some environments — indeed, in most environments that we shall discuss in the next chapter — the choices are restricted, so that we even find environments where no more than one feature-combination is possible. We have al-

ready had an example of this extreme situation, namely where the clause depends on a verb like *need*:

> *Your hedge* needs *cutting.*

In this environment, the embedded clause cannot be [past], nor [perfect],
nor [progressive], nor [active] — hence, presumably, the possibility of using
an active-type verb *cutting* without the usual passive markers.

The hierarchical ordering of tense/aspect and voice features
There is an interesting generalisation that we can make about the environmental exclusion of tense/aspect and voice features: they are always excluded
cumulatively, in the following order:

        (1) [past]
        (2) [perfect]
        (3) [progressive]
        (4) [active] or [passive].

That is, [perfect] is never excluded unless [past] is too; [progressive] is only
if [perfect] and [past] are; and [active] or [passive] only if the other three
are all excluded. As the reader will already have noticed, this order corresponds exactly to the order in which the features are realised: [past] first,
then [perfect], then [progressive], and finally voice. It is as if each exclusion
strips off the outer layer of both meaning and structure from the clause, and
takes us nearer to expressing the meaning of the main verb alone, by means of
the main verb alone.
    We might have reached the same conclusion by two or three other different
routes — for instance, by studying the relative positions of adverbials in the
clause, in cases where there are two or three of them each depending on a
different tense-aspect feature; or by studying the semantic relations among
the features. We cannot go into these other areas here, but the reader will no
doubt already be familiar with the kind of pattern I am referring to.
    Unfortunately, the grammar I shall present in the next section and in the
following chapters does not capture this generalisation. In other words, the
grammar would have been no more or less complex if the features had been
excluded in a completely different order. This is at least partly because my
analysis of tense/aspect is highly oversimplified — for instance, I make no distinction between recurrent events:

The train is late every day,

and non-recurrent ones:

The train is late again.

Nor do I distinguish between 'future':

He is giving his last lecture tomorrow,

and 'non-future':

He is just giving his last lecture.

However, one analysis of tense/aspect has already been prepared, taking these other factors into account; and one of its characteristics is precisely that the features are ordered in the system network in a way corresponding to the order of their realisations. Needless to say, it is too complicated to include ir the present book.

Marked and unmarked features

There is another interesting generalisation that we can make: the features that are excluded are those which have a realisation in the clause's verbs (with two or three exceptions). That is, when the environment is restrictive, it excludes the feature that is 'marked' in the sense of being positively realised (p. 117), and allows only the unmarked, unrealised, feature from the same system to occur. The most striking instance of this is that, so far as I know, there are no environments in which the non-finite clause must be [perfect], although there are plenty where it must be [non-perfect].

Admittedly as many as three exceptions to this rule may seem to weaken it almost to the point of applying only to the [perfect] : [non-perfect] distinction, since there are only four contrasts in question anyway. However, the exceptions are in themselves quite interesting, since they seem if anything to support the original generalisation, rather than weakening it.

The most obvious exception is that, as far as voice is concerned, each of the two features is excluded in one environment or another, [active] in some, [passive] in others. If our generalisation was operative here, we should expect [passive] to be excluded, since it is realised (by an en-form, with or without a preceding form of *be*); but we should not expect [active] to be excluded.

However, in the cases where [active] is excluded, in favour of [passive] , the latter either is not realised at all, or has the shorter of its two realisations.

With *need*, as we have seen, the clause must be [passive] , but contains no realisation of this feature:

> *This clock* needs *winding up*.

And in the second environment which excludes [active] , after verbs like *order*, [passive] is realised just by the en-form:

> The general ordered *them executed*.

There is only one environment where [passive] is excluded: after *watch*:

> The general watched *his men execute the prisoners*,
> *The general watched *the prisoners executed*.

Since the form that is excluded would have been precisely the same as the form that is mandatory after *order*, the relative simplicity of this form cannot in itself explain why it is mandatory; so the exclusion of actives after *order* remains as an exception to the generalisation that where one feature is mandatory, it must be unrealised. The obligatory [passive] after *need* turns out to be regular, however.

The second exception is that our grammar will define certain environments in such a way that the embedded clause has to be progressive in them, although this is a realised feature — realised by an ing-form with or without a form of *be* in front of it. The following is an example:

> We saw *the manager making for us*.

Here again, however, the feature [progressive] has its shorter realisation, and never the longer one, just like [passive] in the environment of *order*, so it is less of an exception to the general rule than it might have been.

The third exception is rather complicated and uncertain. It is possible that we should say that with verbs like *remember* and *recall*, a non-finite clause (which is gerundival) must be [past] , as in

> I don't remember *having met anyone like that at*
> *your Christmas party*.

Here, the embedded clause has the feature [past], which in this case has its full realisation — a form of *have* as well as an en-form — as it must in a gerundival clause. If [past] is obligatory, we shall have a much more serious exception to our generalisation about obligatory features being unrealised. However, at least the *realisation* of [past] is clearly not obligatory, as witness

> I don't remember *meeting anyone like that at your*
> *Christmas party.*

To this it might be objected that the embedded clause *is* in fact [past], even if there is no realisation for [past], since the time-adverbials permitted are those associated with [past] rather than with [non-past]:

> Do you remember *being frightened of policeman when*
> *you were little?*

If we accept this suggestion we shall need to explain why in some of these sentences [past] is realised while in others it is not. We cannot relate this difference to differences in the linguistic environment, since there are none: wherever a gerundival clause which is [past] can occur, it may or may not have a realisation for [past]. So we shall have to have a system contrasting [realised] with [unrealised], and applying only to [past] clauses in this environment. Fortunately, this is not the only possible analysis, and the one I shall argue for later in this section (pp. 127–131) treats the difference as a case of [past] versus [non-past]. In other words, the third exception is not an exception at all: both [past] *and* [non-past] are possible if the clause is object of *remember, recall*, etc.

The definition of environments

The reader is probably rather puzzled by some of the factual claims that I have been making in the last few paragraphs, since they may seem to be blatantly untrue. For instance, it is easy to find counterexamples to the claim that [passive] is obligatory after *order*:

> The general ordered *the execution to take place at once.*

It all depends on what one means by 'environment'. It is clear, and presumably generally accepted, that environments must be defined with reference to factors that are (a) abstract and general — i.e. not simply 'frames' consisting of strings of particular words, and (b) defined by the grammar itself.

This being so, the reader will appreciate that environments are not and cannot be self-explanatory, and in theory at least cannot be understood unless the underlying grammar is also known. I have not yet introduced the underlying grammar, so inevitably the reader is in the unfortunate position of having to simply take the defining environments as given. Because of this, he cannot either agree or disagree with the claims I have made about the relations between a clause's environment and its tense/aspect and voice categories. However, I can at least enlist his sympathy by explaining how I come to define the environments in such a way that I can claim that a clause depending on *order* must be [passive].

First of all, this is really an informal and rather misleading way of saying that in one particular environment, which is characterised by, among other things, the presence of a verb like *order*, only passive clauses are possible. (This being an informal discussion of 'the facts', such inaccuracy is inevitable; the gain in 'readability' seems to justify it.) This more accurate restatement does not use the presence of a verb like *order* as a sufficient criterion for defining the relevant environment, but just as a necessary one. Consequently, an environment which did allow the embedded clause to be active could nevertheless include *order*; so the sentence quoted above need not be a counter-example to our generalisation. In other words, the embedded clauses in the following sentences may appear to have the same environments, but in fact they have different environments:

> The general ordered *the execution to take place*,
> The general ordered *the prisoners executed*.

Secondly, we treat these as two different environments for two reasons. The first, relatively concrete, reason is that some verbs can occur in one environment but not in the other. For instance, although *order* can occur in both, *allow* can occur only in one:

> The general allowed *the execution to take place at once*,
> *The general allowed *the prisoners executed*.

The second reason, which is more abstract, is that it is relatively easy to write the grammar so that the environments are seen as instances of two very different more general environments: in one case, the environments that allow participial clauses, and in the other, those that allow infinitival or gerundival clauses. This analysis automatically generates not only active but also passive clauses in the latter environment:

The general allowed/ordered *the prisoners to be executed*.

It is much harder, however, to write a grammar which defines an environment (allowing *order* but not *allow*) in which the embedded clause can be either infinitival (active or passive), or participial (passive). Needless to say, it is the former grammar that I shall be offering below.

In other words, according to our grammar the following are not active and passive equivalents of each other:

The general ordered *his men to execute the prisoners*,
The general ordered *the prisoners executed*.

Rather, the first is the active equivalent of

The general ordered *the prisoners to be executed*,

and the second has no active equivalent — hence the original, loosely formulated, claim that a clause depending on *order* must be passive.

Past versus non-past and time-reference in non-finite clauses
If we were to consider just simple sentences, we should find that the difference between [past] and [non-past] was relatively straightforward: if we wish to refer to an event (or state) in such a way as to suggest that it took place in a period that is now over, we use a clause that is [past]. One of the consequences of this fact is that an adverbial which can only define a time preceding the present will occur in [past] clauses, but not in [non-past] ones:

We accepted twenty candidates last year,
*We accept twenty candidates last year.

It is therefore tempting to conclude that there is a *grammatical* restriction on adverbials like *last year* which excludes them from [non-past] clauses. Problems arise with examples like

We accept twenty candidates last year, and look
what happens this year!

But we can probably find some way of getting round these.

As far as simple sentences are concerned, these observations are scarcely original. What is the situation in non-finite clauses? If it is the same, we shall be able to use the possibility of an adverbial like *last year* as a criterion for identifying clauses as [past]. This raises again the question that we met in discussing clauses occurring with *remember*: is the gerundival clause in the following [past] or [non-past]?

> I distinctly remember *accepting twenty candidates last year*.

If we treat the presence (or possibility) of *last year* as a sufficient criterion for [past], this clause must be [past]; but what then is the difference between it and

> I distinctly remember *having accepted twenty candidates*
> *last year*?

As I suggested in discussing these constructions, the answer towards which we are tending is to say that these clauses are respectively [non-past] and [past], as their verb-forms indicate, and so the possibility of *last year* is *not* to be taken as a sufficient criterion for [past]. Let us consider evidence in favour of this conclusion from other kinds of non-finite clause.

First, consider the following:

> Most of the candidates *applying last year* were accepted,
> Most of the candidates *who applied last year* were accepted.

It seems reasonable to treat the non-finite clause as well as the finite one as [past] — and in a TG analysis one might even give them both the same deep structure. But how do we explain the fact that the participial clause ceases to be grammatical if the matrix clause ceases to be [past]?

> *Most of the candidates *applying last year* will be accepted,
> Most of the candidates *who applied last year* will be accepted.

The most reasonable explanation is that the possibility of *last year* in the participial clause depends on the environment of this clause being [past] — and not on the tense of the participial clause itself. If this is correct, there is nothing to prevent us from treating *applying last year* as [non-past]: *last year* is compatible with [non-past] provided the larger environment is in some sense 'past'.

Moreover, if the participial clause is passive (instead of active, as in the last example), the above restriction no longer holds: *last year* is possible whether the matrix clause is past or not.

> Most of the candidates *accepted last year* began in October,
> Most of the candidates *accepted last year* will begin this October.

We can easily explain this difference by referring back to the discussion in 3.1.2: *accepted* is ambiguously the realisation of two features (just [passive] and [participial]) or of three ([passive] and [participial] and also either [perfect] or [past]). That is, *accepted last year* can be taken as either [non-past] *or* [past] ; and in particular we can take it as [past] in a non-past environment, just like the corresponding finite relative clause:

> Most of the candidates *who were accepted last year*
> will begin this October.

We could not use *applying last year* in a non-past environment because it is not ambiguous in this way between [past] and [non-past] , but must be [non-past] . The corresponding [past] clause would contain *having applied*, which is only marginally acceptable:

> ? Most of the candidates *having applied last year* will be accepted.

The general rule towards which we are moving is thus as follows: in non-finite clauses, an adverbial like *last year* is possible (a) if the clause is [past] ; or (b) if it is [non-past] but the environment is past. This rule seems to work with all other kinds of non-finite clauses as well. For instance, it explains the following:

> It's a pity *for Basil to have fallen asleep yesterday*
> *during his own lecture*,
> *It's a pity *for Basil to fall asleep yesterday during his own lecture*,
> It was a pity *for Basil to fall asleep yesterday during*
> *his own lecture*.

We can formulate the rule in a rather more general and simple way: tenses in non-finite clauses are never selected deictically. That is, they do not define 'before' ([past]) and 'not before' ([non-past]) with reference to the moment of speaking, but with reference to the time defined by the matrix clause. (If the latter is itself [non-past] , the non-finite clause may appear to be deictic, but this will be only because the time referred to by the matrix clause is the same as the moment of speaking.)

Interestingly, the situation just described seems to be exactly the opposite of the situation that we find with finite clauses whose tense is determined by the 'sequence of tenses' rules. Here, it is the clause that is (apparently, at least) [past] that has the more general time-reference: in a 'past' environment, a [past] clause can refer to an event that is still going on or a state that still exists, but a [non-past] one can only refer to the latter.

> He recognised *that Plato was a genius,*
> He recognised *that Plato's ideas were true* (not odd),
> He recognised *that Plato is a genius* (odd),
> He recognised *that Plato's ideas are true.*

By way of contrast, a [past] non-finite clause in a past environment must refer to a past state, so it could not be used for 'eternal truths'; for these, a [non-past] non-finite clause must be used.

> He recognised *Plato to have been a genius,*
> He recognised *Plato's ideas to have been true* (odd),
> He recognised *Plato to be a genius* (not odd),
> He recognised *Plato's ideas to be true.*

There is undoubtedly much more to be said about the semantics of time-reference in non-finite clauses, but I shall add just one more remark. The reader may have noticed that the word 'past' occurred between square brackets when describing the non-finite clause, but not when it described the latter's environment. This was deliberate, since I did not want to give the impression that the relevant environment could be defined simply with reference to the grammatical tense of the matrix clause: this is only one of the factors involved in the quality of 'pastness'. Another one has already been mentioned: if the verb is *remember* or *recall* (for instance) then the matrix clause qualifies as 'past' even if it is [non-past] :

> I remember *falling over a lot when I was a little boy.*

Others are not hard to find — for instance, *since* and *after* make the environment 'past':

> Since *meeting her first about a month ago* I feel very peculiar.

It would obviously be hard to bring all these environments together into a single grammatical category, but this need not worry us, since it is not necessary: the distinctions we have been discussing here are *semantic* rather than grammatical, so we can leave the problem of formalising them till a much later day. Certainly the most important conclusion we have come to, as far as the present chapter is concerned, is that we need not treat apparently [non-past] non-finite clauses as being in fact [past] : they are grammatically [non-past] , but they may refer to an event or state that was located in the past.

Purely structural restrictions: the ungrammaticality of 'being ...ing'

This completes our discussion of restrictions imposed by the environment. There is another kind of restriction, however, which I have not mentioned so far: purely structural restrictions. These are much less numerous than environmental restrictions, but they reflect a very important characteristic of language: that restrictions on 'form' need not be exactly in line with restrictions on 'content', so that there may be a 'content' without a corresponding 'form' (p. 78).

There is only one example of this phenomenon that is peculiar to non-finite clauses, so far as I know. It was noticed some years ago, and formulated as follows: any pair of adjacent ing-forms is ungrammatical. In particular, the progressive *be*, which is followed by an ing-form, must not itself be an ing-form. This means, in our terms, that a gerundival clause cannot be [progressive] , unless it is also [perfect] :

> **Being still living in the house where one was born when*
> *one dies* is unusual these days,
> *Having been living in the house where one was born till*
> *one dies* is unusual these days.

It is easy to see that there is nothing wrong with the first sentence as far as its meaning is concerned, because we get a fully grammatical sentence if we extrapose the non-finite clause, replacing the gerundival clause (regularly) by an infinitival one (pp. 177−180):

> It is unusual these days *to be still living in the house where*
> *one was born when one dies.*

This is not ruled out, as the earlier one was, simply because it does not contain *being* as marker of [progressive] .

It is interesting to compare gerundival clauses with participial clauses: since [gerundival] and [participial] can both be realised by the first verb being an ing-form, we might expect to find the same restriction on participials that we find with gerundivals. In fact, we do not. It is true, we do not find *being* followed by an ing-form — but then, we would not expect to, since it would break the normal pattern for realising features in the structure of a participial clause: [progressive] and [participial] both allow a simple ing-form among their realisations, so the form of *be* is not needed. Thus whereas the ungrammaticality of *being*-plus-ing-form leads to a gap in the gerundival paradigm, it has no effect at all on that of the participial (or any other) paradigm.

How can we be sure that the missing form in the gerundival paradigm is not in fact some other form? In particular, is it not possible that instead of being the form that we should expect from the normal workings of the rule for forming gerundivals, it is a simple ing-form, just like the corresponding participial form? The following examples should provide the needed evidence: a gerundival clause with just an ing-form (*sleeping*) can only be taken semantically as [non-progressive] so it is semantically anomalous to use it as if it were progresssive.

> He slept soundly when he went to bed,
> He was sleeping soundly when the office phone rang,
> It's very gratifying *to sleep soundly when one goes to bed*,
> It's very trying *to be sleeping soundly when the office phone rings*,
> Anyone *sleeping soundly when he goes to bed* wakes up feeling pleased with life,
> Anyone *sleeping soundly when the office phone rings* wakes up feeling guilty,
> *Sleeping soundly when one goes to bed* is one of youth's boons,
> ? *Sleeping soundly when the office phone rings* is very trying.

The oddness of the last example is just the same as that of

> He slept soundly when the office phone rang.

In other words, the string of words *sleeping soundly when the office phone rings* can be either [progressive] or [non-progressive] if it is [participial], but only [non-progressive] if [gerundival]; but at the same time it is only when it is [progressive] that it makes sense.

How 'being ...ing' can be excluded

It is probably clear why we cannot reasonably use the system-network to prevent [progressive] from combining with [gerundival, non-perfect]. For one thing, it would be extremely complicated to do so: excluding just one

product of the intersection of three otherwise independent systems is something systemic grammar does very clumsily — and rightly so, since this represents a significant claim about the nature of language. In other words, systemic theory is based on the assumption (among others) that this kind of
situation does not arise in natural languages. Consequently, where we appear
to have an instance of it, we look for another explanation.

Secondly, it is extremely easy to exclude this combination of features by
means of a direct restriction on structure.

And thirdly, there seems to be no extrinsic reason for excluding this particular feature-combination as such, beyond the fact that it is ungrammatical
— there is nothing in any way odd about it semantically, as I hope to have
shown. When it comes to excluding *being* followed by an ing-form, however,
it is at least not entirely arbitrary, though it is far from the kind of purely
surface phenomenon that one might rule out on grounds of 'euphony', such
as

> ? Tom ran faster than Bill more often *than than* Fred.

The relatively 'deep' character of our rule can be seen from the fact that
being retiring is possible if *retiring* is an adjective, but not if it is a verb:

> *Being retiring by nature* prevented Sam from going to parties,
> **Being retiring in a year's time* prevented Sam from taking
> on any more commitments.

Moreover, the ing-form has to be an IC of the same clause as *being*, so the
following is grammatical:

> *His biggest vice being drinking ginger beer* made Sam
> feel very virtuous.

These observations, in turn, mean that we must exclude progressive non-
perfect gerundivals by restrictions operating on a relatively deep representation, though not as deep as the features: which leads us naturally to let them
operate on our structures made of function-bundles (p. 153).

3.2. The analysis

3.2.1. *Introduction*
The rest of this chapter will be devoted to a systemic grammar that gener-

ates non-finite clauses with the verb-forms appropriate both to their environment and to their tense/aspect features, and which only allows the range of tense/aspect features that are permitted in each environment. There are of course many facets of these clauses that are *not* covered. since we are concentrating on tense/aspect and voice; but the way in which the verb-forms are specified can be extended to other aspects, and my primary aim is still to illustrate the way in which a systemic grammar works, rather than to give an exhaustive analysis of English non-finite clauses. Apart from the incompleteness of the grammar in not covering all aspects of the non-finite clause's grammar, the grammar in this section will be incomplete in another sense: the environments we shall have to refer to will not be specified formally. However, on this question the reader is invited simply to wait till the next chapter but one, where nearly all the relevant environments will be formally defined.

Tense/aspect and voice in non-finite and finite clauses

One thing that is clear about non-finite clauses is that they can be described in terms of the same categories of tense/aspect and voice as finite clauses. The realisations of these categories may be to some extent different, and in one case ([non-past]) we have even found that the meaning is slightly different (p. 131); but it would obviously make the grammar much longer and less general, with little or no advantage, to set up two separate sets of contrasts, one set for finite clauses and another for non-finite ones. Indeed, this is one of the main reasons for calling non-finite constructions 'clauses' rather than 'phrases'.

One way of allowing the same sets of contrasts to apply to both finite and non-finite clauses is to have a stage in the derivation of both where clauses are not yet divided into 'finite' and 'non-finite', and to let the tense/aspect and voice contrasts apply at that stage. This would be a typical TG approach, and it might take the form of an analysis where TENSE (the marker of finiteness) is present in the deep structure of every clause, but is deleted before the surface structure of some clauses is reached (e.g. Rosenbaum). Alternatively, the marker of finiteness might be *absent* from all deep structures, but added transformationally under certain conditions (e.g. McCawley). In either case, of course, the grammar shows that the tense/aspect and voice contrasts are common to all clauses, finite or non-finite.

Another way of achieving the same result is to let the tense/aspect and voice contrasts cut across the contrast between finite and non-finite. This is the approach we shall use, and it consists simply in including the finiteness contrast as one of the systems that apply to the clause, along with all the others including tense/aspect and voice. One of the characteristics of this analysis is that it makes neither of finite and non-finite prior to the other — which seems something of an advantage in view of the apparent difficulty there is in deciding which one is prior.

Thus in this systemic grammar finite and non-finite clauses will share the same network, which means that there will be at least some features that they will both be able to select. As we have seen, these include the tense/aspect and voice features; but these do not always have the same realisations in non-finite as in finite clauses, so we shall have to make some of the realisation rules for these features environmentally determined — so that [past] has one realisation in [finite] clauses, and another in [non-finite] ones, for instance.

Distributional classes of non-finite clauses

Another fact that the grammar must take account of is that non-finite clauses of different kinds are required in different environments — infinitival in some environments, gerundival in others, and so on. This is not true of finite clauses, of course, or at least not in the same sense, so we shall have to make special statements that apply only to non-finite clauses.

In a TG analysis, the environmental factors could be handled by a range of transformations, each of which modifies the clause's structure in a different way, and operates in a different range of environments from the others (p. 47). It is hard to see how such a grammer could avoid reflecting the distinctions we made in 3.1.1 and 3.1.2, or something very similar to them; and in particular it would need to take account of the complexities that arise with participial clauses, as described in 3.1.2. This means that the transformations needed might be quite numerous and complicated. Moreover, it might well prove difficult to define the relevant environments for each transformation in a simple way. However, assuming that this is possible, the transformation might introduce abstract markers such as INFINITIVAL, GERUNDIVAL and PAR-TICIPIAL into the clause's still relatively deep structure, and these markers might themselves in turn trigger a further set of transformations. This at least seems a promising hypothesis.

In a systemic grammar, the desired result will again be achieved by a combination of subclassification and conditioned realisation rules. Non-finite clauses will be subclassified into the classes already introduced — [infinitival], [gerundival], [participial], the former two being grouped together as [nominal], and [infinitival] and [participial] being further subdivided. In other words, the distinctions made on the horizontal axis in the table on p. 120 will be converted into systems applying to clauses that are [non-finite].

Restrictions on tense/aspect and voice

Thirdly, the grammar has to say what restrictions the various environments place on the selection of tense/aspect and voice – it must formalise the fact, for instance, that with *seem* both [past] and [perfect] are possible, with *tend* only [perfect] is, while with *see* neither is.

seem   (a) *He* seems *to go to lunch unusually early,*
         (b) *He* seems *to have been to lunch already,*
         (c) *He* seems *to have gone to lunch two hours ago.*

tend   (a) *He* tends *to go to lunch unusually early,*
         (b) *He* tends *to have been to lunch by one o'clock,*
         (c) **He* tends *to have gone to lunch two hours ago.*

see   (a) I saw *him go to lunch unusually early,*
         (b) *I saw *him have been to lunch by one o'clock,*
         (c) *I saw *him have gone to lunch two hours ago.*

One way in which these restrictions could be formalised in a TG grammar might be by means of transformations whose range of environments were so defined as to exclude, say, past tense clauses in the environment of *tend* or *see*. If these transformations were among the more essential ones – such as those for inserting lexical items, or for combining affixes with stems – then no acceptable surface structure would be generated corresponding to such deep structures. Alternatively, and preferably, a 'generative semantics' analysis would presumably never generate these deep structures, so they would not need to be filtered out transformationally. How this might be done is not for me to suggest.

In the systemic grammar, the restrictions will be handled in just the same way as all other facts about the distribution of items: by environmentally predetermined selections in the system network. For instance, there is never (as far as I can see) a free choice between [dependent] and [independent] : one or the other is always obligatory because of the clause's environment, and, more precisely, because of its functions. Similarly, in some environments there is no choice between [past] and [non-past], and in these environments the clause's functions select the obligatory feature – i.e. [non-past]. The restricting effect of the environment is mediated by the realisation rules for the clause's functions; that is, among the clause's functions there may be one realised by [dependent], another by [infinitival], another by [non-past], and so on.

Thus the majority of unwanted combinations of features will be ruled out from the start: given the clause's functions, only feature-combinations that are compatible with them will be selected. This means that in most cases there is no question of generating deep representations (feature-combinations, corresponding to TG deep structures) which then turn out to have no grammatical surface representation to match them. In a few cases, however, it is necessary to 'filter out' representations which are unexceptionable as far as the feature combinations involved are concerned, but which require surface representations (viz., structures) that would not be grammatical. The clearest instance of this is the ungrammaticality of [progressive, non-past, non-perfect, gerundival] clauses, described on pp. 131—133: for these the feature-combination will be permitted, but the structure will be ruled out by the 'structure building' rules (see 3.2.5).

3.2.2. *The system network*

Four areas of the total system-network for English are relevant to this chapter: the area in which non-finite clauses are distinguished from other clauses; the area where they are subclassified as [infinitival], etc.; the area where clauses as a whole are subclassified according to tense/aspect and voice; and the area where verbs are distinguished from other words, and then further sub-divided. We shall not need this last part till 3.2.5 below, but I shall introduce it here to remind the reader that it belongs to the same all-inclusive system-network as the other three areas.

These four parts of the total network cover the following systems in the partial network on the next page:
(a) non-finite clauses are distinguished from other clauses by system 4;
(b) the distributional classes of non-finite clauses are distinguished by systems 5 through 9.
(c) the tense/aspect and voice distinctions are made in systems 3 and 10 through 12; unlike the systems under (b), these apply to finite clauses as well as to non-finite ones, but system 3, [past] versus [non-past], is prevented from applying to imperative clauses;
(d) the classification of words as verbs or otherwise, and the sub-classification of verbs, are effected by systems 13 through 20.

The interaction of the features of clauses and of their verbs
Let us take a few examples of non-finite clauses to show how they select features from this network.

(a) He tried not to let *his car skid on the wet road.*

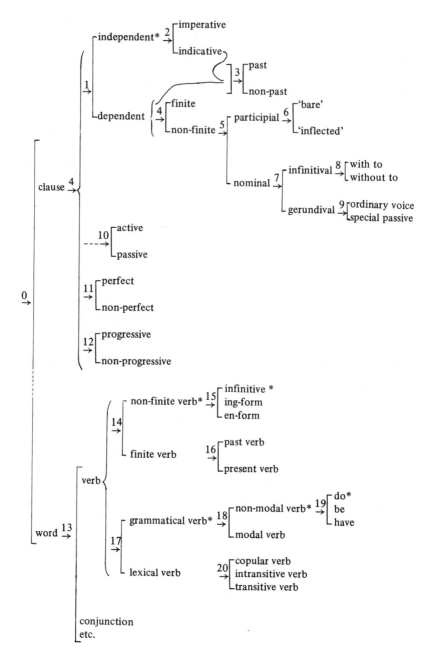

The italicized has the following features from the network: [clause, dependent, non-past, non-finite, nominal, infinitival, without to, non-perfect, non-progressive, active]. Its only verb is *skid*, which has the following: [word, verb, non-finite verb, infinitive, lexical verb].

    (b) I saw *his car skid on the wet road.*

The italicized has the same features as in (a), except that instead of [nominal, infinitival, without to] it has [participial, 'bare']. Its only verb, *skid*, has the same features as *skid* in (a), without exceptions.

    (c) I saw *his car skidding on the wet road.*

The features of the italicized are the same as in (b), except that [progressive] occurs in place of [non-progressive]. The verb *skidding* is the same as *skid*, except that it has [ing-form] in place of [infinitive].

    (d) The car *skidding towards him* appeared to be
         a 1963 Deluxe Mini.

The italicized has the same features as in (c), with ['inflected'] instead of ['bare']. Its verb *skidding* has precisely the same features as in (c).

    (e) *His car skidding on the wet road* made him drive
         more slowly.

Here the italicized looks identical to that in (c), but has quite a different set of features: where the latter had [participial, 'bare'] this has [nominal, gerundival], and where the latter had [progressive] this has [non-progressive]. The verb *skidding*, however, again has exactly the same features.

    (f) *His car* seems *to have been skidding rather a lot*
        on the wet road just before the accident.

The italicized has the same features as (e) except that it has [infinitival, with to] where the latter had [gerundival, ordinary], and [past, non-perfect, progressive] in place of [non-past, non-perfect, non-progressive]. It contains three verbs: *have, been* and *skidding.* These all have the feature [non-finite verb], but *have* also has [infinitive], *been* [en-form] and *skidding* [ing-form];

and *skidding* has [lexical verb] whilst both the others have [grammatical verb, non-modal verb] , with [have] in the case of *have*, and [be] in that of *been*.

This network illustrates rather clearly the importance of allowing classification at different ranks − in particular, of allowing the classification of verbs as [ing-form] , etc. to be separate from the classification of clauses as [gerundival] or [participial] . If we had had to concentrate all the contrasts on one rank − the word − we should have run into the same confusion about whether an ing-form is a gerund or a participle (or both) as arises in traditional grammars. As we have already seen in the preceding sections, the task of relating the two sets of classes − of saying when a participial clause contains an ing-form and when not, or of saying when a clause containing an ing-form is gerundival, and when participial, when progressive and when non-progressive − is not simple. So it is not surprising that trying to merge the two sets of distinctions into one should have led to confusion.

Environmental restrictions on clause features

As I admitted earlier, I shall not formalise the environmental restrictions on the system network in this chapter; this will have to wait till chapter 5. All I can do here is to show the way in which these restrictions will be effected, by means of examples, starting with the following:

They made him *send for a doctor.*

In this grammar we shall assign the following functions to the italicized clause: THIRD, COMPLETER, CLAUSE, INFIN-CL, NONPERF-CL, NONPROG-CL, NONPAST-CL. The first two of these functions are irrelevant to the selection of the clause's features, but each of the other five narrows down the range of features the clause can have: CLAUSE makes it have [dependent], INFIN-CL [infinitival], NONPERF-CL [non-perfect], NONPROG-CL [non-progressive] and NONPAST-CL [non-past]. These five features are features the clause must have because it has the functions listed, and therefore there is no longer a free choice in systems 1, 3, 7, 11, 12.

However, the restrictions in effect extend beyond these systems, for two reasons. Firstly, there are features which an item must have if it has the features just listed, because in the system-network the latter depend on them. For instance, [dependent] presupposes [clause] , so the latter must also be one of the item's features. Similarly, the features [non-finite] and [nominal] are presupposed by [infinitival] , so they too must be present. This adds systems 0, 4 and 5 to the list of systems that are predetermined by the clause's environment.

Secondly, there are some features that are starred in the system-network, meaning that wherever their system applies they are to be selected unless the environment makes another feature obligatory. For instance, [independent] is starred, which reflects the fact that if a clause has *no* environment — that is, if it is a complete 'sentence' on its own — it must be [independent]. Similarly, [without to] is starred, showing that it must be selected in the absence of a function which requires [with to]. In our example there is no such function, so system 8 is also predetermined, and the item must have the feature [without to].

Thus if an item has the functions listed above, it *must* have the features [clause, dependent, non-past, non-finite, nominal, infinitival, without to, non-perfect, non-progressive]. This in effect leaves only one system to be freely chosen from: system 10, [active] versus [passive]. So our example above can be matched by

They made him *be examined by a doctor.*

In both examples the italicized have exactly the same set of functions — in other words their environments are identical — and the difference between them lies only in the features they have selected from system 10, the voice system.

These two examples can be compared with

He was made *to send for a doctor,*
He was made *to be examined by a doctor.*

Once again, the environment is exactly the same for both the italicized clauses, but it is different from the environment in the first two examples. Most obviously, the matrix clause was active in the latter whereas it is passive in the former, but this in itself does not explain why the non-finite clauses should be different too. To do this, we introduce one extra function, TO-FULL, which must be combined with CLAUSE if a matrix clause of the kind illustrated is passive; and this function in turn makes the feature [with to] obligatory. There is no need to drop one of the functions already in the list in order to prevent a conflict with TO-FULL, since the feature [without to] was selected precisely because of the absence of TO-FULL.

Not all environments are as restricting as these, of course. A less restricting one is exemplified in

Everyone believes *Fred to be going to the States next year.*

Here the italicized has just the following functions: SECOND, GOAL, COM-
PLEMENT, CLAUSE, TO-FULL. The first three are irrelevant to the clause's
features, and the last two simply preempt the features [dependent] and [with
to] in systems 1 and 8 respectively. These in turn predetermine systems 0, 4,
5 and 7 but we are still left with systems 3, 10, 11 and 12 — all the tense/
aspect and voice systems. So exactly the same environment equally well
allows the following:

> Everyone believes *the Sun to be hotter than the Earth,*
> Everyone believes *the Vikings to have been the first Europeans*
>   *in America,*
> Everyone believes *Susan to have been being taken out by Fred*
>   *for the last two years.*

3.2.3. *The feature-realisation rules*

The network that I have on p. 138 included two sets of features: one set
that combined with [clause], and one that combined with [word]. In this section I shall give realisation rules for the former — the latter will not concern
us. There were twelve binary systems, so including [clause] itself, we shall
have twenty-five features to account for.

Why these rules are so simple

These realisation rules (on the next page) have been simplified to some
extent by leaving out details that are not relevant to our main topic: tense/
aspect and voice in the non-finite clause and the ways they are reflected by
the verb-forms. For instance, under [passive] I have not mentioned that another realisation is that GOAL is conflated with SUBJECT. These extra
details will be introduced in chapter 5. However, even when we bear in mind
that the rules have been artificially simplified in this way, the reader will
agree that the rules are surprisingly simple: only one feature has a realisation
that is context-sensitive, and only one has a realisation that involves anything
other than simply adding a function to the clause's structure. Considering
how complicated we found the facts to be, we might have expected much
more complexity in these rules.

The main reason why these rules could be so simple is that a lot of the
complexity is handled not in them, but in the structure-building rules or the
function-realisation rules — especially the former. This is not a case of simply
postponing the crisis, but rather of using the most appropriate kind of rule

system	feature	realisation
0	clause	+ PROCESS
1	dependent	—
	independent	—
2	indicative	—
	imperative	—
3	past	+ PAST
	non-past	—
4	non-finite	—
	finite	+ FINITE
5	nominal	—
	participial	+ PARTICIPLE
6	'bare'	—
	'inflected'	+ ING/EN = PARTICIPLE
7	infinitival	—
	gerundival	+ GERUND
8	with to	+ TO
	without to	—
9	ordinary voice	—
	special passive	—
10	active	—
	passive	+ PASSIVE // not [special passive]
11	perfect	+ PERFECT
	non-perfect	—
12	progressive	+ PROGRESSIVE
	non-progressive	—

for handling the facts concerned: the kind of complexity with which we have
to contend is best handled in the structure-building rules.

For instance, the realisation of [perfect] is simply the presence of a function PERFECT. Perhaps surprisingly, PERFECT is the function of an en-form
verb, so we still have to account for the presence of the preceding *have* —
which at first sight one might expect to have had the function PERFECT, as
the basic marker of the feature. However, the structure-building rules will
automatically add a function representing the *have*, in most cases where PER-
FECT occurs, and will ensure that these functions occur in the right order
and are combined with other functions in the right way. So all we need give
as realisation of [perfect] is PERFECT, which will then trigger off the appropriate structure-building rules.

Another characteristic of systemic theory which enables these rules to be relatively simple is the convention about selecting starred features in the absence of any environmental pressures to do otherwise. This means that a lot of the features have no realisation at all, and it is even possible to make a total selection of features from the network which are *all* unrealised — except for [clause], which is always realised by the presence of PROCESS. The combination of features that has this property is [clause, dependent, non-finite, nominal, infinitival, without to, non-past, non-perfect, non-progressive, active]. As far as the rules given above are concerned, all we know about the structure of a clause with these features is·that it contains PROCESS. The realisation rules for PROCESS tell us that it must be a lexical verb, and the starring convention tells us that this must be [non-finite verb, ∅-form]. This description would fit the following, for instance:

He let *her cry for a reasonable period*,
She made him *see red.*

On the other hand, we could also select features which are all realised (except for [dependent]): [clause, dependent, finite, past, perfect, progressive, passive]. The realisation rules tell us that a clause with these features must have a structure containing the following functions: PROCESS, FINITE, PAST, PERFECT, PROGRESSIVE, PASSIVE. Various operations will be performed on these functions by the structure-building rules, and these, together with the function-realisation rules, will tell us that a clause with the features listed will have to contain a cluster of verbs with the following specification: *had* followed by *been* followed by *being* followed by the en-form of a lexical verb.

One consequence of saving some of the complications till the structure-building rules is that two clauses can have not only very nearly the same features, but also very nearly the same structure as far as the realisation rules above are concerned, and yet be very different in their more 'surface' structures, resulting from the structure-building rules. For instance, two clauses might both have the features [dependent, non-finite, non-past, perfect, non-progressive, passive]; and because of these features they would both have structures containing the functions PERFECT and PASSIVE, as well as PROCESS. But if one had the feature [participial] while the other had [infinitival], their final structures would be very different: the former would contain just one verb, the en-form of a lexical verb, while the latter would contain no less than three: *have*; then *been*, then the en-form of a lexical verb. They could be respectively the italicized in the following:

All houses *built since 1930* contain a bath-room,
A lot of good houses seem *to have been built since 1930.*

The realisations of tense/aspect and voice: auxiliaries or affixes?

The tense/aspect and voice features are all either unrealised or realised just by the presence of a single function. As I have already mentioned, PERFECT is not the function of the form of *have*, but of the following en-form. Similarly, PAST, PROGRESSIVE and PASSIVE reflect the presence of an *affix* rather than of the auxiliary verb that is usually considered to mark these categories. This is probably one of the least conventional aspects of the analysis in this chapter (p. 25 ff.), so I ought to try to justify it.

One alternative would be to let each of the features in question be realised by the presence not of one function but of two: one corresponding to the auxiliary, the other to the affix. The main difficulty with this analysis is that sometimes only the affix is present: this is true for [past] in all finite clauses except those that are [modal], and for all the features in some participial clauses. That is, [past] *can* be realized by both a form of *have* and an en-form, just like [perfect], but in finite clauses it is realised just by a past tense form; and all of the realised features are sometimes realised just by an ing-form or en-form of the lexical verb, when the clause is [participial] (p. 117). This being so, one of the two functions realising each of the features would be sometimes present, sometimes absent, and defining the relevant rules would be extremely difficult; certainly the realisation rules would lose any claim to simplicity or generality.

A second alternative would be to have just one function per feature, as in our rules, but to let this function represent the auxiliary verb rather than the affix; a function representing the latter would then be introduced obligatorily by the structure-building rules. The difficulties this analysis would run into would be like those described in the last paragraph: sometimes the affix is present but the auxiliary verb is not, so unless we are to allow deletion rules among the structure-building rules — which otherwise do not appear to be needed — we cannot introduce the auxiliary-function in all cases.

A third alternative would be to introduce two functions, one for the auxiliary verb and one for the affix, and to allow these to be conflated with each other under certain circumstances — notably, in the presence of PARTICIPLE. This was tried, and seemed hopeful, but makes the rules far harder to formulate than they need be — certainly harder than the analysis we have adopted.

The analysis underlying this grammar, on the other hand, justifies itself by the elegance and simplicity of the structure-building rules it allows us to formulate: we can easily define the environments where the auxiliary verb is needed, and formulate the rule that introduces it in such a way that it is introduced in precisely those environments.

Besides this general virtue of our analysis, there are two secondary advantages that it brings. Firstly, the realisation of [past] is just PAST, and this in turn is *in all cases* realised by a particular form of a verb, whether the clause is finite or non-finite. Admittedly, the form in question is a past-tense form in one case, and an en-form in the other, but it is still the same kind of inflectional realisation. If on the other hand we had treated auxiliary verbs, wherever possible, as realisation of the features concerned, then we should have had to say that PAST is sometimes the function of a past-tense form of a verb, and sometimes the function of a form of the verb *have*. On balance, the present analysis, in which [past] is realised just by PAST, and the latter just by one of two forms of a verb, seems preferable to all of the many other analyses that I have tried.

The other secondary advantage of our analysis is that [passive] is realised by PASSIVE which is always realised by the main verb being in the en-form. This means that PASSIVE is always conflated with PROCESS, the function of the main verb; and this makes it very easy to specify that a particular class of verbs either must, or must not, be used in a passive clause: we simply say that it can realise PROCESS only if PROCESS is (is not) conflated with PASSIVE. I shall make use of this possibility in discussing noun clauses; for instance, we shall want to prevent *need* from being used in passive clauses, and *purport* from being used in active clauses (5.2.1).

3.2.4. *The structure-building rules*

The feature-realisation rules on p. 143 introduced the following functions: FINITE, GERUND, ING/EN, PARTICIPLE, PASSIVE, PAST, PROCESS, PROGRESSIVE. By the rule for ['inflected'], ING/EN was conflated with PARTICIPLE, but otherwise these functions are so far completely unordered and un-'structured'. In this section I shall describe rules which will add a number of other functions to these, including those representing the auxiliary verbs — and specify how they combine into a structure, by either being conflated or being arranged in a sequence, or both.

There are the usual four kinds of structure-building rules, called 'sequence rules', 'compatibility rules', 'addition rules', and 'conflation rules'. At the end of this section I shall be able to bring together all the rules of each kind to give an overall picture of the structure-building rules. At the beginning, however, it would only lead to confusion if we introduced the rules one kind at a time, since we should keep on having to refer forward to rules of another kind that had not been introduced yet. Instead, I shall introduce the rules in the order which will be most convenient for presentation, one or two at a time, moving about freely from one type of rule to another.

Portmanteau realisations

Rule (a): + AFFIX = PAST, PERFECT, PROGRESSIVE, PASSIVE, PARTI-
CIPLE, GERUND, FINITE.

This rule identifies all the functions that were introduced by the realisation rules, except for PROCESS and TO, as affixes — or rather, as having to
do with the affix of the verb they represent, and not with its stem. It results
in every occurrence of PAST, etc. being conflated with AFFIX.

Rule (b): AFFIX = AFFIX // AFFIX = PARTICIPLE.

If the clause's structure contains more than one occurrence of AFFIX, and
one of them is conflated with PARTICIPLE, the separate occurrences of
AFFIX are all conflated — which means that the functions with which they
are individually conflated are all conflated too. (This rule is subject to a general restriction which I shall state later.) For instance, a clause whose features
include [participial] and [passive] will have in its structure PARTICIPLE =
AFFIX and PASSIVE = AFFIX. This rule will lead to these two bundles being
conflated into a single bundle: PARTICIPLE = AFFIX = PASSIVE = AFFIX.
Another rule (see below) will also conflate this bundle with PROCESS, giving
PROCESS = PARTICIPLE = AFFIX = PASSIVE = AFFIX — the functions
of the only verb in a clause such as:

Grammars *written late at night* tend to contain errors.

Similarly, if the clause also has [perfect] among its features, as well as [parti-
cipial] and [passive], its structure will include PERFECT = AFFIX, PASSIVE
= AFFIX and PARTICIPLE = AFFIX, which will all be conflated, with
PROCESS, into PERFECT = AFFIX = PASSIVE = AFFIX = PARTICPLE =
AFFIX = PROCESS. These are the functions of the single verb *written* in

Grammars *written since 1960* have tended to be
transformational.

This analysis reflects our claim that in such participial clauses as these several different features all have a single 'portmanteau' realisation (p. 116). This is not in fact a very accurate description of the situation: the features [participial], [perfect] and [passive] do not strictly speaking have a portmanteau realisation, since they are each realised separately, by a separate function; but these functions *do* have a portmanteau realisation, in as much as they are all realised by the same feature of the verb – the feature [en-form].

There is a general restriction on rules such as rule (b) – that is, on 'conflation rules' (p. 87). It is that they must not lead to a conflict with rules of the other kinds and if conflating two functions according to some conflation rule would produce a conflict, the conflation does not take place. The next rules are 'compatibility rules', and will provide an illustration of this general principle.

Adding the auxiliaries

Rule (c): PAST   ≠ PROGRESSIVE.
Rule (d): PERFECT ≠ PROGRESSIVE.
Rule (e): PASSIVE   ≠ PROGRESSIVE.

The three functions PAST, PERFECT and PASSIVE are all realised by an en-form verb, whilst PROGRESSIVE is realised by an ing-form; consequently, none of the former can be conflated with the latter, since this would produce a conflict. This is the first restriction imposed on rule (b), conflating any two occurrences of AFFIX in the environment of PARTICIPLE: it will not apply where one AFFIX is conflated/with PROGRESSIVE and the other with one of the three functions PAST, PERFECT and PASSIVE. If the clause's structure *does* contain PROGRESSIVE as well as one of these, then we know from these rules that they are not conflated with one another; but the rules given so far tell us no more than this. So if the clause's features include [participial, progressive, passive] , we know that there are three functions each of which is conflated with AFFIX: PARTICIPLE, PROGRESSIVE, PASSIVE; and we know that PROGRESSIVE and PASSIVE cannot be conflated; but a lot more information must be given before we can tell that the clause must contain *being* followed by an en-form.

Rule (f): + PREPAST // + PAST ≠ FINITE ≠ PASSIVE.
Rule (g): + PREPERFECT // + PERFECT ≠ PASSIVE.
Rule (h): + PREPROGRESSIVE // + PROGRESSIVE ≠ PARTICIPLE.
Rule (i) : + BE // + PASSIVE ≠ PARTICIPLE.

These are 'addition-rules', which add further functions to the structure, just as rules (a) and (b) did. Unlike rules (a) and (b), however, these rules simply specify that a particular function must be present, without saying what it must be conflated with. They are also different from rule (a) in that they have a conditioning environment stated separately, after the //: rule (h), for instance, means 'PREPROGRESSIVE must be present in any structure if this structure contains PROGRESSIVE not conflated with PARTICIPLE'. However, this difference is more apparent than real, since addition rules are *all* conditional (p. 83 ff.), and rule (a) has an underlying condition: AFFIX must be conflated with PAST *if* the structure in fact contains PAST.

PREPAST, PREPERFECT, PREPROGRESSIVE and BE are the functions that represent the auxiliary verbs *have* (PREPAST and PREPERFECT) and *be* (PREPROGRESSIVE and BE); so these four rules are the means by which the auxiliary verbs are introduced. It will be clear that there is a sense in which, say, a form of *be* is still part of the realisation of [progressive]: it realises PREPROGRESSIVE, and PREPROGRESSIVE is present because of the presence of PROGRESSIVE, which realises [progressive]. But there is still only an indirect relationship between the form of *be* and [progressive].

The last two rules will add PREPROGRESSIVE or BE wherever PRO-GRESSIVE or PASSIVE is present but not conflated with PARTICIPLE. This will obviously be the case in any clause other than a [participial] one, since PARTICIPLE occurs only in the structures of the latter; but it can arise even in [participial] clauses, since PARTICIPLE must not merely be present, but must also be conflated with PROGRESSIVE or PASSIVE. As we have seen, rule (e) prevents PROGRESSIVE from conflating with PASSIVE, whether PARTICIPLE is present or not; so if both PROGRESSIVE and PASSIVE are present, at least one of them cannot be conflated with PARTICIPLE (which only occurs once), and either rule (h) or rule (i), or both, must apply to add PREPROGRESSIVE and/or BE. Similarly, if both PERFECT and PROGRES-SIVE occur, they must not be conflated (rule d) and PROGRESSIVE will not in fact be conflated with PARTICIPLE, so PREPROGRESSIVE must be added.

The rules for adding PREPAST and PREPERFECT (both representing a form of *have*) are similar, but the conditions for adding them are not quite the same. Firstly, of course, PREPAST is never needed if the clause is finite, in which case it will contain FINITE, which will be conflated (for other reasons) with PAST; so PREPAST is not added if PAST is conflated with FINITE. Otherwise the rules for adding PREPAST and PERFECT are the same: there is one circumstance under which neither is added, namely when the clause is [participial]. However, unlike PREPROGRESSIVE and BE, it is not enough for PAST or PERFECT to be conflated with PARTICIPLE in order for the auxiliary to be excluded: they must also be conflated with PASSIVE. (This is how we formalise the claim (p. 115) that a clause containing *taken* can be either [non-past] or [past], [non-perfect] or [perfect], whereas one containing *taking* must be [non-past] and [non-perfect], the corresponding [perfect] or [past] form being one containing *having taken*.) But since they will be conflated with PASSIVE only as a result of rule (b), which presupposes the presence of PARTICIPLE, we need not mention the latter, and can simply mention PASSIVE. Hence the difference between the environmental restrictions on rules (f) and (g) on the one hand, and rules (h) and (i) on the other.

These rules, then, add the functions which will be realised by the auxiliary verbs that are associated with the tense/aspect and voice features. We still have to give quite a lot of information about the functions that have been introduced so far — including, most obviously, information about the sequence in which they occur.

The function 'BE'

Why do we call the function added by rule (i) 'BE' rather than PRE-PASSIVE, to match the names of the other functions? The answer is probably already obvious: this will be the function not only of the 'passive' *be*, but also of the 'main verb' *be*, whether copular, equative or existential/locative. In other words, this function will be introduced by several different rules, and not just by our rule (i), so we need a neutral name for it; and BE is the obvious name to choose.

The reason why we want to give the function BE to these 'main verb' uses of *be* is probably equally obvious: even when used as 'main verb', *be* is still treated syntactically like an auxiliary, as far as the rules for subject-verb inversion for instance are concerned. If we give these uses of *be* the function BE (an 'auxiliary' function), and *not* PROCESS (the 'main verb' function), then we need not explicitly include them in the rules that apply to functions other than PROCESS.

However, I shall also have to modify the grammar given so far, since according to this *every* clause contains the function PROCESS. This is easy to do — we allow PROCESS to represent either an ordinary main verb or a form of *be*, and then introduce another function MAIN VERB, which will distinguish verbs that do not behave like auxiliaries from those that do (including the 'main verb' *be*). I shall not in fact introduce this modification into the grammar, since it is not relevant to any of the other problems we shall encounter.

The ordering of the auxiliaries and affixes

Rule (j): TO   →
           PARTICIPLE ⎫   ⎫ (PREPAST → PAST = (PREPERFECT
           GERUND   ⎬ =   ⎬ → PERFECT = (PREPROGRESSIVE
           FINITE   ⎭   ⎭ → PROGRESSIVE = (BE → PASSIVE
                                   = PROCESS))))

This is a 'sequence rule' — the only sequence rule we shall need, in fact. It tells us *nothing at all* about the circumstances under which the functions concerned are present or absent, and in particular nothing about the dependency relations among them: it is concerned solely with questions of sequence. (This makes it very different from a tagmemic structural formula, for instance.) It tells us that if two functions both occur in the same structure, and both are mentioned in this formula, then they must not infringe the ordering specified.

To help the reader to interpret rule (j), I repeat below the general conventions for sequence rules (p. 90):

$A \rightarrow B$: B must precede A,
$A = B$: if A and B are both present, then they must be conflated,
$A = (B \rightarrow C \dots)$: A, if present, must be conflated with whichever of B and C comes first.

Note that it makes no difference whether the functions concerned are adjacent in rule (j) or not: so, for instance, we can tell that PREPERFECT must precede not only PERFECT, but also anything with which PERFECT is conflated (naturally enough) or anything else which is on the right of PREPERFECT. Similarly, TO precedes not only PREPAST, its neighbour in the rule, but everything else too, whether PREPAST occurs or not.

This rule immediately ensures that the auxiliary verbs will occur in the right sequence, and also that the affixes will be attached to the right verbs. So if PREPERFECT, PROGRESSIVE, BE and PROCESS all occur in the same structure, they must occur in that order; and PERFECT must be conflated with the first function following PREPERFECT, which in this case will be PROGRESSIVE.

In discussing rule (b), conflating AFFIX with AFFIX in the presence of PARTICIPLE, I noted that it did not apply if it conflicted with other rules. I have already given one instance of a possible conflict, involving rules (c), (d) and (e); I can now give another, involving the sequence rule and rules (f)

and (g). The latter rules introduced PREPAST and PREPERFECT respectively if PAST or PERFECT was present and was not conflated with
PASSIVE.

Let us consider how these rules operate in the case of a clause that has the
features [participial, non-past, perfect, non-progressive, passive] . These features are realised by PARTICIPLE, PERFECT and PASSIVE; by rule (a)
AFFIX is conflated with each of these three functions, and by rule (b) they
are all conflated into a single bundle because AFFIX and PARTICIPLE are
conflated. None of the conditions for rules (f) – (i) are satisfied, so no
'auxiliary' functions are added, so the clause must contain just one verb,
whose functions include PARTICIPLE = AFFIX = PERFECT = AFFIX =
PASSIVE = AFFIX, and also, of course, PROCESS; in other words, a verb
like *taken*.

Now let us replace [passive] by [active] , but leave the features otherwise
the same. In this case the features will be realised by just PARTICIPLE and
PERFECT, which will each be combined with AFFIX by rule (a), giving
PARTICIPLE = AFFIX and PERFECT = AFFIX. Let us see what happens if
we let rule (b) operate, to conflate these two bundles, giving PARTICIPLE =
AFFIX = PERFECT = AFFIX. This partial structure does not include
PASSIVE, but does include PERFECT, so it will allow rule (g) to apply,
adding PREPERFECT. Now comes the conflict: according to the sequence
rule, PREPERFECT must precede PERFECT, but it must *also* be conflated
with PARTICIPLE; since PERFECT is already conflated with PARTICIPLE,
there is no way of resolving the conflict. So rule (b) does *not* apply, and
PARTICIPLE is left free to conflate with PREPERFECT when this is introduced by rule (g); and the clause's structure must include PARTICIPLE =
AFFIX = PREPERFECT (i.e. *having*) followed by PERFECT = AFFIX,
which will be conflated by the sequence rule with PROCESS, to represent a
verb like *taken*.

Before leaving the sequence rule, it is perhaps worth pointing out that not
every function need be mentioned in it: if a function is always conflated with
some other function, then the position of the latter always determines that
of the former, so the former can be left out of the sequence rule. An instance
of this is the function ING/EN, which is always conflated with PARTICIPLE
and therefore does not figure anywhere in our sequence rule. If anything this
rule is unusual in mentioning explicitly such a high percentage of the functions affected by it.

The realisations of past and perfect

Rule (k): PAST = PERFECT // PAST ≠ FINITE.
Rule (l) : PREPAST = PREPERFECT.

If a non-finite clause is [past], this feature is usually realised by the presence of a form of *have* followed by an en-form; and exactly the same applies if it is [perfect]. But if it is both [past] *and* [perfect], there is still only a single instance of *have* followed by a single instance of an en-form. The two rules given here reflect this fact, by ensuring that if both PAST and PERFECT are present, they will be conflated — and likewise for PREPAST and PRE-PERFECT. Thus the form of *have* will have *both* the latter two functions, and the en-form both the former two. This will not cause any conflict, since both PAST and PERFECT require the same realisation in this environment, as do PREPAST and PREPERFECT.

If the clause is finite, on the other hand, [past] and [perfect] do not have the same realisations, and these rules do not apply. That is, PAST will not be conflated with PERFECT but rather with PREPERFECT, as in *had* (PAST = PREPERFECT = FINITE) *taken* (PERFECT = PROCESS). We can contrast this situation with the parallel one in non-finite (say, gerundival) clauses: PAST is conflated with PERFECT, and PREPAST with PREPERFECT, as in *having* (GERUND = PREPAST = PREPERFECT) *taken* (PAST = PERFECT = PROCESS).

Progressive gerundivals

Rule (m): GERUND ≠ PREPROGRESSIVE.

This rule excludes all clauses that are [gerundival, non-perfect, progressive], thus explaining the two gaps in the gerundival paradigm (p. 131 ff.): the first verb cannot have the function GERUND and *also* the function PREPROGRES-SIVE. If this combination was possible, it would be realised by *being*, which would be followed by an ing-form, realising PROGRESSIVE; but as we found in 3.1.3, clauses like the following are ungrammatical:

  **John being still lecturing* is a nuisance.

Why does our rule not simply prevent GERUND from combining with PREPROGRESSIVE, and make some alternative realisation for [progressive] necessary? If this were the case, then there would not be gaps in the gerundival paradigm, but instead forms which were in some way out of step with the others. This is not the case, however, because our grammar does not allow any alternative realisation for [progressive] : the only alternative is to have no PREPROGRESSIVE, but the latter is obligatory, according to rule (h), wherever there is no PARTICIPLE. Moreover, the grammar is *right* to allow no alternative, because, as a matter of fact, there *is* no alternative, as we saw in 3.1.3.

   This rule is a 'compatibility rule', like rules (c), (d) and (e); but it is unlike these in being relatively unmotivated. These three rules ruled out combinations of functions which would in any case have led to conflict when it came to realising them, because one function would have required an ing-form, while another required an en-form. For our present rule, however, there is no such easy way of explaining it (see again the discussion in 3.1.3). All we can do is to state it as a fact of English.

The structure-building rules summarised

   I have now introduced all the structure-building rules, and can bring them together, arranged into their four kinds. For the reader's convenience, their reference-letters are given in the margin.

Sequence rules

(j)   TO   → ⎫
      PARTICIPLE   ⎫   ⎬ (PREPAST → PAST = (PREPERFECT
      GERUND   ⎬ = ⎨   → PERFECT = (PREPROGRESSIVE
      FINITE   ⎭   → PROGRESSIVE = (BE → PASSIVE
                               = PROCESS))))

Compatibility rules

(c)   PAST ≠ PROGRESSIVE
(d)   PERFECT ≠ PROGRESSIVE
(e)   PASSIVE ≠ PROGRESSIVE
(m)   GERUND ≠ PREPROGRESSIVE

Addition rules

(a)   + AFFIX = PAST, PERFECT, PROGRESSIVE, PASSIVE, PARTICIPLE,
      GERUND, FINITE
(f)   + PREPAST // + PAST ≠ FINITE ≠ PASSIVE
(g)   + PREPERFECT // + PERFECT ≠ PASSIVE

(h) + PREPROGRESSIVE // + PROGRESSIVE ≠ PARTICIPLE
(i) + BE // + PASSIVE ≠ PARTICIPLE

Conflation rules
(b) AFFIX = AFFIX // AFFIX = PARTICIPLE
(k) PAST = PERFECT // PAST ≠ FINITE
(l) PREPAST = PREPERFECT

3.2.5. *The function-realisation rules*

In this section I shall relate the various functions that I have introduced so far to the system-network, and more precisely to the lower part of the network on p. 138, depending on the feature [word]. I have intentionally introduced only those functions that are realised by features of words, although some of the features of non-finite clauses should have been realised by functions that are realised by phrasal features, such as SUBJECT. Consequently, all the functions that have been introduced have realisations that can be treated in our system-network — with the exception of TO, realised by a word having whatever features *to* has. The rules are as follows.

function	realisation
AFFIX	—
BE	[be]
FINITE	[finite verb]
GERUND	[ing-form]
ING/EN	—
PARTICIPLE	[en-form] // = PASSIVE [ing-form] // = ING/EN, *and not* = PASSIVE [infinitive] // otherwise
PASSIVE	[en-form]
PAST	[past-verb] // = FINITE [en-form] // otherwise
PERFECT	[en-form]
PREPAST	[have]
PREPERFECT	[have]
PREPROGRESSIVE	[be]
PROCESS	[lexical verb]
PROGRESSIVE	[ing-form]

There are two kinds of realisation rule in this list, corresponding to the two sub-networks that depend on [verb] . One kind classify the verb according to systems 14–16, which have to do with its inflections; these rules realise 'inflection' functions such as FINITE, GERUND and PAST. The other kind classify it according to systems 17–20, reflecting its stem; and the functions thus realised can be referred to as 'stem' functions. There are only five of these: BE, PREPAST, PREPERFECT, PREPROGRESSIVE and PROCESS.

Let us take a simple example. The function PROCESS is realised by [lexical verb] and GERUND by [ing-form] , so if a word has both these functions it must have both these features too. Naturally, each of these features might also imply that other features must be present – for instance, [ing-form] can be present only if [non-finite verb] is too.

In a slightly more complicated example, let us assume that a word has the four functions PARTICIPLE = ING/EN = PASSIVE = PROCESS. Because of PROCESS, it must have the feature [lexical verb] ; and because of PASSIVE, [en-form] . But PARTICIPLE *also* requires it to have [en-form] , since this is the realisation it always has when combined with PASSIVE. This does not mean that the verb must therefore have two occurrences of [en-form] ; rather, it means that both functions make the same feature necessary. As far as the fourth function, ING/EN, is concerned, it does not contribute anything to the word's features.

Now let us take the case where the word's functions are just PARTICIPLE = ING/EN = PROCESS. Again PROCESS requires [lexical verb], but PARTICIPLE is conflated with ING/EN but not with PASSIVE, so it is realised by [ing-form] instead of [en-form] .

Reducing the functions still further, it is possible for PROCESS to occur all on its own – when all the relevant features of the clause are unrealised: [infinitival, without to, non-past, non-perfect, non-progressive, active] . Here there is no function to predetermine the selections from systems 14–17, so the starring convention comes into play, and [non-finite verb, infinitive] are chosen.

3.2.6. *Summary of the analysis*

In this little grammar we have stated completely explicitly what the relations are between various features that clauses can have and various features that verbs can have. We explored these relations in a more informal way in section 1, and discovered that they were complex: a difference of one feature in the clause might make the difference between having one verb and having three; a particular feature of the clause need not always be reflected by its verbs in the same way; there are odd gaps in the paradigm caused by purely structural restrictions internal to the clause's structure; and so on. And yet we have taken account of all these complications in our formal statement without using transformations to relate a 'deep structure' to a 'surface structure', and without the grammar reaching a degree of complexity that is obviously unreasonable. Chapter 5 will extend this grammar 'upwards', so that we shall be able to see not only how the non-finite clause's features relate to the features of its verbs, but also how they relate to features of the larger clause containing it. Again, the facts are complex, but can be handled without too much difficulty in a systemic formalisation.

Probably the most helpful way to summarise the overall structure of the grammar we have given in this chapter is to take some examples and show how the various kinds of rule contribute to their generation.

Let us start with an example that involves a lot of verbs and a lot of functions, but not much complexity in the relations between the clause's features and these functions:

They appear *to have been being supported by the Albanians.*

Let us assume that the italicized has the following features:

[clause, dependent, non-finite, nominal, infinitival, with to, non-past, perfect, progressive, passive] .

(Actually it is ambiguous: it could be [past] as well as or instead of [perfect] .) Of these features, [dependent] (and therefore [clause] too) and [with to] (and therefore also [nominal, infinitival]) are present because the clause's environment requires them. The rest are freely chosen.

Only five of these features are in fact realised, according to our realisation rules, and each of them is realised by the presence of one function: [clause] by PROCESS, [with to] by TO, [perfect] by PERFECT, [progressive] by PROGRESSIVE and [passive] by PASSIVE. So we know that the clause's structure must contain at least these five functions.

The structure-building rules tell us that AFFIX must be conflated with each of PERFECT, PROGRESSIVE and PASSIVE, but the rule which conflates instances of AFFIX does not apply. They also tell us that PRE-PERFECT, PREPROGRESSIVE and BE must be added, because of the presence of these three functions; and that the functions must occur in the following pattern:

TO → PREPERFECT → PERFECT = AFFIX = PREPRO-
GRESSIVE → PROGRESSIVE = AFFIX = BE
→ PASSIVE = AFFIX = PROCESS.

According to the function-realisation rules, the five bundles of functions
are realised by the following feature-combinations:

TO: ? [to]
PREPERFECT: [non-finite verb, infinitive, grammatical verb, non-modal
verb, have]
PERFECT = AFFIX = PREPROGRESSIVE: [non-finite verb, en-form, gram-
matical verb, non-modal verb, be]
PROGRESSIVE = AFFIX = BE: [non-finite verb, ing-form, grammatical
verb, non-modal verb, be]
PASSIVE = AFFIX = PROCESS: [non-finite verb, en-form, lexical verb] .

The grammatical description of our example will thus include the following:

features of clause	[clause, dependent, non-finite, nominal, infinitival, with to, non-past, perfect, progressive, passive]				
structure of clause	... TO	PREPERFECT	PERFECT AFFIX PREPRO- GRESSIVE	PROGRESSIVE AFFIX BE	PASSIVE ... AFFIX PROCESS
features of verbs	?	non-finite verb infinitive grammatical verb non-modal verb have	non-finite verb en-form grammatical verb non-modal verb be	non-finite verb ing-form grammatical verb non-modal verb be	non-finite verb en-form lexical verb
items thus represented	*to*	*have*	*been*	*being*	*supported*

By way of contrast, we shall finish by taking an example where the structure-building rules play a bigger part:

They did not reach the point *reached on previous occasions*
by three o'clock till much later.

We shall take the features of the italicized to be

[clause, dependent, non-finite, participial, 'inflected', past, perfect, non-progressive, passive] .

Six of these features are realised: [clause, participial, 'inflected', past, perfect, passive] ; and, according to the realisation rules for features, they make the following functions appear in the clause's structure: PROCESS, PARTICIPLE, ING/EN (which must be conflated with PARTICIPLE), PAST, PERFECT and PASSIVE.

From the structure-building rules we derive the following information:
(a) PARTICIPLE, PAST, PERFECT and PASSIVE must each occur conflated with AFFIX;
(b) if possible, all four of these functions, plus ING/EN and the four occurrences of AFFIX, must be conflated with each other, since one of them is PARTICIPLE;
(c) since PAST and PERFECT are conflated with PASSIVE, there is no need for PREPAST and PREPERFECT to be added; and similarly BE is not added, because PASSIVE is conflated with PARTICIPLE;
(d) PAST and PERFECT must be conflated in any case; and there is in fact nothing to prevent all the functions from being conflated together, as demanded by (b). In other words, the clause's structure will include the following functions, all conflated together: PARTICIPLE = AFFIX = ING/EN = PAST = AFFIX = PERFECT = AFFIX = PASSIVE = AFFIX = PROCESS.

For these functions, the function-realisation rules require the following features: [non-finite verb, en-form, lexical verb] .

The description of our example will include the following:

features of the clause	[clause, dependent, non-finite, participial, 'inflected', past, perfect, non-progressive, passive]
structure of clause	... PARTICIPLE ... AFFIX ING/EN PAST AFFIX PERFECT AFFIX PASSIVE AFFIX PROCESS
features ot verb	$\begin{bmatrix} \text{non-finite verb} \\ \text{en-form} \\ \text{lexical verb} \end{bmatrix}$
item thus represented	*reached*

4. INTRODUCTION TO NOUN-CLAUSES

4.1. The kinds of constructions to be covered

The grammatical description in chapter 5 is intended to cover a wide variety of constructions, and the term 'noun-clause' seems the best term to use to refer to them, in spite of, or perhaps even because of, its vagueness. In traditional grammars, noun-clauses are clauses acting as (or like) nouns; nowadays we should prefer to describe them as clauses functioning in ways characteristic of noun-phrases (rather than 'nouns'), but the term is otherwise a suitable one for the present purposes, in that it at least covers the majority of the constructions which we shall be considering here.

Traditional noun-clauses, like other kinds of clauses, have to have a finite verb, but I shall include non-finite constructions as well, since the traditional restriction is no longer necessary, as I argued in the last chapter (3.1). This means that our term 'noun-clause' will be applied not only to clauses like the italicized in

He told me *that it would be ready by Friday*,

but also to items like those italicized below:

Sitting in front of the fire makes me feel drowsy,
He enjoyed *just watching her*,
Everyone likes *to be needed by someone.*

These are all examples in which the clause (in our extended definition of 'clause') can be replaced by a noun-phrase. However, there are also a variety of constructions which will be covered by the discussion in this chapter and

161

the next but which cannot be replaced by a noun-phrase; two examples are

> Women tend *to live longer than men*,
> Everyone seemed *to be talking about the same thing.*

There is no noun-phrase which can replace the italicized items in these examples, nor is there one which can replace the clause if we extend it to include
the subject of the main clause (*women, everyone*), as I shall argue that we
should in 4.2.5. This being so, even a term as vague as 'noun-clause' is too
precise.

Nevertheless, what is important is the range of reference of the term,
rather than the term itself, and the former was determined by the relationships within the grammar, rather than by a prior decision as to what ought to
be covered by the term 'noun-clause'. That is to say, the constructions concerned are all related to each other in a fairly direct way, so that it is more or
less unavoidable that a grammar describing one construction should refer to
all the others as well. The choice of a term to cover all the constructions thus
grouped together is a secondary matter, and 'noun-clause' can be seen merely
as a name that is mnemonically helpful, but in principle not self-defining.

Other terms that could have been used include 'reported clause' and 'predicate complement construction' (following Rosenbaum, 1967). The former is
too specific, since there is no sense in which any of the clauses quoted above
(except the first one) could be said to be reported versions of actual utterances. The other term, 'predicate complement construction', is vague enough
to be used here, but it is unsuitable, because I shall not make any use of the
idea of 'complementation' in the grammar of chapter 5 — nor for that matter
in this chapter.

The range of constructions to be covered

It is not only the choice of name that is to some extent arbitrary, however:
precisely the same kinds of reason that lead us to group together all the constructions in question could also have persuaded us to include a wide range of
other constructions too. Indeed, ideally the grammar would automatically
have become more and more comprehensive until it reached the point where
the entire range of English constructions was covered. Rather than aim for
this ideal, and risk waiting till many years and linguists had elapsed, it seemed
better to draw a line around the constructions that I had already taken
account of in the grammar by early 1970; and this range it is that the grammar in chapter 5 is intended to cover. Consequently, it should be remembered

that the grammar is provisional in two senses: in the obvious sense that it will certainly be imperfect in the way it handles the given range of constructions, but also in the sense that it will even more certainly need to be radically changed when a wider range of constructions is taken into account.

In order to define the constructions that the reader should expect to find described, informally in this chapter and more formally in the next chapter, it is probably easier to say what constructions he should *not* expect the grammar to cover: to define the boundaries of the area by saying what is out-side it rather than what is inside it. The constructions listed below are *not* covered by the grammar.

(i) *Constructions involving phrases but no embedded clauses*
That is, the grammar will not even cover constructions in which there is a noun-phrase that could have been replaced by a clause, such as *the truth* in

She told him the truth.

The one exception is that rules will be given to generate sentences containing the items *so* and *as*, acting as 'substitute clauses' (or 'clause-substitutes'):

I think *so*,
George has been taking bribes, *so* his wife told me,
He had never even left the flat, *as* we suspected all along.

The grammar could very easily be expanded to allow for ordinary sentences without embedded clauses, as the reader will realise by comparing it with the grammar given in chapter 2, which does allow for such clauses. But leaving out the more commonplace constructions makes the grammar a little simpler than it would otherwise have been, and allows us to concentrate on the more complicated kinds of constructions involving embedded clauses.

(ii) *Constructions involving clauses embedded in phrases*
Even the following are excluded, although they include clauses that clearly ought to be treated as 'noun-clauses':

The fact *that no-one came to her party* has cast Cleo
into a black despair,
I can't understand Geoffrey's determination *to be
considered boorish*,
I'm well aware *that they don't like each other*,

He'd be glad *to help you*, I'm sure,
Several candidates failed through *writing on both sides
of the paper*.

The grammar will not generate any sentences in which there is a clause of any
kind acting as an IC in a phrase of any kind, whether nominal, adjectival, adverbial or prepositional. One exception has been made, however: for cases
where a gerund-clause is complement of the preposition *by*, as ACTOR in a
passive clause; so the following will be covered by the grammar:

We were slowed down a lot by *having to carry so much baggage*,
She was outraged by *such a small boy using such a rude word*.

(iii) *Constructions where an embedded clause has an adverbial function*
This category is not a clear one, of course, but is intended to cover cases
where an embedded clause is an IC of another clause, and has a function such
as 'purpose', 'time' or 'manner'. Most such clauses are clearly different from
our noun-clauses, but there are some which are not too easy to keep separate
and which should have been treated in the same grammar:

She encouraged him *to run for the presidency* (noun-clause),
She encouraged him *to stop him giving up*   (adverbial clause),
He heard *her coming back from her midnight rendezvous*
                                      (noun-clause),
He ran into her *coming back from her midnight rendezvous*
                                      (adverbial clause).

(iv) *Constructions where an embedded clause has an adjectival function*
This category is not much clearer than the preceding one, but it covers a
rather smaller range of constructions, such as the following:

They all rushed out *screaming wildly*,
He left her *puzzled by his behaviour*,
Seen from behind, they look rather like giraffes,
The room was *as the goblins had left it*.

Roughly speaking, these constructions are those in which the embedded
clause can be replaced by an adjective, as the name implies, and in which the
clause can itself be clearly participial — and in particular, where it can have an
en-form verb, as in some of the examples above. Here again, an exception will

be made: where such a clause is embedded in a main clause of 'perception', it will be treated as a noun-clause:

> I saw *all my friends taken to the gallows*,
> We heard *them coming in together*.

(v) *Constructions involving reported questions*
In our terms, these constructions involve clauses with the features [dependent, interrogative] . Again, these could have been quite easily integrated into our grammar, but they involve a number of special complications, such as that in some cases they define a question, whereas in others they refer to the answer to the question:

> He asked me *what I could do with the grammar*,
> He told me *what I could do with the grammar*.

(vi) *Cleft sentence and pseudo-cleft sentence constructions*
These will not be generated by our grammar, since this would have taken us into a whole new area of grammar, but a number of references will be made to the circumstances under which noun-clauses can be treated as focus in a cleft or pseudo-cleft sentence:

> What she really hoped was *that he would keep on trying*,
> It was *her not apologising for forgetting the appointment*
> that really made him see red.

This list of exclusions may well strike the reader as a very long and comprehensive one, but the constructions that are left offer enough variety and complexity for one book, especially when the book is intended primarily as an explanation of systemic theory.

4.2. Some facts regarding noun-clauses
Many of the facts noted below have already been mentioned in recent discussions of noun-clauses, notably Rosenbaum (1967), Kiparsky and Kiparsky (1968), Stockwell et al. (1969), Huddleston, in Huddleston et al. (1968), and Huddleston (1969). However, it seems worth bringing them all together here in order to give the reader an overall view of the problems that our grammar will have to deal with.

One of the most striking characteristics of this list of facts is how hetero-

geneous it is, and the interesting question is how each fact should be incorporated into a grammar. Clearly, they cannot all be handled in the same way:
some will be stated explicitly, and others will be left implicit; some will
appear among the systemic contrasts in the system-network, others among
the feature-realisation rules or the function-realisation rules, and others again
among the structure-building rules. In the sections that follow, however,
I shall as far as possible present them simply as facts, without prejudging the
question of how they will be incorporated into the grammar.

4.2.1. *The structure of the matrix-clause and the noun-clause's functions*

The noun-clause, like any other of the matrix-clause's ICs, has a number of
functions which identify its contribution to the realisation of the matrix-
clause's features, and which form part of the matrix-clause's structure. For
instance, the underlined is a noun-clause with the functions SUBJECT and
ATTRIBUANT:

> *To accept a bribe* would be most unusual for Herbert.

These two functions, together with a number of others, will form one of the
bundles of functions that make up the matrix-clause's structure. If we
ignore the other functions that will combine with SUBJECT, the structure of
this matrix-clause will be just the same as that of the following, where it is a
noun-phrase rather than a noun-clause that has the functions SUBJECT and
ATTRIBUANT:

> Such behaviour would be most unusual for Herbert.

SUBJECT and COMPLEMENT

Both SUBJECT and ATTRIBUANT can be replaced as functions of the
noun-clause. For instance, the noun-clause is not SUBJECT in either of the
following:

> Herbert condescended *to accept a bribe*,
> Herbert intended *to accept a bribe*.

However, these two sentences are also different from each other, in that one
of them is parallelled by a pseudo-cleft sentence with the noun-clause as
focus, but the other is not:

> *What Herbert condescended was *to accept a bribe*,
> What Herbert intended was *to accept a bribe*.

Wherever a noun-clause is SUBJECT (with two major exceptions), there is a parallel pseudo-cleft sentence in which the noun-clause is focus, as witness:

> What would be unusual for Herbert would be *to accept a bribe*.

So the question of whether or not pseudo-clefting is possible for SUBJECT clauses does not arise in the first instance.

There are thus three possibilities according to (a) whether or not the noun-clause is SUBJECT and (b) whether or not there is a corresponding pseudo-cleft sentence with the noun-clause as focus. If the noun-clause is SUBJECT, the pseudo-cleft construction will be possible, so this information is implicit in the function SUBJECT. If it is not SUBJECT, then we can distinguish between those cases where the pseudo-cleft construction is possible and those where it is not, by giving the function COMPLEMENT (not to be confused with COMPLETER, to be introduced below) to the noun-clause in the former cases but not in the latter. In other words, where the pseudo-cleft construction is not possible, the noun-clause will have no function at all corresponding to SUBJECT or COMPLEMENT.

I mentioned that there are two exceptions to the rule that pseudo-cleft is always possible where the noun-clause is SUBJECT. One of these is when the SUBJECT clause is 'extraposed' (see 4.2.2 below):

> It would be most unusual for Herbert *to accept a bribe*,
> *What it would be most unusual for Herbert would be
>   *to accept a bribe*.

The other is where the SUBJECT clause is 'split' (see 4.2.5, 4.2.6):

> *Herbert* tended *to accept bribes*,
> *What tended was (*for*) *Herbert to accept bribes*.

ATTRIBUANT, ACTOR, GOAL, COMPLETER and ADDRESSEE

The other kind of functions that noun-clauses can have are 'transitivity' functions, such as ATTRIBUANT, GOAL and ACTOR. ATTRIBUANT is the function of the SUBJECT in an [attributive] clause — i.e. a clause containing a copular verb (*be, seem*, etc.) and a 'predicative complement' (represented

by our function ATTRIBUTE). ACTOR is the function of the SUBJECT in
any other kind of non-passive clause, and GOAL is the function of the SUB-
JECT in a passive clause or the COMPLEMENT (as defined above) in an
active one:

> ATTRIBUANT: *To accept a bribe* would be unusual for Herbert,
> ACTOR: *To accept a bribe* would ruin his reputation,
> GOAL: He didn't intend *to accept a bribe*.

These three functions are also available for noun-phrases, and it is when a
clause has one of them that it most resembles a noun-phrase syntactically.

One characteristic of noun-clauses, however, is that there are some active
clauses in which they occur which do not have a corresponding passive, even
though the noun-clause's function is GOAL. Take the following, for instance:

> Herbert wants *to accept the bribe*.

According to the 'pseudo-clefting' criterion, the italicized is COMPLEMENT:

> What Herbert wants is *to accept the bribe*.

Consequently, according to the last paragraph, it is also GOAL; but there is
no corresponding passive, whether the noun-clause is extraposed or not:

> **To accept the bribe* is wanted (by Herbert).
> *It is wanted (by Herbert) *to accept the bribe*.

In passing, it is interesting to note, with Stockwell et al. (1969: p. 548), that
if the matrix-clause is pseudo-clefted, even *want* allows a passive:

> What is wanted by most people is *to get rich*.

Alongside these cases where there is no corresponding passive, there are
even a few cases where there is no corresponding active — when the main verb
is *repute*, for instance:

> *They repute *that Herbert accepted a bribe*,
> It is reputed *that Herbert accepted a bribe*.

Returning to the cases where a noun-clause cannot be used as SUBJECT in a passive matrix-clause even though it has the function GOAL, this also arises where there is an 'indirect object' as well as the noun-clause — with the verb *tell*, for instance. The 'indirect object' has the function ADDRESSEE.

> They told us *that the party was off*,
> What they told us was *that the party was off*,
> **That the party was off* was told us,
> *It was told us *that the party was off*.

Where ADDRESSEE is present, along with a GOAL noun-clause, the matrix-clause can be passive, but it is ADDRESSEE that combines with SUBJECT, not GOAL:

> We were told *that the party was off*.

If the matrix-clause is not passive but active, neither ADDRESSEE nor GOAL is combined with SUBJECT, but ADDRESSEE must precede GOAL.

If a noun-clause is not SUBJECT, and does not allow pseudo-clefting, then is has none of the functions ATTRIBUANT, ACTOR and GOAL; instead, it has COMPLETER, since it has no more precise a function than to 'complete the meaning' of the matrix-clause's main verb. Thus, the noun-clause's function is COMPLETER with the verb *condescend*, and also with *enable*:

> Herbert condescended *to accept the bribe*,
> His position enabled Herbert *to accept bribes*.

Where the main verb is *enable*, however, the matrix-clause's structure *also* contains GOAL (*Herbert*), and can be matched by a passive construction:

> Herbert was enabled by his position *to accept bribes*.

What I am claiming, then, is that if a noun-clause has the function COMPLETER, it cannot also have SUBJECT, whereas if it has GOAL, it can also have SUBJECT (except in the cases mentioned above). Besides this difference between COMPLEMENT and GOAL, however, there is another one: GOAL allows *as* to replace the noun-clause, but COMPLEMENT does not (see 4.2.11). Thus, *as* is compatible with *intend*, but not with *condescend*:

> (Herbert accepted the bribe), *as* he had always intended,
> *(Herbert accepted the bribe), *as* he always condescended.

I have introduced six 'transitivity' functions: ATTRIBUANT, ATTRI-
BUTE, ACTOR, GOAL, ADDRESSEE and COMPLETER. If we were extending the discussion to include all kinds of clause, I should of course have to
extend this list considerably, to take account for instance of Fillmore (1968)
and Halliday (1967, 1968). However, as far as our present purposes are concerned there is no need to do so, since this would mean either bringing in
functions like BENEFICIARY which do not occur with noun-clauses, or
replacing (say) ACTOR by more specific functions (DATIVE, NOMINATIVE,
ERGATIVE, etc.). This second development would obviously be a desirable
improvement in many ways, but as far as I can see it makes little difference
for our grammar whether we make these finer distinctions or not; so in order
to avoid unnecessary complexities I shall not in fact make them.

However, there is one whole range of constructions which I have intentionally omitted entirely from the grammar: those where the matrix-clause is
'equative' or 'identifying' — i.e. where the main verb is *be*, and the clause
equates the referents of the SUBJECT and the COMPLEMENT:

His greatest mistake was *to accept the bribe*.

These constructions are different from ordinary 'attributive' constructions in
a number of ways (see Halliday, 1967); for instance, the order of SUBJECT
and COMPLEMENT is reversible in equative clauses but not in attributive
ones:

To accept the bribe was his greatest mistake,
To accept the bribe was a great mistake,
*A great mistake was *to accept the bribe.*

However, I have omitted the equative type of construction for a number of
reasons, the main reason being that it is not yet clear — to me, at any rate —
how they relate to the other kinds of construction that we have just discussed.
In other words, the main problem with equative clauses is not how to handle
the noun-clauses — that is in fact quite easy — but rather how to handle the
matrix-clause.

SUBJECT and MOOD-SUBJECT

Among the rules of our grammar that will mention 'subject' will be the
following two:
(a) in interrogative clauses (of certain kinds) the 'subject' follows the finite
verb, and precedes the main verb;

(b) the function ATTRIBUANT always combines with the function SUBJECT; and ACTOR or GOAL also does, according to whether the clause is active or passive.

In the simplest cases the item that is 'subject' as far as rule (a) is concerned also has the function SUBJECT for rule (b). However, this need not be so, and is not so where there is an extraposed noun-clause acting as 'subject', as in

> It would be most unusual *for Herbert to accept a bribe*,
> It would surprise everyone *for Herbert to accept a bribe*.

The next section will discuss extraposition in detail, and all I have to do here is to point out the conflict between the two definitions of 'subject' that arises where there is extraposition. As far as the first usage is concerned, the 'subject' is always the expletive *it*, and only this, since the noun-clause itself always follows both the finite verb and the main verb, whether the matrix-clause is interrogative or not. But the second usage of 'subject' applies to the noun-clause and not to the *it* (according to the analysis in this book, which seems the easiest to justify). Clearly if we were to use the same function, SUBJECT, to correspond to *both* of these uses of 'subject' we should find ourselves in serious confusion; so I shall use SUBJECT just in the second sense, and introduce another function-name for the first sense: MOOD-SUBJECT (abbreviated to M-SUBJECT).

According to the present analysis, then, if a 'subject' item is not extraposed it will have both of the two functions SUBJECT and M-SUBJECT; but if it is extraposed, M-SUBJECT will be the function of the expletive *it*, and SUBJECT of the extraposed noun-clause. Moreover, as far as the grammatical rules are concerned, the rule for inverting the 'subject' and the finite verb will refer to M-SUBJECT, and that for treating GOAL as the function of the 'subject' in a passive clause will refer to SUBJECT. So if we have a passive matrix-clause in which the 'subject' is an extraposed clause, the expletive *it* will have the function M-SUBJECT, and the noun-clause will have SUBJECT and GOAL:

> It was hinted *that Herbert had accepted a bribe*.

Summary

The matrix-clause can contain any of the following functions: ATTRIBU-ANT, ATTRIBUTE, ACTOR, GOAL, ADDRESSEE, COMPLETER. Any of

these except ADDRESSEE and ATTRIBUTE can be among the functions of
the noun-clause.

If the noun-clause's function is GOAL, the matrix-clause may also contain
ADDRESSEE in its structure; if it is COMPLETER, there may also be GOAL;
and if it is ACTOR, then again there may also be GOAL in the matrix-clause's
structure.

In general, if the matrix-clause has GOAL in its structure, it may be either
active or passive, irrespective of whether the GOAL is a noun-phrase or a
noun-clause. But (a) there are some constructions in which a noun-clause is
GOAL but the clause must be active – as when the matrix-clause's main verb
is *want* – and some where it must be passive – as where the verb is *repute*;
and (b) if ADDRESSEE is present as well as GOAL, it is the former, not the
latter, which is subject of the passive clause.

If an item's functions include ATTRIBUANT, ACTOR, ADDRESSEE or
GOAL, then it should be possible to construct a pseudo-cleft sentence in
which the item is focus (provided the item is neither extraposed nor 'split').
This is reflected in the analysis by the fact that the item in question has either
SUBJECT or COMPLEMENT in addition to its other functions.

If a noun-clause is extraposed it must have the function SUBJECT; the
expletive *it*, which substitutes for it, has the function M-SUBJECT. In most
cases, however, these two functions are both assigned to the same item.

The diagram below shows most of these relations between the various
functions, and also between them and the classes 'noun-clause' and 'noun-
phrase'. Any two categories that are joined by lines are compatible, provided
the connecting lines do not connect more than one higher node to any one
lower node.

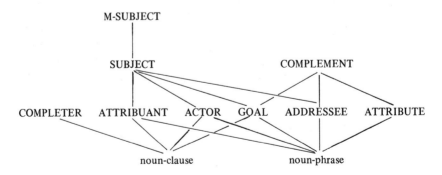

4.2.2. Extraposition

Functions of extraposed clauses

If the noun-clause's function is SUBJECT, it may or may not be extraposed — that is, transferred to after the main verb and any complements, while an 'expletive' *it* is introduced to take its place as the M-SUBJECT:

> *For the pubs to close so early* is ridiculous,
> It's ridiculous *for the pubs to close so early.*

This applies whether the noun-clause is SUBJECT in an active or a passive clause; in the latter case, if the ACTOR is specified the noun-clause may either precede it or follow it:

> *That we might go to the seaside* was suggested by
>   little Amanda herself,
> It was suggested *that we might go to the seaside*
>   by little Amanda herself,
> It was suggested by little Amanda herself *that we might go*
>   *to the seaside.*

In our grammar we shall take account only of extraposed clauses that are SUBJECT, whereas in other analyses (e.g. Langendoen, 1969) extraposition has also been allowed for clauses that are COMPLEMENT. In most cases such extraposition is 'vacuous': the only sign that it has taken place is its effect on later transformations, since it does not alter the noun-clause's place in sequence. Since transformations play no part in this grammar, we shall not use the notion of 'vacuous extraposition'. There are, however, a few verbs with which extraposition is not vacuous, but results in an expletive *it*. For my dialect at least such verbs are rare, and the only examples that come to mind are *resent* and *take*, and possibly *understand*:

> She resented it *that he was taking her sister out,*
> I take it *that you don't want this,*
> ? I understand it *that you feel upset.*

Because this construction is so limited I shall ignore it entirely from now on, but it will be seen that it would not be hard to change our grammar in order to accommodate it.

Environments where extraposition is impossible or obligatory

In perhaps the majority of constructions the choice between extraposing and not extraposing a SUBJECT noun-clause is a free one, and is determined only by considerations of length (the longer the noun-clause, the more likely it is to be extraposed) and information distribution (on the principle that what is functionally 'new' is put at the end of the clause). However, there are some cases where the choice is not free, extraposition being either obligatory or impossible.

Extraposition is *obligatory* for a SUBJECT noun-clause under the following conditions:
(i) If the matrix-clause specifies the 'modality' of the noun-clause, and contains no COMPLEMENT; 'modality' includes semantic factors such as the reliability of the information in the noun-clause or the source of the information (see 4.2.12):

> It seems *that no-one had locked the door*,
> It is presumed *that he was drunk*.

The non-extraposed equivalents of these sentences are ungrammatical, but this would not have been so if there had been a COMPLEMENT of some kind in the matrix clause:

> **That no-one had locked the front door* seems,
> **That he was drunk* is presumed,
> *That no-one had locked the front door* seems quite likely.

(ii) If the noun-clause is SUBJECT and GOAL — i.e. SUBJECT in a passive matrix-clause — and is infinitival:

> **To do it immediately* was agreed,
> It was agreed *to do it immediately*.

(iii) If the noun-clause's SUBJECT is 'fronted' (see 4.2.5).
(iv) If the noun-clause's COMPLEMENT is 'fronted' (see 4.2.6).

Extraposition is *impossible* if the noun-clause is gerundival, unless the matrix-clause expresses an emotional reaction to the event described by the noun-clause (see 4.2.11). The normal pattern is represented by the following:

> *Going out this evening* is out of the question,
> **It's out of the question *going out this evening*,

> *Climbing up that hill* always exhausts me,
> *It always exhausts me *climbing up that hill*.

The exceptional pattern on the other hand is represented by these:

> *Working so late in the evening* is ridiculous,
> It's ridiculous *working so late in the evening*.

4.2.3. *The finiteness of the noun-clause*

Noun-clauses fall into a number of different classes according to the 'finiteness' of their first verb, and for this classification we can take over part of the system-network given on p. 138:

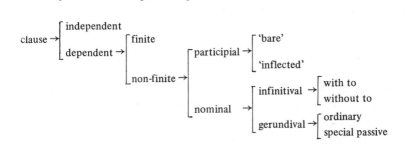

The distinctions formalised in this network are closely related to the environments in which clauses can appear: no two classes have the same distribution, though there is quite a lot of overlap, as we shall see. But we shall also see — indeed, we saw this already in the last chapter — that many other ways of classifying a clause have something to do with the environments in which it can occur: for instance, clauses of different tense/aspects have different distributions. Thus we do not need to elevate the distinctions in the network above to any special status, as the main basis for setting up distributional classes of clause.

All noun-clauses are of course [dependent] ; and none are ['inflected'] — these occur only as postmodifiers in noun-phrases. With these two exceptions, all the classes listed in the net work above will have to be referred to in our grammar. As we make further distinctions in the course of the present chapter we shall find them cutting across these finiteness distinctions as well as running parallel to them, so in this section there is no point in trying to relate the finiteness distinctions to distinctions to be made later; but we can refer back to the distinctions that we have already made.

The functions of participial clauses

If a clause is [participial] , then it must have the function GOAL; more-over, the matrix-clause must be active. Most constructions of this kind involve verbs of 'perception' — *see*, *hear*, etc.:

> She saw *him fall over the edge*,
> She saw *him pushed over the edge*.

It is true that in such cases we cannot produce a corresponding pseudo-cleft sentence, as we should be able to if the noun-clause is GOAL, but this is be-cause the SUBJECT is 'fronted' — i.e. the clause is in fact in two parts, and pseudo-clefting does not apply in these cases, as I shall explain in 4.2.5.

The evidence that we have that the noun-clause's functions include GOAL in such cases is that passivization of the matrix-clause is possible:

> *He* was seen *to fall over the edge*,
> *He* was seen *to be pushed over the edge*.

However, it will be noticed that the noun-clause is no longer [participial] but [infinitival, with to] . This is why I had to say that participial clauses only occur in active matrix-clauses.

A possible counter-example to this claim might be

> She saw *him falling over the edge*,
> He was seen *falling over the edge*.

Here the embedded clause is [participial] even when the matrix-clause is pas-sive. However, there are reasons for not giving these constructions the same analysis as the previous examples, or, for that matter, the same analysis as each other. We shall in fact distinguish three constructions in 4.2.9:

(i) [non-progressive] noun-clause in an active or passive matrix-clause:

> She saw *him fall over the edge*,
> *He* was seen *to fall over the edge*.

(ii) [progressive] noun-clause in an active matrix-clause:

> She saw *him falling over the edge*.

(iii) [progressive] adverbial clause in an active or passive matrix-clause:

> She saw him *falling over the edge,*
> He was seen *falling over the edge.*

If I am right in making this three-way distinction, then the passive matrix-clause with a [participial] clause in it is not in fact a counter-example to my claim that the noun-clause must be infinitival if the matrix-clause is passive, since the [participial] clause is not a noun-clause at all.

There is also another construction that should be distinguished from the above: those cases where the verb may be one of perception, but where the noun-clause has to be [infinitival] whether the matrix-clause is active or passive:

> She saw *him to be falling over the edge,*
> *He* was seen *to be falling over the edge.*

These are straightforward instances of 'factive' constructions (see 4.2.12), and have nothing to do with the 'perception' constructions involving [participial] noun-clauses.

The functions of infinitival and gerundival clauses

If a clause is infinitival, without *to*, it is restricted to active matrix-clauses, just as participial clauses are. Again, the corresponding passive matrix-clause will contain a clause that is infinitival, with *to*:

> They made him *sit down,*
> He was made *to sit down.*

There are only three verbs that allow a noun-clause of this kind: *let, make, help.* We analyse the noun-clause in each case as having the function COMPLETER, but with *make* and *help* the noun-phrase between the two verbs is GOAL of the matrix-clause — hence the possibility of passivization.

Clauses that are [finite] , [infinitival, with to] , or [gerundival] , make up the vast majority of noun-clauses. Only [infinitival, with to] is possible if the clause is COMPLETER; otherwise there appear to be no restrictions on the functions these classes of clause can have.

Extraposition

Whether or not the clause is extraposed has some bearing on its finiteness, though the details vary from one environment to another. In general, [finite] clauses are not affected, so the following discussion will deal only with noun-clauses that are [gerundival] or [infinitival, with to] .

There are a number of constructions where the noun-clause, which is SUBJECT, can be either [gerundival] or [infinitival] : for instance, with the adjectives *normal* and *regrettable*:

> *To have nude scenes on the stage* is normal nowadays,
> *Having nude scenes on the stage* is normal nowadays,
> *To have nude scenes on the stage* is regrettable,
> *Having nude scenes on the stage* is regrettable.

However, the reader will probably agree that when the noun-clause is not extraposed, as in all these examples, the gerundival form is much more natural than the infinitival one.

When the noun-clause *is* extraposed, however, the relation between the two forms is reversed: the infinitival form is normal, and the gerundival form is either relatively abnormal or even ungrammatical, as witness the following:

> It is normal nowadays *to have nude scenes on the stage*,
> *It is normal nowadays *having nude scenes on the stage*,
> It is regrettable *to have nude scenes on the stage*,
> It is regrettable *having nude scenes on the stage*.

For me at least, the fourth example is possible, but less likely than the third example, whilst the second example is simply impossible. This means that we shall have to distinguish two constructions: those involving adjectives like *normal* and those with adjectives like *regrettable*. There are other reasons for distinguishing them (see, for instance, 4.2.9), which suggests that I may be right in assessing the grammaticality of the second example above as different in kind from that of the fourth example.

This is perhaps an appropriate point at which to make it clear that I am distinguishing *extraposition* from *apposition*. This distinction is important, because the two constructions can look identical in print, and sound very similar in speech, although they are subject to very different restrictions. For instance, it may be that the reader disagreed with me about the second example above:

> It is normal nowadays *having nude scenes on the stage*.

I said that this was ungrammatical, but the reader may have found it quite grammatical. If so, the chances are that he was treating it as an example of apposition rather than of extraposition, so there is really no disagreement between us: as an example of apposition, it seems unexceptionable to me, but not as an example of extraposition. The difference between the two constructions is primarily marked by the presence or absence of an intonational boundary before the noun-clause; if there has to be a boundary, then the sentence is an instance of apposition, and involves precisely the same construction as we find in

> They're rather expensive, those geraniums,

so it is not relevant to our discussion of extraposition.

Returning to the question of the relation between extraposition and the finiteness of the noun-clause, there seems to be another factor which complicates the rules: the presence or absence of SUBJECT in the noun-clause (see 4.2.4). If there is *no* SUBJECT — as in all the examples given so far — then what I have said holds true, but if there *is* a SUBJECT, it seems more natural for an infinitival clause not to be extraposed than it would have been if there had been no SUBJECT:

> *For actors to undress on the stage* is normal nowadays,
> *For actors to undress on the stage* is regrettable.

These seem if anything more natural than the corresponding gerundival forms, although the latter would have been much more natural had there been no SUBJECT:

> *Actors undressing on the stage* is normal nowadays,
> *Actors undressing on the stage* is regrettable.

The grammar I shall offer is incapable of distinguishing degrees of acceptability, however, so we shall simply have to exclude the gerundival extraposed clauses with adjectives like *normal*, as ungrammatical, and allow the rest as grammatical, on an equal footing.

4.2.4. *The presence or absence of SUBJECT in the noun-clause*

If the noun-clause is [finite], its structure must contain SUBJECT, but if it is [non-finite], it need not. This can be seen most clearly in noun-clauses which themselves have the function SUBJECT:

That he didn't know her was news to all of us,
*That didn't know her was news to all of us,
His children being so young has made it possible for him
     to travel a lot,
Being so young has made it possible for him to travel a lot.

Identifying the SUBJECT in a non-finite clause

   When the noun-clause is SUBJECT, it is clear whether or not it has a SUB-
JECT in its own structure, since if it has one there is a nominal item (noun-
phrase or noun-clause) which could not be analysed in any other way, such as
his children in the third example above. This applies whether the non-finite
clause is [gerundival] or [infinitival] (it could not be [participial], since
[participial] clauses do not occur as SUBJECT); if it is [infinitival], however,
the clause must be introduced by *for* (see 4.2.8):

            To be popular with girls would be a new experience for Stanley,
            For girls to like him would be a new experience for Stanley.

   The situation is more complicated, however, if the noun-clause is not
SUBJECT, since there are two ways of analysing a noun-phrase coming between the main-clause's and the noun-clause's verbs: either it is SUBJECT in
the noun-clause, or it is GOAL in the matrix-clause, the noun-clause itself
being COMPLETER. In some environments it should be analysed one way, in
others in the other way; for instance, after *expect* the first analysis is the correct one — *expect* + (NP + verb) — whereas after *persuade* we need the other
analysis — *persuade* + NP + noun-clause. Thus the noun-clauses will be the
italicized items in the following examples (just as they have been in all the
other examples so far):

            Susan expected *Bert to propose to her sister*,
            Susan persuaded Bert *to propose to her sister*.

   There are two main criteria justifying this distinction. One is the semantic
effect of passivizing the noun-clause: if it makes no difference to the sense
(beyond the differences that passivization normally effects), then the construction is of the *expect*-type; but if it does make a difference, it is of the
persuade-type. Clearly, the passive version of our sentence containing *expect*
has the same meaning as the active version quoted above:

Susan expected *her sister to be proposed by Bert*.

This is not true, however, of the sentence containing *persuade*:

Susan persuaded her sister *to be proposed to by Bert*.

The second criterion underlying this distinction is the possibility or impossibility of the 'anticipatory' *there* (see Huddleston, 1969 and Stockwell et al, 1969), as in

There was a fight,
There are some people outside.

Wherever this *there* occurs, it always has the function M-SUBJECT, so if it can occur in the place of the noun-phrase in between the verbs of the matrix-clause and the noun-clause, then the noun-phrase itself must also have the function M-SUBJECT in the noun-clause. Consequently, *there* is possible with *expect*, but not with *persuade*:

Susan expected *there to be a lot of fuss*,
*Susan persuaded *there to be a lot of fuss*.

Conditions for the occurrence of SUBJECT

According to these two criteria, quite a wide range of constructions allow the noun-clause to have its own SUBJECT — a much wider range than the constructions in which the doubtful noun-phrase would be COMPLEMENT in the matrix-clause. Indeed, there appear to be only two (or possibly even just one) sets of constructions of this type: those involving verbs like *persuade*, *encourage*, *invite* and *tempt*; and (possibly) those involving *help*, with a to-less infinitive:

Susan helped her sister *find a husband*,
*Susan helped *there be lots of suitors for her sister*,
? Susan helped *a husband be found for her sister*.

In all other constructions that allow a noun-phrase before the noun-clause's verb, this noun-phrase is SUBJECT in the noun-clause. If the latter is [infinitival] , *for* may be a necessary companion to the SUBJECT, as when the noun-clause itself is SUBJECT:

> They promised *for the matter to be looked into*.

However, in most constructions this *for* is not necessary, as witness the examples involving *expect* given above.

A noun-clause can have a SUBJECT whatever its finiteness-type is, so we also find [gerundival] examples like

> He imagined *there being lots of work to do*,
> He was put off by *there being so many people there*.

SUBJECT can also be present in a [participial] clause; here the *there* test is relatively hard to apply, but the passivization test works:

> Bill heard *the neighbours discussing his roses*,
> Bill heard *his roses being discussed by the neighbours*.

The referent of a 'missing' SUBJECT

If a noun-clause does not contain SUBJECT, this means that the clause's structure will also lack whichever transitivity function should have been combined with SUBJECT according to the noun-clause's features — i.e. ACTOR, ATTRIBUANT or GOAL. The semantic characteristics of the clause can often be reconstructed, however, by postulating a referent for this absent function — that is, by 'supplying' a (referent for) a subject. In some cases there is no way of identifying the referent from the linguistic environment:

> It is hard *to ride a monocycle*,
> Bill suggested *washing the dishes*,
> The bishop advocated *being friendly to strangers*.

However, in many cases there is a noun-phrase in the matrix-clause whose referent can be taken also as the referent of the 'missing' item. This item may be GOAL in the matrix-clause, as it is with *persuade*, or SUBJECT, as with *expect*.

We find, then, that a noun-clause sometimes does contain a SUBJECT, and sometimes does not; but if it does not, it may be possible to find a referent for a hypothetical SUBJECT-item, which can be included in the sentence's semantic representation.

As we might expect, the relation between the presence of SUBJECT and the noun-clause's environment is not a simple one, and all three logical possibilities are found: some environments (as with *expect*) allow SUBJECT to be either present or absent; in others (e.g. with *condescend*) it must be absent; and in others still (e.g. after *hear* or *believe*) it must be present:

> We all expected *them to pass,*
> We all expected *to pass,*
> *The managing director condescended *(for) his secretary*
>   *to see the deputation,*
> The managing director condescended *to see the deputation,*
> Everyone believed *him to be someone important,*
> *Everyone believed *to be someone important.*

4.2.5. *The position of SUBJECT in the noun-clause; 'SUBJECT-fronting'*

SUBJECT-fronting defined

If a noun-clause has the function GOAL, it is generally possible for the matrix-clause to be either active (with GOAL following the main verb) or passive (with GOAL combined with SUBJECT). This applies to [non-finite] as well as to [finite] noun-clauses:

> They haven't yet suggested *that lecturers should work*
>   *night-shifts,*
> It hasn't been suggested *that lecturers should work night-shifts,*
> They hoped *for the rain to stop before tea-time,*
> It was hoped *for the rain to stop before tea-time.*

The examples just quoted raise no particular problems, but there are problems with cases like those discussed in 4.2.4, where a [non-finite] clause is GOAL and contains SUBJECT:

> Many people believe *there to be a life after death.*

I gave arguments above for saying that *there* is an IC of the noun-clause, not of the matrix-clause, so if the noun-clause is GOAL, we should expect the corresponding passive to be

> *(For) there to be a life after death* is believed by many people.

In fact, however, this is not possible, and instead of it we find

There is believed by many people *to be a life after death.*

The italics in this example reflect the fact that I am assuming a particular analysis of it: in which the noun-clause is discontinuous, as in Jespersen's 'split-subject' analysis. An alternative analysis would be to avoid this by treating *there* as an IC of the matrix-clause, not of the noun-clause; but this would have been much more complicated to generate. For one thing, it would make it impossible to generalise about the relation between *there* and the 'true subject' that it anticipates, since sometimes they would be ICs of the same clause, and sometimes not. For another thing, we should have a very complicated relation between active and passive matrix-clauses in such constructions. So on balance the 'split-subject' analysis is simpler than the other one in spite of the discontinuity that it involves.

We can refer to the process by which SUBJECT is separated from the rest of the noun-clause as 'SUBJECT-fronting'. By choosing this term I am presupposing a particular analysis of such sentences, in which what has to be explained is the position of the SUBJECT rather than that of the rest of the noun-clause. If we had adopted this latter analysis, we should have said that the noun-clause's SUBJECT occupies the normal position for the noun-clause as a whole, and the rest of the noun-clause has been shifted to a later position in the matrix-clause; we could perhaps have referred to this as 'predicate-shifting'. The two alternatives are both equally good candidates, since there are two positions that a SUBJECT noun-clause can occupy, according to whether it is extraposed or not (see 4.2.2):

> *To refuse an invitation from Pat* would be sheer madness,
> It would be sheer madness *to refuse an invitation from Pat.*

If we assume that the noun-clause in a split-subject construction is *not* extraposed, then its SUBJECT is in the right place, but the rest of the noun-clause is later in the matrix-clause than it ought to be. But if we take it that the noun-clause *is* extraposed, it is the position of its SUBJECT that has to be explained, since the rest of the clause is in the right place.

Extraposition

As the term 'SUBJECT-fronting' suggests, then, I am taking split-subject constructions as examples of extraposition. There are a number of reasons why this analysis is simpler than the alternative. Firstly, it is easier to define the part that has to be 'shifted' if it is just one IC of the noun-clause, the SUBJECT. Secondly, the fronted SUBJECT is in complementary distribution with the 'expletive' *it*, so that we can say that the latter occurs only if there is no fronted SUBJECT:

> *There* was expected *to be a thunderstorm*,
> It was expected *that there would be a thunderstorm*,
> It was expected *to finish by the end of the month*.

We can thereby explain why the usual marker of extraposition is absent in these cases. And thirdly, there are some verbs with which extraposition is obligatory (see 4.2.2), and so when these occur with split-subject noun-clauses we must say that the latter are extraposed — or change the rule given in 4.2.2:

> It is presumed *that he was drunk*,
> **That he was drunk* is presumed,
> *He* is presumed *to have been drunk*.

It follows from this analysis of split-subject constructions that if some environment requires a noun-clause to contain a fronted SUBJECT, then it will also require the noun-clause to be extraposed.

SUBJECT and M-SUBJECT in the noun-clause's structure

So far I have been implying that the item that is 'SUBJECT-fronted' must have the function SUBJECT in the noun-clause's structure. However, this is not in fact so. We have already met one situation in which it is not so: the 'test-case' of the anticipatory *there*, in which *there* is M-SUBJECT though (probably) not SUBJECT. Thus, in an example like

> *There* was expected *to be a thunderstorm*,

it is likely that we shall treat the fronted item, *there*, not as SUBJECT but as M-SUBJECT, the SUBJECT of the noun-clause being *a thunderstorm*. Another instance of M-SUBJECT, rather than SUBJECT, being fronted is where the noun-clause itself contains an extraposed noun-clause:

> *It* seems *to be hard to get a job as a linguist*.

Here the fronted item, *it*, is again M-SUBJECT in the noun-clause, whose SUBJECT is the extraposed noun-clause *to get a job as a linguist*.

Thus, where M-SUBJECT is distinct fromSUBJECT, as it is in the *there* construction and in straightforward extraposition with *it*, what is fronted is the M-SUBJECT, and the position of SUBJECT is not affected. In most cases, of course, M-SUBJECT and SUBJECT are *not* distinct, so SUBJECT automatically occupies the same position, whether fronted or not, as M-SUBJECT, and it is because of this that it has not been too misleading to use the term 'SUBJECT-fronting' rather than the more accurate 'M-SUBJECT fronting'. I shall in fact continue to use the former term, as the two are not in contrast with each other, and 'SUBJECT-fronting' is shorter and slightly easier to verbalise.

Recursive SUBJECT-fronting

The effect of SUBJECT-fronting is to identify the M-SUBJECT of the noun-clause with the M-SUBJECT of the matrix-clause; so, for instance, *Sam* is both M-SUBJECT of the noun-clause and M-SUBJECT of the matrix-clause in

> *Sam* seems *to work too hard.*

This being so, there is no reason why the M-SUBJECT of the matrix-clause should not itself be identified with the M-SUBJECT of a still larger matrix-clause:

> Sam tends to seem to work too hard.

Here there are two noun-clauses: *Sam ... to seem to work too hard*, and *Sam ... to work too hard*; but *Sam* is M-SUBJECT in each of these and also in the larger matrix-clause, whose verb is *tends*. This identification of M-SUBJECT's is completely recursive, so that any number of such constructions can be embedded in one another, allowing such monstrosities as

> Sam happens to keep starting to tend to seem to work too hard.

Environments allowing SUBJECT-fronting

So far I have illustrated SUBJECT-fronting with reference to two kinds of constructions: where the matrix-clause is passive, so that it is easy to reconstruct a corresponding active form in which the 'fronted' item is next to the rest of the noun-clause; and where the matrix-clause is intransitive, with verbs like *seem, happen, tend, begin*. In the latter cases we can see that the matrix-clause's SUBJECT is split from the fact that the item in M-SUBJECT position in the matrix-clause can be a *there* which belongs clearly to the structure of the noun-clause:

There seems *to be a mistake,*
There happened *to be a power-cut,*
There began *to be some mould on top of all the cheeses,*
There needs *to be more discipline in schools,*
There kept *being too much background noise to hear.*

Besides these kinds of construction, there are others which allow split-subject noun-clauses. Firstly, there are cases where the noun-clause is SUBJECT, as in the above examples, but has a different transitivity function: ATTRIBUANT — that is, cases where the matrix-clause is [attributive] , with a verb like *be* or *seem* and an ATTRIBUTE in its structure:

There is certain *to be some opposition to your suggestion,*
There were bound *to be difficulties for the first few years.*

This kind of construction, like the other two, is covered by Jespersen's term 'split-subject', since the matrix-clause's SUBJECT is in fact split in two, one part coming before the main verb, and the other coming after it.

However, there are reasons for extending the 'SUBJECT-fronted' analysis to other constructions which do *not* come within the scope of Jespersen's term, since they involve a noun-clause which is neither SUBJECT nor split (at least, not split in the obvious sense in which I have been taking the term so far).

SUBJECT-fronting when the noun-clause is not SUBJECT

There are three kinds of construction in which we shall say that the noun-clause's SUBJECT is fronted although the noun-clause itself is not SUBJECT; in all of them, the noun-clause is GOAL in an active matrix-clause, and we can distinguish them in terms of the matrix-clause's main verb. Firstly, there are those constructions where the main verb defines some kind of cognitive process, such as *believe, claim, realise* (for this class of verbs, see 4.2.11):

Everyone believes *her to be his mistress,*
At last they realised *her to be speaking Mohawk.*

As the italics show, *her* is to be treated in each case as an IC of the noun-clause, according to the principles outlined in 4.2.4, and it has the functions SUBJECT and M-SUBJECT in the noun-clause's structure. However, although *her* is an IC of the noun-clause, and is in fact immediately next to the rest of the noun-clause, I shall analyse such noun-clauses as being in two parts, the

SUBJECT and everything else. In other words, in these cases we have 'vacuous' SUBJECT-fronting, in the sense in which extraposition is vacuous in some TG analyses of similar constructions.

The other two kinds of construction in which we get this vacuous SUB-JECT-fronting involve respectively verbs of 'causation', like *cause* and *enable*, and verbs of 'perception', like *hear* and *watch*:

> The strike caused *there to be frequent delays on the railways*,
> He watched *them walk to the other side of the room.*

Here too, the noun-clause's M-SUBJECT is analysed as being separate from the rest of the noun-clause, although there is no other item from the matrix-clause in between the two parts of the noun-clause.

This analysis may well seem thoroughly perverse, since it in effect generalises an awkward analysis (with the noun-clause in two parts) from the cases where it is unavoidable to cases where it could easily be avoided. However, it does in fact result in a simplification of the grammar, for two reasons.

Firstly, it allows us to account for the fact that the pseudo-cleft-sentence construction is possible for some noun-clauses acting as GOAL, but not for others. For instance, it is possible if the matrix-clause's main verb is *want* (though *for* must be added to the noun-clause, as we should expect from 4.2.8 below), but not if it is *believe*:

> Joe wanted *there to be lots of people at his party*,
> What Joe wanted most of all was *for there to be lots of people
>   at his party*,
> Joe expected *there to be lots of people at his party*,
> *What Joe expected was (*for*) *there to be lots of people
>   at his party*.

A very general rule will automatically cover this difference between *want* and *believe*, provided we have SUBJECT-fronting after *believe* but not after *want*: no item can be the focus of a pseudo-cleft sentence if it would be in two parts in the corresponding un-clefted sentence. We need a rule of this kind in order to prevent pseudo-clefting from applying to split-subject constructions:

> *There* seemed *to be two possibilities*,
> *What seemed was (*for*) *there to be two possibilities.*

But if we formulate it as I have just done, it will automatically make pseudo-clefting just as impossible after *expect*, where there is no actual discontinuity, as with *seem*. Similarly, it will rule out pseudo-clefting with verbs of causation and of perception:

> He caused *there to be a recount*,
> *What he caused was (*for*) *there to be a recount*,
> He heard *his roses being discussed by the neighbours*,
> *What he heard was *his roses being discussed by the neighbours*.

In contrast with these cases, we find that pseudo-clefting is possible with *want*, *intend* and so on, as we should expect if the noun-clause in such cases is in one piece, not two.

The second advantage of this analysis is that it allows the generalisation that if a noun-clause involves SUBJECT-fronting when it is GOAL in a passive matrix-clause, it will also involve SUBJECT-fronting when the matrix-clause is active. In other words, we can then ignore the difference between active and passive matrix-clauses, and have one rule covering both of them. So for instance an infinitival clause occurring as GOAL with *believe* will always have a fronted SUBJECT, whether the matrix-clause is active or passive:

> Girls always believed *him to be sincere*,
> *He* was always believed *to be sincere*.

Summary

To summarise this rather complicated discussion, if a [non-finite] noun-clause contains SUBJECT, this may or may not be 'fronted'. If it is fronted, there are two possibilities, according to the function of the noun-clause itself: if the noun-clause is SUBJECT, then extraposition is obligatory, but its own M-SUBJECT is moved back to replace the expletive *it*, and consequently the noun-clause is discontinuous; if however the noun-clause is not SUBJECT, there is no discontinuity, but the fronting prevents the occurrence of the pseudo-cleft-sentence construction.

4.2.6. *The position of COMPLEMENT in the noun-clause;* *'COMPLEMENT-fronting'*

COMPLEMENT can be combined with a number of other functions, namely (from those introduced in 4.2.1) GOAL, ATTRIBUTE and ADDRESSEE; and in the simplest cases any item which has the function COMPLEMENT follows the main verb, whether the clause containing it is a

noun-clause or not. Indeed, one of the main reasons for having this function
in addition to the functions just mentioned is to enable us to say in a single
generalisation that these functions follow the main verb when they are not
combined with SUBJECT. Another reason is to allow a distinction to be
made between 'adverbial' functions, like TIME, PURPOSE, and so on, and
'participant' functions like ACTOR, ATTRIBUANT, GOAL, ATTRIBUTE
and COMPLETER.

COMPLEMENT-fronting

There is, however, a construction in which COMPLEMENT is 'fronted' in
just the same way as SUBJECT, and which we must be able to generate. This
involves a noun-clause which is ATTRIBUANT and an adjective such as *easy*
or *difficult* acting as ATTRIBUTE in the matrix-clause:

> *The drawbridge* was difficult *to raise*.

This analysis of such sentences is justified partly on the grounds that it
matches the meaning more closely than would an analysis in which *the draw-*
bridge is treated as an IC of the matrix-clause, not of the noun-clause: the
adjective describes a characteristic of the action denoted by the noun-clause
as a whole, rather than of the object denoted by the fronted noun-phrase.
This can be seen clearly in examples like

> *An easy life* is hard *to achieve*.

Another justification is that it avoids the need to postulate clauses with structures that lack COMPLEMENT, grammatically, but which have a semantic
representation as though they did have a COMPLEMENT, with the same
referent as an item elsewhere in the sentence. And thirdly, it reflects the fact
that such sentences can always be paralleled by sentences such as the following, where there is no fronting:

> It was difficult *to raise the drawbridge*,
> It is hard *to achieve an easy life*.

If this analysis is accepted, then we have yet another condition under
which extraposition is obligatory: fronting presupposes that the rest of the
noun-clause is extraposed, whether the fronted item is M-SUBJECT or COM-
PLEMENT. However, the constructions allowing COMPLEMENT-fronting are
different from those allowing SUBJECT-fronting in that for them extraposi-

tion is otherwise optional, rather than obligatory. That is, not only is the fronting of COMPLEMENT not obligatory, but where COMPLEMENT is not fronted, extraposition is not obligatory either:

> *To raise the drawbridge* was difficult,
> It was difficult *to raise the drawbridge.*

Related constructions

Where COMPLEMENT is not fronted, the sentence is in fact an instance of a construction that is much more comprehensive than the COMPLEMENT-fronted construction: as well as adjectives like *easy* and *difficult*, which do allow COMPLEMENT-fronting, they can involve adjectives like *normal* and *usual*, which do not:

> *To raise one's drawbridge in the evening* was normal
>   in those days,
> **One's drawbridge* was normal *to raise in the evening*
>   in those days.

Apart from not allowing COMPLEMENT-fronting, these constructions are indistinguishable from those involving *easy*, etc.; for instance, extraposition is optional:

> It was normal in those days *to raise one's drawbridge*
>   *in the evening.*

Similarly, in neither case can the noun-clause be [finite] :

> *It was usual *that they raised their drawbridges in the evening*,
> *It was easy *that they raised their drawbridges in the evening.*

In all cases, whether COMPLEMENT is fronted or not, the presence of SUBJECT in the noun-clause is optional. It has been absent in all the examples given so far, but it is present in the following:

> *The turn* was easy *for anyone driving fast to miss completely*,
> It was easy *for anyone driving fast to miss the turn completely*,
> It was usual *for the sexes to be segregated* in mediaeval churches.

What can be fronted

The choice of the term 'COMPLEMENT-fronting' is deliberate, since it is necessary to exclude all adverbial functions from this kind of fronting:

> It was difficult *to get up this morning,*
> **This morning* was difficult *to get up.*

It is tempting to include under this construction cases like the following, where ATTRIBUTE is the function of a noun-phrase rather than of an adjective:

> That was an easy turn to miss.

However, these are different from the examples with adjectives in that they allow fronting not only of COMPLEMENT but also of at least some adverbial functions:

> That was an easy morning to get up,
> London is an expensive place to live.

If we convert *an expensive place* into an adjective, *expensive*, the sentence ceases to be grammatical:

> *London is expensive to live,

showing how important the difference between an adjective and a noun-phrase is. Consequently, I shall not try to make the rules cover both kinds of construction; indeed, I shall have no more to say about the construction involving noun-phrases, partly because it is possible that their analysis should not involve COMPLEMENT-fronting at all, but should treat the infinitival clause as being embedded in a noun-phrase, like the similarly incomplete one in

> He has just bought too big a house *to paint on his own.*

There is another gap in our grammar, where the discussion of COMPLE-MENT-fronting ought to cover cases like the following:

> *This subject* is quite easy *to talk about,*
> *This subject* is quite easy *to write books about.*

Here the item that is fronted (*this subject*) is complement of a preposition, and therefore does not have the function COMPLEMENT, according to the present analysis. Part of the reason why these are not covered is that it is not clear what the restrictions are; for instance, where do we draw the line between cases where an item embedded in a noun-phrase can be fronted and those where it cannot?

> *Some subjects* are easy *to find books about*,
> **Some children* were hard *to find the parents of*.

Another reason, however, is simply that prepositional constructions as a whole are difficult to handle in any satisfactory way at the present stage of development of systemic grammars.

4.2.7. *The mood of the matrix-clause; 'QUESTION-fronting'*

On the whole, the mood of the matrix-clause — whether it is [imperative] or [non-imperative], and so on — can be completely ignored in discussing noun-clauses, but there is one respect in which it is relevant to the discussion: if the matrix-clause is [wh, interrogative], the item on which the question is focussed may be an IC of the noun-clause:

> *What* do you think *they'll do to him*?
> *Where* did he promise *to be*?

Here too we have an instance of 'fronting': the main body of the noun-clause is where we should expect it to be, but one of its ICs is separated from it and moved to an earlier position in the matrix-clause, so that the noun-clause itself is discontinuous. The similarities to constructions involving SUBJECT-fronting and COMPLEMENT-fronting are clear.

However, there are also very great differences between the fronting of an item in a [wh, interrogative] matrix-clause — which I shall call 'QUESTION-fronting' — and the fronting of M-SUBJECT and COMPLEMENT as described in the preceding two sections. These differences will become clear in the following discussion of the characteristics of QUESTION-fronting.

The class of the fronted item and of the noun-clause

QUESTION-fronting does not simply involve the moving of one of the noun-clause's ICs: it also involves a 'change' in this IC's class-membership, changing a [non-questioning] phrase into a [questioning] phrase (see p. 68 for these classes). For instance, compare the following:

> Marcus thought *that Julia had a lot of money*,
> *How much money* did Marcus think *that Julia had*?

Where the matrix-clause is [declarative], GOAL in the noun-clause is an ordinary noun-phrase, *a lot of money*; but when the matrix-clause is [wh, interrogative], it is possible for the noun-clause's GOAL to be a [questioning] noun-phrase, *how much money*.

This makes it look as though the noun-clause itself is [declarative] in one example, but [wh, interrogative] in the other; but this analysis is impossible, for a variety of reasons. For instance, it is hard to reconcile it with the presence of *that* in the noun-clause; and QUESTION-fronting is possible in constructions which otherwise never allow [interrogative] noun-clauses:

> *What* did he least regret *her buying*?
> *He regretted *what her buying.*

Therefore we must recognise that with QUESTION-fronting the noun-clause has among its ICs one that is a [questioning] phrase, and to which we shall assign the function QUESTION, but that in spite of this the noun-clause itself is not [wh, interrogative]. In other words, we must show that the fronted item is a [questioning] phrase because the *matrix-clause* is [wh, interrogative], and not because the noun-clause itself is.

The position of the noun-clause

The way in which fronting affects the class of the fronted item makes QUESTION-fronting different from the other kinds of fronting. However, these are like QUESTION-fronting in one respect, that the *position* of the fronted item (as distinct from its class-membership) is determined by the features of the matrix-clause: with SUBJECT- or COMPLEMENT-fronting the fronted item precedes or follows the finite verb, and so on, according to the usual rule determining the position of MOOD-SUBJECT; and similarly, the item affected by QUESTION-fronting occurs in the position, in the matrix-clause, which is usual for QUESTION in a wh-interrogative clause.

The finiteness of the noun-clause and its functions

QUESTION-fronting is possible with noun-clauses of any finiteness-type, and not just with infinitival clauses as was the case with SUBJECT- and COMPLEMENT-fronting:

> *Who* did you most enjoy *seeing*?

Where does he want *her to live?*
Who do you think *I met the other day?*

Similarly there are no restrictions on the 'transitivity' functions that the noun-clause can have: it can be ACTOR, ATTRIBUANT, GOAL or COMPLETER. However, if it is SUBJECT, extraposition is obligatory (as with the other types of fronting):

> *To distrust bald-headed men* seemed natural to John,
> It seemed natural to John *to distrust bald-headed men,*
> **Who* did *to distrust* seem natural to John?
> *Who* did it seem natural to John *to distrust?*

As far as the functions of the noun-clauses are concerned, then, QUESTION-fronting is similar to SUBJECT-fronting; but they differ again with regard to the functions that the fronted item can have: with SUBJECT- and COMPLEMENT-fronting, only SUBJECT and COMPLEMENT can be fronted, but with QUESTION-fronting, any function can be fronted, provided only that it can normally be combined with QUESTION (with one exception). Thus the fronted item can be a time-, place-, manner- or reason-adverbial, for instance:

> *When* does the time-table say we *should arrive at Budapest?*
> *On which side of the paper* did he say *we were to write?*
> *How firmly* is it necessary *to fix the back-plate?*
> *Why on earth* do you think *she married him in the first place?*

The exception to this rule is that SUBJECT cannot be QUESTION-fronted from a noun-clause that is itself SUBJECT:

> **Who* is it mostly likely *invited her?*

By way of contrast, COMPLEMENT can be QUESTION-fronted from such a noun-clause:

> *Who* is it most likely *that he invited?*

and SUBJECT can be QUESTION-fronted from a noun-clause that is not itself SUBJECT:

> *Who* do you think *invited her*?

No such restriction applies when the fronting is of the other kind, SUB-JECT-fronting; indeed, the standard examples involve precisely the construction that is excluded for QUESTION-fronting: fronting of SUBJECT from a noun-clause that is SUBJECT:

> *Herbert* is most likely *to have invited her*.

On the other hand, there is no restriction on the mood of the matrix-clause when there is SUBJECT-fronting, so there is no reason why the matrix-clause should not be a wh-question here too, just as it is with QUESTION-fronting. In a wh-question, the item that has been SUBJECT-fronted may itself be the focus of the question:

> *Who* is most likely *to have invited her*?

This looks like a case of QUESTION-fronting, but is in fact a case of SUB-JECT-fronting, in a wh-question.

QUESTION-fronting in 'factive' constructions

In 4.2.11 below we shall distinguish between constructions in which the noun-clause is 'factive' in meaning and those where it is not; *recognise*, but not *think*, will typically occur in a 'factive' construction, since what one recognises is usually taken to be a fact, whereas what one thinks need not be seen as a fact. On the whole, in 'factive' constructions, QUESTION-fronting is not possible, whereas in the other kinds of construction it is:

> *Why* does he think *that it happened*?
> **Why* does he realise *that it happened*?

In examples like these it is clear that, although the non-factive construction is possible, the factive one is not. However, I must admit (following Huddleston, 1969) that not all examples are as clear as these, and it does seem to be possible to have QUESTION-fronting even in a factive construction, especially where the fronted item does not have an adverbial function:

> *How much* do they realise *that we know*?
> *What* did he admit *that he stole*?

The general point remains, however, although I do not know what the detailed rules are: that QUESTION-fronting is far more restricted in factive constructions than in non-factive constructions.

No such restriction applies to SUBJECT-fronting, of course: this is just as possible in a construction that is factive as in one that is not, as witness

He was thought *to be a serious candidate*,
He was recognised *to be a serious candidate*.

Differences between QUESTION-fronting and SUBJECT- or COMPLEMENT-fronting

The characteristics of QUESTION-fronting which distinguish it from SUBJECT- or COMPLEMENT-fronting thus include the following:
(i)   QUESTION-fronting affects not only the position but also the class of the fronted item;
(ii) QUESTION-fronting is not restricted to non-finite noun-clauses;
(iii) QUESTION-fronting is not restricted to ICs of the noun-clause that have the function SUBJECT or COMPLEMENT;
(iv) QUESTION-fronting is impossible for the SUBJECT in a noun-clause that is itself SUBJECT;
(v)   QUESTION-fronting is relatively difficult in a 'factive' construction.

Though it is unnecessary to add to this list in order to prove that the two kinds of fronting are different, there is one more related fact that is worth noting: QUESTION-fronting and SUBJECT- or COMPLEMENT-fronting can both apply to the same noun-clause.

What is *Nelson* believed nowadays *to have said to Hardy*?
How well does *this government* seem *to be managing
    the economy*?

In case it was still needed, this could be taken as clinching evidence that the two kinds of fronting were the reflexes of completely independent sets of factors, although in their effects on the surface structuring of the sentence they are similar.

Our grammar will generate QUESTION-fronted construction, as well as those involving the other kind of fronting. However, there is another kind of construction which is very similar to QUESTION-fronting, but which I shall not include in the grammar: those where an IC of the noun-clause is a 'rela-

tive phrase' (instead of a 'question-phrase') because the matrix-clause itself is
a relative clause:

> The steam-roller *that* he claimed *that he had ordered in March*
> wasn't delivered till September,
> The place *where* he said *he lived* was a gas-works.

Precisely the same rules seem to apply here as with QUESTION-fronting, with
one possible difference: it seems easier to front adverbial functions in factive
clauses, as witness the following, which can be compared with examples of
QUESTION-fronting:

> They searched all the places *where* she admitted
> *she had put bombs,*
> ? *Where* did she admit *she had put bombs*?

Recursive QUESTION-fronting

Finally, we can note a point of similarity between QUESTION-fronting
and SUBJECT-fronting: they are both recursive.

In a wh-question, there is one item which defines what is unknown, and
this has the function QUESTION; so in

> What did she want?

the item *what* has the function QUESTION. With QUESTION-fronting, the
item that defines the unknown is not an IC of the wh-question itself but of a
noun-clause within it; and the effect of this is that the noun-clause has an IC
whose function is QUESTION:

> *What* did she say *that she wanted*?

However, this in a sense turns the noun-clause itself into a wh-question
(I shall refer to it as a 'pseudo-interrogative clause' in the grammar), since the
QUESTION item has to be located in its structure just as it would if the
noun-clause were a genuine wh-question. Consequently, the same rules apply
to it as to a genuine wh-question, and once more QUESTION-fronting is possible if there is a noun-clause inside the noun-clause:

> *What* did she say *that she thought she wanted*?

Thus QUESTION-fronting is not in fact restricted to wh-questions proper: it is found either in them or in noun-clauses that themselves have an IC that is QUESTION-fronted. There is no limit to the number of different clauses in whose structures the same item can have the function QUESTION, and it is not hard to construct examples like the following:

> What did she say that she felt instinctively that he was likely
> to expect her to say that she wanted?

4.2.8. *The presence or absence of BINDER in the noun-clause*
A noun-clause may contain a BINDER in its structure if it is finite or infinitival, but rules determining whether BINDER should be present or not are different in the two cases, and reasonably complicated. What is not complicated is the identity of the item with the function BINDER: if the clause is finite, it is *that*, and if it is infinitival it is *for*, as in the following:

> I suspect *that Judy's got someone else's eye-lashes on*,
> It would be a shame *for the outing to be called off just
> because of a little war*.

The occurrence of 'that'
Taking the rules for *that* first, in the simplest cases, *that* is optional, and it seems to make no difference to the meaning whether it is present or not:

> People say *that Corfu is a nice place for a holiday*,
> People say *Corfu is a nice place for a holiday*.

However, in one environment it is obligatory, and in another it is impossible. It is *obligatory* if the noun-clause is SUBJECT and not extraposed:

> *That he'll ever finish* is open to question,
> **He'll ever finish* is open to question.

More generally, it is obligatory if the noun-clause precedes the matrix clause's main verb, so that a 'thematic' (i.e. clause-initial) COMPLEMENT-clause will also have to contain *that*:

> *That she was as keen on him as you say* I didn't know,

She was as keen on him as you say I didn't know.

However, I am not trying to cover special thematic structures like these in this description, so we can define the relevant environment as 'un-extraposed SUBJECT'.

That is *impossible*, on the other hand, if SUBJECT is fronted. Since *that* occurs only in finite clauses, and SUBJECT-fronting as such is possible only in infinitival clauses, the environment in question will arise only as the result of QUESTION-fronting, where the fronted item happens to be SUBJECT:

> *Who* did you say *was coming*?
> *Who* did you say *that was coming*?

This pair can be compared with the following, where *that* is optional because the QUESTION-fronted item is not SUBJECT in the noun-clause:

> *Who* did you say *you invited*?
> *Who* did you say *that you invited*?

The occurrence of 'for'

Turning now to the rules for the conjunction *for*, this is found only if the noun-clause both is infinitival (with *to*) and contains SUBJECT; under these circumstances, it is obligatory, unless one of two extra factors is present.

The first of these possible factors is that the noun-clause's SUBJECT is fronted: if this is so, *for* is impossible.

> *The earth* is said *not to be quite round*,
> *For the earth* is said *not to be quite round*.

It should be remembered that SUBJECT-fronting is not restricted to noun-clauses acting as SUBJECT (2.5), but can also occur in COMPLEMENT clauses, although in these cases it does not lead to discontinuity in the noun-clause; but the rule given above applies here too, and *for* is excluded:

> We were all expecting *Harry to fall madly in love with her*,
> *We were all expecting *for Harry to fall madly in love with her*.

The second case where *for* is not possible is when the noun-clause is COM-PLEMENT after certain verbs such as *want*, which do not allow SUBJECT-

fronting but do not allow *for* either. The differences between these constructions and the apparently similar ones involving verbs like *believe* were discussed in 2.5; the reader will remember that one difference is that with *want*
the pseudo-cleft sentence construction is possible;

> I want *everybody to be happy*,
> What I want is *for everybody to be happy*,
> I believe *all the people here to be staunch Conservatives*,
> *What I believe is *for all the people here to be staunch
>   Conservatives.*

Notice that in the pseudo-cleft sentence construction the *for* is required, since
it can be absent only under the strict conditions that the noun-clause is COM-
PLEMENT and follows its main verb.

4.2.9. *Tense and aspect in the noun-clause*

In some environments, all the eight combinations of tense/aspect categories are possible for the noun-clause, whether it is finite or non-finite. One
such environment is when the matrix-clause has a verb like *believe* as its main
verb:

> I believe *that he reads/read The Times*,
> I believe *that he has/had read The Times*,
> I believe *that he is/was reading The Times*,
> I believe *that he has/had been reading The Times*.

> I believe *him to read/to have read The Times*,
> I believe *him to have read/to have read The Times*,
> I believe *him to be reading/to have been reading The Times*,
> I believe *him to have been reading/to have been reading
>   The Times.*

In such environments there is nothing to say about tense/aspect, except to
state the rules for the 'sequence of tenses', which I shall not try to cover.
However, in other environments there is more to be said, because the environment restricts the choice of tense/aspect in one way or another. (For some
general remarks on this topic as it applies to non-finite clauses, see 3.1.3.)

Restrictions on [past]

In the majority of constructions that we shall eventually distinguish, the noun-clause is obligatorily [non-past] : it cannot be [past] . For instance, after *intend* this is obviously so.

> *She intends *to have mended it last week.*

However, perhaps less obviously, it also seems to be the case after *normal*:

> *It is normal *for her to have mended it last week.*

There are a number of apparent counter-examples to these claims, but these all turn out not to involve a [past] noun-clause. For instance, in

> She intended *that he should take the initiative*,

the noun-clause may seem to be [past] , but, if we treat the verb *should* as [past verb] , it will be due to the rule for sequence of tenses, and the noun-clause itself will be [non-past] . Alternatively, we might take it as an instance of the same clause as in

> She intends *that he should take the initiative.*

But here again the noun-clause is [non-past] , and *should* is present (rather than *shall*) because of the particular modality of the clause.

Another kind of confusion can arise in non-finite clauses from the fact that [past] and [perfect] always have the same realisations: what looks like a [past] clause can turn out to be in fact [non-past, perfect] . An instance of this is

> She intends *to have mended it soon.*

This noun-clause can easily be analysed as [perfect] , so there is no need to analyse it as [past] — indeed, semantically there is every reason for not doing so.

A more troublesome kind of counter-example is the kind in which the noun-clause contains a noun-phrase with indefinite reference:

> She intends *her husband to have graduated at least ten years ago.*

If this is grammatical, the noun-clause must be [past] rather than [perfect] , since *at least ten years ago* is (normally at least) incompatible with [perfect] .

This kind of example is rather special, however, so I feel justified in ignoring it in this analysis.

Environments permitting [past]

It is easier to define the environments where the noun-clause can be [past] than those where it cannot. Thus, [past] is excluded from any environment that does not come under one of the following three groupings:

(a) Where the matrix-clause specifies the 'modality' of the noun-clause, as this term was used in 4.2.2 (p. 174): that is, where the noun-clause is simply a proposition, without any kind of 'truth-value' (e.g. true or false, certain or likely) specified in the noun-clause itself, and where the matrix-clause specifies this 'truth-value':

> It is clear *that she pushed him*,
> I suppose *she pushed him*.

(b) Where the matrix-clause specifies some kind of subjective reaction to the fact stated in the noun-clause (like the first environment, this was mentioned in the discussion of extraposition (p. 174):

> It is a pity *that she pushed him*,
> Everyone regrets *that she pushed him*.

(c) Where the matrix clause specifies some kind of cognitive process applied to the fact stated in the noun-clause (p. 187). Note that, as in (b), the noun-clause defines a *fact*, and not just a 'proposition', as in (a):

> The insurance company discovered *that she pushed him*.

Finite clauses that must be [non-past]

Outside these constructions, there are none that allow the noun-clause to be [past]. As it happens, too, nearly all constructions other than these three kinds require the noun-clause to be non-finite — though non-finite clauses are also common in the above three kinds of constructions.

Nevertheless, there are a few verbs that occur in the constructions that exclude [past] noun-clauses, and which do allow finite noun-clauses. One such verb is *intend*, which was discussed on the previous page:

> I intend *that the play shall be a success*,

       I recommend *that he give her a receipt.*

However, such clauses are not simply [non-past] : if we were to use an ordinary [finite non-past] clause it would be ungrammatical, in some cases at least:

       *I intend *that the play is a success,*
       ? I recommend *that he gives her a receipt.*

    In other words, the noun-clause in the environments where [past] is not possible must be [modal] or 'subjunctive' — but again, not all modal verbs are possible:

       *I intend *that the play may be a success.*

I do not know what the facts are with regard to such modal or 'subjunctive' clauses, let alone how to make the grammar reflect them. So these extra details, important though they are, will have to be simply ignored in what follows.

Restrictions on [perfect]
    Some constructions that do not allow [past] in the noun-clause do not allow [perfect] either. The restriction is perhaps at its clearest in constructions of 'perception', involving verbs like *see, hear, feel* and *watch*:

       I saw *George go to lunch,*
       *I saw *George have gone to lunch.*

The reason why [perfect] seems to be excluded here is, presumably, that the object of perception must be the event itself rather than a state resulting from it.
    Similarly, [perfect] seems to be excluded when the verb in the matrix-clause is *make*, though it is permitted with *oblige*:

       The pressure of work during term-time obliged George
           to have got all his lectures prepared by the end
           of the holidays,
       *The pressure of work during term-time made George *have got*
           all his lectures prepared by the end of the holidays.

These two verbs thus seem to be semantically different: the object of causation must be an event with *make*, but can be a more diffuse state of affairs with *oblige*. The same kind of difference seems to exist between *let*, which does not allow [perfect] , and *allow*, which does.

The constructions which do not permit the noun-clause to be [perfect] include all those in which the noun-clause is [participial] — as with *see* — and also those where it is [infinitival, without to] — as with *make* and *let*. However, they also include constructions in which the noun-clause is [gerundival] or [infinitival, with to] , provided all the following are ungrammatical:

> **George* kept *having got through his lecture material by*
>   *half-way through the term,*
> **George* started *having got through his lecture material by*
>   *half-way through the term,*
> **These letters* need *having signed by two o'clock this afternoon,*
> **George* started *to have got through his lecture material by*
>   *half-way through the term,*
> ***The lack of interruptions in his lectures helped George *to have*
>   *got through his lecture materials by half-way*
>   *through the term.*

I shall assume that these are all ungrammatical, and prevent the grammar from generating them.

The number of verbs that do not allow [perfect] in the noun-clause is relatively small — my lists in 4.2.15 and the appendix include only 32, and it seems unlikely that there are very many more. The majority of verbs which do not allow [past] *do* allow [perfect] — my lists are certainly far from complete but already include 182 such verbs. In spite of this big difference in the numbers of verbs involved, however, the two kinds of constructions will figure equally prominently in our grammar, because the kind which do not permit [perfect] include a relatively wide range of different constructions, each involving just a handful of verbs, or even just one verb.

Restrictions on [progressive] and [non-progressive]

There are some constructions in which the noun-clause must be [non-progressive] , and others where it must be [progressive] , but both kinds are sub-divisions of the class of constructions which do not permit [perfect] . In fact, the [progressive] versus [non-progressive] system is predetermined for *all* constructions where the noun-clause must be [non-perfect] (and for no other constructions); so this class of constructions fall into two classes: those where the noun-clause must be [non-progressive], and those where it must be [progressive].

Taking the first of these classes, it seems to include (inter alia) all constructions where the noun-clause is [gerundival] or [infinitival], whether [with to] or [without to]. That is, I am claiming that sentences like the following are ungrammatical:

> *The interruptions in his lectures made George *be still*
>   *lecturing on the first topic at the end of term,*
> **George* has started *to be still lecturing five minutes after*
>   *the lectures should have ended,*
> *George's determination helped him *still to be working long*
>   *after everyone else had fallen asleep.*

With a gerundival noun-clause, of course, it is hard to find a [progressive] example, since a [gerundival] clause can be [progressive] only if it is also [perfect], as we saw in discussing non-finite clauses (3.1.3).

[Progressive] and [non-progressive] 'perception' clauses

Apart from these constructions, however, some constructions prevent a [participial] clause from being [progressive]; for instance, there is no [progressive] counterpart to:

> Bill saw *Fred's rock give way.*

This claim is harder to justify than the earlier ones, however, since it does not rest on the ungrammaticality of the corresponding [progressive] form, which clearly *is* grammatical:

> Bill saw *Fred's rock giving way.*

Rather, what I am claiming is that the difference between [progressive] and [non-progressive] is not the *only* difference between these two. There are in fact two other differences.

First, the [progressive] noun-clause allows pseudo-clefting, whilst the [non-progressive] does not:

> *What Bill saw was *Fred's rock give way,*
> What Bill saw was *Fred's rock giving way.*

It is tempting to conclude from this that the progressive form must in fact be [gerundival], while the [non-progressive] is participial, and to make a general rule that [participial] clauses cannot be the focus of a pseudo-cleft construction. However, as we saw in 3.1.3 there are good reasons for saying that this feature, [progressive], is the one feature that gerundival clauses *cannot* have (except with [perfect]), so we cannot use this way of explaining why pseudo-clefting is possible in one case but not in the other.

Instead, we can explain it by saying that the noun-clause's SUBJECT is fronted when it is [non-progressive], but not when it is [progressive]. In either case, of course, *Fred's rock* will be an IC of the noun-clause, but when it is fronted pseudo-clefting will automatically be excluded, according to the principles of 4.2.5 (p. 188).

The second difference, which is related to the first, is that the matrix-clause can be passive if the noun-clause is [non-progressive], but not if it is [progressive]; in other words, there is no [progressive] equivalent of

Fred's rock was seen *to give way*.

Here again, my claim may seem to be blatantly false, since there are in fact two different forms which might be considered to fill this role:

Fred's rock was seen *to be giving way*,
Fred's rock was seen *giving way*.

However, these can both be identified as instance of a different construction from the one containing the [non-progressive] clause. The first, containing *to be giving*, is the passive counterpart of

We saw *Fred's rock to be giving way*,

which is a 'cognition' construction — of the kind which allows verbs like *understand, realise, admit, recognise* — rather than a 'perception' construction. And the second is an instance of a construction that I have explicitly excluded from our discussion (p. 164), found in:

We last sighted her sailing west from Liverpool,
She was last sighted sailing west from Liverpool.

What is true of 'perception' verbs like *see* also seems to be true of the verb *have*: it too can occur in either the [progressive] or the [non-progressive] kind of construction.

> She had *the butler show them into the drawing-room*,
> She had *the butler receiving her guests as they arrived.*

As with *see*, the [non-progressive] noun-clause can be active or passive, and it is when it is [passive] that it is most clearly [participial] :

> She saw *them shown into the drawing-room*,
> She had *them shown into the drawing-room.*

There are thus two sets of verbs that can occur when the noun-clause must be [progressive] : perception verbs like *see*, and the verb *have*. There is also a third set: verbs like *need*:

> He needs *someone standing over him all the time.*

This third set of verbs will be found in several other constructions apart from this one, which again makes it quite hard to 'prove' that this example has no [non-progressive] counterpart unless we change the construction; this does, however, seem to be the case.

Restrictions on [progressive] and [non-progressive] summarised
To sum up, constructions in which the noun-clause has to be [non-perfect] are of two kinds: those where the noun-clause must be [progressive], and those where it must be [non-progressive]. In the former, 'pseudo-clefting' is possible, since the noun-clause's SUBJECT is not fronted; but in the latter it is fronted, so pseudo-clefting is ruled out. And in the latter, given an appropriate verb, the matrix clause can be passive (with the noun-clause's SUBJECT fronted to act as the matrix-clause's MOOD-SUBJECT, of course), whereas in the former it cannot.

Restrictions on 'non-stative'
The facts that I outlined above will be reflected in the grammar, but those that follow will not. The former concerned tense/aspect in the sense of the three systems [past] versus [non-past], [perfect] versus [non-perfect], [progressive] versus [non-progressive] ; the latter will concern a different dimension which I have not yet been able to incorporate into my grammar: 'stative' versus 'non-stative'. This distinction seems to be relevant to constructions where there is no other restriction on tense/aspect at all — i.e. those constructions that even allow the noun-clause to be [past], as when the verb

is *believe*. In this respect, as in others, it is completely different from the ordinary tense/aspect restrictions.

The restriction seems to be that in these constructions the referent of the noun-clause must in general be a 'state' rather than an 'event':

> I didn't believe *John to be dying,*
> *I didn't believe *John to die.*

However, if the 'event' is earlier in time than the time of 'believing' (or whatever type of cognition may be involved), then the restriction is waived:

> I didn't believe *John to have died so long before.*

In discussing 'perception' clauses that have to be [non-progressive], I mentioned the verbs like *see* and *hear*, and suggested that they could be used not only in 'perception' constructions but also in 'cognition' constructions (p. 177). For instance, in a discussion of examples like

> *Fred's rock* was seen *to be giving way.*

I claimed that the corresponding active form would be

> We saw *Fred's rock to be giving way,*

and not the [participial] form

> We saw *Fred's rock giving way.*

As a 'cognition' verb, *see* is subject to the restriction on 'non-stative' clauses: thus the corresponding [non-progressive] form is the ungrammatical

> *We saw *Fred's rock to give way,*

whereas in a 'perception' construction it would of course be fully grammatical:

> We saw *Fred's rock give way.*

However, although the 'stative' versus 'non-stative' contrast is to some extent related to our tense/aspect contrasts, the relation is a very complicated one, and may well be better treated as semantic rather than grammatical. As I have already admitted, our grammar will have nothing at all to say about it.

4.2.10. *Voice in the noun-clause, and constructions involving 'need', 'want', etc.*
    In most constructions there are no restrictions on the voice of the noun-clause: wherever an active noun-clause is possible, so is a passive one, and vice versa. There are just three constructions where voice is restricted.

Voice-restrictions with 'watch'
    When the verb in a 'perception' construction (as described in 2.9) is *watch*, the noun-clause has to be [active] whereas it can be either [active] or [passive] if the verb is *see*:

> We saw *Bob beat Harry*,
> We saw *Harry beaten by Bob*,
> We watched *Bob beat Harry*,
> *We watched *Harry beaten by Bob.*

I have alread said that in 'perception' constructions the noun-clause cannot be [perfect] or [past], so this extra restriction associated with *watch* means that the only contrast left to affect the verbs in the noun-clause is that between [progressive] and [non-progressive]:

> We watched *Bob beat Harry*,
> We watched *Bob beating Harry*.

But we have also seen (p. 206) that these two classes occur in different constructions, so that the latter are instances not of the same larger construction, with the difference located simply in the noun-clause, but of two different constructions. Consequently, where the verb in the matrix-clause is *watch*, the form of the verb in the noun-clause is determined entirely by the latter's environment.
    As well as restricting the voice of the noun-clause, *watch* is also unusual in restricting the voice of the matrix-clause: this too has to be active:

> We saw *Bob beat Harry*,
> *Bob* was seen *to beat Harry*,
> We watched *Bob beat Harry*,
> *Bob* was watched *to beat Harry*.

It is true that the matrix-clause can be passive if the embedded clause is [progressive]:

The lollipop-man watched the children *crossing the road*,
The children were watched *crossing the road.*

However, this is not an example of a noun-clause, but of the purely 'participial' kind of construction which can even involve verbs like *meet* and which we are excluding from our grammar (p. 164).

I am aware of only two other verbs that are like *watch* in any of these respects: *notice* and *observe.* Even with these verbs it is not at all certain that they are in fact like *watch* with regard to all the rules I have just formulated.

Voice-restrictions with 'order', etc.

There are some verbs, including *order*, that allow two different forms for a passive noun-clause, one [participial], and the other [infinitival, with to]:

The butler ordered *the maids to lay the table immediately*,
The butler ordered *the table to be laid immediately*,
The butler ordered *the table laid immediately.*

In the active voice, however, the noun-clause must be [infinitival, with to], as above, and cannot be [participial]:

* The butler ordered *the maids lay the table immediately.*

Not all the verbs that allow a [participial] noun-clause provided it is [passive] are like *order*, however. For instance, *get* is another such verb:

The butler got the maids *to lay the table immediately*,
The butler got *the table laid immediately.*

This verb is different from *order* in that the two different forms for a [passive] noun-clause do not mean the same — indeed, in our last example the infinitival form would make nonsense:

The butler got the table *to be laid immediately.*

This difference between *order* and *get* arises from the fact that the noun-clause contains a SUBJECT with *order*, but not with *get*: in the latter case, as with *persuade*, the noun-phrase between the two sets of verbs is GOAL in the matrix clause, not SUBJECT in the noun-clause.

It appears then that in these constructions, the [participial, passive] noun-

clause has no exact active counterpart, either [infinitival] or [participial].
Morever, not all verbs that are otherwise similar to either *order* or *get* can also
be used with a [passive, participial] noun-clause: for instance, *forbid* seems to
be otherwise like *order*, and *persuade* like *get*, but neither of them allows a
[participial, passive] noun-clause:

> The butler forbade *the maids to open the wine-bottles*,
> The butler forbade *the wine-bottles to be opened*,
> *The butler forbade *the wine-bottles opened*,
> The butler persuaded the maids *to lay the table immediately*,
> *The butler persuaded *the table laid immediately*.

These arguments all favour the same analysis: the [participial, passive]
noun-clauses do not occur in the same constructions as the [infinitival] noun-
clauses, although all the verbs that occur with the former also occur with the
latter. So the construction in which the former occur only allows [passive]
noun-clauses, so that in this environment too the voice of the noun-clause is
restricted.

Voice-restrictions with 'need', etc.
    One of the most obviously special facts about *need* is that it allows the
noun-clause to be [gerundival, special passive] — that is, a [gerundival] clause
that is [passive] but does not contain the function PASSIVE in its structure:

> *These books* need *putting back on the shelves.*

This clearly constitutes a separate construction, with no corresponding form
containing an [active] noun-clause. I know of only three verbs that can occur
in the matrix-clause: *need, require* and *want*.
    However, this is not the only construction in which these three verbs are
found. First of all, we can match the above example with one containing an
[infinitival] noun-clause, which may be either [active] or [passive].

> *These books* need *to go back onto the shelves*,
> *These books* need *to be put back onto the shelves.*

Secondly, both these constructions can be matched by constructions in which
there is a second noun-phrase, acting as SUBJECT of the matrix-clause, whilst
the noun-phrase above is moved after *need*:

He'll need *these books putting back on the shelves,*
He'll need *these books to go back onto the shelves,*
He'll need *these books to be put back onto the shelves.*

(The first of these seems to be ungrammatical in many dialects, but it is certainly grammatical in my dialect.) Thirdly, there are two other possibilities with the noun-phrase after *need*, in both of which the noun-phrase is [participial] : in one it is [passive, non-progressive] , and in the other it is [progressive] .

He'll need *these books put back on the shelves,*
He always needs *his books lying within easy reach.*

For those speakers who did reject the construction mentioned above, the first of these last two constructions would probably be used in preference to it. In my dialect the two passive constructions coexist.

In other words, *need*, *require* and *want* occur in the following six constructions.

	NP need −	NP need NP −
free choice of voice and aspect	[infinitival, with to]	[infinitival, with to]
passive only	[gerundival, special passive]	[gerundival, special passive] [participial, passive]
progressive only		[participial, progressive]

Of these constructions, the voice of the noun-clause is limited to [passive] in three, exemplified in

These books need *putting back on the shelves,*
He'll need *these books putting back on the shelves,*
He'll need *these books put back on the shelves.*

The other three constructions are not relevant to the question of restrictions on voice.

The SUBJECT of the noun-clause with 'need', etc.

The way in which I have italicized the examples given so far clearly implies that I am taking one noun-phrase as SUBJECT in the noun-clause. How do I justify this analysis? And in which cases is this SUBJECT fronted?

When the noun-clause is [active] and [infinitival] it is easy to construct an example involving the 'dummy' *there*, which has to be taken as SUBJECT of the noun-clause; hence the italics in the following:

> *There* needs *to be more cooperation between departments,*
> We need *there to be more cooperation between departments.*

Since the SUBJECT is clearly fronted in the first example, it is natural to assume it is also fronted in the second; and if the following is ungrammatical, this assumption must be correct:

> *What we need is *for there to be more cooperation between*
> *departments.*

When the noun-clause is [participial, progressive] , it is simply an instance of the obligatorily [progressive] constructions that are mentioned in 4.2.9 (p. 206); and like the other instances of this construction, it allows pseudo-clefting:

> What he needs is *his books lying within easy reach.*

This shows that *his books* is SUBJECT, but *not* fronted.

As far as the obligatorily [passive] constructions are concerned, none of them seem to allow pseudo-clefting:

> *What these books need is *putting back on the shelves,*
> *What he'll need is *these books putting back on the shelves,*
> *What he'll need is *these books put back on the shelves.*

This suggests that, here too, *these books* is SUBJECT, but fronted. This would not be unprecedented for gerundival clauses, since we shall in any case have to allow SUBJECT-fronting with *keep*, for instance:

> *There* kept *being somebody else on our line.*

I am aware that the arguments do not very clearly favour one analysis rather than another, except in those cases where we can use the test with *there.* I shall assume, for the sake of our grammar, that the noun-clause has a fronted SUBJECT except where it is obligatorily [progressive] ; but if the reader finds another analysis more convincing, then it will be quite easy to adapt our grammar to reflect his analysis.

4.2.11. *Reaction and cognition*

Semantic differences

In 4.2.9 we divided constructions into two classes: those that do allow the noun-clause to be past tense, and those that do not (p. 201). The latter include a wide range of semantic types, but the former, where the tense of the noun-clause is not predetermined by its grammatical environment, cover two main types: constructions defining someone's emotional reaction to the content of the noun-clause, and those defining some kind of cognitive process applied to it. We can call them respectively 'reaction-type' and 'cognition-type' constructions; the following illustrate the difference between them:

> Samson regretted *that he had told Delilah his secret,*
> Samson realised *that he had told Delilah his secret.*

'Regretting' is a kind of emotional reaction, whilst 'realising' is simply a cognitive process.

Formal differences

As well as the semantic distinction between the two types of construction, there are eight formal differences.
(i) *Finiteness of the noun-clause.* In constructions of either kind the noun-clause can be finite, as in the above examples; as far as I know, there are no verbs or adjectives that can occur in such constructions but cannot occur with a finite noun-clause. However, the noun-clause can also be non-finite, and in some cases it is infinitival while in others it is gerundival. There are differences between reaction-type and cognition-type constructions in the rules for using these two finiteness-types. Taking reaction-type constructions first, if the noun-clause is ACTOR or ATTRIBUANT, either finiteness-type is possible.

> It worried Samson *to see Delilah with the scissors,*
> It worried Samson *seeing Delilah with the scissors.*

But if it is GOAL, it must be gerundival:

Samson didn't mind *telling Delilah his secret*,
*Samson didn't mind *to tell Delilah his secret*.

As far as cognition-type constructions are concerned, the restrictions are more
complicated, and we can best leave them till section 4.2.12 below (pp. 219–
226). Briefly, there are three classes of verbs and adjectives: (a) those with
which the noun-clause cannot be non-finite:

It is probable *that Samson told her*,
*It is probable *for Samson to have told her*,
**Samson* is probable *to have told her*;

(b) those with which it may be either gerundival or infinitival, and which are
in this respect like reaction-type constructions, though in other respects they
are not:

Samson remembered *her to be very inquisitive*,
Samson remembered *her being very inquisitive*;

(c) those with which it must be infinitival:

Samson realised *her to have tricked him*,
*Samson realised *her having tricked him*.

(ii) *Presence or absence of SUBJECT.* If the noun-clause is infinitival, the
presence of SUBJECT is optional in reaction-type constructions, but obligatory in cognition-type constructions (with one exception, noted in 4.2.12,
p. 223).

It worried Samson *for Delilah to be so affectionate*,
It worried Samson *to be in the dark*.

Samson believed *Delilah to be in love with him*,
*Samson believed *to be able to trust Delilah*.

(iii) *Fronting of SUBJECT.* If the noun-clause is infinitival, and contains
SUBJECT, this must be fronted (see 4.2.5 above) in a cognition-type construction, but must not be fronted in a reaction-type construction; consequently, the former are never introduced by *for*, while the latter always are,
and also the former but not the latter can involve the split-subject construction.

It was ridiculous *for Samson to trust Delilah in the first place,*
*Samson was ridiculous *to trust Delilah in the first place,*
*It is likely *for Samson to have been bemused by her charms,*
Samson is likely *to have been bemused by her charms.*

(iv) *QUESTION-fronting.* As I noted in 4.2.7 (p. 196), QUESTION-fronting is often not possible in a construction where the noun-clause is semantically 'factive'. Such constructions include those of the reactor type, so we should not expect QUESTION-fronting in these. This assumption seems correct:

How long did Samson think *that his hair had to be?*
*How long did Samson regret *that his hair had to be?*

(v) *'Negative-raising'.* In a cognition-type construction, the noun-clause can be negative, but the negative marker can be transferred into the structure of the matrix-clause (in other words, 'negative-raising' is possible); this is not possible in a reaction-type construction:

He didn't think *that he'd told her a single thing,*
*He didn't regret *that he'd told her a single thing.*

I shall not be able to incorporate this fact into the grammar, since it would take us into the subject of negation, which is too big to be dealt with here.

(vi) *'Indefinite' noun-clauses.* In a reaction-type construction, the noun-clause can be of a particular kind, which we can call 'indefinite', and which is not possible in cognition-type constructions. One of the characteristics of 'indefinite' noun-clauses is that they can contain the modal verb *should* or the adverb *ever*, each with a rather special meaning. These meanings are very hard to define, and can best be explained by examples:

It is rather strange *that Samson ever married Delilah,*
It is rather strange *that Samson should have married Delilah in the first place,*
*It is likely *that Samson ever married Delilah,*
*It is likely *that Samson should have married Delilah in the first place.*

(vii) *The functions of the noun-clause.* The functions (see 4.2.1) that the noun-clause can have in reaction-type and cognition-type constructions are different: in reaction-type constructions, it can be ACTOR in an intransitive clause, ACTOR in a transitive clause, or ATTRIBUANT, while in cognition-type constructions it can be ACTOR in an intransitive clause, ATTRIBUANT, GOAL or COMPLETER. That is, only in reaction-type constructions can the noun-clause be ACTOR of a transitive clause, and only in cognition-type constructions can it be GOAL or COMPLETER.

Reaction-type:

> It doesn't really matter to us *that Delilah cut off Samson's hair*,
> It hurt Samson *that Delilah should do such a thing to him*,
> It's strange *that Samson ever trusted Delilah.*

Cognition-type:

> It appears *that Samson didn't learn from his mistakes*,
> It is clear *that Delilah was working for Samson's downfall*,
> Nowadays we all know *that Delilah was wicked*,
> Nobody told Samson *that Delilah was against him.*

(vii) *Use of 'as' in place of the noun-clause.* A cognition-type construction can contain *as* in place of the noun-clause, but a reaction-type construction cannot. This *as* has the function BINDER — i.e. it acts as a kind of subordinating conjunction or relative pronoun:

> (Delilah knew his secret) *as* Samson had suspected for some time,
> *(Delilah knew his secret) *as* Samson regretted.

This *as* is not restricted to constructions of the kind we are discussing — i.e. those where the noun-clause can be past tense; it can in fact occur in any construction which permits a noun-clause with a function other than COMPLETER:

> (Samson's hair grew longer), *as* he wanted,
> * (Samson's hair grew longer), *as* it tended.

Consequently we must make a special statement for the reaction-type constructions, in order to exclude *as*, rather than one for the cognition-type constructions to allow *as*.

4.2.12. *Factive and modal constructions*

The preceding section distinguished between two types of construction, both of which allow the noun-clause to be of any tense: reaction-type and cognition-type constructions. In this section we shall further sub-divide cognition-type constructions into 'factive' and 'modal' constructions, and show how this classification applies to reaction-type constructions. The distinction between 'factive' and 'modal' was suggested by the distinction between 'factive' and 'non-factive' (Kiparsky and Kiparsky, 1968) or between 'facts' and 'reports' (Halliday, personal communication). From a semantic point of view it is clearly very important indeed, but, as the reader will see in the next chapter, it does not occupy a particularly prominent place in our grammar.

Semantic differences

The semantic difference between 'factive' and 'modal' constructions is clear if we compare examples such as the following:

Baden-Powell realised *that wearing uniforms was good for boys*,
Baden-Powell thought *that wearing uniforms was good for boys.*

With *realise*, the noun-clause defines a proposition which the speaker wants to be taken as a fact — i.e. as factually true. It may or may not be true in a historical sense, but this is not relevant: what is relevant is how the speaker wants it to be taken. So for instance the example above is no more or less 'factive' than the following:

Theseus realised *that he was getting closer to the Minotaur.*

Thus, in these examples containing *realise*, the speaker is committing himself to the views attributed to Baden-Powell and Theseus. In the example containing *think*, however, there is no such implication: the speaker is simply quoting a hypothesis, and saying what its status is (it was believed by Baden-Powell), without thereby committing himself to accepting it as true.

It is clear why we use the term 'factive' to refer to the first kind of construction, but the term 'modal', applied to the second kind, may need some explanation. The reason is simply that the semantic function of such constructions is just the same as that of modal verbs, used in a 'true modal' sense (Halliday, 1969). For instance, there is little semantic difference between the following pair, although one involves a 'modal' construction with an em-

bedded noun-clause, and the other involves a single clause with a modal verb
may.

> It is possible *that Theseus got a clue from Ariadne,*
> Theseus may have got a clue from Ariadne.

In both cases, there is a 'thesis' and a 'modal component' which defines the
status of the thesis: in the first example, the thesis is defined in the noun-
clause, and its status in the matrix clause, while in the second example, the
thesis is in the whole clause less *may*, and its status is defined by *may*.

The polarity of the matrix-clause
   One consequence of the semantic characteristics of factive constructions is
that the implied truth of the noun-clause will be unaffected by any change in
the polarity (positive or negative) of the matrix clause. So for instance, the
object of *realise* is implied to be true whether the matrix-clause is positive or
negative:

> Theseus realised *that he was near the Minotaur,*
> Theseus didn't realise *that he was near the Minotaur.*

   With a modal construction, in most cases it also makes no difference
whether the matrix clause is positive or negative: the speaker does not vouch
for the truth of the noun-clause in either case:

> Theseus thought *that he was near the Minotaur,*
> Theseus didn't think *that he was near the Minotaur.*

However, in some cases it can make a difference: namely, where the meaning
of the matrix clause, when positive, is precisely 'I, as speaker, commit myself
to the following proposition'. Naturally, if such a clause is negated, we can no
longer conclude that the speaker believes the noun-clause to be true. The
effect of negating the matrix clause can be seen in the following two pairs of
examples:

> I think *we're getting near the Minotaur,*
> I don't think *we're getting near the Minotaur.*

> It's true *that Theseus is after the Minotaur's blood,*
> It's not true *that Theseus is after the Minotaur's blood.*

Formal differences

Turning to more formal differences between factive and modal constructions, we can identify the following seven differences.

(i) *The possibility of 'the fact'.* If the noun-clause is finite, it can be put in apposition to *the fact* if the construction is factive, but not if it is modal:

> Theseus recognised the fact *that he was lost,*
> *Theseus thought the fact *that he was lost.*

With some verbs, however, *the fact* seems rather unnatural although for other reasons the construction will be classified as factive:

> ? Theseus admitted the fact *that he was lost,*
> ? Theseus realised the fact *that he was lost.*

Another restriction is that *the fact that* ... cannot be extraposed, since it is an ordinary noun-phrase (and is therefore not generated by our grammar — see p. 163):

> *It has been recognised for a long time the fact
>   *that Theseus provoked the Minotaur.*

(ii) *The use of 'so' in place of the noun-clause.* If the construction is modal, the clause-substitute *so* or *not* can be used instead of a noun-clause; this is not possible in factive constructions:

> *Theseus realised so/not,
> Theseus thought so/not.

However, the use of these clause-substitutes is rather restricted by other factors: even if the construction is modal, *so* is not possible (a) if it would be SUBJECT but not extraposed:

> *So was thought in those days,
> It was thought so in those days.

or (b) if it would be ATTRIBUANT:

> *It is possible so,
> It seems so.

(iii) *Extraposition.* In both factive and modal constructions the noun-clause can be SUBJECT without being ATTRIBUANT: it can be SUBJECT either in a passive transitive clause, or in an intransitive clause. The following pair are both factive:

> It was recognised long ago *that Minotaurs were a nuisance,*
> It emerged from the investigation *that Theseus had no license.*

These can be matched by the following modal examples:

> It was believed at one time *that the Minotaur was really*
>   *killed by Ariadne,*
> It seemed to the Minotaur *that Theseus had already had*
>   *some experience.*

The difference between factive and modal constructions is that extraposition is optional in the former, but appears to be obligatory in the latter if the noun-clause is not ATTRIBUANT:

> *That Minotaurs were a nuisance* was recognised long ago,
> *That Theseus had no license* emerged from the inquiry,
> ? *That the Minotaur was really killed by Ariadne* was believed
>   at one time,
> *That Theseus had already had some experience* seemed to
>   the Minotaur.

Even in factive constructions, extraposition is sometimes obligatory: namely, if the noun-clause is infinitival. This follows automatically from two facts that I have already noted: that such clauses must contain a fronted SUBJECT (4.2.11) and that extraposition is obligatory if a noun-clause acting as SUBJECT has a fronted SUBJECT (4.2.2). In this respect, there is no difference between factive and modal constructions:

> Theseus realised *Ariadne to be in danger from the Minotaur,*
> *Ariadne* was realised *to be in danger from the Minotaur,*
> Theseus thought *Ariadne to be in danger from the Minotaur,*
> *Ariadne* was thought *to be in danger from the Minotaur.*

(iv) *The finiteness of the noun-clause.* In both factive and modal constructions, the noun-clause is either [finite] or [non-finite], and if [non-finite] it

is usually [infinitival] , as in the examples quoted so far. However, there are
also some factive constructions in which the noun-clause can be [gerundival];
these all involve verbs like *remember, forget* and *recall*. With these verbs the
noun-clause can be either infinitival or gerundival:

> Theseus remembered *Ariadne to have given him some thread*,
> Theseus remembered *Ariadne giving him some thread*.

Thus, we must further divide factive constructions according to whether or
not they allow gerundival noun-clauses; those that do we can call 'recall' constructions, and the others 'non-recall'. Apart from the 'finiteness' differences,
there is a difference between infinitival and gerundival noun-clauses: the
former must contain SUBJECT (as noted in 2.11) but the latter need not.

> *Theseus remembered *to have been along that passage
> five minutes earlier*,
> Theseus remembered *having been along that passage
> five minutes earlier*.

(v) *The presence or absence of SUBJECT in the noun-clause.* In 4.2.11 we
noted that in cognition-type constructions (as opposed to reaction-type constructions) an infinitival noun-clause has to contain SUBJECT:

> Theseus realised *Ariadne to have let the thread go*,
> *Theseus realised *to be lost*.

However, we also mentioned that there was an exception to this rule. This
exception is that if the verb in the main clause is *claim*, SUBJECT is optional.
(I do not know of any other verbs like *claim* in this respect, with the possible
exception of *admit*.)

> Theseus claimed *the Minotaur to have been neutralised*,
> Theseus claimed *to have neutralised the Minotaur*.

Since *claim* occurs in modal constructions rather than in factive ones, we
must now subdivide modal constructions into two classes: those in which
SUBJECT is present in the noun-clause, and those where it is absent. (The
verb *claim* will thus appear in both kinds of construction.) This fact distinguishes modal from factive constructions in as much as we do not need to
subclassify the latter simply in order to show whether SUBJECT is present or

absent in the noun-clause. (Paragraph (iv) contains a basis for subdividing 'factive' which is on some respect similar, but not identical.)

(vi) *QUESTION-fronting.* In 4.2.7 we noted that QUESTION-fronting is generally impossible if the construction is semantically 'factive', whilst otherwise it is possible:

> *How long* did Theseus think *that he had been in the Labyrinth*?
> **How long* did Theseus realise *that he had been in the Labyrinth*?

(vii) *The functions of the noun-clause.* The ranges of functions (4.2.1) available to the noun-clause in the two types of construction are not the same. In either type it can be GOAL or COMPLETER:

factive: Theseus realised *that he was lost,*
            Ariadne reminded Theseus *that he was supposed to be
                 rescuing her*;
modal: Theseus assumed *that he was lost,*
            Theseus assured Ariadne *that he would vanquish the Minotaur.*

However, modal constructions also allow the noun-clause to be either ATTRIBUANT or ACTOR in an intransitive clause:

> It was possible *that Theseus would never come back*,
> It seems *that nobody had ever told him about Minotaurs.*

The constructions to which this contrast applies

So far in this section I have applied the distinction between factive and modal to just one class of constructions, those called cognition-type constructions in 4.2.11. We must now consider how the distinction applies, if at all, to other kinds of construction.

First, let us consider the most closely related class of constructions, the 'reaction'-type constructions defined in 4.2.11. These are all clearly factive, both from the semantic point of view and from the formal point of view. Semantically, there is always the implication that the noun-clause defines a *fact*, and not just a hypothesis; and formally, the noun-clause can appear in apposition to *the fact.*

> *That the Minotaur was so small* surprised Theseus.
> The fact *that the Minotaur was so small* surprised Theseus.

In these two respects, reaction-type constructions are like factives, and different from all other kinds of construction; but the similarities between the two constructions are outnumbered by the differences between them, so I shall treat them as two separate grammatical classes. In other words, reaction-type constructions will not be treated as a sub-class of factives.

When we consider all other constructions in which noun-clauses occur, we find that none of them have either the semantic or the formal properties of factive clauses, so we might be tempted to group them together under the heading 'non-factive' (including 'modal' as a particular kind of non-factive). For instance, none of the following imply anything about the truth of the noun-clause's meaning:

> Theseus had never heard *the Minotaur moo*,
> Theseus wanted *to go home*,
> Theseus enjoyed *exploring the labyrinth*,
> Theseus couldn't stop *worrying about Ariadne*,
> *Theseus' sword* needed *sharpening.*

On the other hand, none of these other constructions have any of the formal characteristics that distinguish modal constructions from factives, such as the possibility of *so* or *not*, or obligatory extraposition if the matrix clause has no COMPLEMENT. Consequently there seems to be no advantage in grouping all constructions that are not factive into one grammatical class, called 'non-factive', and indeed this would make the grammar considerably more complicated.

'Factive' versus 'modal' summarised

To summarise this section, we shall divide cognition-type constructions (and only these) into two classes, 'factive' and 'modal'. There is a clear and consistent semantic difference between these two classes: in one, the noun-clause defines a 'fact', whose truth is presupposed, while in the other it defines a 'thesis' whose degree of reliability is defined by the matrix-clause. In addition to this semantic difference, there are a number of formal differences: where a finite noun-clause can occur, we may find *the fact that* ... (factive) or *so* (modal), and if the noun-clause is SUBJECT in a clause which contains no COMPLEMENT, extraposition is optional for factive constructions, but obligatory for modals. For one class of factives (called 'recall'-type constructions), the noun-clause can be gerundival, but otherwise it must be infinitival for both factive and modal constructions. In one class of modal constructions, the noun-clause contains no SUBJECT (the verb in the matrix clause being *claim*); and in gerundival clauses of the kind just mentioned, SUBJECT is optional; but otherwise SUBJECT is always present in the noun-clause.

4.2.13. *The possibility of a governing preposition*

In section 4.1.2 I admitted that I should be ignoring constructions in which the noun-clause is the object of a preposition (with one exception), but it is necessary to say something about the use of noun-clauses as prepositional objects, partly in order to define more clearly the range of constructions that we are ignoring, and partly in order to discuss the exception just mentioned.

The basic facts are simple: only gerundival noun-clauses can be object of a preposition. (Actually, interrogative clauses can also be object of a preposition, but we are ignoring these throughout, according to 4.1.) More precisely, finite clauses (with or without the binder *that*) and infinitival clauses (with or without the binder *for*) can be object of a preposition only under rather special circumstances — such as when the preposition is *except*:

> Schroeder enjoys nothing except *playing Beethoven*,
> Schroeder told Lucy nothing except *that he was going away*
>   *for a while*,
> Schroeder wanted nothing except *to be left alone with his piano*.

The presence or absence of the agentive 'by' before a noun-clause

One consequence of this rule is that there are some complications when a noun-clause is ACTOR in a passive clause, since the normal rule is that ACTOR in a passive clause is a prepositional phrase with *by* as preposition. There are no difficulties if the noun-clause is gerundival, since the normal rules can apply:

> *Lucy leaning on his piano* upset Schroeder,
> Schroeder was upset by *Lucy leaning on his piano*,
> *Having to listen to Lucy* upset Schroeder,
> Schroeder was upset by *having to listen to Lucy*.

As far as the other kinds of noun-clause are concerned, there are two possible situations that might obtain.

One is that the rule preventing them from being governed by a preposition would simply block the generation of constructions requiring this combination; that is, an active clause with a finite or infinitival clause as ACTOR could never be parallelled by a passive clause with the ACTOR specified. For instance, take the following active clauses:

> *That Lucy spent so much time with him* puzzled Schroeder,
> *To hear the things Lucy said* amazed Schroeder.

If this first situation obtained, there would be nothing to be said once we had said that the expected passive parallel constructions are excluded by the rule about prepositions governing noun-clauses:

> *Schroeder was puzzled by *that Lucy spent so much time with him,*
> *Schroeder was amazed by *to hear the things Lucy said.*

The other possibility is that the normal rule for forming passives does not apply if the ACTOR is a finite or infinitival noun-clause. This is in fact the situation I shall assume. Instead of the normal rule, a simpler rule applies in such cases: the ACTOR in a passive clause is no different in form from the ACTOR in an active clause, as witness the following:

> *That Lucy spent so much time with him* puzzled Schroeder,
> Schroeder was puzzled *that Lucy spent so much time with him,*
> *To hear the things Lucy said* amazed Schroeder,
> Schroeder was amazed *to hear the things Lucy said.*

As the reader will remember from 4.2.11 (pp. 217–218) this construction is found only in reaction-type constructions since it is only then that a finite or infinitival noun-clause can be used as ACTOR in a transitive clause.

Phrasal-verb prepositions suppressed before noun-clauses

There is a second complication that arises out of the basic rule preventing some noun-clauses from acting as object of a preposition: a preposition that is otherwise needed in COMPLEMENT may be absent if the COMPLEMENT is a finite or infinitival clause. This complication, unlike the first, is one we shall not be able to handle in the grammar in the next chapter, since again it involves large areas of English grammar that I have not yet formalised. The problem can be seen clearly when the matrix clause has a verb like *long*, taking an infinitival noun-clause as COMPLETER. In the simple cases, no preposition is involved:

> Schroeder longed *to be left alone.*

However, in the pseudo-cleft sentence construction the preposition *for* appears:

What Schroeder longed for was *to be left alone*,
*What Schroeder longed was *to be left alone*.

This discrepancy clearly has to be explained somehow, but until both the treatment of prepositional phrases and that of cleft-sentence constructions has been formalised I shall have to ignore it, and treat verbs like *long* in the same way as verbs such as *hate*:

Schroeder hated *to be left alone*,
What Schroeder hated was *to be left alone*.

4.2.14. *The interaction of these factors with each other; 'construction-sets'*

Each of the preceding thirteen subsections has defined a parameter, or a number of parameters, on which constructions involving noun-clauses can differ from one another. For some of the parameters I showed how they related to other parameters: for instance, I showed how the possibility or otherwise of extraposition (4.2.2) depended on:
(a) the function of the noun-clause (4.2.1): for extraposition to be possible, it must be SUBJECT;
(b) the finiteness-type of the noun-clause (4.2.3): in most cases it must not be gerundival if it is extraposed;
(c) whether or not the SUBJECT (4.2.5) or COMPLEMENT (4.2.6) of the noun-clause is fronted: if it is, then extraposition is obligatory;
(d) whether or not there is QUESTION-fronting (4.2.7): if there is, and if the noun-clause is SUBJECT, then extraposition is obligatory;
(e) whether or not the construction is 'modal' (4.2.12): if it is, and if the matrix-clause has no COMPLEMENT, extraposition is obligatory.
However, we have not yet attempted to do this in a systematic way, and this is the first thing I shall undertake in this subsection.

Free and deterministic relations between parameters

It is not easy to set these interrelations down in a clear and concise way, one of the main sources of difficulty being that the interrelations are of many different kinds. It will be helpful to distinguish between two kinds of inter-relation: one kind which is to some extent free, and the other which is com-pletely deterministic. The relations between extraposition and the other four parameters just quoted are an instance of the first category: under some con-ditions extraposition is either obligatory or impossible, but there are also some under which it is not possible to tell from other parameters whether the noun-clause is extraposed or not. As an instance of the second category we can take the relations between the possibility of a preposition governing the noun-clause (4.2.13) and other parameters: if we know the finiteness-type of the clause, and if we know that it is ACTOR in a passive matrix-clause, then we can predict whether *by* will govern it or not.

In describing the interrelations of the parameters I shall ignore interrelations of the second kind, since they are already given explicitly in the preceding subsections. Likewise, we can ignore the relations between the mood of the matrix-clause and the other parameters, since the former is on the whole independent of the latter, and the few restrictions are given explicitly in 4.2.7. This is in fact one of the only two parameters that we can ignore, the other being the question of whether or not the noun-clause can be governed by a preposition, mentioned in the last paragraph.

'Construction-sets'

Excluding these two parameters leaves us with the task of relating eleven parameters which are at least to some extent independently variable. The easiest way of doing this is in the form of a table (pp. 230–231), where each column represents one parameter, and each row represents one set of compatible selections from all the parameters (called a 'construction-set'). Plotting the parameters against each other yields in fact quite a small number of 'construction-sets': 47, to be precise.

One reason why this number is relatively small (in comparison, that is, with the theoretically possible number of $2^{11} = 2,048$, which would be the number of 'construction-sets' if all the parameters were completely independent of each other) is that many of the parameters are either not relevant or are completely determined for certain selections in other parameters.

Another reason, however, is simply that we have define 'construction-sets' in such a way that they include more than one selection in some parameters. For instance, where there is a free choice between extraposing and not extraposing a subject noun-clause, this is treated as one possibility ('free selection') rather than two ('extraposed' and 'not extraposed').

This decision is not arbitrary: the reason for defining the construction-sets as I have done is that as so defined construction-sets can be used for defining the verbs or adjectives that can occur in the matrix-clause. To do this, we simply take each construction-set and define the range of verbs or adjectives it allows (adjectives if the matrix-clause is attributive, otherwise verbs). If we had treated 'extraposed' and 'not extraposed' as distinct entries in the 'extraposition' column, they would have defined a large number of otherwise similar pairs of construction-sets allowing precisely the same ranges of verbs

Table 4.1

Construction-set		Typical verb or adjective	1 Function	2 Extra-position	3 Finiteness	SUBJECT 4 present	SUBJECT 5 fronted	COMP. 6 fronted	COMP. 7 for	Tense/aspect 8 [past] [perfect] [progressive]	9 Voice	10 Reaction or cognition	11 Factive or modal
I	a	demand	GOAL		finite					[perfect] +/− [progressive] +/−			
	b	promise	GL/ADDR										
II		see	GL/-PASS				−						
III	a	watch	GL/-PASS		participial	+					−pass		
	b	see	GOAL				+						
IV	a	have	GL/-PASS			−					+pass		
	b	order	GOAL										
V	a	need	GL/-PASS										
VI	a	make	COMP/TRANS		inf./-to								
	b	let	COMP/INTR										
VII		need	AC/GL		spec.pass	+	−						
VIII	a	keep	AC/INTR		gerundival		+				+pass		
	b	stop	GOAL										
IX	a	cease	AC/INTR			−							
	b	help	COMP/TRANS										
X	a	tend	AC/INTR		infinitival	+	+		−				
	b	need	AC/GL										
	c	allow	GOAL			−	−						
XI	a	command	GOAL										
	b	persuade	COMP/TRANS										
	c	condescend	COMP/INTR										
XII		easy	ATTR	+/−	gerundival or infinitival			+					
XIII	a	normal	ATTR	+/−					+ −				
	b	wake	AC/TRANS										
	c	enjoy	GOAL										
XIV	a	desire	GOAL		infinitival	+/−	+		+ −				
	b	want	GL/-PASS										
	c	promise	GL/ADDR										
	d	long	COMP/INTR										
XV	a	regrettable	ATTR	+/−	finite or gerundival or infinitival				+ −	[perfect] +/− [progressive] +/−		Reaction	
	b	matter	AC/INTR		fin. or ger.								
	c	amaze	AC/TRANS										
	d	resent	GOAL										

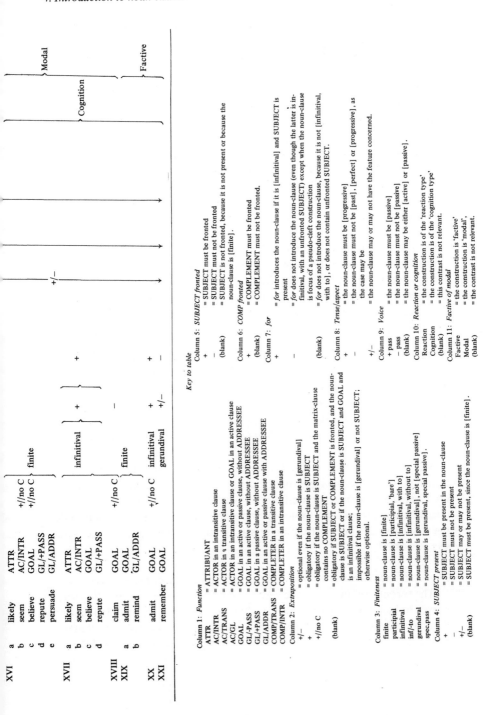

Key to table

Column 1: Function
ATTR = ATTRIBUANT
AC/INTR = ACTOR in an intransitive clause
AC/TRANS = ACTOR in a transitive clause
AC/GL = ACTOR in an intransitive clause or GOAL in an active clause
GOAL = GOAL in an active or passive clause, without ADDRESSEE
GL/PASS = GOAL in an active clause, without ADDRESSEE
GL/+PASS = GOAL in a passive clause, without ADDRESSEE
GL/ADDR = GOAL in an active or passive clause with ADDRESSEE
COMP/TRANS = COMPLETER in a transitive clause
COMP/INTR = COMPLETER in an intransitive clause

Column 2: Extraposition
+/– = optional even if the noun-clause is [gerundival]
+ = obligatory if the noun-clause is SUBJECT
+//no C = obligatory if the noun-clause is SUBJECT and the matrix-clause contains no COMPLEMENT
(blank) = obligatory if SUBJECT or COMPLEMENT is fronted, and the noun-clause is SUBJECT or if the noun-clause is SUBJECT and GOAL and is an infinitival clause; impossible if the noun-clause is [gerundival] or not SUBJECT; otherwise optional.

Column 3: Finiteness
finite = noun-clause is [finite]
participial = noun-clause is [participial, 'bare']
infinitival = noun-clause is [infinitival, with to]
inf/to = noun-clause is [infinitival, without to]
gerundival = noun-clause is [gerundival] ,not [special passive]
spec.pass = noun-clause is [gerundival, special passive].

Column 4: SUBJECT present
+ = SUBJECT must be present in the noun-clause
– = SUBJECT must not be present
+/– = SUBJECT may or may not be present
(blank) = SUBJECT must be present, since the noun-clause is [finite].

Column 5: SUBJECT fronted
+ = SUBJECT must be fronted
– = SUBJECT must not be fronted
(blank) = SUBJECT is not fronted, because it is not present or because the noun-clause is [finite].

Column 6: COMP fronted
+ = COMPLEMENT must be fronted
(blank) = COMPLEMENT must not be fronted.

Column 7: for
+ = for introduces the noun-clause if it is [infinitival] and SUBJECT is present
– = for does not introduce the noun-clause (even though the latter is infinitival, with an unfronted SUBJECT) except when the noun-clause is focus of a pseudo-cleft construction
(blank) = for does not introduce the noun-clause, because it is not [infinitival, with to], or does not contain unfronted SUBJECT.

Column 8: Tense/aspect
+ = the noun-clause must be [progressive]
– = the noun-clause must not be [past], [perfect] or [progressive], as the case may be
+/– = the noun-clause may or may not have the feature concerned.

Column 9: Voice
+ pass = the noun-clause must be [passive]
– pass = the noun-clause must not be [passive]
(blank) = the noun-clause may be either [active] or [passive].

Column 10: Reaction or cognition
Reaction = the construction is of the 'reaction type'
Cognition = the construction is of the 'cognition type'
(blank) = this contrast is not relevant.

Column 11: Factive of modal
Factive = the construction is 'factive'
Modal = the construction is 'modal'
(blank) = the contrast is not relevant.

		Function	Extraposition	Finiteness		Reaction/Cognition	Factive/Modal
XVI	a	likely	ATTR		finite		Modal
	b	seem	AC/INTR	+//no C			
	c	believe	GOAL	+//no C			
	d	repute	GL/+PASS				
	e	persuade	GL/ADDR				
XVII	a	likely	ATTR		infinitival	+	Cognition
	b	seem	AC/INTR				
	c	believe	GOAL				
	d	repute	GL/+PASS				
XVIII		claim	GOAL	+//no C	finite	–	
XIX	a	admit	GOAL	+//no C			Factive
	b	remind	GL/ADDR				
XX		admit	GOAL	+//no C	infinitival	+	
XXI		remember	GOAL		gerundival	+/–	

or adjectives; so we include both extraposed and non-extraposed constructions under the same construction-set.

The table is intended to be self-explanatory, in conjunction with the key
for interpreting the entries, and the relevant discussion of each parameter in
the previous subsections. However, the reader may find a few comments on it
helpful, in addition to the general comment that all the relations represented
in the table will be formalised in the next chapter.

The numbering of the construction-sets

Each construction-set is given a label consisting of a roman number with or
without a letter (a−e) following it. This rather complicated indexing system
will be helpful in the next chapter, and its justification will have to wait till
then (see 5.2.1 and 5.6). The basis of the system is simple, however: construction-sets in which the noun-clauses have different functions, but which are
otherwise similar, have the same roman number, and the letters following this
correspond to different functions of the noun-clause. For instance, each of
the sentences below belongs to a different construction-set, but the differences between them lie only in the noun-clause's function, so their respective
construction-sets are all labelled with the same roman number (XVI) followed
by different letters:

XVIa: It's likely *that we shall have at least a dozen kittens soon,*
XVIb: It seems *that we shall have at least a dozen kittens soon,*
XVIc: The cat's size has persuaded us *that we shall have at least*
          a dozen kittens soon,
XVId: We believe *that we shall have at least a dozen kittens soon,*
XVIe: It is reputed *that we shall have at least a dozen kittens soon.*

The ordering of the construction-sets in the table obviously reflects the
roman numbers used to label them, but as far as the discussion in this chapter
is concerned, this ordering itself is wholly arbitrary. Once again it is introduced here in preparation for the next chapter, where it will be used to reflect
the way in which the construction-sets are grouped together into more inclu-
sive classes.

The relation between the verbs or adjectives and the construction-sets

The second column gives one verb or adjective for each construction-set,
simply to help the reader to imagine what constructions are included under
that construction-set. The items chosen are intended to be just typical members of the classes that can occur in the constructions concerned, and the

classes that they represent will have to be defined separately. We shall return to this problem in subsection 4.2.15 below. Here I can point out simply that there is quite a large degree of overlap between the classes permitted by different construction-sets; for instance, *start* can occur either in IV or in VIa:

IV :   *The cat* started *getting pear-shaped.*
VIa: *The cat* started *to get pear-shaped.*

In some cases the overlap is complete; there are two instances of this in the table, involving construction-sets VIIa and VIIb (both allowing *need, require* and *want*) and IXa and IXb (both allowing *help*). There are other cases where the same verb or adjective is given for two construction-sets (e.g. Ia and XIa), but the overlap in these other cases is just partial.

4.2.15. *The choice of verb or adjective in the matrix-clause*

The functions of the item reflecting the construction-set
    The item with the function PROCESS or ATTRIBUTE in the matrix-clause reflects the construction-set, in the sense that different construction-sets allow different ranges of items with these functions. The relevant item's function is ATTRIBUTE if the main clause is [attributive] ; otherwise it is PROCESS — i.e. the item concerned is the main verb.
    For instance, construction-set XVIa allows both *likely* and *probable* to act as ATTRIBUTE, whereas XVIIa allows *likely* but not *probable*:

XVIa :   It is likely *that we shall have at least a dozen kittens soon,*
          It is probable *that we shall have at least a dozen kittens soon,*
XVIIa: *We* are likely *to have at least a dozen kittens soon,*
          *We are probable *to have at least a dozen kittens soon.*

And *normal* can be ATTRIBUTE if the construction-set is XIIIa, but not if it is either of the above two kinds:

XIIIa :   It is normal *for cats to produce several kittens at a time,*
XVIa :   **It is normal *that cats produce several kittens at a time,*
XVIIa: **Cats* are normal *to produce several kittens at a time.*

    Similarly, the main verb can be either *seem* or *emerge* if the construction-set is XVIb, but only *seem* if it is XVIIb:

XVIb :   It seemed *that the proud father was the neighbour's ginger-tom,*
          It emerged *that the proud father was the neighbour's ginger-tom,*

XVIIb: *The proud father* seemed *to be the neighbour's ginger-tom,*
            **The proud father* emerged *to be the neighbour's ginger-tom.*

The choice of main verb does not seem to be connected with the construction-set, however, when the matrix-clause is [attributive]: whatever the construction-set, the same range of copular verbs (be, seem, become, etc.) appear
to be possible.

Thus the construction-set restricts one IC of the matrix-clause by obliging
it to fall within a specified range, and this item is either the one functioning
as ATTRIBUTE, or the main verb (PROCESS), but not both. This simplifies
the task of stating the restrictions, since it means that we can simply specify
one list of items for each construction-type, and let the noun-clause's function determine whether these items must function as PROCESS or
ATTRIBUTE.

The kinds of item occurring as ATTRIBUTE

However, there is a difference between the two kinds of item, since items
functioning as PROCESS must be just single words — which we can treat for
simplicity as lexical items — whereas those that function as ATTRIBUTE may
be complex items: as well as being single adjectives, they can be phrases of
various kinds, or even clauses. For instance, the following are the same except
for the items functioning as ATTRIBUTE in the matrix-clauses:

> *To ask for help* would be advisable,
> *To ask for help* would be highly advisable,
> *To ask for help* would be a wise move,
> *To ask for help* would be in your own interests,
> *To ask for help* would be to invite a refusal.

Strictly speaking, then, there is no question of listing the items that can occur
as ATTRIBUTE, since the list would be completely open-ended — in contrast
to the lists of verbs whose membership is in principle finite, even where it is
large and somewhat indeterminate.

Nevertheless, I shall offer lists of items occurring as ATTRIBUTE, on the
understanding that the reader should bear in mind that these lists only represent one particular kind of item that can have this function. The items in
these lists will all be adjectives, like *advisable, probable* and *likely*, and the
presentation will imply that they have the function ATTRIBUTE *qua* adjectives — i.e. *qua* single words, just as the verbs have the function PROCESS.
However, this may not be strictly true, since it will probably be better in a

complete grammar to allow adjective-*phrases*, but not single adjective words, to act as ATTRIBUTE. Thus, when the ATTRIBUTE is just *advisable*, this would be an adjective-phrase consisting of one word, an adjective, whose function is HEAD (rather than ATTRIBUTE).

The relation between verb/adjective classes and construction-sets

I defined the forty-seven construction-sets in such a way that they could be used for describing the distribution of verbs and adjectives among the various constructions that involve noun-clauses. This being so, it might be expected that the relation between the construction-sets and the distributional classes of verbs and adjectives would be a simple one — even a one-one relation, so that there would be forty-seven classes of verbs or adjectives, each corresponding to one construction-set. However, the relations I shall in fact describe between the construction-sets and the verb/adjective classes will be quite complicated, since there is a good deal of overlap between the sets of verbs or adjectives allowed by different construction-sets.

For instance, I have already shown that the adjectives permitted by construction-sets XVIa and XVIIa overlap, since both allow *likely* whereas only the former allows *probable*. We can now compare fuller lists of the adjectives allowed by the two construction-sets:

XVIa : certain, clear, false, likely, obvious, possible, probable, provable, sure, true;

XVIIa: bound, certain, likely, meant, supposed, sure.

If we compare these two lists, we find three adjectives that occur in both: *certain, likely, sure*. We might say this is simply 'chance' overlap, except that we then have to explain why as many as three items should belong to both of these classes, while no item in either class also belongs to any of the other classes we shall define with respect to the construction-sets.

In other words, the overlap is *systematic*, and in order to show this, we must try to cover all these three items by one statement. This can easily be done by putting them in a single distributional class, whose distribution includes both XVIa and XVIIa. Thus, instead of just two overlapping classes we shall have three discrete ones.

XVIa :⟨— clear, false, obvious, possible, probable, provable, true;

   certain, likely, sure;

XVIIa:⟨— bound, meant, supposed.

The approach to classification

We have used two different approaches to classification in the above discussion. I started off by setting up one class for each of the two construction-sets XVIa and XVIIa, so that there was a one-one match between construction-sets (i.e. environments) and distributional classes. Then I destroyed this one-one match by setting up three classes, in place of the original two, and allowing one of these classes to be shared by the two environments. These two different classifications represent two different analyses, and in fact two different grammars, since either makes the other redundant. It is the second approach that I shall take in this grammar.

This second approach has two main advantages over the other one. Firstly, as I have pointed out, it shows that the overlap between the environments is systematic and not just due to chance: there are cases of overlap which we shall *not* treat in this way because too few items are involved for the overlap to be clearly systematic. In other words, the second approach allows us to distinguish between systematic and 'sporadic' overlap.

The second advantage is that it forces the analyser to test every verb or adjective for use in every environment, whereas the other approach allows one to compile lists of items found in one environment without reference to the lists compiled for other environments. That is, the approach I have adopted is better than the other as a heuristic device.

However, this approach also has disadvantages corresponding to these two advantages. First of all, it is not clear *how* we should draw the line between systematic and sporadic overlap: I have done it in a purely impressionistic way, and it may be that other linguists would have drawn the line in different places. Possibly a statistical basis could be found for making the distinction in a principled way, but this is still just speculation.

Secondly, it seems to be in the nature of language for the borders between the larger classes of lexical items to be fuzzy, so it is often hard to decide which environments an item can occur in — and therefore, which classes it ought to be assigned to. Worse still, this uncertainty can involve so many items that it is even hard to decide what classes should be set up, since the extent of overlap between two environments is not certain. On top of this, there is a certain amount of dialectal variation regarding the environments that particular items can occur in.

In view of these difficulties, it will not be at all surprising if the reader finds that he disagrees with my classification of verbs and adjectives, on a factual if not on a theoretical level. He will find a complete list of my classes and the items included in them in the Appendix. Many of the items listed are taken from the very useful lists given by Rosenbaum, though our classes of course are quite different from his.

The classes in detail

If we had adopted the first approach to classification, and allowed extensive overlapping of classes, I should have listed something like 670 word-tokens. By adopting the second approach, we reduce this total to around 510 tokens. The first approach would have yielded 47 classes, one for each construction-set; the second approach (by chance) yields very nearly the same number: 46. Using the first approach, we should have had a very simple relationship between environments and classes (one-one); but by the second approach we arrive at a relatively complex set of relations.

The tables below show what these relations are. The construction-sets are divided into groups according to the function of the noun-clause, since this corresponds to the way in which the classes are numbered. Where, as far as I know, a class has four or less members, I list them all; otherwise, I quote just two members, and use dots to show that the list is not complete.

Table 4.2

Function of noun-clause	Construction-set	Number of class	Members of class
ATTRIBUANT	XII	A.1	bad, interesting, ...
		A.2	dangerous, difficult, ...
	XIII	A.3	characteristic, normal, ...
	XV	A.4	exciting, regrettable, ...
	XVI	A.5	clear, probable, ...
		A.6	certain, likely, sure
	XVII	A.7	bound, meant, supposed
ACTOR in an intransitive clause	VII	V.1	need, require, want
		V.2	finish, keep, quit (?)
	VIII	V.3	start, stop
		V.4	get
	IX	V.5	begin, cease, ...
	X	V.6	come, tend, ...
	XV	V.7	count, matter, rankle
	XVI	V.8	come (to pass), emerge, eventuate
	XVII	V.9	appear, chance, ...
ACTOR in a transitive clause	XIII	V.10	bore, wake, ...
	XV	V.11	alarm, amaze, ...
GOAL in an active or passive clause	I	V.12	promise
		V.13	agree, ask, ...
	XI	V.14	command, order, ...
	XIV	V.15	desire, expect, ...
		V.16	advocate, allow, ...
	II	V.17	demand, request, ...
	IV	V.18	hear, see, feel
	V	V.4	get
	VIII	V.3	start, stop
	X	V.19	cause, oblige, ...
		V.20	avoid, enjoy, ...
	XIII	V.21	dislike, like, ...
	XV	V.22	deplore, mind, regret, resent
	XVI	V.23	complain, say, ...
	XVII	V.24	allege, believe, ...
	XVIII	V.25	claim, admit (?)
	XIX	V.26	accept, gather
	XX	V.27	deny, forget, recall, remember
	XXI		

Table 4.2 (continued)

Function of noun-clause	Construction-set	Number of class	Members of class
GOAL in an active clause only	II IV III V VII X	V.1 V.28 V.29	need, require, want have notice (?), observe (?), watch
	XIV	V.21	dislike, like, ...
GOAL in a passive clause only	XVI XVII	V.30	repute, rumour, say, whisper
GOAL in an active or passive clause containing ADDRESSEE	I XIV	V.12	promise
	XVI	V.31 V.32	answer, assure, ... advise, persuade, ...
	XIX	V.33	notify, remind, tell
COMPLETER in a transitive clause	VI IX	V.34 V.35	make help
		V.4	need, require, want
	XI	V.21 V.32 V.33 V.36	dislike, like, ... advise, persuade, ... notify, admonish, invite, ...
COMPLETER in an intransitive clause	VII XI XIV	V.37 V.38 V.39	let attempt, condescend, ... aim, long, ...

Table 4.3
Function of noun-clause (see key to table 4.1).

Construction set	ATTR	AC/INTR	AC/TRANS	GOAL	GL/-PASS	GL/+PASS	GL/ADDR	COMP/TRANS	COMP/INTR
I				V.12, 13, 14, 15 16, 17			V.12		
II				V.18	V.1, 28				
III					V.29				
IV				V.18	V.28				
V				V.4, 14, 15	V.1				
VI								V.34, 35	V.37
VII		V.1			V.1				
VIII		V.2, 3, 4, 5		V.3, 4					
IX		V.5						V.35	
X		V.1, 6		V.14, 16, 19	V.1				
XI				V.14				V.3, 21, 32, 33, 36	V.38
XII	A.1, 2								
XIII	A.1, 3		V.10						
XIV				V.12, 13, 15, 17	V.21		V.12		V.39
XV	A.2, 4	V.7	V.11	V.22					
XVI	A.5, 6	V.8, 9		V.18, 23, 24		V.30	V.31, 32		
XVII	A.6, 7	V.9		V.18, 24, 25		V.30			
XVIII				V.25					
XIX				V.26, 27			V.33		
XX				V.26, 27					
XXI				V.27					

5. A GRAMMAR FOR NOUN-CLAUSES

This chapter contains a systemic grammar that formalises all the facts that we described in the last chapter — except for those which I admitted to be beyond it. The way in which I shall explain the grammar will be oriented towards these facts: I shall give priority throughout to showing how each set of facts is handled by the grammar, rather than to taking a perhaps neater and more logical route through the various parts of the grammar. This orientation will lead to a certain amount of repetition and referring forward to later sections of the discussion, but this seems a reasonable price to pay for being able to build on the previous chapters. It will also have an added advantage of allowing — even forcing — us to refer to more than one part of the grammar in the same discussion, so that the reader will gain a clearer impression of the way in which the various kinds of facts are distributed among the various parts of the grammar.

It is quite possible, of course, that the reader has rejected some of the claims I made in the last chapter, and that he would not agree that all of our 'facts' *are* facts. Probably every reader will have disputed at least some of my claims, and to that extent he will certainly also find shortcomings in the grammar. If the reader is very dissatisfied with the facts that the grammar is going to formalise, he will probably have little interest in seeing how the grammar does this formalising of non-facts. But I am hoping that he will adopt one of two positions: either he accepts most of the facts, and can see that the grammar could quite easily be corrected to formalise the facts as he sees them; or there are a lot of our 'facts' which he denies, but he nevertheless recognises that they are the *kinds* of phenomena which we might well expect to find in a natural language. If his reaction is of the second kind, he may still find the grammar interesting as an example of the way in which complex data can be handled by a systemic grammar, even if some of these complex data seem to him to be incorrect.

I shall start by presenting the whole of the grammar in its final form, with only a few general comments; and in the later sections we shall take the various sets of facts one at a time and relate them back to the grammar. I shall group the facts into five larger sets, and re-order them, but otherwise they will be grouped in just the same way as in the last chapter.

5.1. The grammar

The grammar, as usual, has four parts: a system-network, a set of feature-realisation rules, a set of structure-building rules, and a set of function-realisation rules.

5.1.1. *The system-network*

The system-network has to cover two rather different ranges of options: those relating to the matrix clause, and those relating to its ICs, including, of course, the noun-clause itself. The first range of options applies to any kind of clause, provided only that it contains a noun-clause; whereas the second range applies on the one hand to clauses that are [dependent], and on the other to words or phrases of the kinds that occur as ICs of clauses. In principle, all these options are integrated into a single catch-all network, covering clauses, phrases and words. But in practice a network as comprehensive as this is too big to present in a single diagram: even if it was practicable from the publisher's point of view, it would not be helpful for the reader.

To make the network easier to refer to and to present, we shall divide it into three separate networks: one for matrix clauses, another for noun-clauses, and a third for verbs. I shall not offer a network for phrases, since we know too little about these, and in any case they are fairly peripheral to a discussion of complex sentences as such. Nor, unfortunately, shall I offer a network which integrates our forty classes of lexical verbs, or our seven classes of adjectives, with each other. We shall return to this point below (p. 249).

Some systems will occur in more than one of these three separate networks, but they will have the same reference-number each time. This means that there will be gaps in the system-numbers in any one network. The names of many of the features have been abbreviated by using 'n-c' instead of 'noun-clause'.

Network A

The main divisions of network A

Network A falls into four sub-networks, each dealing with a different area of grammar:

(a) In systems 1 through 12 we make various distinctions having to do with the mood and 'dependency' of the matrix clause. For instance, these systems will reflect the differences among the following:

> Merlin persuaded Arthur *to have a round table*,
> Did Merlin persuade Arthur *to have a round table*?
> (I gather) that Merlin persuaded Arthur *to have a round table*,
> Merlin persuading Arthur *to have a round table* (marked
>   the beginning of Western democracy),
> Since Merlin persuaded Arthur *to have a round table* (his
>   court has been famous).

These same contrasts apply equally to clauses that do not contain noun-clauses, so their relevance is not, on the whole, specific to the discussion of clauses that do contain noun-clauses. We have to include them in the system network, however, because we shall need to refer to two features that they define when we come to discuss QUESTION-fronting (6.1) and the use of the substitute item *as* instead of a noun-clause (5.1). These two possibilities are covered by systems 21 and 22.

(b) Systems 23 through 37 distinguish a variety of different constructions which require different kinds of noun-clause (differing in their finiteness, in the presence or absence of SUBJECT, etc.) and different classes of verb or adjective in the matrix clause. It is in this part of the network that most of the distinctions are located that are reflected in our 'construction-sets' (see 4.2.14), namely those which we labelled with roman numbers (I through XXI). The reader will see that these numbers are shown in network A; for instance, the feature [progressive noun-clause] identifies construction-set II, and [modal, finite] identify XVIa, XVIb, XVIc, XVId or XVIe. The systems in this second block make distinctions of quite a different kind from those made by the first set; so for instance they will show the following as being different:

> Merlin persuaded Arthur *to have a round table*,
> Merlin persuaded Arthur *that round tables are best*,
> Merlin made Arthur *have a round table*.

Network A: matrix clauses.

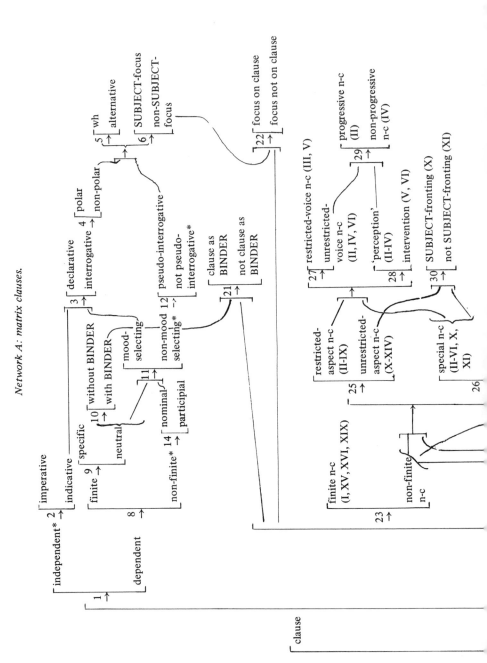

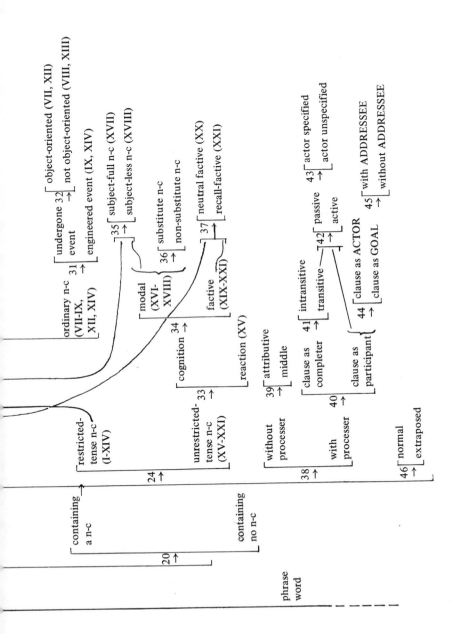

(c) Systems 38 through 45 have to do with the structural environment of the noun-clause: its functions, and the structure of the matrix clause. This set of systems is entirely independent of the previous set, so that the two kinds of classification cut across each other, and it is the present set which accounts for the remaining classification of 'construction-sets', as 'a', 'b', etc. So for instance, all the following are the same as far as the previous sets of contrasts are concerned — they all have the features [modal, finite], identifying them as construction-set XVI — but are different for the present set, since the noun-clause's environment is different in each case:

It's likely *that a round table was the best solution*   (XVIa),
It seems *that a round table was the best solution*   (XVIb),
Many people think *that a round table was the best solution*
                                                                                          (XVIc),
It's reputed *that a round table was the best solution*   (XVId),
Merlin persuaded Arthur *that a round table was the best
          solution*   (XVIe).

(d) System 46 shows whether the noun-clause is extraposed or not. I have made it entirely independent of all the other systems, but we know that there are some environments where extraposition is impossible and others where it is obligatory (4.2.2), so we shall have to use some other means to show these restrictions. This system allows us to distinguish the following:

That the round table would work seemed unlikely,
It seemed unlikely *that the round table would work.*

Deficiencies of network A

Some aspects of the total network have been deliberately simplified in network A, so that we could concentrate on the more relevant parts. This applies in particular to three areas of the network: (a) systems 1 through 12, (b) system 20 and (c) systems 38 through 45.

In systems 1 through 12 a good number of questions have been begged — for instance, we have made it impossible for a clause to be both [dependent] and [imperative]. This means that we cannot treat the following as a dependent equivalent of an imperative clause.

Merlin told Arthur *to have a round table.*

Although it is possible that Merlin's words to Arthur were

> Have a round table!

we cannot, in our analysis, show a parallel between this pair and the following:

> Merlin told Arthur *that round tables are best*,
> Round tables are best.

This analysis is clearly debatable, but it is unlikely that it would make a great deal of difference to our grammar even if the debate showed our analysis to be wrong.

The trouble with system 20, whose terms are [containing a noun-clause] and [containing no noun-clause], is that it is thoroughly ad hoc in the worst sense: its purpose is simply to delimit the area to be covered by our grammar, but as I have admitted (4.1) there is no 'natural' way of doing this. That is, the range of constructions covered by [containing a noun-clause] tells the reader rather more about the time available to the analyst than about English grammar. Moreover, it is most unlikely that constructions containing noun-clauses would be completely isolated from all other constructions in a fully integrated grammar of English. So we can be fairly confident that integrating our grammar into a more comprehensive one would mean, among other things, doing away with system 20.

Systems 38 through 45 suffer from much the same defect: their value is confined to this grammar of noun-clauses, and if we were to expand this to take in other kinds of construction as well, these systems would have to be replaced. For instance, systems 40 and 44 apply only where there is a noun-clause, but they are surrounded by systems that apply to any kind of clause, whether it contains a noun-clause or not. Indeed, it is likely that most of the systems will have to be changed, since they have been arranged here in such a way as to be most useful for our present purposes, rather than in order to reflect the suggestions of Halliday (e.g. 1967, 1968) and Fillmore (e.g. 1968) on 'transitivity' and voice.

Network B

Network B is an expanded version of the top half of the system network on p. 138. The systems added are those applying to [finite, dependent] clauses — systems 9 and 10; systems 11 and 12, contrasting [mood-selecting] with [non-mood-selecting] and [pseudo-interrogative] with [not pseudo-interrogative]; and system 15, contrasting [with for] and [without for]. This network

Network B: noun-clauses.

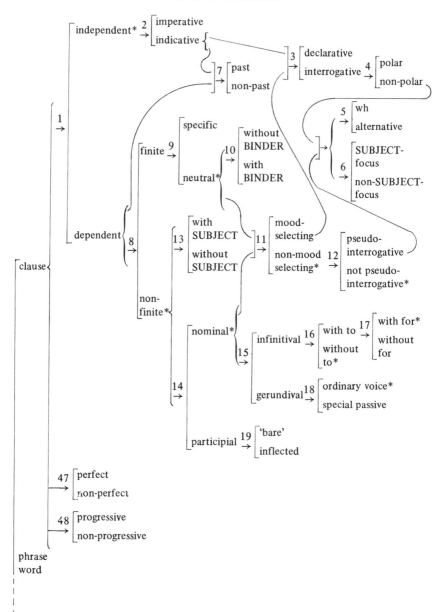

is also an expanded version of the first part of network A, and the reader will
see that a number of systems occur in both of networks A and B. Since we are
not generating reported questions, we do not need to show how [interroga-
tive, dependent [clauses] are sub-classified, and noun-clauses are always [de-
pendent] , so we have been able to leave out a number of the systems of network A.

Network C: verbs

Network C is precisely the same as the bottom half of the network on
p. 138, and needs no comment in itself. What does need some comment, however, is the fact that it does not offer a sub-classification of lexical verbs.

The sub-classification of lexical verbs and adjectives

In 4.2.15 we distinguished 39 classes of verbs and 7 of adjectives, according to the kinds of matrix clause in which they can occur as 'predicate'. We
shall of course need to incorporate into our grammar all the facts we gave in
that section about the distribution of these classes, and this we can do.

But there is a theoretical difficulty: it is hard to see how to describe the
relations between these classes in terms of a system network. It may be that
we could find some grounds for grouping some of the classes together: one
obvious basis for grouping would be according to the noun-clause's functions
and the matrix-clause's structure, giving nine larger classes, each corresponding to one column in table 4.3 (p. 240). But it is not obvious that there is any

Table 5.1.
Feature-realisation rules.

System	Feature	Realisation
	clause	+ PROCESS + LEX = ATTRIBUTE // [attributive] + LEX = PROCESS // *otherwise*
1	independent dependent	– –
2	imperative indicative	– + FINITE + SUBJECT
3	declarative interrogative	– + MOOD-FOCUS // [independent] + BINDER + QUESTION = BINDER } // [dependent]
4	polar non-polar	– –
5	wh alternative	+ QUESTION = MOOD-FOCUS // [independent] + QUESTION // [pseudo-interrogative] + ALTERNATIVE
6	SUBJECT-focus non-SUBJECT focus	QUESTION = SUBJECT // [wh] ALTERNATIVE = SUBJECT // [alternative] QUESTION = COMPLEMENT // [wh] *and not* [focus on clause] ALTERNATIVE = COMPLEMENT // [alternative] *and not* [focus on clause]
7	past non-past	+ PAST –
8	finite non-finite	+ FINITE + SUBJECT –
9	neutral specific	+ THAT = BINDER // *not* [interrogative] –
10	with BINDER without BINDER	+ BINDER // *not* [interrogative] –
11	mood-selecting non-mood-selecting	– –
12	pseudo-interrogative not pseudo-interrogative	– –
13	with SUBJECT without SUBJECT	+ SUBJECT –

Table 5.1 (continued)

System	Feature	Realisation
14	nominal	−
	participial	+ PARTICIPLE
15	infinitival	−
	gerundival	+ GERUND
16	with *to*	+ TO
	without *to*	−
17	with *for*	+ BINDER ⎫
		+ FOR = BINDER ⎬ // [with SUBJECT]
	without *for*	−
18	ordinary voice	−
	special passive	−
19	'bare'	−
	inflected	+ ING/EN = PARTICIPLE
20	containing a noun-clause	+ CLAUSE // *not* [clause as ACTOR, actor unspecified]
	containing no noun-clause	−
21	clause as BINDER	CLAUSE = BINDER
	not clause as BINDER	−
22	focus on clause	+ Q-FRONTED = QUESTION ⎫ // [wh]
		+ PSEUDO-WH = CLAUSE ⎬
		ALTERNATIVE = CLAUSE // [alternative]
	focus not on clause	−
23	finite noun-clause	+ FIN-CL = CLAUSE
	non-finite noun-clause	−
24	restricted-tense noun-clause	+ NONPAST-CL = CLAUSE
		+ I = LEX // [finite noun-clause]
	unrestricted-tense noun-clause	−
25	restricted-aspect noun-clause	+ NONPERF-CL = CLAUSE
		+ NONPROG-CL = CLAUSE // *not* [progressive noun-clause]
	unrestricted-aspect noun-clause	−
26	special noun-clause	+ TO-FULL = CLAUSE // [unrestricted-aspect noun-clause]
		or [restricted-aspect noun-clause, passive]
	ordinary noun-clause	+ FRONTED // [restricted-aspect noun-clause] *and not* [clause as completer]

Table 5.1 (continued)

System	Feature	Realisation
27	restricted-voice noun-clause	+ PASSIVE-CL = CLAUSE // [intervention] + ACTIVE-CL = CLAUSE // ['perception'] + FRONTED
	unrestricted-voice noun-clause	–
28	'perception'	+ PARTICIPIAL-CL = CLAUSE // *not* [passive] + III = LEX // [restricted-voice noun-clause]
	intervention	+ PARTICIPIAL-CL = CLAUSE // [restricted-voice noun-clause] *and not* [passive] + INFIN-CL = CLAUSE // [unrestricted-voice noun-clause] *and not* [passive] + SUBJECTLESS = CLAUSE // [transitive] + SUBJECTFULL = CLAUSE // [intransitive] + V = LEX // [restricted-voice noun-clause] + VI = LEX // [unrestricted-voice noun-clause]
29	progressive noun-clause	+ SUBJECTFULL = CLAUSE + PROGRESSIVE-CL = CLAUSE + II = LEX
	non-progressive noun-clause	+ FRONTED + IV = LEX
30	SUBJECT-fronting	+ FRONTED + X = LEX
	not SUBJECT-fronting	+ SUBJECTFULL = CLAUSE // [clause as participant] + SUBJECTLESS = CLAUSE // [clause as completer] + XI = LEX
31	undergone event	+ GERUND-CL = CLAUSE // [restricted-aspect noun-clause] *or* [not object-oriented] + TO-FULL = CLAUSE // [unrestricted-aspect noun-clause]
	engineered event	+ TO-FULL = CLAUSE + FOR-LESS = CLAUSE // [without ADDRESSEE] + SUBJECTLESS = CLAUSE // [transitive] + IX = LEX // [restricted-aspect noun-clause] + XIV = LEX [unrestricted-aspect noun-clause]
32	object-oriented	+ CRYPTO-PASSIVE = CLAUSE } + VII = LEX // [restricted-aspect noun-clause] + VII = LEX

Table 5.1 (continued)

System	Feature	Realisation
		+ FRONTED + COMPLEMENT ‖ FRONTED } // [unrestricted-aspect noun-clause] + XII = LEX
	not object-oriented	+ GERUND-CL = CLAUSE // [unrestricted-aspect noun-clause] + VIII = LEX // [restricted-aspect noun-clause] + XIII = LEX // [unrestricted-aspect noun-clause]
33	cognition	+ FRONTED // [non-finite noun-clause] *and not* [subject-less noun-clause] *and not* [recall-factive]
	reaction	+ INDEFINITE = CLAUSE + FACT = CLAUSE + XV = LEX
34	modal	+ REPORT = CLAUSE // *not* [attributive] + TO-FULL = CLAUSE // [non-finite noun-clause] + XVI = LEX // [finite noun-clause]
	factive	+ FACT = CLAUSE + XIX = LEX // [finite noun-clause]
35	subject-full noun-clause	+ XVII = LEX
	subject-less noun-clause	+ SUBJECTLESS = CLAUSE + XVIII = LEX
36	substitute noun-clause	+ SUBSTITUTE = CLAUSE
	non-substitute noun-clause	—
37	neutral-factive	+ TO-FULL = CLAUSE + XX = LEX
	recall-factive	+ GERUND-CL = CLAUSE + XXI = LEX
38	without processer	CLAUSE = SUBJECT
	with processer	+ ACTOR // *not* [actor unspecified]
39	attributive	+ ATTRIBUANT = CLAUSE + ATTRIBUTE + COPULAR = PROCESS
	middle	+ ACTOR = CLAUSE + INTRANS = PROCESS
40	clause as completer	+ COMPLETER = CLAUSE + INCOMPLETE = PROCESS

Table 5.1 (continued)

System	Feature	Realisation
	clause as participant	+ GOAL
41	intransitive	+ INTRANS = PROCESS ACTOR = SUBJECT
	transitive	+ GOAL + TRANSITIVE = PROCESS
42	passive	ADDRESSEE = SUBJECT // [with ADDRESSEE] GOAL = SUBJECT // *otherwise* + PASSIVE // *not* [special passive]
	active	ACTOR = SUBJECT
43	actor specified	+ AGENT = ACTOR
	actor unspecified	−
44	clause as ACTOR	CLAUSE = ACTOR + ACTOR-CLAUSE = PROCESS
	clause as GOAL	CLAUSE = GOAL + GOAL-CLAUSE = PROCESS
45	with ADDRESSEE	+ ADDRESSEE + ADDRESSED = PROCESS
	without ADDRESSEE	−
46	normal	−
	extraposed	+ LATE = CLAUSE
47	perfect	+ PERFECT
	non-perfect	−
48	progressive	+ PROGRESSIVE
	non-progressive	−

reason for grouping these into still larger classes, so we are likely to have systems contrasting a dozen different classes, rather than just two classes, at a time. There is no theoretical reason why systems should be binary, and it may be that the predominance of binary systems in our grammar is due to the primitive stage of the analysis as much as to any inherent characteristic of language. Nevertheless, there is obviously a very big difference between a two-term system and a twelve-term system − a difference of kind rather than degree, it would seem. And if we find that there is in fact no reason for grouping the classes at all, we shall have a thirty-nine term system, which is even more blatantly a different kind of object from our 'normal' systems.

All we can do here is to note the difficulty, and simply give the classes as an unordered list, as in the appendix (the reference numbers are in principle arbitrary, so the fact that we can order the classes according to them is irrelevant).

5.1.2. *The feature-realisation rules*

We shall not give realisation rules for the features in systems 49 through 55, since this would involve describing the morphology of the English verb. Nor shall we give realisations for the features [phrase] and [word]. Otherwise there is a realisation rule in table 5.1 for every feature in the network. We make no distinction between network A and network B, but give the features that appear in either or both in a single list, ordered according to the reference-number of the system.

The relations between the features and the functions

One of the most striking characteristics of this set of rules is how complicated the relations between the features and the functions realising them are. In a few cases there is a one-one match between them — for instance, [past] (system 7) is always realised just by the presence of PAST, and PAST never realises any feature except [past] — but this isomorphism is the exception rather than the rule.

At the opposite extreme, we find no less than six features realised by the presence of FRONTED (allowing for the fronting of SUBJECT or COMPLEMENT): [ordinary noun-clause] (26), [restricted-voice noun-clause] (27), [non-progressive noun-clause] (29), [SUBJECT-fronting] (30), [object-oriented] (32), [cognition] (33). Moreover, each one of these six features is also realised by other patterns in the structure, in addition to the presence of FRONTED, or instead of it: for instance [ordinary noun-clause] (27) is realised either by the presence of FRONTED, or by the presence of SUB-JECTLESS (conflated with CLAUSE), depending on whether or not it occurs in combination with [clause as completer]. These relations can be represented diagrammatically as follows.

Features   *Structural patterns*

[ordinary noun-clause] (26) ⟵————— + SUBJECTLESS = CLAUSE
[restricted-voice noun-clause] (27)
[non-progressive noun-clause] (29)
[SUBJECT-fronting] (30) ⟶ + FRONTED
[object-oriented] (32)
[cognition] (33)

Apart from the lack of one-one correspondence between features and functions, there are other sources of complexity in these rules. For instance, there are two ways in which a feature may help to determine the structure: directly, by having some structural pattern as its own realisation, or indirectly, by acting as conditioning environment for some other feature's realisation. For instance, [transitive] (41) is directly realised by the presence of GOAL and of TRANSITIVE conflated with PROCESS, but it also appears in the realisation-rule of, for instance [unrestricted-voice noun-clause] (27), which is realised by the presence of SUBJECTLESS conflated with CLAUSE only when in combination with [transitive].

Indeed, some features have no realisation of their own, but do act as conditioning environments for other features. For instance, [special passive] (18) has no realisation of its own. The reader will recall that [special passive] clauses are gerundival passive clauses that do not contain the usual passive verb-forms, and that are found with verbs like *need*:

These mysterious telephone-calls need *investigating.*

If we were to give [special passive] a realisation of its own this would have to in some way get rid of the PASSIVE which is required by [passive] − e.g. by deleting it. There is an easy way of avoiding this very un-systemic expedient, however: we make the realisation-rule for [passive] (42) introduce PASSIVE only provided [passive] is *not* combined with [special passive].

In some cases there is an obvious connection between the feature and the structural pattern realising it − as with [clause as BINDER], which is realised by CLAUSE being conflated with BINDER. This is not always so, however, since characteristics tend to go in 'bundles' − that is, a class will be characterised by more than one property. For instance, [progressive noun-clause] (29) is realised, as we might expect, by the presence of PROGRESSIVE-CL conflated with CLAUSE; but less predictably, it is also realised by the presence of SUBJECTFULL conflated with CLAUSE, because the feature [progressive noun-clause] is reflected not only by the tense/aspect of the noun-clause but also by the fact that it contains an unfronted SUBJECT.

The relations among the functions

The feature-realisation rules introduced a total of 78 functions, but we can group these into a number of large groups according to the ways they combine with each other. They fall into three groups, according to whether they conflate with CLAUSE, with LEX, or with neither.

A function that conflates with CLAUSE is a function of the noun-clause (since this always has the function CLAUSE), and determines some of the noun-clause's features, or its position in the matrix clause, or both. For instance, if a noun-clause has the function FIN-CL it must have the feature [finite], and if it has the function LATE it must come towards the end of the matrix clause — i.e. it must be extraposed.

Some functions indicate the noun-clause's relation to the matrix-clause's transitivity, without determining any of its features: ACTOR, ATTRIBUANT, COMPLETER, GOAL; but these also help to determine the clause's place. The other functions that do this are AGENT, LATE, REPORT and SUBJECT.

The functions that restrict the features that the noun-clause can have are the following: ACTIVE-CL, AGENT, ALTERNATIVE, CRYPTOPASSIVE, FIN-CL, FOR-LESS, GERUND-CL, INDEFINITE, INFIN-CL, ING/EN, NONPAST-CL, NONPERF-CL, NONPROG-CL, PARTICIPIAL-CL, PASSIVE-CL, PROGRESSIVE-CL, PSEUDO-WH, SUBJECTFULL, SUBJECTLESS, SUBSTITUTE, TO-FULL.

The 'CL' occurring as the second part of some of these function-names stands for 'CLAUSE'; it is added in order to distinguish these functions from the functions of verbs in the clause's structure — for instance, to distinguish PASSIVE-CL, the function of an obligatorily [passive] noun-clause, from PASSIVE, the function of the [en-form] verb whose presence marks the clause as [passive].

LEX is the function of the matrix-clause's 'predicate' — i.e. its main verb or the item acting as ATTRIBUTE in it; so according to the realisation-rule for [clause] LEX conflates with PROCESS or ATTRIBUTE. Apart from these two functions, there are two distinct sets of functions which conflate with LEX: those which reflect the construction-set of which the matrix-clause is an instance, and those which reflect its 'transitivity' structure and the noun-clause's transitivity function(s). The former simply consist of the roman numbers I through XXI corresponding to the numbers used for referring to the construction-sets in 4.2.14. The latter include ACTOR-CLAUSE, ADDRESSED, COPULAR, GOAL-CLAUSE, INCOMPLETE and INTRANS.

Apart from the functions listed so far, there are a group which are the functions of verbs — FINITE, GERUND, PARTICIPLE, PASSIVE, PAST, PERFECT, PROCESS, PROGRESSIVE; a group that conflate with BINDER — CLAUSE, FOR, THAT; and a handful of miscellaneous functions — ADDRESSEE, COMPLEMENT, FRONTED, MOOD-FOCUS, Q-FRONTED, QUESTION, and TO.

5.1.3. *The structure-building rules*

We find the usual four kinds of structure-building rules — sequence rules, compatibility rules, addition rules and conflation rules – and this distinction allows us to divide the rules into four groups. However, there is no reason for ordering one of these groups before any of the others, nor is there any basis for ordering the rules *within* any of the groups, so the ordering in the following list is in principle arbitrary.

The structure-building rules

1. The sequence rules

(1a) $\text{TO} \rightarrow$

$\left. \begin{array}{l} \text{PARTICIPLE} \\ \text{GERUND} \\ \text{FINITE} \end{array} \right\} = \left. \begin{array}{l} (\text{PREPAST} \rightarrow \text{PAST} = (\text{PREPERFECT} \rightarrow \text{PERFECT} = \\ (\text{PREPROGRESSIVE} \rightarrow \text{PROGRESSIVE} = (\text{BE} \rightarrow \\ \text{PASSIVE} = \text{PROCESS})) \end{array} \right\}$

(1b)   BINDER $\rightrightarrows$ M-SUBJECT $\rightarrow$ PROCESS $\rightarrow$ POST-VERB

(1c)   FIRST $\rightarrow$ SECOND $\rightarrow$ THIRD $\rightarrow$ LATE

(1d)   MOOD-FOCUS $\rightrightarrows$ (PRE-SUBJECT $\rightarrow$ M-SUBJECT) $\rightarrow$ POST-SUBJECT $\rightarrow$ PROCESS

2. The compatibility rules

(2a)   PAST $\neq$ PROGRESSIVE

(2b)   PERFECT $\neq$ PROGRESSIVE

(2c)   PASSIVE $\neq$ PROGRESSIVE

(2d)   GERUND $\neq$ PREPROGRESSIVE

(2e)   PRE-SUBJECT $\neq$ PROCESS

(2e') PRE-SUBJECT $\neq$ POST-SUBJECT

(2f)   PASSIVE $\neq$ II

(2g)   BINDER $\neq$ INDEFINITE

(2h)   BINDER $\neq$ COMPLETER

(2i)   SUBSTITUTE $\neq$ BINDER

(2j)   SUBSTITUTE $\neq$ ATTRIBUANT

(2k)   FRONTED $\neq$ CLAUSE

(2l)   POST-VERB $\neq$ QUESTION

(2m) LATE $\neq$ CLAUSE // CLAUSE $\neq$ SUBJECT

(2n)   SUBSTITUTE $\neq$ CLAUSE // CLAUSE $\neq$ FIN-CL

(2o)   SUBSTITUTE $\neq$ SUBJECT // CLAUSE $\neq$ LATE

(2p)   REPORT $\neq$ SUBJECT // CLAUSE $\neq$ LATE

(2q)   LATE $\neq$ GERUND-CL // GERUND-CL $\neq$ TO-FULL

(2r)   CLAUSE $\neq$ SUBJECT // CLAUSE $\neq$ LATE *and* + PRE-CLAUSE

(2s)   TO-FULL $\neq$ SUBJECT // CLAUSE $\neq$ LATE *and* SUBJECT = GOAL

3. The addition rules

(3a)   + AFFIX = PAST, PERFECT, PROGRESSIVE, PASSIVE, PARTICIPLE, GERUND, FINITE

(3b)   + PREPAST // + PAST $\neq$ FINITE $\neq$ PASSIVE

(3c)   + PREPERFECT // + PERFECT $\neq$ PASSIVE

(3d)   + PREPROGRESSIVE // + PROGRESSIVE $\neq$ PARTICIPLE

(3e)   + BE // + PASSIVE $\neq$ PARTICIPLE

(3f)   + FIRST = ADDRESSEE // + ADDRESSEE ≠ SUBJECT
(3f′) + FIRST = FRONTED // + CLAUSE ≠ SUBJECT
(3g)   + SECOND = GOAL // + GOAL ≠ SUBJECT
(3h)   + THIRD = ATTRIBUTE, COMPLETER
(3i)   + POST-VERB = FIRST, SECOND, THIRD, AGENT, LATE
(3j)   + COMPLEMENT = FIRST, SECOND
(3k)   + PRE-CLAUSE = FRONTED, Q-FRONTED
(3l)   + M-SUBJECT // + SUBJECT
(3m)   + M-SUBJECT ‖ FRONTED // *not* COMPLEMENT ‖ FRONTED
(3n)   + PRE-SUBJECT // + MOOD-FOCUS ≠ SUBJECT
(3n′) + POST-SUBJECT = MODAL, PREPAST, PREPERFECT, PREPROGRESSIVE,
       BE
(3o)   + FOR-LESS = CLAUSE // + M-SUBJECT ‖ FRONTED *and* CLAUSE =
       TO-FULL
(3p)   + QUESTION ‖ Q-FRONTED

4. The conflation rules

(4a)   AFFIX = AFFIX // AFFIX = PARTICIPLE
(4b)   PAST = PERFECT // PAST ≠ FINITE
(4c)   PREPAST = PREPERFECT
(4d)   PRE-SUBJECT = FINITE
(4e)   PRE-SUBJECT = MOOD-FOCUS // MOOD-FOCUS ≠ QUESTION
(4f)   M-SUBJECT = SUBJECT // SUBJECT ≠ LATE
(4g)   FRONTED = M-SUBJECT // + CLAUSE = SUBJECT

Some of the rules in this list are already familiar, since they are taken over without change from the grammar of non-finite clauses (3.2.4). These rules are at the head of the list in each section — viz. rules (1a), (2a−d), (3a−e) and (4a−c). The rules are to be interpreted in the usual way, as in the grammar of non-finite clauses; the meaning of ‖ will be explained on p. 263.

Compared with the system-network and the feature-realisation rules, the structure-building rules show very few general patterns that we could bring out in this section. This seems to reflect a general tendency for rules to be less integrated and interrelated in the structure-building part of the grammar: the role of this part is a rather 'messy' one, since it has to operate on the output of earlier parts and simply tidy it up in a variety of ways. Certainly there is no question of discovering here anything corresponding to the independent sub-networks into which the system-network naturally falls. To a lesser extent, of course, the same is true of the feature-realisation rules — but when we come to the function-realisation rules we shall find order returning again. This is easy to explain: in these rules, the 'lower' term of the realisation relation is once again located in the system-network. In other words, the further we are from the system-network, the less organised the grammar is.

SUBJECT and M-SUBJECT

One of the facts that these rules account for is the difference between the 'real subject' and the strict 'grammatical subject' when the noun-clause is extraposed (see 4.2.1); for instance, in

It is difficult *to speak French,*

the noun-clause is the 'real subject' but *it* is the grammatical subject. That is, when it comes to the rules for inverting subject and finite verb (for instance), all that is relevant is the position of *it*, but the restrictions affecting the class of the subject all apply to the noun-clause, and not to *it*.

This distinction is made in a simple way: there is an addition-rule, rule (31), which says that a second function, M-SUBJECT, must be present when SUBJECT is present. Thus any feature-realisation rule which introduces SUBJECT is indirectly introducing M-SUBJECT as well. Then there is a conflation-rule (rule (4f)) which conflates M-SUBJECT with SUBJECT wherever SUBJECT is not conflated with LATE, the function of extraposed clauses. Consequently, if the SUBJECT clause *is* extraposed, SUBJECT will be conflated with LATE, and this will prevent it from being conflated with M-SUBJECT.

Having made this distinction, we shall now be able to refer to M-SUBJECT, rather than SUBJECT, in formulating the rules having to do with the relation between 'the subject' and the finite verb — such as the sequence-rules that we shall discuss at the end of this section. I shall also make great use of the distinction in discussing our way of handling 'fronted' items (below) and the grammar of extraposition (5.2.2).

FRONTED and Q-FRONTED   ——

FRONTED is a function of an item that is fronted by SUBJECT- or COM-PLEMENT-fronting, and Q-FRONTED is a function of one that is fronted by QUESTION-fronting. As I showed in 4.2.7 these two kinds of fronting are completely independent of each other, and both are possible in the same sentence:

Who	does	*Mabel*	seem *to like best*?
Q-FRONTED		FRONTED	

The noun-clause here is *who ... Mabel ... to like best*, and *Who* and *Mabel* are both fronted.

The two functions FRONTED and Q-FRONTED are each introduced by one or more feature-realisation rules (see the realisation-rules for the following features: [focus on clause] (22), [ordinary noun-clause] (26), [restricted-voice noun-clause] (27), [non-progressive noun-clause] (29), [SUBJECT-fronting] (30), [object-oriented] (32), [cognition] (33)). There are two ways in which the structure-building rules have to expand the structure generated by the feature-realisation rules in order to account adequately for fronting: firstly, FRONTED and Q-FRONTED must be related 'sideways' to the rest of the noun-clause, and secondly they must be related 'downwards' to one IC of the noun-clause.

The discontinuity of the noun-clause

The first demand is met by addition-rule (3k), which adds the function PRE-CLAUSE and conflates it with any instance of FRONTED or Q-FRONTED. That is, both *who* and *Mabel* will have the function PRE-CLAUSE in addition to Q-FRONTED and FRONTED respectively. A general rule, which is not of the kind that can be formalised algebraically but is no less explicit for all that, states that wherever a structure includes both PRE-CLAUSE and CLAUSE, these are functions of the same item even though they are not conflated into a single bundle. In other words, as a rule every item has just one bundle of functions, but exceptionally a single item may have two (or even three) bundles, provided the earlier bundle(s) include PRE-CLAUSE.

But although these bundles of functions belong to the same item — namely the noun-clause — the distribution of functions between them is not arbitrary: certain functions are conflated with PRE-CLAUSE (in the first bundles) and others with CLAUSE (in the last bundle), and the former are *not* to be considered as being conflated with CLAUSE, nor the latter with PRE-CLAUSE. For instance, in our example *who* has QUESTION among its functions, and *Mabel* has M-SUBJECT; but this does not mean that CLAUSE is conflated with either of these functions. If we did interpret the structure in this way, we should run into considerable difficulties and confusion: for instance, CLAUSE is conflated with LATE, so if we treated CLAUSE as being conflated with M-SUBJECT, LATE would be conflated with M-SUBJECT — which would make it impossible to use the distinction between the two to handle extraposition.

Thus the noun-clause in our example has three completely separate bundles of functions, including the following:

Who	does	Mabel	seem	to like best?
Q-FRONTED		FRONTED		CLAUSE
PRE-CLAUSE		PRE-CLAUSE		LATE
QUESTION		M-SUBJECT		TO-FULL
MOOD-FOCUS				FOR-LESS
				REPORT
				ACTOR
				SUBJECT

When it comes to relating the noun-clause's features to its environment, the only bundle which is directly relevant, in that it imposes restrictions via the function-realisation rules, is the bundle containing CLAUSE: none of the functions in the other bundles has any realisation. However, we shall see below (p. 264) that the other bundles do indirectly influence the noun-clause's structure, and thereby restrict its features.

The FRONTED item's function in the noun-clause

The second way in which the structure-building rules must extend the structures involving FRONTED and Q-FRONTED is by extending them 'downwards', into the structure of the noun-clause itself. For instance, we have to show not only that *Mabel* is M-SUBJECT in the matrix-clause, but also that it is M-SUBJECT in the noun-clause: we have to show not only that it is an IC of the noun-clause, but also what its function in the noun-clause must be. Given the kind of matrix-clause in which it occurs, it cannot be anything but M-SUBJECT — whereas if the matrix-clause had been of the kind which involves COMPLEMENT-fronting, the fronted item would have had to be COMPLEMENT in the noun-clause:

Our National Anthem is hard *to whistle.*

However, although we can tell from the environment whether an item that is FRONTED is M-SUBJECT or COMPLEMENT in the noun-clause's structure, we cannot predict any of its other functions: for instance, it could be ACTOR, GOAL or ATTRIBUANT as well as M-SUBJECT. Therefore we must introduce these two functions (M-SUBJECT and COMPLEMENT), and only these, by the rules which follow from the matrix-clause's features. COMPLE-MENT is introduced by the realisation-rule for [object-oriented] (32), and M-SUBJECT by a structure-building rule:

(3m)   + M-SUBJECT || FRONTED // *not* COMPLEMENT || FRONTED.

The up-ended 'equals' sign means that the first function (M-SUBJECT or COMPLEMENT) is immediately below the second (FRONTED), but in a different structure, that of the noun-clause.

The rules not only introduce M-SUBJECT and COMPLEMENT beneath FRONTED, but also introduce QUESTION beneath Q-FRONTED:

(3p)   + QUESTION ‖ Q-FRONTED.

Given these rules, we can extend the structure of our example to include two functions in the structure of the noun-clause:

Q-FRONTED	PRE-SUBJECT	FRONTED	PROCESS	CLAUSE
PRE-CLAUSE	FINITE	PRE-CLAUSE		LATE
QUESTION		PRE-SUBJECT		TO-FULL
MOOD-FOCUS				FOR-LESS
				REPORT
				ACTOR
				SUBJECT
QUESTION		M-SUBJECT		
Who	does	*Mabel*	seem	*to like best?*

There is nothing unusual about being able to predict part of the structure of a noun-clause from the structure of the matrix-clause; for instance, given that the latter includes TO-FULL we can predict that the former will include TO. What is unusual about structures like the above is that the presence of QUESTION and M-SUBJECT are required *directly* by the realisation-rules for the matrix-clause's features or the structure-building rules that supplement these: we do not have to go through the features of the noun-clause in order to find what kind of structure it must have, as we have to when we predict TO from TO-FULL.

The FRONTED item's effect on the noun-clause's features

There is just one more point to be made in connection with FRONTED and Q-FRONTED: the functions that are introduced because of them into the structure of the noun-clause (M-SUBJECT, COMPLEMENT or QUESTION) must *also* be permitted by the features of the noun-clause itself. For instance, the noun-clause must not have the feature [without SUBJECT] if its structure has to contain M-SUBJECT because of FRONTED in the matrix-clause's structure: the presence of M-SUBJECT requires the noun-clause to have a feature which would in any case lead to the presence of M-SUBJECT, which means that it must have [with SUBJECT]. It is in this sense that the functions of the noun-clause that are not in the bundle containing CLAUSE do influence the noun-clause's selection of features, although only indirectly.

Sequence-rules

Returning to the structure-building rules, there is another question that may be puzzling the reader: why is there more than one sequence-rule? We needed only one in the grammar for non-finite clauses (viz. the first sequence-rule in this chapter, rule (1a)), so why should we need more than one here? Or, approaching the matter from a different point of view, since there is only one left-right dimension in a structure, it should be enough to have one sequence formula, so why have five different formulae?

As I explained in 2.4, the answer is that the sequence restrictions are in fact too complicated to handle in a single formula. To take an obvious instance of this, the first formula could not be expanded to include M-SUBJECT, since M-SUBJECT can occur either before all the verbs, or after the finite verb. In order to allow for these two possibilities the formula would have to contain M-SUBJECT in many different places:

$$
\text{M-SUBJECT} \rightarrow
\left\{
\begin{array}{l}
\text{TO} \rightarrow \\
\text{PARTICIPLE} \\
\text{GERUND} \\
\text{FINITE}
\end{array}
\right\}
=
\left\{
\begin{array}{l}
(\text{PREPAST} \rightarrow \text{M-SUBJECT} \rightarrow \text{PAST} = \\
(\text{PREPERFECT} \rightarrow \text{M-SUBJECT} \rightarrow \text{PER-} \\
\text{FECT} = (\text{PREPROGRESSIVE} \rightarrow \text{M-} \\
\text{SUBJECT} \rightarrow \text{PROGRESSIVE} = (\text{BE} \rightarrow \\
\text{M-SUBJECT} \rightarrow \text{PASSIVE} = \\
\text{PROCESS})))))
\end{array}
\right.
$$

In other words, the formula would impose *no* restrictions on the place of M-SUBJECT, except that it cannot follow PROCESS. This would have the disadvantage, among others, of allowing

PREPERFECT	→	PREPROGRESSIVE	→	M-SUBJECT	→	PROGRESSIVE
FINITE		PERFECT				PROCESS
has		*been*		*he*		*taking*

Instead of this, we describe the sequence-relations among the verbal functions (including FINITE) in one formula, and the relations between PRE-SUBJECT and M-SUBJECT in another, and link the two by conflating PRE-

SUBJECT with FINITE. The former formula is the one we have just been discussing, and the latter is (1d):

$$\text{MOOD-FOCUS} \supseteqq (\text{PRE-SUBJECT} \rightarrow \text{M-SUBJECT}) \rightarrow \text{PROCESS}.$$

The function PRE-SUBJECT is introduced by addition-rule (3m):

$$+ \text{PRE-SUBJECT} \;//\; + \text{MOOD-FOCUS} \neq \text{SUBJECT}.$$

That is, it is obligatory wherever the clause is [independent, interrogative] (realised by MOOD-FOCUS) but is not a wh-question in which the wh-item is SUBJECT — in other words, it is obligatory in those environments where inversion of the finite verb with the subject takes place. Our sequence-rule ensures that PRE-SUBJECT precedes M-SUBJECT (and is conflated with MOOD-FOCUS), and conflation-rule (4d) gets PRE-SUBJECT conflated with FINITE, thus bringing into play all the sequence-restrictions involving FINITE.

As the reader will see, it would be quite impossible to handle all these relations in a single formula.

5.1.4. *The function-realisation rules*

Functions with and without realisations

Some of the functions that we have introduced so far help to restrict the *place* of the item concerned, others restrict its *features*, and others do both things. For instance, FIRST, SECOND and THIRD have nothing to do with features, since they simply help to get the item in the right place in the clause's structure; whereas PASSIVE-CL is concerned only with features, and not at all with position: it simply ensures that the item concerned has the feature [passive]. Many functions restrict the item's features as well as its position; for instance, LATE is the function of extraposed clauses, and is subject to a rule that it must come at the end of the matrix-clause's structure (structure-building sequence-rule (1c)), but it also restricts the features that the noun-clause can have, since a gerundival cannot (normally) be extraposed (see 4.2.2).

In the function-realisation rules below I shall list *all* the functions that we have introduced already, whether they have a realisation (i.e. whether they restrict the item's features) or not; so some functions will simply have a dash in the realisation column. However, in some cases it is to some extent arbitrary whether we assign a realisation to one function or to another.

For instance, there are three functions (among others) that the main verb

Table 5.2
The function-realisation rules.

Function	Realisation
ACTIVE-CL	*not* [passive]
ACTOR	[phrase, nominal] // *not* = CLAUSE *or* AGENT
ACTOR-CLAUSE	[V10/11]
ADDRESSED	[V12/31/32/33]
ADDRESSEE	[phrase, nominal]
AFFIX	—
AGENT	[finite] *or* [infinitival] *or* [gerundival, prepositional // = CLAUSE [phrase, prepositional] // *otherwise*
ALTERNATIVE	[pseudo-interrogative, alternative] // = CLAUSE
ATTRIBUANT	[phrase, nominal] // *not* = CLAUSE
ATTRIBUTE	[phrase, adjectival, A1/2/3/4/5/6/7]
BE	[be]
BINDER	[word, conjunction] // *not* = QUESTION *or* SUBJECT *or* COMPLEMENT *or* CLAUSE
CLAUSE	[dependent] // *not* = SUBSTITUTE *or* BINDER [as] // = BINDER
COMPLEMENT	—
COMPLETER	—
COPULAR	? [copular verb] ?
CRYPTO-PASSIVE	[special passive, passive]
FACT	[declarative]
FIN-CL	[finite] // *not* = SUBSTITUTE [with BINDER] // = M-SUBJECT
FINITE	[finite verb]
FIRST	—
FOR	[for]
FOR-LESS	[without *for*] // + M-SUBJECT ‖ FRONTED *or* *not* = SUBJECT
FRONTED	—
GERUND	[ing-form]
GERUND-CL	[gerundival] // *not* = TO-FULL *or* LATE
GOAL	[phrase, nominal] // *not* = CLAUSE
GOAL-CLAUSE	[V1/3/4/12/13/.../29] // *not* = ADDRESSED *or* PASSIVE [V3/4/12/13/.../27/30] // = PASSIVE *and* *not* = ADDRESSED
INCOMPLETE	[V12/13/17/37/38/39] = INTRANS
INDEFINITE	[gerundival] *or* [with to] // *not* = GOAL *or* FINITE [gerundival] // = GOAL *and* *not* = FINITE

Table 5.2 (continued)

Function	Realisation
INFIN-CL	[without to]
ING/EN	–
INTRANS	[V1/2/.../9] // *not* = INCOMPLETE
LATE	[with to] // *not* = FIN-CL *or* INDEFINITE
LEX	–
MOOD-FOCUS	–
M-SUBJECT	[it] // *not* = SUBJECT *or* FRONTED
NONPAST-CL	[non-past]
NONPERF-CL	[non-perfect]
NONPROG-CL	[non-progressive]
PARTICIPIAL-CL	['bare']
PARTICIPLE	[en-form] // = PASSIVE [ing-form] // = ING/EN *and not* = PASSIVE [infinitive] // *otherwise*
PASSIVE	[en-form]
PASSIVE-CL	[passive]
PAST	[past verb] // = FINITE [en-form] // *otherwise*
PERFECT	[en-form]
POST-SUBJECT	–
POST-VERB	–
PRE-CLAUSE	–
PREPAST	[have]
PREPERFECT	[have]
PREPROGRESSIVE	[be]
PRESUBJECT	–
PROCESS	[lexical verb]
PROGRESSIVE	[ing-form]
PROGRESSIVE-CL	[progressive]
PSEUDO-WH	[pseudo-interrogative, wh] [non-SUBJECT focus] // = SUBJECT
Q-FRONTED	–
QUESTION	[phrase, questioning] // = SUBJECT *or* COMPLEMENT, *and* *not* = PRE-CLAUSE [whether/if] // *not* = SUBJECT *or* COMPLEMENT *or* PRE- CLAUSE
REPORT	–
SECOND	–
SUBJECT	–

Table 5.2 (continued)

Function	Realisation
SUBJECTFULL	[with SUBJECT]
SUBJECTLESS	[without SUBJECT]
SUBSTITUTE	[so]
THAT	[that]
THIRD	–
TO	[to]
TO-FULL	[with to] *or* [gerundival] // = GERUND-CL *and not* = LATE [with to] // *otherwise*
TRANSITIVE	[V4/21/32/34/35/36]
I	[V12/13/14/15/16/17]
II	[V1/18/28]
III	[V29]
IV	[V18/28]
V	[V1/4/14/15]
VI	[V34/35/37]
VII	[V1]
VIII	[V2/3/4/5]
IX	[V5/35]
X	[V1/6/14/16/19]
XI	[V4/14/21/32/36/38]
XII	[A1/2]
XIII	[A1/3] *or* [V10/16/20/21/22]
XIV	[V1/21] // = GOAL-CLAUSE *and not* = PASSIVE [V12/13/15/17/39] // otherwise
XV	[A2/4] *or* [V7/11/22]
XVI	[A5/6] *or* [V8/9/18/23/24/30/31/32]
XVII	[A6/7] *or* [V9/18/24/25/30]
XVIII	[V25]
XIX	[V26/27/33]
XX	[V26/27]
XXI	[V27]

can have: INTRANS, TRANSITIVE and INCOMPLETE (meaning that the accompanying noun-clause has the function COMPLETER rather than GOAL). The first two cannot be conflated with each other, but they can be conflated with INCOMPLETE, yielding just three possible combinations: INTRANS,

without INCOMPLETE; INTRANS = INCOMPLETE; and TRANSITIVE =
INCOMPLETE. Each of these three combinations allows a different range of
lexical verb classes, and for the first combination, without INCOMPLETE, it
is clear that these classes should be treated as the realisation of INTRANS.
But with the other two combinations, should they be treated as the realisation
of INCOMPLETE or of the other function? I have arranged the realisation
rules in such a way that each of these functions has some realisation, but if
the reader considers the realisations given for INCOMPLETE, INTRANS and
TRANSITIVE he will see that the rules could have been different. The same
applies in several cases where one function acts as conditioning environment
for the realisation of another.

To make it easier for the reader to refer to these realisation rules I have
ordered them alphabetically, according to the name of the function, and
grouped them into a single list. The disadvantage with this approach, however,
is that the list gives no kind of overall picture of the relations among the rules.
I shall try to remedy this in tables 5.3 and 5.4.

The systemic relations of the realising features

The functions listed in the function-realisation rules all occur in the structures of matrix-clauses, but they cover a very wide range. Apart from the distinction already made between functions that are realised and those that are
not, we can distinguish functions according to the area of the system-network
from which they select features as their realisations. Some functions select
features of the noun-clause itself; some select features of a verb; some select
features of the 'predicate' (main verb or adjective phrase); and some select
features of a phrase or a word of some kind.

When we have a more complete system network for English, all the features
given as realisations in the above rules will presumably have a place in it, and
the network will show clearly how they are related to each other. Unfortunately, we are some way from being able to do this at present, and the best we
can do is to show how the first two kinds of feature are related, by referring
to the system-network given (in three different diagrams) in 5.1.1 above. That
is, we can locate the first kind of features in network B, giving features of
noun-clauses, and the second kind in the network giving features of verbs,
network C. As for the third and fourth kinds of feature, I have already admitted the difficulty in integrating the third kind into a system-network:
these are the 39 verb-classes and 7 adjective-classes that are distinguished in
4.2.15. All we can do with these is to list them. The fourth kind of features
are even more unsatisfactory: they are just a miscellany of phrase- and word-
features.

Table 5.3
Functions realised by features of the noun-clause.

Function	Realisation	
	Systems	Features
CLAUSE	1	[dependent] // *not* = SUBSTITUTE *or* BINDER
	?	[as] // = BINDER
NONPAST-CL	7	[non-past]
FIN-CL	8	[finite] // *not* = SUBSTITUTE
INDEFINITE	8, 15, 16	[finite] *or* [gerundival] *or* [with *to*] // *not* = GOAL
	8, 15	[finite] *or* [gerundival] // = GOAL
AGENT	8, 15, ?	[finite] *or* [infinitival] *or* [gerundival, prepositional] // = CLAUSE
	?	[phrase, prepositional] // *otherwise*
SUBJECTFULL	13	[with SUBJECT]
SUBJECTLESS	13	[without SUBJECT]
GERUND-CL	15	[gerundival] //·*not* = TO-FULL *or* LATE
TO-FULL	15, 16	[gerundival] *or* [with *to*] // = GERUND-CL *and not* = LATE
	16	[with to] // *otherwise*
INFIN-CL	16	[without *to*] // *not* = TO-FULL
LATE	16	[with *to*] // *not* = FIN-CL *or* INDEFINITE
FOR-LESS	17	[without *for*] // + M-SUBJECT ‖ FRONTED *or not* = SUBJECT
CRYPTO-PASSIVE	18, 42	[special passive, passive]
PARTICIPIAL-CL	19	['bare']
PASSIVE-CL	42	[passive]
ACTIVE-CL	42	*not* [passive]
NONPERF-CL	47	[non-perfect]
NON PROG-CL	48	[non-progressive]
PROGRESSIVE-CL	48	[progressive]

For the functions realised by the first two kinds of feature, we can thus offer them in a rather more revealing way, ordering them according to the systems from which they select features rather than alphabetically – hence tables 5.3 and 5.4.

These two lists include 35 functions out of a total of 94 functions. Of the remaining 59 functions, 16 have no realisation; 28 are realised by subclasses

Table 5.4
Functions realised by features of a verb.

Function	Realisation	
	Systems	Features
FINITE	49	[finite verb]
PAST	50	[past-verb] // = FINITE
	52	[en-form] // *otherwise*
GERUND	52	[ing-form]
PROGRESSIVE	52	[ing-form]
PASSIVE	52	[en-form]
PERFECT	52	[en-form]
PARTICIPLE	52	[en-form] // = PASSIVE
	52	[ing-form] // = ING/EN *and not* = PASSIVE
	52	[infinitive] // *otherwise*
PROCESS	53	[lexical verb]
BE	55	[be]
PREPROGRESSIVE	55	[be]
PREPAST	55	[have]
PREPERFECT	55	[have]

of lexical verbs or adjectival phrases; and 15 are realised by features which are ad hoc, notably those identifying classes pf phrases (nominal, adjectival, prepositional) and classes of conjunctions (*that, for*) or other kinds of words (*it, as*). Even the functions that *are* included in the above lists are not without problems, since some of them have alternative realisations that are not defined in our system-network − viz. CLAUSE and AGENT.

Although our system-network covers the realisations of only just over a third of the functions − or just under half of the realised functions − this should nevertheless be enough at least to give the reader a clear idea of the principles underlying this kind of grammar − and in particular, how the grammar links the system-network back to itself through the structure-building rules and function-realisation rules.

5.2. The noun-clause's place in the structure of the matrix clause

We now move on to the main task of this chapter: showing how the grammar that I have just presented handles the facts that I described in the last

Transitivity and voice in the matrix-clause.

A. System-network.

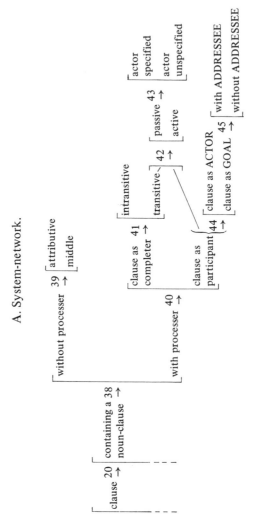

B. Feature-realisation rules.

System	Feature	Realisation
	clause	+ PROCESS + LEX = ATTRIBUTE // [attributive] + LEX = PROCESS // *otherwise*
20	containing a noun-clause	+ CLAUSE // *not* [clause as ACTOR, ACTOR unspecified]
38	without processer with processer	CLAUSE = SUBJECT + ACTOR // *not* [ACTOR unspecified]
39	attributive middle	+ ATTRIBUANT = CLAUSE + ATTRIBUTE + COPULAR = PROCESS + ACTOR = CLAUSE + INTRANS = PROCESS
40	clause as completer clause as participant	+ COMPLETER = CLAUSE + INCOMPLETE = PROCESS + GOAL
41	intransitive transitive	+ INTRANS = PROCESS ACTOR = SUBJECT + GOAL + TRANSITIVE = PROCESS
42	passive active	ADDRESSEE = SUBJECT // [with addressee] GOAL = SUBJECT // *otherwise* + PASSIVE // *not* [special passive] ACTOR = SUBJECT
43	actor specified actor unspecified	+ AGENT = ACTOR −
44	clause as ACTOR clause as GOAL	CLAUSE = ACTOR + ACTOR-CLAUSE = PROCESS CLAUSE = GOAL + GOAL-CLAUSE = PROCESS
45	with ADDRESSEE without ADDRESSEE	+ ADDRESSEE + ADDRESSED = PROCESS −

C. Structure-building rules

---

1. *The sequence-rules*

    (1b) BINDER $\leqq$ M-SUBJECT $\rightarrow$ PROCESS $\rightarrow$ POST-VERB
    (1c) FIRST $\rightarrow$ SECOND $\rightarrow$ THIRD $\rightarrow$ LATE

2. *The compatibility rules*

    (2h) BINDER $\neq$ COMPLETER
    (2l) POST-VERB $\neq$ QUESTION

3. *The addition rules*

    (3f) + FIRST = ADDRESSEE // + ADDRESSEE $\neq$ SUBJECT
    (3g) + SECOND = GOAL // + GOAL $\neq$ SUBJECT
    (3h) + THIRD = ATTRIBUTE, COMPLETER
    (3i) + POST-VERB = FIRST, SECOND, THIRD, AGENT, LATE
    (3j) + COMPLEMENT = FIRST, SECOND

---

chapter. We start off by looking at the way in which it allows the noun-clause to occur in a variety of places, with a variety of functions, in the matrix-clause. This discussion will be in three parts, each corresponding to a different section from the last chapter:

(1) The structure of the matrix-clause and the functions of the noun-clause (= 4.2.1);

(2) Extraposition (= 4.2.2);

(3) The possibility of a governing preposition (= 4.2.13).

5.2.1. *The structure of the matrix-clause and the functions of the noun-clause*

Transitivity and voice in the matrix-clause

The noun-clause can have any one of the functions ATTRIBUANT, ACTOR, GOAL and COMPLETER, and it may also have SUBJECT or COMPLEMENT. Which of these functions it has clearly depends partly on the 'transitivity' and voice of the matrix-clause, since it is this which determines which of these functions are present in the matrix-clause's structure. However, if both ACTOR and GOAL are present, the noun-clause may have either of them, so we have to assign one or the other to it. All these ranges of possibilities are formalised in systems 38 through 45, together with the relevant feature-realisation, structure building and function-realisation rules, which are brought together here (pp. 272–275) for ease of reference.

The noun-clause always has the function CLAUSE, introduced as realisa-

D. Function-realisation rules

Function	Realisation
1. Functions of the 'predicate'	
ACTOR-CLAUSE	[lexical verb, V10/11]
ADDRESSED	[lexical verb, V12/31/32/33]
ATTRIBUTE	[phrase, adjectival, A1/2/3/4/5/6/7]
COPULAR	[copular verb]
GOAL-CLAUSE	[lexical verb, V1/3/4/12/13.../29] // *not* = ADDRESSED *or* PASSIVE
	[lexical verb, V3/4/12/13.../27/30] // = PASSIVE *and not* = ADDRESSED
INCOMPLETE	[lexical verb, V12/13/17/37/38/39] // = INTRANS
INTRANS	[lexical verb, V1/2/.../9] // *not* = INCOMPLETE
LEX	–
PASSIVE	[en-form]
PROCESS	[lexical verb]
TRANSITIVE	[lexical verb, V4/21/32/34/35/36]
2. Other functions	
ACTOR	[phrase, nominal] // *not* = CLAUSE *or* AGENT
ADDRESSEE	[phrase, nominal]
AGENT	[finite] *or* [infinitival] *or* [gerundival, prepositional] // = CLAUSE
	[phrase, prepositional] // *otherwise*
ATTRIBUANT	[phrase, nominal] // *not* = CLAUSE
CLAUSE	[dependent] // *not* = SUBSTITUTE *or* BINDER
	[as] // = BINDER
COMPLEMENT	–
COMPLETER	–
FIRST	–
GOAL	[phrase, nominal] // *not* = CLAUSE
POST-VERB	–
SECOND	–
SUBJECT	–
THIRD	–

tion of [containing a noun-clause] (20), so the grammar has to introduce the other functions that the noun-clause can have, and arrange for CLAUSE to be conflated with them. The functions with which it has to be conflated are, according to 4.2.1, the following: SUBJECT or COMPLEMENT; and ATTRI-BUANT, ACTOR, GOAL or COMPLETER. We have to explain how these are introduced and how the right conflations are brought about.

ATTRIBUANT, COMPLETER, ACTOR and GOAL

ATTRIBUANT and COMPLETER are easy: they are introduced by the realisation-rules for [attributive] (39) and [clause as completer] (40) respectively, and as they are introduced they are already conflated with CLAUSE. ACTOR and GOAL are more complicated, since they are each introduced by two different realisation rules, and the conflations are not necessarily done by the same rules.

ACTOR is introduced by the rules for [middle] (39) and for [with processer] (38); if a clause does not have either of these features, it must have the feature [attributive], so one condition under which clauses do not have ACTOR in their structure is where they have the feature [attributive]. However, there is also an environmental condition on the presence of ACTOR: it is *not* present if the clause has the feature [actor unspecified] (43). This condition prevents ACTOR from being inserted only to be 'deleted' in some way in generating the structure of a clause like

> It is no longer believed *that the moon is made of cheese,*

which has the feature [actor unspecified] but is otherwise like

> It is no longer believed by reputable astronomers *that*
> *the moon is made of cheese.*

Thus not all clauses other than [attributive] ones contain ACTOR: if the clause is passive, ACTOR is optional. This condition is stated in the realisa-tion-rule for [with processer] (38).

As for the conflation of ACTOR with CLAUSE, this is effected by two realisation-rules: by the rule for [middle] (39), which is also one of the rules that introduces ACTOR; and by the rule for [clause as ACTOR] (44). Sys-tem 44 contrasts this latter feature with [clause as GOAL], and reflects the fact that if the matrix clause defines (or implies) two participants — one re-ferred to by the noun-clause, the other by another item — then either of them can be treated as the 'actor'. The following pair, for instance, are distinguished by this system (and only by this system);

His typing the letter hurt her	[clause as ACTOR] ,
She resented *his typing the letter*	[clause as GOAL] .

Turning now to GOAL, this is introduced by the rules for two different features: [clause as participant] (40) and [transitive] (41). According to this rather oversimplified grammar, if the noun-clause is a participant in the clause, whether its own function is ACTOR or GOAL, the matrix clause's structure must always contain GOAL — unlike ACTOR, which can be absent if the matrix-clause is [passive] . But if the noun-clause is not a 'participant' but just a 'completer' of the verb, the matrix-clause may or may not contain GOAL; the choice between having and not having GOAL is reflected by system 41. The following is an example of a minimal pair contrasted by this system:

She remembered *to switch the engine on*	[intransitive] ,
He reminded her *to switch the engine on*	[transitive] .

So if GOAL realises the feature [transitive] , it is not the function of the noun-clause but of a noun-phrase (*her*).

For the conflation of CLAUSE with GOAL, the rules are relatively straightforward: if the matrix-clause has the feature [clause as GOAL] (44), CLAUSE is always conflated with GOAL, otherwise they are never conflated. That is, it is only if GOAL is introduced by the *first* of the two rules above — that for [clause as participant] — that it can be conflated with CLAUSE.

Let us review the four functions ATTRIBUANT, COMPLETER, ACTOR and GOAL. They are introduced by feature-realisation rules, and the same kinds of rules — and, in some cases, the same rules — conflate them with CLAUSE where appropriate. The rules are formulated in such a way that none of these functions will conflate with each other — though this can be proved only by considering the whole grammar, which the reader can do for himself. Consequently, there is no need to explicitly prevent them from conflating with each other, by means of structure-building compatibility-rules. However, although they cannot conflate with each other, they can conflate with SUBJECT and COMPLEMENT, which we shall consider below.

ATTRIBUTE and ADDRESSEE
Three of the four functions we have just discussed are functions that

phrases can have as well as noun-clauses: these are ATTRIBUANT, ACTOR and GOAL. And, in fact our grammar will generate both kinds of structure: CLAUSE is combined with only one of these functions in any one structure, so the other(s) must be realised by noun-phrases. There are two other functions which it includes, however, and which are always realised by phrases, never by clauses (at least as far as the grammar goes): ATTRIBUTE and ADDRESSEE. According to the grammar — which is here vastly oversimplified — ATTRIBUTE allows only adjective-phrases as its realisation; and ADDRESSEE allows only noun-phrases. (ADDRESSEE is the noun-phrase that occurs as 'indirect object' with verbs like *tell*, *remind* and *promise*.)

These two functions are introduced in a simple way: by the realisation-rules for [attributive] (39) and for [with ADDRESSEE] (45) respectively.

SUBJECT

We now turn to SUBJECT, and start by considering the rules for conflating it with other functions. If the matrix-clause is [without processer] (38) or [intransitive] (41) — i.e. if it is not subject to the [active] : [passive] contrast — then SUBJECT must conflate with ATTRIBUANT or ACTOR. This is effected by the realisation-rules for these features, though only indirectly in the case of [without processer] : this feature itself requires the conflation of CLAUSE with SUBJECT, but since CLAUSE is conflated with ATTRIBUANT and ACTOR respectively by the realisation-rules for [attributive] and [middle], this automatically ensures the conflation of SUBJECT with these two functions as well.

If the matrix-clause *is* open to the voice contrast, SUBJECT is conflated with ACTOR or GOAL (or ADDRESSEE), according to whether the clause is [active] or [passive]. If it is [active], ACTOR is conflated with SUBJECT, but if [passive], it is ADDRESSEE or GOAL that is conflated with SUBJECT (see the realisation-rules for [active] and [passive] (42)). If ADDRESSEE is present, then it must be SUBJECT in the passive clause:

The audience were told *that they should applaud vigorously.*

Otherwise the SUBJECT of the passive is also GOAL:

It was suggested *that they should applaud vigorously.*

The function with which SUBJECT conflates is thus determined by one of the realisation-rules just mentioned. There remains the question where SUBJECT comes from — that is, what decides whether it shall be present or not.

For this, we must turn to a completely different set of features, which are out-side the network that I repeated at the beginning of this section: [indicative] (2), [finite] (8), and [with SUBJECT] (13). In other words, whether or not a clause contains a subject depends not on its transitivity and voice, but on its mood — [indicative] or [imperative] — and its 'dependency-type' — [finite] or [non-finite], and if [non-finite], then [with SUBJECT] or [without SUB-JECT]. So for instance, the following pair of clauses are the same except that one is [indicative] (and therefore does have a SUBJECT) while the other is [imperative] (and does not):

> You can tell her *that you stayed late at the office*,
> Tell her *that you stayed late at the office*.

The fact that SUBJECT may or may not be present, independently of all the contrasts we have described so far, obviously has important implications for the structures realising the latter: a rule which realises one of these fea-tures by conflating some function (say, ACTOR) with SUBJECT will not work if there *is* no SUBJECT. Moreover, not only must the other function not be conflated with the non-existent SUBJECT, but the former must not be present at all. In order to ensure this, we have taken advantage of the general convention for interpreting rules of the form '(+) F = F' (p. 83): if the second function (F) is not present in the structure, then the first one must not be present either.

In other words, a clause whose features do not require SUBJECT to be present, may also have features which normally require other functions to be conflated with SUBJECT. In the absence of SUBJECT, any function which would have been conflated with SUBJECT by other rules is simply not intro-duced into the clause's structure. Thus the last two examples quoted have the same features except that one has [imperative] where the other has [indica-tive] : they both have [with processer, clause as participant, active, clause as GOAL, with ADDRESSEE] for instance. The first of these features is nor-mally realised by the presence of ACTOR, and the third by the conflation of ACTOR with SUBJECT; but since SUBJECT is never introduced into the structure of the second example, ACTOR cannot be conflated with it, and therefore is not introduced by the realisation-rule for [with processer].

COMPLEMENT

The grammar has to assign the function COMPLEMENT to any noun-clause that is a 'participant' — i.e. that is not simply a 'completer' — and that is not SUBJECT. In order to do this, there is no need to use a feature-

realisation rule at all – and, in fact, the reader will find that COMPLEMENT
is not mentioned in any of the feature-realisation rules. Instead, it is introduced by a structure-building addition-rule (rule 3j):

+ COMPLEMENT = FIRST, SECOND.

As for the functions FIRST and SECOND, they too are introduced by
addition-rules (rules 3f and 3g):

+ FIRST = ADDRESSEE // + ADDRESSEE ≠ SUBJECT,
+ SECOND = GOAL // + GOAL ≠ SUBJECT.

We shall return below to these two functions, to see how they fit into the
grammar. From the point of view of our present discussion, it should be clear
how they help to get COMPLEMENT conflated with the right functions: they
themselves conflate with ADDRESSEE or GOAL (provided these are not conflated with SUBJECT, as they are in passive clauses), and therefore COMPLE-
MENT must also conflate with these functions if it conflates with FIRST or
SECOND.

Moreover, COMPLEMENT will *not* conflate with COMPLETER, since this
is conflated with THIRD (rule 3h) and not with FIRST or SECOND; nor will
it conflate with SUBJECT, since ADDRESSEE and GOAL do not conflate
with FIRST and SECOND when they are subject in a passive clause. Thus our
rules conflate COMPLEMENT with the right functions – GOAL and
ADDRESSEE – and only do so under the right circumstances.

Summary of the introduction and conflation of these functions
It may help the reader if I bring together the various functions I have discussed and the things I have said about them. The easiest way to do this is by
running through the network comprising systems 38 through 45, showing the
effect that each feature has on the matrix-clause's structure (table 5.5). To do
this we can pretend that the systems are ordered, and that each time we select
a feature we apply its realisation-rule to the structure defined by the previous
feature, so that the structure will be built up cumulatively until we reach the
right-hand edge of the network.

For instance, we start off with a structure consisting simply of CLAUSE,
realising [containing a noun-clause] (20); then we select [without processer],
which conflates CLAUSE with SUBJECT; and finally we select [attributive],
which adds ATTRIBUANT and conflates it with CLAUSE, which is itself
already conflated with SUBJECT. Thus, the combination of features [con-

Table 5.5

Features	Structure
containing a noun-clause	[+ CLAUSE]
┌without processer	+ CLAUSE = SUBJECT
│ ┌attributive	* + *ATTRIBUANT = CLAUSE = SUBJECT*
│ └middle	* + *ACTOR = CLAUSE = SUBJECT*
└with processer	[+ ACTOR], [+ CLAUSE]
┌clause as completer	+ COMPLETER = CLAUSE, [+ ACTOR]
│ ┌intransitive	* + *ACTOR = SUBJECT, + COMPLETER = CLAUSE*
│ └transitive	+ GOAL, + COMPLETER = CLAUSE, [+ ACTOR]
│ ┌passive	+ GOAL = SUBJECT, + COMPLETER = CLAUSE, [+ ACTOR]
│ ┌actor specified	* + *AGENT = ACTOR, + GOAL = SUBJECT, + COMPLETER = CLAUSE*
│ └actor unspecified	* + *GOAL = SUBJECT, + COMPLETER = CLAUSE*
│ └active	* + *ACTOR = SUBJECT, + GOAL, + COMPLETER = CLAUSE*
└clause as participant	+ GOAL, [+ ACTOR], [+ CLAUSE]
┌clause as ACTOR	[+ CLAUSE = ACTOR], + GOAL
│ ┌passive	+ GOAL = SUBJECT, [+ CLAUSE = ACTOR]
│ ┌actor specified	* + *AGENT = CLAUSE = ACTOR, + GOAL = SUBJECT*
│ └actor unspecified	* + *GOAL = SUBJECT*
│ └active	* + *CLAUSE = ACTOR = SUBJECT, + GOAL*
└clause as GOAL	+ CLAUSE = GOAL, [+ ACTOR]
┌with ADDRESSEE	+ ADDRESSEE, + CLAUSE = GOAL, [+ ACTOR]
│ ┌passive	+ ADDRESSEE = SUBJECT, + CLAUSE = GOAL, [+ ACTOR]
│ ┌actor specified	* + *AGENT = ACTOR, + ADDRESSEE = SUBJECT, + CLAUSE = GOAL*
│ └actor unspecified	* + *ADDRESSEE = SUBJECT, + CLAUSE = GOAL*
│ └active	* + *ACTOR = SUBJECT, + ADDRESSEE, + CLAUSE = GOAL*
└without ADDRESSEE	+ CLAUSE = GOAL, [+ ACTOR]
┌passive	+ CLAUSE = GOAL = SUBJECT, [+ ACTOR]
┌actor specified	* + *AGENT = ACTOR, + CLAUSE = GOAL = SUBJECT*
└actor unspecified	* + *CLAUSE = GOAL = SUBJECT*
└active	* + *ACTOR = SUBJECT, + CLAUSE = GOAL*

taining a noun-clause, without processer, attributive] requires a structure in which ATTRIBUANT, CLAUSE and SUBJECT are conflated.

In the table above, I only show the structural patterns that result directly from the feature-realisation rules — in other words, I do not include COMPLEMENT or FIRST and SECOND among the functions. Some functions are present only if [actor unspecified] is *not* selected, but this feature is one of the last ones that we introduce, being on the right-hand edge of the network. To simplify the diagram, I introduce these functions right from the start, but enclose them in square brackets so long as the feature [actor unspecified] could be selected; but as soon as I select a feature which excludes [actor specified], I remove the brackets — and when I select [actor specified] itself, I remove the contents of the brackets. When I have selected from all the available systems, I asterisk the structure: as far as the rules I have discussed so far are concerned, the italicized structures cannot be specified any more precisely. Note, incidentally, that I have not yet mentioned the question of *sequence* in the structures, and even the asterisked structures are still unordered sets of function-bundles. I shall come to the question of sequence on p. 285.

The selection of the lexical verb

The distinctions that I have been discussing so far clearly have a lot to do with the selection of the main verb in the matrix clause: different combinations of features will allow different ranges of verbs. For instance, if the matrix clause's features include [without processer, middle], it will have an 'intransitive' verb that allows a clause as subject — like *seem* or *matter* — but if it is [without processer, attributive], it will have a 'copular' verb. In principle, the systems relating to voice, [passive]:[active] (42) and [actor specified]:[actor unspecified] (43), are irrelevant to the selection of the main verb, but otherwise the systems are all relevant, and every feature allows a different range of verbs.

These restrictions are formalised in our grammar as follows. Certain of the features have realisations which include a function conflated with PROCESS, the function of the main verb. For instance, [middle] (39) is realised (in part) by the presence of INTRANS conflated with PROCESS. Each of these functions is in turn realised by some range of classes of lexical verb, taken from our list of thirty-nine classes, as shown in the first set of function-realisation rules quoted on p. 275. For instance, INTRANS (when not conflated with INCOMPLETE, for which see below) is realised by classes V1, 2, 3, 4, 5, 6, 7, 8 and 9. That is, a verb which has the function INTRANS (but not INCOMPLETE) must belong to one of these nine classes.

The functions that restrict the main verb in this way are: ACTOR-CLAUSE, ADDRESSED, COPULAR, GOAL-CLAUSE, INCOMPLETE, INTRANS and TRANSITIVE. The features they realise are as follows:

[attributive] ——————— COPULAR
[middle] ——————
[intransitive] ———— INTRANS
[transitive] ——————— TRANSITIVE
[clause as completer] ————INCOMPLETE
[clause as ACTOR]——————ACTOR-CLAUSE
[clause as GOAL]—————— GOAL-CLAUSE
[with ADDRESSEE]——————ADDRESSED

However, a complication arises from the way in which the features are related in the network: [transitive] and [intransitive] occur only if [clause as completer] also occurs, so their realisations (TRANSITIVE and INTRANS) will also be bound to occur with the realisation of [clause as completer] (IN-COMPLETE); and the same goes, mutatis mutandis, for [with ADDRESSEE] and [clause as GOAL]. On the other hand, [middle] cannot occur with [clause as completer], so the latter's realisation will always be absent and we can use INTRANS as the realisation of [middle] without danger of it being confused with INTRANS realising [intransitive], since the latter will always be conflated with INCOMPLETE.

Thus the functions found with the features that I listed above will in fact be the following:

[attributive]	COPULAR
[middle]	INTRANS
[clause as completer, intransitive]	INCOMPLETE = INTRANS
[clause as completer, transitive]	INCOMPLETE = TRANSITIVE
[clause as ACTOR]	ACTOR-CLAUSE
[clause as GOAL, without ADDRESSEE]	GOAL-CLAUSE
[clause as GOAL, with ADDRESSEE]	GOAL-CLAUSE = ADDRESSED

The function-realisation rules define the verb-classes possible for each of these combinations of functions. Except for [copular verb], these classes are those listed in the appendix.

The selection of the 'predicate'

Except where the matrix clause is [attributive], the main verb is sensitive to the 'construction-set' represented by the clause — e.g. to whether it is a 'perception' construction or a 'factive' one, and so on. We shall return to this question in 5.7.2 below, but I can give here part of the solution to the problem of how we are to relate the larger construction to the matrix clause's main verb: to the extent that 'transitivity' differences are involved in the distinction between construction-sets, they will automatically lead to the selection of different classes of verbs as I have described above.

There is a small complication though: where the matrix clause is [attributive], it is the adjective-phrase acting as ATTRIBUTE, and not the main verb, that is sensitive to the construction-set. For instance, the difference between *suppose* and *regret* in the following pair:

> I suppose *that she provoked him,*
> I regret *that she provoked him.*

is parallelled by the difference between *likely* and *regrettable* in the following:

> It's likely *that she provoked him,*
> It's regrettable *that she provoked him.*

In each pair the first example is a 'modal' construction, while the second is a 'reaction' one.

Consequently, when it comes to distinguishing the classes of lexical item associated with each construction-set, we shall want to refer to the 'predicate' item, including both the main verb of a non-attributive clause and the adjective-phrase of an attributive clause. In order to do this, we introduce the function LEX (see the realisation-rule for [clause]) and conflate it with PROCESS or ATTRIBUTE as the case may be; and then we simply locate in LEX all the relevant grammatical restrictions on the lexical predicate. This means among other things that of the seven function combinations listed above, all but COPULAR occur conflated with LEX.

Voice in the matrix-clause

One of the facts that I noted in 4.2.1 was that for some constructions the matrix clause must not be [passive] even if for other reasons we identify one of its ICs as GOAL: for instance, *want* cannot occur in a passive clause (except when 'pseudo-clefted'), whereas *intend* can:

> *It is wanted *for the programme to start soon.*
> It is intended *for the programme to start soon.*

It is easy to build this restriction into the grammar, since one of the realisations of [passive] is PASSIVE conflated with PROCESS (by the sequence-rule (1a)): we simply prevent verbs like *want* from having the function PASSIVE. That is, when defining the realisation of GOAL-CLAUSE, we give two different realisations, one with PASSIVE, the other without (the rule is quoted in the list on p. 275). The verb *want* belongs to class V1, which realises GOAL-CLAUSE in the absence of PASSIVE, but not otherwise.

Conversely, there are a few verbs for which the matrix clause *has* to be [passive] — such as *repute* and *rumour*:

It is rumoured *that bank-rate is going up*,
*They rumour *that bank-rate is going up.*

The same kind of expedient can be used for stating this restriction: we simply make PASSIVE an obligatory function for this class of verbs. In other words, we include them (viz., class V30) in the realisation of GOAL-CLAUSE when it is conflated with PASSIVE, but not otherwise.

The sequence of elements in the matrix-clause

So far the rules I have quoted have accounted for the presence of a function, or for the fact that it is conflated with some other function; but none of them have given any information about the *order* in which functions occur in the matrix-clause's structure. For instance, in the 'structures' that we built up by applying the feature-realisation rules one after the other (see the last table) the function-bundles are completely unordered; one of them was quoted as follows:

+ AGENT = ACTOR, + GOAL = SUBJECT, + COMPLETER = CLAUSE,

but the three bundles could equally well have been listed in a different order — or put one above the other in a column.

To the extent that we can define an order for the functions, this is done by the structure-building rules, as follows. By addition-rules (3f), (3g) and (3h), the functions FIRST, SECOND and THIRD are added and conflated with ADDRESSEE (FIRST), GOAL (SECOND) and (THIRD) ATTRIBUTE or COMPLETER, provided only that these functions are not conflated with SUBJECT. Then sequence-rule (1c) applies to get these three functions in the right order:

FIRST → SECOND → THIRD.

This ensures, for instance, that when ADDRESSEE and GOAL are both present, ADDRESSEE precedes GOAL:

He assured all the people in the room *that there was no danger*,

rather than following it:

*He assured *that there was no danger* all the people in the room.

Similarly, it guarantees that GOAL and COMPLETER will occur in that order:

He persuaded all the people in the room *to keep quiet*,
*He persuaded *to keep quiet* all the people in the room.

Another addition-rule (31) adds POST-VERB and conflates it with FIRST, SECOND or THIRD, and also with AGENT and LATE (which has not yet been introduced). Sequence-rule (1b) tells us that POST-VERB must follow PROCESS, so these two rules between them make sure that ADDRESSEE, GOAL, ATTRIBUTE and COMPLETER follow the main verb, except when they are conflated with SUBJECT. Note, incidentally, that they do *not* tell us the sequence relation between AGENT and these functions: they simply tell us that AGENT must follow PROCESS. This is intentional, since AGENT can either precede or follow any of them — though it is probably more usual for it to come before the noun-clause than after it:

People have often been persuaded by unscrupulous politicians
    to go to war,
People have often been persuaded *to go to war*
    by unscrupulous politicians.

The rules as stated so far work for the simple cases, but they need qualify-ing to cover more complicated constructions. For instance, the functions just listed do *not* follow PROCESS if they are conflated with QUESTION, as ADDRESSEE is in

Who did you tell *that you were working here*?

This particular complication is in fact covered by our rules: there is a compatibility rule (21) which prevents POST-VERB from conflating with QUES-TION, and a general convention (p. 87) that the addition-rules (including the one that adds POST-VERB) apply only if they do not lead to a conflict with any of the other rules. Since adding POST-VERB and conflating it with ADDRESSEE in the above example *would* lead to a conflict (with compatibility rule (21)), POST-VERB is not added. Thus our generalisation that POST-VERB always follows PROCESS is saved.

I have not yet mentioned the position of SUBJECT, which is obviously a crucial function since its position determines the position of other functions conflated with it. We must leave this question to the discussion of extraposition in the next section.

Summary

This section has dealt at some length with the way in which our grammar generates a range of feature-combinations for matrix-clauses and the structures associated with each combination of features. We have shown how we can classify matrix-clauses according to their 'transitivity' and voice, and map these class-distinctions onto fairly complicated structural-distinctions, which in turn are mapped onto class-distinctions at a lower 'rank', that of verbs.

The grammar has formalised all the facts that I described in 4.2.1, with one exception: I have not tried to formalise the rules for forming pseudo-cleft sentences. All I have been able to do on this score is to lay the basis for such an analysis by making distinctions that it will need to refer to, such as that between COMPLEMENT and COMPLETER.

It should not be surprising that the grammar turns out to be quite complicated: in this grammar I have in fact gone *beyond* the facts in 4.2.1, in order to cover some topics that are not restricted to constructions involving noun-clauses; but even if we had kept strictly to the facts there, the grammar would have been complicated.

5.2.2. Extraposition

In this section we have to account for the two possible positions of a SUBJECT noun-clause: before the main verb or extraposed; and we have also to account for various restrictions on extraposition.

The position of an extraposed noun-clause

Basically, the generation of extraposed noun-clauses is very simple: there is a system (system 46) which contrasts [normal] with [extraposed] , and which applies to all clauses with the feature [containing a noun-clause] , completely independently of all the other systems that apply to such clauses. Thus the matrix-clauses in the following have the features [normal] and [extraposed] respectively:

> *For the gear-box to wear out* is fairly common with this model,
> It's fairly common with this model *for the gear-box to wear out*.

Only one of these features has any realisation: [extraposed] is realised by the presence of the function LATE conflated with CLAUSE; and LATE is mentioned in one of the sequence-rules (1c), part of which was quoted in the previous section:

> FIRST → SECOND → THIRD → LATE.

This sequence-rule gets the extraposed clause in the right place in the clause — after GOAL, ATTRIBUTE, and so on, but not necessarily at the absolute end of the clause, since our rules say nothing about adverbials. Thus our grammar allows the following just as much as the second of the examples above:

> It's fairly common *for the gear-box to wear out* with this model.

There are a number of other structure-building rules which refer to LATE. First of all, there is one which guarantees that the extraposed clause will be SUBJECT:

(2m)   LATE ≠ CLAUSE // CLAUSE ≠ SUBJECT.

That is, LATE cannot conflate with CLAUSE if CLAUSE is not conflated with SUBJECT: in other words, LATE must conflate with SUBJECT.

Before we turn to the other rules which impose restrictions on the extraposed clause, I must say how our grammar generates noun-clauses that are *not* extraposed. It may seem odd to have accounted for the extraposed ones before the normal ones, but there is a reason for this: it is easy to define the latter by excluding the former, and then we can formulate rules to put the latter in the right place in the matrix-clause's structure.

The 'normal' SUBJECT noun-clauses are those that do not have the function LATE, and their place is defined by the place of SUBJECT, so we have the following conflation-rule

(4f)   M-SUBJECT = SUBJECT // SUBJECT ≠ LATE.

The place of M-SUBJECT itself is defined by sequence-rules (1b) and (1d), especially the latter:

(1d)   MOOD-FOCUS ≅ (PRE-SUBJECT → M-SUBJECT) → PROCESS.

That is, it must precede the main verb, and must follow the finite verb when the latter has the function PRE-SUBJECT (see the discussion of these relations in 5.1.3 above) — i.e. when the finite verb and the 'subject' are inverted.

The position of SUBJECT is thus determined by the position of one of two othe functions, LATE and M-SUBJECT, according to whether it is extraposed or not. This is why we could not deal with it in the last section.

Restrictions on extraposition

The grammar so far suggests that extraposition is always the result of a free choice, with only one constraint: that the noun-clause should have the function SUBJECT. We know from 4.2.2 that this is far from true, since extraposition is obligatory in some environments, and impossible in others.

Let us start with the environments where it is *impossible*: it is impossible if the noun-clause is [gerundival], unless the matrix-clause has the feature [reaction]:

> *It's common *having a puncture when one's in a hurry*,
> It's irritating *having a puncture when one's in a hurry*.

This time the restriction is located not in the structure-building rules, but in the function-realisation rules: the realisation-rule for LATE is as follows:

[with to] // *not* = FIN-CL *or* INDEFINITE.

In other words, an extraposed clause must have the feature [with to] (implying [infinitival]) unless it also has one of the functions FIN-CL (which makes it have [finite] instead) and INDEFINITE, which is the function of the noun-clause in a [reaction] environment — i.e. in precisely the environment where [gerundival] clauses *are* possible. Thus the noun-clause with *irritating* has the function INDEFINITE, so it does not have to be [infinitival], but can be [gerundival]; whereas with *common* it does not have this function, and does have to be [infinitival].

There are three environments in which extraposition is *obligatory*. First of all, if the matrix-clause is [modal] and contains no COMPLEMENT:

> It seems/is generally assumed *that she forgot*,
> **That she forgot* seems/is generally assumed.

The noun-clause in these constructions has the function REPORT, but only if the matrix-clause is *not* [attributive] : this is ensured by the realisation-rule for [modal] (34):

> + REPORT = CLAUSE // *not* [attributive] .

It is only when the matrix-clause is [attributive] that there is a COMPLE-MENT when the noun-clause is SUBJECT, so this rule has REPORT conflated with CLAUSE just in those cases where the noun-clause has to be extraposed. We can now formulate a simple compatibility rule which makes extraposition obligatory for the noun-clause:

(2p)   REPORT ≠ SUBJECT // CLAUSE ≠ LATE.

Secondly, extraposition is obligatory if the noun-clause is SUBJECT and GOAL − i.e. subject in a passive noun-clause − and is infinitival.

> **To reject him* was agreed,
> It was agreed *to reject him*.

The only circumstances which allow this situation to arise also require the noun-clause to have the function TO-FULL (meaning that it has to be an infinitival clause containing *to*), so we can make extraposition obligatory by applying another compatibility rule:

(2s)   TO-FULL ≠ SUBJECT // CLAUSE ≠ LATE *and*
                 SUBJECT = GOAL.

Thirdly, it is obligatory if QUESTION or SUBJECT or COMPLEMENT is fronted − that is, if the function PRE-CLAUSE is present.

> **He to be asleep* seemed,
> *He* seemed *to be asleep*.

Once again, we use a compatibility rule to state this restriction:

(2r)   CLAUSE ≠ SUBJECT // CLAUSE ≠ LATE *and* + PRE-CLAUSE.

The expletive 'it'

The last of these restrictions on the choice between extraposing and not extraposing raises another question: when does extraposition lead to the use of the 'expletive' *it*? For instance, the last example was:

He seemed *to be asleep*,

which involves extraposition but no *it*, whereas all the earlier examples did involve *it*. The factual answer is that *it* occurs whenever there is no fronting of SUBJECT or COMPLEMENT (see 4.2.5); but how do we show in our grammar whether *it* occurs or not?

This is done by the function-realisation rules — unlike the other facts relating to extraposition, which have been reflected by systems or structure-building rules. The relevant rule is the one that gives the realisation for M-SUBJECT:

[it] // *not* = SUBJECT *or* FRONTED.

The feature [it] is an ad hoc feature introduced to define the word-class whose one member is *it*. The rule in effect says that M-SUBJECT operates its own realisation restrictions (requiring the feature [it]) only if there is no other function conflated with it that might do so: if it is combined with SUBJECT or FRONTED these functions will themselves be conflated with other functions, such as ACTOR and CLAUSE, that have realisations, but failing such functions, the 'unmarked' realisation of M-SUBJECT occurs.

How then do SUBJECT and FRONTED get conflated with M-SUBJECT, thereby preventing it from being realised as *it*? We have already seen the rule which conflates SUBJECT with it:

(4f)   M-SUBJECT = SUBJECT // SUBJECT ≠ LATE.

The rule which conflates FRONTED with M-SUBJECT is

(4g)   FRONTED = M-SUBJECT // + CLAUSE = SUBJECT.

5.2.3. *The possibility of a governing preposition*

The fact that we have to handle here was described in 4.2.13: if a noun-clause is ACTOR in a passive matrix-clause, it may or may not be preceded by the preposition *by*:

> *Losing all her friends* depressed her,
> She was depressed by *losing all her friends*,
> *That all her friends had deserted her* depressed her,
> She was depressed *that all her friends had deserted her.*

If the noun-clause is [gerundival], *by* occurs — though it often seems to be replaced by other prepositions in this environment, such as *at* for the above example; but if it is [infinitival] or [finite] there is no *by*.

This fact too is reflected by a function-realisation rule, namely that for AGENT, with which ACTOR is always conflated in passive clauses (by the realisation-rule for [actor specified] (43)):

> [finite] *or* [infinitival] *or* [gerundival, prepositional] //
>   = CLAUSE
> [phrase, prepositional] // *otherwise.*

This rule involves an ad hoc feature, or rather combination of features: [gerundival, prepositional] . These features are intended to define the class of items consisting of *by* followed by a gerundival clause — a sub-class of [phrase] rather than of [clause] , although, exceptionally, it would have the function CLAUSE. Otherwise, the rule is self-explanatory, except that it should be seen in conjunction with the realisation-rule for ACTOR, which is formulated in such a way that it does *not* require ACTOR to be a noun-phrase when conflated with AGENT:

> [phrase, nominal] // *not* = CLAUSE *or* AGENT.

5.3. Finite and non-finite noun-clauses

In this section I shall show how the grammar handles the distinctions between finite and non-finite clauses, and between the various kinds of non-finite clause: participial, infinitival, gerundival; with or without SUBJECT; and with or without BINDER. All of these distinctions are closely related to the noun-clause's environment, but I should like to draw the reader's attention to the different ways in which the environment restricts the 'finiteness' of the noun-clause, and the correspondingly wide range of ways in which the restrictions are formalised in the grammar.

There will be three sub-sections, which again each correspond to one sub-section in the last chapter:
(1) The finiteness of the noun-clause (= 4.2.3);
(2) The presence or absence of SUBJECT in the noun-clause (= 4.2.4);
(3) The presence or absence of BINDER in the noun-clause (= 4.2.8).

5.3.1. *The finiteness of the noun-clause*

In 4.2.3 we were not able to do much more than define the various finiteness-types for noun-clauses, and make some very general observations concerning the environments in which these types occurred. Now that we have not only 4.2.3 but the whole of chapter 4 to build on, we can relate the noun-clause's finiteness to many other factors in its environment.

The finiteness options regardless of environment

Before we define the restrictions which the environment imposes on the noun-clause's finiteness, we have to define the range of possibilities on which these restrictions are imposed. This is done by systems 1, 8, 14, 15, 16 and 19, which are to be found in the network that applies to noun-clauses (network B, p. 248). They are repeated below for convenience.

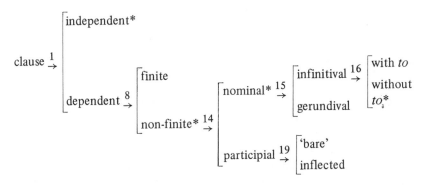

The noun-clause is always [dependent], and it cannot be [inflected] — such clauses are typically used as post-modifiers, rather than as noun-clauses. Otherwise all the possibilities defined by the network are found in noun-clauses, and are illustrated by the following.

[finite]   She saw *that he was eating her sandwiches,*

[non-finite, nominal, infinitival, with *to*]	He wanted *to eat her sandwiches,*
[non-finite, nominal, infinitival, without *to*]	She let him *eat her sandwiches,*
[non-finite, nominal, gerundival]	He enjoyed *eating her sandwiches,*
[non-finite, participial, 'bare']	She watched *him eat(ing) her sandwiches.*

I have already described the way in which the grammar generates the structures and correct verb-forms for these features, in the chapter on non-finite
clauses, so there is nothing more to be added on that question.

Environmental restrictions
    The environment always constrains the noun-clause's choice from these
systems to some extent, and in most cases it leaves only one combination of
features possible; but it should be remembered, when one works through the
relevant parts of the grammar, that the network is not restricted if no restriction is explicitly stated, although this situation arises in only one kind of environment.
    The environments that restrict the finiteness of the clause are first and
foremost those that are distinguished by systems 23 through 37 — that is, the
twenty-one 'construction-sets' — and secondarily those distinguished by the
presence or absence of extraposition.

Structural differences between construction-sets
    The realisation-rules for the features in systems 23 through 37 are rather
complicated, since a lot of them offer alternative, environmentally conditioned, realisations, and each realisation may involve more than one function.
However, not all functions are relevant to the noun-clause's finiteness, so we
can ignore some of the complexity. However, it would still take too long to
go through the realisation rules for all the features in each of the possible
combinations of features, so I shall just take one combination as an example.
    Consider the following combination, which is generated by the system-
network: [clause, containing a noun-clause, non-finite noun-clause, restricted-
tense noun-clause, restricted-aspect noun-clause, special noun-clause, un-
restricted-voice noun-clause, 'perception', non-progressive noun-clause]. The
realisation rules for these features are repeated in table 5.6 for convenience,
omitting all the irrelevant functions — e.g. PROCESS, LEX, NONPAST-CL,
and so on.

Table 5.6

System	Feature	Realisation
	clause	–
20	containing a noun-clause	+ CLAUSE // *not* [clause as ACTOR, ACTOR unspecified]
23	non-finite noun-clause	–
24	restricted-tense noun-clause	–
25	restricted-aspect noun-clause	–
26	special noun-clause	+ TO-FULL = CLAUSE // [unrestricted-aspect noun-clause] *or* [restricted-aspect noun-clause passive]
27	unrestricted-voice noun-clause	–
28	'perception'	+ PARTICIPIAL-CL = CLAUSE // *not* [passive]
29	non-progressive noun-clause	–

Only three rules contribute to the relevant parts of the clause's structure, but these are all conditional. We can ignore the condition on the rule for [containing a noun-clause] (20), and assume that CLAUSE is present. As far as the rule for [special noun-clause] is concerned, we know that one of the alternative conditions for it to apply is not satisfied: the feature [unrestricted-aspect noun-clause] cannot be present, because it would conflict with [restricted-aspect noun-clause] (25). The other alternative condition may or may not be satisfied, depending on whether or not the clause is [passive]: if it is, then the realisation-rule for [special noun-clause] applies. If it is not, however, that for ['perception'] applies.

Thus, if we add [passive] to the list of features, the matrix-clause's structure must include CLAUSE = TO-FULL; otherwise it includes CLAUSE = PARTICIPIAL-CL. (Note that the rules are formulated in such a way that TO-FULL and PARTICIPIAL-CL cannot conflate with each other; if they could, their realisation-rules would conflict.) This accounts for the alternation between pairs such as the following, both of which have all the features in our original list:

We saw *him fall over*,
He was seen *to fall over*.

Table 5.7

Construction sets	Environment	Structural patterns
XV	[non-finite noun-clause]	CLAUSE
I, XV, XVI, XIX	[finite noun-clause]	CLAUSE = FIN-CL
II III, IV, V	*not* [passive]	} CLAUSE = PARTICIPIAL-CL
VI	*not* [passive]	CLAUSE = INFIN-CL
IX, X, XI, XIV, XVII, XVIII, XX III, IV, V, VI VIII, XII	[passive] [attributive]	} CLAUSE = TO-FULL
VII, VIII, XXI		CLAUSE = GERUND-CL
XIII		CLAUSE = GERUND-CL = TO-FULL

We shall consider below the question of how the realisation-rules for the functions TO-FULL and PARTICIPIAL-CL account for the differences between these two noun-clauses, one [participial] and the other [infinitival, with *to*]

If we list all the combinations of features allowed by systems 23 through 37 (ignoring system 36), we find that there are twenty-one of them, each corresponding to one of our twenty-one construction-sets labelled I through XXI (see 4.2.14). However, if we then apply the relevant realisation-rules to the features defining the construction-sets, we find that we produce just seven different structural patterns, each of which allows noun-clauses of a different 'finiteness' class (or classes). They are shown in table 5.7.

The function-realisation rules

The relevant function-realisation rules are those for the functions mentioned in the structural patterns above — CLAUSE, FIN-CL, PARTICIPIAL-CL, INFIN-CL, TO-FULL and GERUND-CL — and also for INDEFINITE and LATE. It will be seen from table 5.8 that the relations between the noun-clause's functions and its features are quite complicated, just as those between the matrix-clause's features and structure were.

One of the most noteworthy characteristics of these realisation-rules, taken in conjunction with the structural patterns that the feature-realisation rules generated, is that they do *not* always restrict the noun-clause to a single combination of finiteness features; in other words, in some cases a clause's finiteness features will include some which are not determined by the environment,

Table 5.8

Function	Realisation
CLAUSE	[dependent] // *not* = SUBSTITUTE *or* BINDER [as] // = BINDER
FIN-CL	[finite] // *not* = SUBSTITUTE
PARTICIPIAL-CL	['bare']
INFIN-CL	[without to]
TO-FULL	[with to] *or* [gerundival] // = GERUND-CL *and not* = LATE [with to] // *otherwise*
GERUND-CL	[gerundival] // *not* = TO-FULL *or* LATE
INDEFINITE	[gerundival] *or* [infinitival] // *not* = GOAL or FINITE [gerundival] // = GOAL *and not* = FINITE
LATE	[with to] // *not* = FIN-CL *or* INDEFINITE

but are freely selected from the system-network. In particular, the choice between [infinitival] and [gerundival] is sometimes undetermined by the grammatical environment.

The cases where this is so are of course those where it is factually possible for a noun-clause to be of either kind — as, for instance, when it is used with an adjective like *normal* or like *regrettable* (p. 178):

> *To wear glasses* is normal/regrettable,
> *Wearing glasses* is normal/regrettable.

More generally, it is possible when the construction-set is either XIII or XV — represented by *normal* and *regrettable* respectively. However, this alternation is allowed in a different way for each construction-set: for XIII by the realisation-rule for TO-FULL conflated with GERUND-CL, and for XV by the realisation-rule for INDEFINITE.

To be more precise, the features that define construction-set XIII require both GERUND-CL *and* TO-FULL to be conflated with CLAUSE, as the table of structural patterns showed. This allows us to use one of these functions (GERUND-CL) as a conditioning environment for the realisation of the other, and to say that in this environment both [with to] and [gerundival] are possible. With construction-set XV, on the other hand, *neither* GERUND-CL *nor* TO-FULL is conflated with CLAUSE — nor, when it has [non-finite noun-clause] among its features, is FIN-CL. However, another function,

unique to XV, *is* conflated with CLAUSE: INDEFINITE; and it is to this
function that we give the alternative realisations [infinitival] or [gerundival].

Why should we treat these two constructions so differently, if the facts are
so similar from one to the other? The reason is that the function-realisation
rules are subject to different conditions in the two constructions: in either
case there is one environment in which the otherwise free choice is restricted,
but the environments relevant to this restriction are different.

In construction-set XIII, illustrated by the examples with *normal*, the extra
restriction is imposed when the clause is extraposed: if it is, it cannot be
[gerundival]:

> *To wear glasses* is normal,
> It is normal *to wear glasses*,
> *Wearing glasses* is normal,
> *It is normal *wearing glasses*.

This is formalised by restricting the pair of realisations to cases where TO-
FULL is conflated with GERUND-CL but not with LATE.

In construction-set XV, on the other hand, it is the transitivity-function of
the noun-clause that is relevant: if this is GOAL then the noun-clause *must* be
[gerundival]. In the examples that I gave above with *regrettable*, the function
was ATTRIBUANT; these examples can be contrasted with examples involving *resent*:

> *To wear glasses* is regrettable,
> *Wearing glasses* is regrettable,
> *She resents *to wear glasses*,
> She resents *wearing glasses*.

To formalise this, we allow both [gerundival] and [infinitival] only on condition that INDEFINITE is not conflated with GOAL.

Turning to the realisation-rules for the other functions, there is little to be
said about them, except to point out that the rules for GERUND-CL and
LATE have to be made conditional in order to ensure that they do not conflict with rules in which they appear as conditioning environments. For instance, we have to prevent the realisation-rule for GERUND-CL from demanding a [gerundival] noun-clause at the same time that the rule for TO-FULL is
demanding an [infinitival] one.

The structure-building rules

There are just two structure-building rules that are relevant to the noun-clause's finiteness, and both of them are compatibility rules:

(2q) LATE $\neq$ GERUND-CL // GERUND-CL $\neq$ TO-FULL,
(2s) TO-FULL $\neq$ SUBJECT // CLAUSE $\neq$ LATE *and* SUBJECT
      = GOAL.

Both of these rules involve extraposition, but they do so in different ways.

The first rule makes extraposition *obligatory* for a noun-clause if it has TO-FULL, SUBJECT and GOAL among its functions – that is, if it is like

> It is hoped *to organise another excursion next month*,
> **To organise another excursion next month* is hoped.

In other words, if a noun-clause is the unextraposed subject of a passive clause, it cannot be infinitival.

The second rule in effect makes extraposition *impossible* if the noun-clause is [gerundival], except when it is in a 'reaction'-type construction; but the relation between the rule and this factual exclusion is fairly indirect. First of all, if the clause has the function TO-FULL as well as GERUND-CL it can be extraposed (i.e. be conflated with LATE); but as we have already seen, GERUND-CL in the environment of LATE and TO-FULL is not realised as [gerundival], so this rule (2q) does not allow [gerundival] clauses to occur extraposed: it simply allows the function GERUND-CL to conflate with LATE, since otherwise we should be treating as ungrammatical sentences such as:

> It is normal *to wear glasses.*

Secondly, there *is* one situation under which our grammar allows a gerundival clause to be extraposed: when it has the function INDEFINITE, since in this case it does not have the function GERUND-CL and the restrictions on the latter's conflating with LATE are irrelevant. And in fact, gerundival clauses *can* be extraposed when their function is INDEFINITE (4.2.2)

> It is irritating *having to wear glasses.*

This completes our discussion of the ways in which the grammar defines the finiteness-classes of clause that are permitted in each environment. From the point of view of linguistic theory it is quite an interesting area, since it shows how helpful it is to have a number of different ways of handling restrictions — as restrictions on the selection of a feature in the system-network, or on the application of a feature- or function-realisation rule, or on the conflation of two functions. However, the facts that have to be handled seem too untidy to allow us to write for them a grammar that is completely satisfying; and the grammar that I am offering here is no exception as far as this area of the grammar is concerned.

5.3.2. *The presence or absence of SUBJECT in the noun-clause*

The question of whether or not the noun-clause contains SUBJECT is similar in many respects to the question of the noun-clause's finiteness. One similarity is that, as far as the grammar of the noun-clause taken in isolation is concerned, the facts are simple. For instance, there is a single system — system 13 — whose terms are [with SUBJECT] and [without SUBJECT] and which applies to non-finite clauses completely independently of all the other systems that apply to them; and this system distinguishes in a straightforward way between noun-clauses that do and those that do not contain SUBJECT. On the other hand, when we come to describe the environmental restrictions which may cause a noun-clause to have or to lack SUBJECT, we find the facts are much more complicated, and the grammar cannot but reflect this complexity. Again, the restrictions are handled in more than one way by the grammar — though not in as many different wasy as the restrictions on finiteness. But in spite of these similarities, this section will have to describe far less interlocking relations in the grammar than the last subsection had to deal with.

The grammar for the noun-clause itself

As far as the grammar for the noun-clause itself is concerned, there is little to be said. System 8 contrasts [finite] with [non-finite] and system 13, applying in the environment of [non-finite], contrasts [with SUBJECT] and [without SUBJECT]. Two of these features are realised by the presence of SUBJECT in the noun-clause's structure: [finite] and [with SUBJECT]. Moreover, wherever SUBJECT occurs in the structure of a noun-clause, the latter must have one of these two features. Consequently, in order to account for the presence or absence of SUBJECT in the structure of noun-clauses, all we need to do is to describe the circumstances under which these two features occur. But we have already done this for the first feature [finite] (5.3.1), so all that remains is to say when noun-clauses have the other feature [with SUBJECT].

Direct restrictions imposed by 'SUBJECTFULL' and 'SUBJECTLESS'

There are two functions that conflate with CLAUSE and that directly restrict the noun-clause to one or the other of the features [with SUBJECT] or [without SUBJECT]: SUBJECTFULL and SUBJECTLESS. The realisation-rules for these functions are simple: they require [with SUBJECT] and [without SUBJECT] respectively, without any kind of environmental restriction. The question, then, is how these two functions are introduced.

Before addressing ourselves to this question, however, we must make two observations. Firstly, it is possible for CLAUSE to be conflated with *neither* of these functions, which means that in principle the choice between [with SUBJECT] and [without SUBJECT] is free. This is the case, as the reader will see from the table on pp. 230 and 231, in construction-sets XII, XIII, XV and XXI:

This book is hard (*for a non-specialist*) *to read*,
He wanted (*someone else*) *to do the washing-up*.

And, secondly, there is a third function which is relevant to the presence of SUBJECT in the noun-clause: namely, SUBJECT itself; and even if CLAUSE is not conflated with SUBJECTFULL it may be necessary for it to have the feature [with SUBJECT]. I shall say more about this point later.

Returning to the question of the conditions under which SUBJECTFULL and SUBJECTLESS occur, what we must do is identify the feature-realisation rules which introduce them, and we shall thereby identify the features that the matrix-clause must have in order for these functions to occur in its structure. If the reader will refer to the table on pp. 230 and 231 summarising the interrelations among the variable characteristics of noun-phrase constructions, he will see that there is no very clear pattern in the distribution of +, −, and ± in column 4, representing the presence, absence or optionality of SUBJECT. Accordingly, we find our two functions realising a number of different features.

The relevant feature-realisation rules are as in table 5.9 on the next page, omitting functions other than SUBJECTLESS and SUBJECTFULL.

There is only one system of the matrix-clause that is set up specifically to account for the presence or absence of SUBJECT in its noun-clause: system 35. This system applies to clauses like the following:

He claimed *to have been working late*,
He claimed *her to be his secretary*.

Table 5.9

System	Feature	Realisation
28	intervention	+ SUBJECTLESS = CLAUSE // [transitive] + SUBJECTFULL = CLAUSE // [intransitive]
29	progressive noun-clause	+ SUBJECTFULL = CLAUSE
30	not SUBJECT-fronting	+ SUBJECTFULL = CLAUSE // [clause as participant] + SUBJECTLESS = CLAUSE // [clause as completer]
31	engineered event	+ SUBJECTLESS = CLAUSE // [transitive]
35	subjectless noun-clause	+ SUBJECTLESS = CLAUSE

The first of these matrix-clauses has [subject-less noun-clause] among its features, and the second has [subject-full noun-clause].

The reader may be wondering why I do not treat these as instances of a construction in which the noun-clause's SUBJECT is optional — as with *want* — in which case there would be no difference at all between the matrix-clauses, and the distinction would appear only when we came to the noun-clauses themselves. There are three reasons for not following this suggestion. Firstly, even if we postulated a construction in which SUBJECT was optional, only one verb (*claim*) would occur in it; secondly, we should in any case have to have a different construction for the cases where SUBJECT was obligatory; and thirdly there is no other difference between constructions containing *claim* and SUBJECT and constructions containing other verbs and SUBJECT, beyond the fact that SUBJECT is obligatory with *claim* and optional with the other verb. So instead of making a systemic distinction according to whether SUBJECT is optional or obligatory, we make one according to whether SUBJECT is actually present or absent, with *claim* possible in either case.

The other features that are realised by SUBJECTLESS or SUBJECTFULL were set up primarily to reflect other distinctions to which the presence or absence of SUBJECT is incidental. As the reader will see, it would be hard to establish any kind of semantic or syntactic explanation for the particular distribution of SUBJECTLESS and SUBJECTFULL that we find in these rules, and I shall not try to offer any such explanation. It seems likely that the arbitrary associations in these rules reflect a bad analysis as much as the facts of English, but it will probably be hard to find an analysis that does not err at least to some extent in this direction.

Indirect restrictions imposed by SUBJECT

We can now turn to the second way in which the choice between [with SUBJECT] and [without SUBJECT] can be predetermined by the environment: if the noun-clause's SUBJECT is fronted, then it follows that the noun-clause must have [with SUBJECT] among its features; but it will not have the function SUBJECTFULL. For instance, the feature [neutral-factive], which defines construction-set XX, is realised by the presence of FRONTED; this in turn has to be conflated with SUBJECT, according to the structure-building rules (3m), and with PRE-CLAUSE (3k), which means that SUBJECT is in fact a part of the structure of the noun-clause itself as well as of the matrix-clause; and this means that the noun-clause does contain SUBJECT and therefore must have the feature [with SUBJECT]. An instance of this construction is the following, where *the crash* is fronted, though this does not lead to discontinuity:

He admitted *the crash to be his fault*.

Thus the noun-clause must have [with SUBJECT] wherever the matrix-clause has SUBJECT conflated with FRONTED in its structure; but SUBJECT is added by a structure-building rule, so we shall find FRONTED but not SUBJECT mentioned in the feature-realisation rules. The relevant realisation-rules, ignoring all functions but FRONTED, are as in table 5.10.

Table 5.10

System	Feature	Realisation
26	ordinary noun-clause	+ FRONTED // [restricted-aspect noun-clause] *and not* [clause as completer]
27	restricted-voice noun-clause	+ FRONTED
29	non-progressive noun-clause	+ FRONTED
30	SUBJECT-fronting	+ FRONTED
35	subject-full noun-clause	+ FRONTED
37	neutral-factive	+ FRONTED

I shall have more ·to say about the fronting of SUBJECT in 5.6.2 below, so there is no need to say anything else about it here. We can finish this discussion by relating the distinctions that have been described to the construction-sets. In some cases a single construction-set, such as VI, has to be subdivided according to the noun-clause's function, but we can show these distinctions by using the more detailed reference numbers that I used in 4.2.14, involving letters as well as the roman numbers: VIa, VIb, etc.

There are five mutually exclusive possibilities for any one clause:
(1) its structure contains SUBJECTLESS = CLAUSE;
(2) its structure contains SUBJECTFULL = CLAUSE;
(3) its structure contains FRONTED, with SUBJECT beneath it;
(4) its structure contains FINITE = CLAUSE;
(5) its structure contains none of the above.

In case (1) the noun-clause contains no SUBJECT; in (2), (3) and (4) it does contain SUBJECT; and in (5) it may or may not contain SUBJECT. These possibilities are distributed among the construction-sets as in table 5.11.

Table 5.11

Structure of matrix-clause	Construction-sets
(1) SUBJECTLESS = CLAUSE	VIa, IXb, XIb, XIc, XVIII
(2) SUBJECTFULL = CLAUSE	II, VIb, XIa
(3) FRONTED over SUBJECT	III, IV, V, VII, VIII, IXa, X, XVII, XX
(4) FINITE = CLAUSE	I, XV, XVI, XIX
(5) –	XII, XIII, XIV, XV, XXI

5.3.3. The presence or absence of BINDER in the noun-clause

There are just two items that we have to deal with as BINDER in the noun-clause: *that* and *for*. When it comes to defining the conditions under which they are present, the facts are very different for the two items, as we saw in 4.2.8, so we gain nothing by trying to formulate general rules which will apply equally to either.

'That' in the grammar for noun-clauses

In the simplest cases a finite noun-clause (other than an interrogative one, which we are ignoring) may or may not be introduced by *that*, and it seems to make no difference to the meaning whether it is present or absent: ·

> I suspect *that it's going to rain soon,*
> I suspect *it's going to rain soon.*

These simplest cases are taken as the 'normal' state of affairs, and there is a system in the network for noun-clauses which allows a choice between having and not having *that*: system 10, which fits into the network as follows:

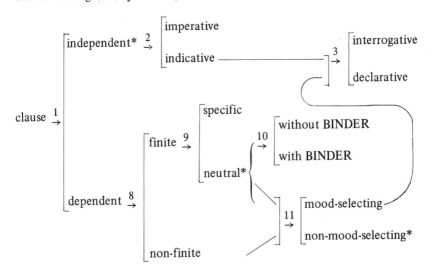

The relevant feature-realisation rules are as in table 5.12.

Table 5.12

System	Feature	Realisation
3	declarative	—
	interrogative	+ MOOD-FOCUS // [independent]
		+ BINDER ⎱
		+ QUESTION = BINDER ⎰ // [dependent]
9	neutral	+ THAT = BINDER // *not* [interrogative]
	specific	—
10	with BINDER	+ BINDER // *not* [interrogative]
	without BINDER	—

The rule for [neutral] introduces THAT, but only if BINDER is available for it to be conflated with; and whether or not BINDER is present depends on system 10. The function THAT is realised by [that] — an ad hoc feature defining the one-member class containing *that*. Thus if the clause is introduced by *that* it must have both the features [neutral] and [with BINDER], but it is also possible for it to have the feature [neutral] without containing *that*: namely if it also has the feature [without BINDER].

A grammar that goes beyond the generation of noun-clauses will have to take account of another fact: *that* is optional not only in noun-clauses, but also in adverbial clauses, such as clauses of degree-result:

> He was so cold that he couldn't feel his fingers,
> He was so cold he couldn't feel his fingers.

Clearly this is the same phenomenon as we find in noun-clauses so we shall want to be able to handle it by means of the same rules. I have prepared for this in the grammar, by not restricting [neutral] to noun-clauses; thus, the two adverbial clauses above can be classified as neutral, just like the noun-clauses with *realise*, in the earlier examples. The only difference between these two pairs of clauses is that those with *realise* are [mood-selecting], in system 11, whilst the adverbial ones are [non-mood-selecting]. Otherwise they are the same as far as the class-membership is concerned, and the differences between them are located entirely in their functions – i.e. in their environments.

Although we are not trying to cover constructions where the noun-clause is [interrogative], it is necessary to mention such constructions here, to explain why two of the feature-realisation rules quoted have conditioning environments that refer to [interrogative]. The reason is that [neutral] covers not only clauses introduced by *that*, but also clauses introduced by an interrogative item like *whether* or *who* – [interrogative, dependent] clauses. In other words, [neutral] is compatible with either [non-mood-selecting] or [mood-selecting, declarative], and in either case it allows *that*; but it is also compatible with [mood-selecting, interrogative], and in this case the clause will not be introduced by *that*. In terms of the clause's abstract structure, the first two feature-combinations allow BINDER = THAT, whilst the third allows BINDER = QUESTION. But whereas the former functions are optional, depending on the selection made in system 10, the latter are not: [interrogative, independent] clauses are *always* introduced by an interrogative item, functioning as BINDER.

Turning to our realisation-rules, if we had not explicitly prevented it, the rule for [neutral] would have conflated THAT with BINDER in [interrogative] clauses, producing bundles of functions in which THAT was conflated with QUESTION. This we have excluded. We have also made sure that BINDER is always present in the structure of [interrogative, dependent] clauses by introducing BINDER in the realisation-rule for [interrogative] in the environment of [dependent]; but [interrogative] is compatible with [with BINDER], so we have to prevent the latter's realisation-rule from introducing a *second* instance of BINDER, and this we have done by making the rule inoperative in the environment of [interrogative].

One consequence of our analysis is that system 10 applies completely vacuously in the environment of [interrogative]: it makes no difference to the structure of the clause whether it has [with BINDER] or [without BINDER]. This would be less worrying if there was any difference of meaning between the two features, but since there is none, we must say that every [interrogative, dependent] clause is ambiguous for system 10, without there being any corresponding semantic ambiguity.

As the reader will probably have guessed, the feature that [neutral] contrasts with, [specific], is given to any clause introduced by an item other than *that* (or *whether* or *if*).

Environmental restrictions on 'that'

There are two environmental restrictions on the occurrence of *that*: it *must* occur if the noun-clause is M-SUBJECT, and it must *not* occur if M-SUBJECT is fronted. These two restrictions are effected in different ways in the grammar.

That is made obligatory in a finite noun-clause by one part of the realisation-rule for FIN-CL:

[with BINDER] // = M-SUBJECT.

Thus the choice between [with BINDER] and [without BINDER] is preempted in the environment of M-SUBJECT, explaining the difference between the following:

> *That he should imagine she loved him* is extraordinary,
> **He should imagine she loved him* is extraordinary.

Similar environmental restrictions could explain the parallel situation where the noun-clause is clause-initial but not M-SUBJECT:

> *That she could love him* I can't believe,
> ' **She could love him* I can't believe.

I have not tried to formalise this restriction though, since our grammar does not cover 'thematic' constructions of any kind.

For the other restriction on *that* we make use of a structure-building rule, rather than a function-realisation one: sequence-rule (1b):

BINDER $\supseteq$ M-SUBJECT → PROCESS → POST-VERB.

According to this rule, it is not permitted under any circumstances for BINDER to *follow* M-SUBJECT. The construction in which BINDER would follow M-SUBJECT, if it were not for this rule, is illustrated by

What did she say (*that) *happened*?

Here the M-SUBJECT of the noun-clause is fronted by question-fronting, but BINDER, if present, must come at the beginning of the unfronted part of the noun-clause — which means that it must follow M-SUBJECT. This conflicts with rule (1b), so it does not occur. That is, the restriction is imposed directly on the noun-clause's structure rather than on its features, and the feature [with BINDER] is ruled out because it would lead to an ungrammatical structure.

There are a number of points that are worth noting with regard to the operation of this rule. First, it prevents nothing except M-SUBJECT from occurring before BINDER, since as a matter of fact M-SUBJECT is the only function that is restricted in this way: if the fronted item does not have the function M-SUBJECT, then BINDER is optional.

What did she say (*that*) *he wanted*?

Secondly, the same restriction applies if the noun-clause is [interrogative], but here BINDER is obligatory, so we should never expect to be able to front M-SUBJECT:

*What did she ask *whether happened*?

Thirdly, the restriction imposed by sequence-rule (1b) explains a phenomenon that otherwise is quite unrelated to the one we have been discussing. A few conjunctions, notably *though* (not *although*) and *as*, can be second in the clause's structure, rather than in the usual initial place:

Intelligent though he is, (he can't understand his wife).

However, this is possible only provided the absolute initial item (*intelligent* in the above example) is *not* M-SUBJECT:

> Many friends though he has, (no-one came to see him
>   in hospital),
> Many people though know him, (no-one came to see him
>   in hospital).

This exclusion is explained by our rule which prevents BINDER (*though*) from following M-SUBJECT (*many people*).

'For' in the grammar for noun-clauses

Turning now to the other item that occurs as BINDER, *for*, the rules for introducing it into the structure of the noun-clause are simpler than those for *that*. There is a system, system 17, which contrasts [with *for*] and [without *for*], and which applies to any clause that is [infinitival, with to]. However, *for* occurs only if the clause contains SUBJECT, so the realisation-rule for [with *for*] introduces FOR = BINDER only in the environment [with SUB-JECT]. The other feature [without for] has no realisation, so an infinitival clause containing *to* will contain *for* only if it has both the features [with *for*] and [with SUBJECT]. The following does have these features:

> It is normal *for old people to wear glasses.*

But the two below do not: the first one lacks [with *for*] but not [with SUB-JECT], and the second lacks [with SUBJECT] but not [with *for*]:

> I want *you to be happy,*
> It is normal *to wear glasses.*

Allowing system 17 to apply to all clauses that are [with to], rather than only to those that are also [with SUBJECT], means that it can apply vacuously, just as did the system contrasting [with BINDER] and [without BINDER] which we discussed above. The two situations are quite different, though, since the present system does not lead to irresolvable ambiguity: the environment always determines which of the two features the clause must have, whereas the choice between [with BINDER] and [without BINDER] is in most cases free.

Environmental restrictions on 'for'

What we have to account for are the environmental restrictions on the features [with for] and [without for], since these are in a one-one relation to the presence and absence of *for* respectively. Of these two features, [with for] is unmarked, as shown by the asterisk against it in the network; that is, this feature is obligatory unless the environmental requires the other. Thus if we compare the clauses found with, say, *hope* and *want*, we are claiming that the former are 'normal', and it is only the latter which require any special explanation:

> We all hoped *for it to stop raining*,
> We all wanted *it to stop raining*.

Using this 'markedness' convention means that we only need to define one set of environments, instead of two; and we do this by means of the function FOR-LESS. This has the following realisation:

> [without for] // + M-SUBJECT ‖ FRONTED *or not* = SUBJECT.

We shall return to the environmental conditioning on this rule below. All we need to note here is that merely the absence of the function FOR-LESS is enough to make [with for] obligatory if a clause has the features [with to, with subject].

The earlier question, then, is reduced to the question: when does FOR-LESS occur? There are two conditions for its occurrence. Firstly it is introduced by the realisation-rule for one feature, [engineered event] in system 31; the realisation-rule for this feature includes the following:

> + FOR-LESS = CLAUSE // [without ADDRESSEE].

The environmental restriction in effect confines the rule to two constructions belonging to construction-set XIV: those involving verbs like *desire* and *want*. In the table on pp. 230 and 231 it is only for these constructions that there is a '—' in column 8, meaning that *for* is absent although it otherwise would be present.

The second condition for the presence of FOR-LESS is the presence of a fronted SUBJECT: if SUBJECT is fronted, then *for* is never present. This accounts for the absence of *for* after *believe*, for instance:

> He believed *it to be his right*.

(We could not have used this explanation for constructions involving *want*, since SUBJECT is not fronted after *want* (see (4.2.5).) In order to introduce

FOR-LESS in the former cases, we use a structure-building rule, the addition-rule (30):

$$+ \text{FOR-LESS} = \text{CLAUSE} \, // + \text{FRONTED} = \text{SUBJECT}$$
$$and \; \text{CLAUSE} = \text{TO-FULL}.$$

(It is necessary to specify that CLAUSE must be conflated with TO-FULL because subject can be fronted from a gerundival clause, in which case of course we do not need FOR-LESS.)

There remains to be explained the condition on the realisation of FOR-LESS: it is *not* realised by [without for] if it is conflated with SUBJECT, unless FRONTED = SUBJECT is present. This proviso is needed because the object of a verb like *desire* (or *intend*) lacks *for* only if the matrix clause is [active] ; otherwise *for* occurs:

> We intended *there to be lots of non-linguists at the party,*
> It was intended *for there to be lots of non-linguists at the party.*

In the second example, the noun-clause has the function FOR-LESS, but it also has SUBJECT, which cancels out the effect of FOR-LESS, so the un-marked feature [with for] is chosen.

5.4. Restrictions on tense/aspect and voice

In this section I shall show how the grammar formalises the restrictions on tense/aspect and voice described in 4.2.9 and 4.2.10. These restrictions are different from those described in the last section in that they involve contrasts that apply to finite clauses, as well as to non-finite ones.

5.4.1. *Tense and aspect in the noun-clause*

There are three sets of restrictions on tense/aspect to be formalised: restrictions on [past], on [perfect] and on [progressive]. Although the cir-cumstances under which [past] is excluded are different from those that ex-clude [perfect], and likewise for [perfect] and [progressive], there is a simple relationship between them: the conditions that do not allow [past] subsume those that exclude [perfect], and the latter subsume those that exclude [pro-gressive]. (For a discussion of the hierarchic relation among the tense/aspect categories, see pp. 122–123.) Thus when we come to classify constructions according to whether they allow [past], [perfect] or [progressive] in the noun-clause, we find that the class that excludes [perfect] is a sub-class of the one that excludes [past], and so on.

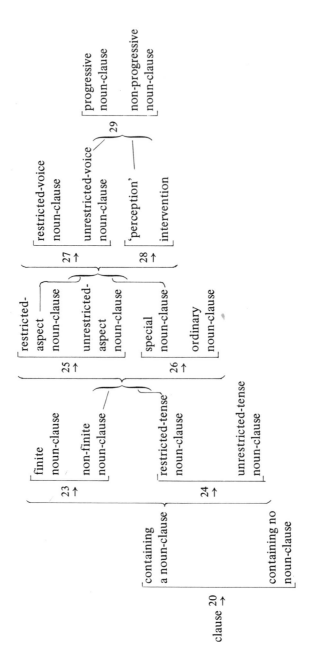

It is easy to handle this kind of relationship in a system-network, so we have given these contrasts a prominent place in the system-network. The relevant systems are systems 24, 25 and 29, but they are inextricably related to a number of other systems, as the system-network on page 312 shows.

If the matrix clause has the feature [restricted-tense noun-clause], then the noun-clause must have [non-past]; and similarly [restricted-aspect noun-clause] in the matrix clause requires [non-perfect] in the noun-clause. The restrictions on [progressive] are slightly more complicated: if the matrix clause has [restricted-aspect noun-clause], then the noun-clause must have [non-progressive] unless the matrix clause *also* has the feature [progressive noun-clause], in which case the noun-clause must be [progressive]. The realisation-rules for these features include those in table 5.13.

Table 5.13

System	Feature	Realisation
24	restricted-tense noun-clause	+ NONPAST-CL = CLAUSE
25	restricted-aspect noun-clause	+ NONPERF-CL = CLAUSE + NONPROG-CL = CLAUSE // *not* [progressive noun-clause]
29	progressive noun-clause	+ PROGRESSIVE-CL = CLAUSE

The reason why the restrictions on [progressive] are dealt with in a different way from those on [past] and [perfect] are rather involved, but I gave them in 4.2.9, to which the reader is referred.

The four functions NONPAST-CL, NONPERF-CL, NONPROG-CL and PROGRESSIVE-CL have simple realisations: [non-past], [non-perfect], [non-progressive] and [progressive] respectively.

The effects of these restrictions can be seen by comparing the following examples:

> Harry believed *Harriet to be angry*,
> He forbad *there to be any demonstrations*,
> Johnny's parents watched *him take his first step*.

In all three examples the noun-clause is [non-past, non-perfect, non-progressive], but in the first it need not have had any of these features, in the second it had to have [non-past] but need not have had [non-perfect] or [non-progressive] and in the third it had to have all three, as a result of the restrictions imposed by the environment.

In the table on pp. 230 and 231, the simple relation between the tense/aspect restrictions and the construction-sets can be plainly seen: construction-sets I through XIV exclude [past], II through IX [perfect], III through IX [progressive], and II [non-progressive]. Construction-set I is out of place simply because of the way in which the system-network defines it, as the reader will see.

5.4.2. *Voice in the noun-clause and constructions involving 'need', 'want', etc.*

There are three separate sets of environments in which the voice of the noun-clause is restricted; in some it is [active] that is obligatory, while in others it is [passive]. The restrictions are discussed in 4.2.10.

Restrictions imposed by 'watch'

If the main-verb in the matrix clause of a 'perception' construction is *watch*, the noun-clause has to be [active] :

> We watched *them fell the tree,*
> *We watched *the tree felled.*

These clauses belong to construction-set III, and they are to be distinguished from otherwise similar constructions with progressive noun-clauses:

> We watched *them felling the tree,*
> We watched *the tree being felled.*

If the noun-clause is [progressive] , then it need not be [active] ; this is one reason for treating examples like the last two as instances of a different construction-set from the earlier ones – viz. construction-set II.

Where the noun-clause is [non-progressive] and it is object of *watch*, the matrix clause has the features [restricted voice noun-clause] , reflecting the voice-restriction. However, this feature in itself does not identify the class concerned, since it is also assigned to the constructions involving *order*, which we shall discuss below. These two constructions are distinguished by another pair of features: ['perception'] for *watch*, and [intervention] for *order*.

The restriction with *watch* is imposed by a function ACTIVE-CL conflated with CLAUSE by the realisation-rule for [restricted-voice noun-clause] in the environment ['perception'] . The function ACTIVE-CL is realised by '*not* [passive]' – not by [active] , since this feature does not cover 'intransitive' clauses, as the reader will see from the system-network.

Restrictions imposed by 'order', etc.

There are a number of verbs including *order*, *get* and *expect*, which allow a [participial, passive] noun-clause:

I expect *this mess cleared up immediately*.

As I argued in 4.2.10 these constructions have no corresponding active forms so we must restrict the noun-clause to [passive]. The construction-set in question is V, and this is identified by the feature [restricted-voice noun-clause, intervention], as I said above.

For these constructions we introduce a function PASSIVE-CL and conflate it with CLAUSE. It realises [restricted-voice noun-clause] in the environment [intervention], and is itself realised by [passive].

Restrictions imposed by 'need', etc.

There are three verbs — *need*, *require* and *want* — which allow a [special passive] noun-clause, as in:

This letter needs *signing by the manager*.

Wherever such a noun-clause occurs, the construction-set is the same: VII; and in this construction-set only the three verbs just mentioned are found. However, the noun-clause can be either ACTOR — as in the above example — or GOAL:

I need *this letter signing by the manager*.

The matrix-clause in construction-set VII is characterised by the features [object-oriented, restricted-aspect noun-clause], from systems 29 and 22 respectively; it is [restricted-aspect noun-clause] because it has to be [non-perfect] and [non-progressive] as well as [passive] and [special passive]. The voice of the noun-clause is restricted by the function CRYPTO-PASSIVE (conflated with CLAUSE), which realises [object-oriented] in the environment [restricted-aspect noun-clause] and which is realised by [special passive, passive].

In order to allow for the noun-clause having the two different transitivity-functions, ACTOR and GOAL, we simply allow the verb-class containing *need*, *require* and *want* (class V1) to occur in either environment: in other words, we allow class V1 to realise either ACTOR-CLAUSE (the function of the main verb where the noun-clause is ACTOR) or GOAL-CLAUSE (its function when the noun-clause is GOAL).

However, construction-set VII is not the only one in which *need, require* and *want* can occur. In 4.2.10 I listed six different constructions, counting construction-set VII as two constructions. One of the other constructions also limits the voice of the noun-clause, but we have already dealt with it: *need* etc. can be used like *order, get, expect* and so on, with a [participial, passive] noun-clause:

> I need *this letter signed by the manager.*

The grammar allows for such sentences in just the same way as for those containing *order*, etc.

Apart from these three constructions, there is another pair of constructions both belonging to the same construction-set – X – with the noun-clause as ACTOR in one and GOAL in the other:

> *This letter* needs *to be signed by the manager,*
> I need *this letter to be signed by the manager.*

The sixth construction involving *need*, etc. belongs to construction-set II:

> He needs *someone else standing over him all the time.*

However, in none of these last three constructions is the voice of the noun-clause restricted, so we need say no more about them here.

5.4.3. *Constructions allowing past-tense noun-clauses*

In this section we shall concentrate on the contrasts that apply to one particular subset of all the constructions containing noun-clauses: those that impose no restrictions at all on the tense/aspect of the noun-clause. These include the constructions generally referred to under the heading of 'reported speech', and it is here that the important contrasts between 'factive' and 'modal' (or 'non-factive'), and between 'reaction' and 'cognition', apply.

In 4.2.11 I listed a number of formal differences between 'reaction-type' and 'cognition-type' constructions, and in 4.2.12 I did the same for 'factive' and 'modal' constructions; but in the following discussion it will be best if we treat these two contrasts together, since their corresponding formal differences are hard to disentangle from each other. For instance, it is not possible

A. The network

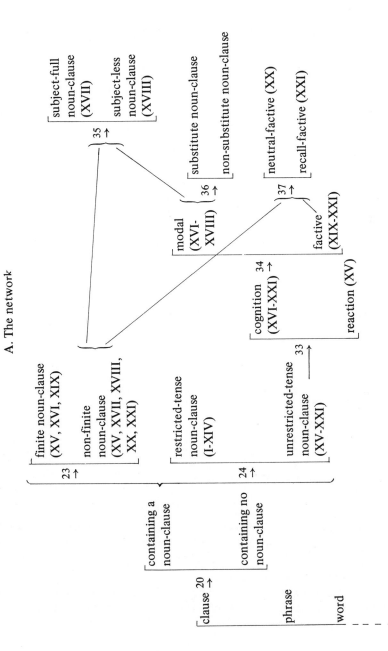

B. The feature-realisation rules.

System	Feature	Realisation
33	cognition	+ FRONTED // *not* [subject-less noun-clause] *and not* [recall-factive]
	reaction	+ INDEFINITE = CLAUSE + FACT = CLAUSE + XV = LEX
34	modal	+ REPORT = CLAUSE // *not* [attributive] + TO-FULL = CLAUSE // [non-finite noun-clause] + XVI = LEX [finite noun-clause]
	factive	+ FACT = CLAUSE + XIX = LEX // [finite noun-clause]
35	subject-full noun-clause	+ XVII = LEX
	subject-less noun-clause	+ SUBJECTLESS = CLAUSE
36	substitute noun-clause	+ SUBSTITUTE = CLAUSE
	non-substitute noun-clause	–
37	neutral-factive	+ TO-FULL = CLAUSE + XX = CLAUSE
	recall-factive	+ XXI = LEX

C. The structure-building rules (compatibility-rules).

(2g)	BINDER ≠ INDEFINITE
(2i)	SUBSTITUTE ≠ BINDER
(2j)	SUBSTITUTE ≠ ATTRIBUANT
(2n)	SUBSTITUTE ≠ CLAUSE // CLAUSE ≠ FIN-CL
(2o)	SUBSTITUTE ≠ SUBJECT // CLAUSE ≠ LATE
(2p)	REPORT ≠ SUBJECT // CLAUSE ≠ LATE

to fully describe the differences in the noun-clause's finiteness corresponding to one contrast without referring to the distinctions made by the other one.

The grammar for these contrasts

The distinctions that we are concerned with are made in systems 33 through 37 of the system-network, which are repeated here together with their associated realisation-rules and structure-building rules.

D. The function-realisation rules.

Function	Realisation
FACT	[declarative]
FRONTED	–
GERUND-CL	[gerundival] // *not* = TO-FULL *or* LATE
INDEFINITE	[gerundival] *or* [with to] // *not* = GOAL *or* FINITE
	[gerundival] // = GOAL *and not* = FINITE
REPORT	–
SUBJECTFULL	[with SUBJECT]
SUBSTITUTE	[so]
TO-FULL	[with to] *or* [gerundival] // = GERUND-CL *and not* = LATE
	[with to] // *otherwise*

[Reaction], [cognition], [modal] and [factive]

As the network shows, the contrast between [modal] and [factive] pre-supposes [cognition], contrasting with [reaction] ; I presented arguments in favour of this analysis in 4.2.12. These four features thus allow just three different combinations, which the following examples illustrate.

[reaction]	We didn't mind *that the lecture was cancelled,*
[cognition, factive]	We didn't realise *that the lecture was cancelled,*
[cognition, modal]	We didn't think *that the lecture was cancelled.*

It is worth pointing out that this is *not* a classification of noun-clauses, but of matrix-clauses. We shall also make some distinctions in the noun-clauses, but the classification that I have just outlined does not apply to them. Locating the contrasts in the matrix-clause makes it easy to relate them to the various characteristics of the matrix-clause itself — especially its main verb — that are associated with them.

Semantic differences

In this chapter I am not trying to go beyond the *grammatical* description of our constructions, so I shall not offer any kind of formalisation of the semantic differences between [reaction] and [cognition], or between [factive] and [modal]. However, we can at least provide points to which the semantic descriptions can be related, whatever form the latter may take.

Most simply, [reaction] and [cognition] define classes of matrix-clauses that are relatively homogeneous semantically, so we can use these features as reference-points for the semantics. Moreover, the classes of verbs and adjectives that are allowed by these two features do not overlap, as the reader can see from table 4.2 (pp. 238–239), in which [reaction] corresponds to construction-set XV and [cognition] to sets XVI through XXI: [reaction] allows items like *dangerous, difficult, exciting, regrettable*; *count, matter, rankle*; *alarm, amaze*; *deplore, mind, regret, resent*, whilst [cognition] allows items like *certain, clear, bound*; *emerge, appear, hear, say, believe, claim, accept, remember, repute, assure, persuade*. These verbs and adjectives define processes that could be described as 'reactions' in the one case and 'cognitive processes' in the other.

Turning to the difference between [factive] and [modal], we could easily relate the features themselves directly to the semantic characteristics in question. However, the same semantic distinction appears in other environments than in [cognition] matrix-clauses.

For instance, compare the following pair:

He didn't ring her because she rang him first,
He didn't ring her as she rang him first.

From the second sentence it is clear that she did ring him first, but this is not unequivocally clear from the first sentence: it is possible that what is denied is that he rang her because she rang him first, and that the reason why this is denied is precisely that she did not in fact ring him. The difference is thus just the same as the one we find between pairs like the following:

He said *that she rang him first*,
He admitted *that she rang him first*,

where the first is [modal] and the second is [factive].

Even if we disregard examples like these, which take us beyond the field of noun-clauses, we shall need to generalise the semantic contrast that is associated with the [factive] versus [modal] contrast: we shall need to give the 'factive' semantic description to matrix-clauses that have the feature [reaction]. The thing that is reacted to is a fact, and not just a report (a 'hypothetical fact'). For instance, in English it is possible to *regret* a fact:

I regret *that the Tories are still in control of Haringey*, but it is not possible both to *suppose* a thing (without knowing it to be a fact) and to *regret* it, although there would be nothing logically anomalous about this:

> *I suppose and regret *that the Tories are still in control*
> *of Haringey*.

Given then that we shall need to describe as 'factive' some constructions other than those that we are labelling grammatically as [factive], we shall need to provide some distinction between [factive] and [modal] constructions other than simply the difference between the features [factive] and [modal]. We do this by classifying the noun-clause as [mood-selecting] (system 11) and [declarative] (3) if the matrix-clause is [factive], but not if it is [modal], in which case the noun-clause is [non-mood-selecting]. Similarly, in the other cases where a dependent clause is semantically 'factive' we can classify it as [mood-selecting, declarative], and make a general rule that if a clause is [declarative] it is to be taken as a factual claim. (We shall note below another advantage of treating the noun-clause in factive constructions as [mood-selecting]; see pp. 325 and 347.)

The relevant rules in the grammar are as follows. The feature [factive] is realised by the presence of the function FACT, and so is the other feature which allows a 'factive' noun-clause, [reaction]. This function FACT is conflated with CLAUSE by the feature-realisation rules that introduce it. Then FACT is realised by the feature [declarative], which implies the feature [mood-selecting]. Wherever the function FACT is *not* present, however, the feature [non-mood-selecting] has to be chosen, because it is the unmarked term in the system (and therefore is starred in the system-network); and if the noun-clause has the feature [non-mood-selecting], this rules out the feature [declarative].

In the examples of this contrast that I have given so far in this section, the dependent clause has in each case been finite; but in fact the same contrasts apply when the noun-clause is non-finite. For instance, *think* appears in [modal] clauses and *recognise* in [factive] ones, but with either the noun-clause can be non-finite as easily as it can be finite, and the same semantic contrasts hold in either case:

> I thought *that she was lying / her to be lying*,
> I recognised *that she was lying / her to be lying*.

The grammar allows for these two possibilities by allowing the contrast be-

tween [mood-selecting] and [non-mood-selecting] to presuppose either
[finite, neutral] or [non-finite, nominal] (see network B on p. 248).

The finiteness of the noun-clause
    The noun-clause can be either [finite] or [non-finite] whether the matrix-
clause has the feature [reaction], [modal or [factive]; this is allowed for in
the grammar by system 23 — [finite noun-clause] versus [non-finite noun-
clause] — being independent of the contrasts between these features. If the
matrix-clause has [finite noun-clause], then its structure will include FIN-CL
conflated with CLAUSE by virtue of the realisation rule for this feature, and
the realisation-rule for FIN-CL will ensure that the noun-clause is [finite].
Where the matrix-clause has [non-finite noun-clause], on the other hand,
there is no FIN-CL, and the noun-clause must have the unmarked feature
[non-finite].
    Having distinguished between the environments for [finite] and [non-
finite] noun-clauses, we still have to show whether a [non-finite] clause
should be [infinitival, with to] or [gerundival]. The facts are as follows:
    (a) [modal] allows only [infinitival, with to]:

        I supposed *her to have deserted him.*

    (b) [factive] allows [gerundival] only with verbs like *remember*; other-
wise the noun-clause must be [infinitival, with to];

        He remembered *her having deserted him,*
        He recognised *her to have deserted him.*

    (c) [reaction] allows only [gerundival] if the noun-clause is GOAL; other-
wise it allows either [gerundival] or [infinitival, with to]

        He regretted *her having deserted him,*
      *He regretted *her to have deserted him,*
        Her having deserted him amazes me,
        For her to have deserted him amazes me.

    These facts are reflected by the following rules:
    (a) [modal] is realised by the presence of TO-FULL conflated with
CLAUSE, which obliges the noun-clause to be [infinitival, with to].
    (b) [factive] allows a selection from a further system, contrasting
[neutral-factive] with [recall-factive]; these features are realised by the pres-

ence of TO-FULL and GERUND-CL respectively, conflated with CLAUSE, and these functions result in the noun-clause having the right finiteness-feature.

(c) [reaction] is realised by the presence of INDEFINITE conflated with CLAUSE, and INDEFINITE has two different sets of realisations: [gerundival] in the environment of GOAL but not of FIN-CL, and either [gerundival] or [with to] in the environment of neither GOAL nor FIN-CL.

The different kinds of restriction are thus handled in different ways: where the restriction is semantically relevant (b) different features are assigned to the matrix-clause, each requiring a different finiteness feature in the noun-clause; but where the restriction is only structural (c), it is stated as an environmental restriction on the realisation of a function.

As far as the lexical predicates are concerned, they all allow the noun-clause to be [finite], but there are some which do not allow it to be anything else. For instance, the adjective in an [attributive, modal] clause can be either *likely* or *probable*, but only with the former can the noun-clause be [non-finite] :

> It is likely *that it will rain soon*,
> It is probable *that it will rain soon*,
> *It* is likely *to rain soon*,
> **It* is probable *to rain soon*.

We shall cover these distributional differences by assigning the matrix-clause to a different construction-set according to whether the noun-clause is [finite] or [non-finite], as described in 5.7.1 below.

The presence or absence of SUBJECT in the noun-clause

If the noun-clause is [non-finite], it may or may not have SUBJECT in its structure. In some environments, SUBJECT is obligatory, in others impossible, and in others optional.

(a) If the matrix-clause has the feature [reaction], SUBJECT is optional whether the noun-clause is [infinitival] or [gerundival] :

> *Forgetting to plant the roses* upset Horace,
> *Agnes forgetting to plant the roses* upset Horace,
> *To have forgotten to plant the roses* upset Horace,
> *For Agnes to have forgotten to plant the roses* upset Horace.

Consequently, the choice between [with SUBJECT] and [without SUBJECT] in system 13 is free in this environment, and nothing is introduced into the matrix-clause's structure to restrict the choice.

(b) The same seems to be true where the matrix-clause has the feature [recall-factive] :

> I remember *saying that before*,
> I remember *someone saying that before*.

Once again, the choice between [with SUBJECT] and [without SUBJECT] is left free.

(c) Any other [factive] matrix-clause requires SUBJECT to be present:

> He admitted *her not to be his sister*,
> *He admitted *not to be her brother*.

However, this SUBJECT must be fronted, so it is introduced by the rules for fronting SUBJECT, described below.

(d) If the matrix-clause is [modal], in nearly all cases SUBJECT must be present; but it can be absent if the noun-clause is object of *claim*. We therefore distinguish two kinds of [modal] clause: those where SUBJECT is absent, the verb being *claim*, and those where SUBJECT is present, the verb being *claim* or any other relevant verb:

> He claimed *to be her brother*,
> He maintained *her to be his sister*.

To reflect this distinction we have a system, system 32, contrasting [subject-full noun-clause] with [subject-less noun-clause]. The latter feature is realised by the presence of SUBJECTLESS conflated with CLAUSE, which in turn is realised by [without SUBJECT] ; and the former is realised by the presence of a fronted SUBJECT, as described below.

The fronting of SUBJECT

SUBJECT is never fronted if the matrix-clause has either of the features [reaction] or [recall-factive] ; these are the two features with which SUBJECT is optional.

Where SUBJECT is obligatory, on the other hand, it must be fronted: that is, where the matrix-clause has either [modal, subject-full noun-clause] or [neutral-factive] among its features. In other words, one of the characteristics of [cognition] clauses as a whole is that when SUBJECT is obligatory, it must be fronted. To reflect this generalisation, we let FRONTED be introduced by the realisation-rule for [cognition], except in the environment of [subject-less noun-clause] or [recall-factive]. The presence of FRONTED permits various structure-building rules to apply, producing the correct structure for fronted SUBJECT as described in 5.6.2 below.

QUESTION-fronting

I shall assume, following 4.2.7, that QUESTION-fronting is possible for [modal] clauses, but not for either of the other constructions:

> *How old* did you think *that she was*?
> *How old did you recognise *that she was*?
> *How old did you regret *that she was*?

The two constructions from which QUESTION-fronting is excluded are the two in which the noun-clause's meaning is 'factive'; in these cases, it has the function FACT and must have the feature [declarative] (see the realisation-rule for FACT).

If the reader will look at network B on p. 248 he will find that we do not need to have any extra rules in the grammar in order to exclude QUESTION-fronting where the noun-clause is [declarative]. If there is QUESTION-fronting, then the noun-clause must be [pseudo-interrogative] (see 5.6.1 below), but [pseudo-interrogative] is incompatible with [declarative]: the former presupposes [non-mood-selecting], whereas the latter presupposes [mood-selecting]. Therefore the noun-clause in a 'factive' construction can never belong to the class which is needed for QUESTION-fronting.

Incidentally, precisely the same conflict automatically makes QUESTION-fronting impossible with reported questions:

> *How old did you wonder *whether she was*?

The noun-clause here will be [dependent, interrogative], which means it must also be [mood-selecting] and therefore cannot be [pseudo-interrogative].

There are thus two justifications for the otherwise perhaps rather unpromising contrast between [mood-selecting] and [non-mood-selecting]: it allows us to make the semantic generalisation that a [dependent] clause is always 'factive', whether it is [independent] or [dependent]; and it allows us to restrict QUESTION-fronting to [non-mood-selecting] clauses, thereby ruling it out in the environment of 'factive' noun-classes.

The use of 'so'

It is possible for the word *so* to occur where we should expect a noun-clause:

> I think *that she had to pay for it*,
> I think *so*.

But this is possible only if the matrix-clause has [modal] among its features, so it is excluded by both the features which permit 'factive' noun-clauses:

> *I realise *so*,
> *I regret *so*.

In order to allow for *so* in [modal] clauses, we have a system (system 36) contrasting [substitute noun-clause] with [non-substitute noun-clause], and presupposing [modal] but neither of the other features. The feature [substitute noun-clause] is realised by the presence of SUBSTITUTE conflated with CLAUSE; and the realisation-rule for SUBSTITUTE requires the feature [so] — an ad hoc feature defining the word *so*. In this way we avoid having to 'pronominalise' a noun-clause into *so*: we show that *so* is being used in an environment that otherwise requires a noun-clause, but we do not postulate a noun-clause which is later to be replaced by *so*.

I have used the term 'substitute noun-clause' to refer to *so*, but the same term could have been used for *it*, which can also be used in place of the noun-clause:

> I don't believe it.

Indeed, *it* is possible in a much wider range of constructions than *so*, and could be considered more important and therefore more deserving of the name 'substitute noun-clause'. However, the grammar does not generate descriptions for clauses containing *it*, because this would have meant a major excursion into pronominalisation, which it seemed better to avoid.

In addition to the restriction that we have already taken into account — that the matrix-clause must be [modal] — there are a number of restrictions on the use of *so*, which we can best formalise by means of structure-building rules. First it seems best to prevent the contrast between [finite noun-clause] and [non-finite noun-clause] (system 23) from applying in this environment, since almost every case of *so* would be ambiguous. This can be done by preventing SUBSTITUTE from conflating with CLAUSE except where FIN-CL is also conflated with it (rule 2n); thus the matrix-clause always has the feature [finite noun-clause] .

Secondly, *so* must be extraposed if it has the function SUBJECT, so by rule (2o) we prevent SUBSTITUTE from conflating with CLAUSE if CLAUSE is conflated with SUBJECT but not with LATE. This rules out the second of the following:

> It was believed so in those days,
> *So was believed in those days.

The possibility of extraposition with *so* is of course very strong evidence that it is being used like a noun-clause. Note that the other 'substitute' item, *it*, need not be extraposed:

> It was believed in those days.

Indeed, extraposition is never possible with *it*, which confirms my conclusion that the uses of *it* and of *so* are very different kinds of phenomena.

Thirdly, *so* cannot be used as ATTRIBUANT:

> It seems so,
> *It seems clear so.

This is easily prevented by rule (2j), SUBSTITUTE ≠ ATTRIBUANT.

The use of 'as'

If the matrix-clause is a particular kind of [dependent] clause, there is another 'substitute' item which can be used in place of the noun-clause: *as*. Unlike *so*, this is a 'subordinating conjunction' — that is, it has the function BINDER, and helps to define its clause's relation to its syntactic environment:

> As we expected, (it rained all day).

The only relevant restriction on the use of *as* is that it *cannot* be used in a clause with the feature [reaction] :

> *As we regretted, (it rained all day).

As far as the other two features, [modal] and [factive] , are concerned, *as* is allowed by either of them, so its exclusion from [reaction] clauses has nothing to do with the factivity associated with these, and the distribution of *as* is not at all parallel to that of *so*.

The grammar allows *as* to replace the noun-clause by including a system, system 21, which contrasts [clause as BINDER] with [not CLAUSE as BINDER] , and which depends on features which require both BINDER and CLAUSE to be present. The feature [clause as BINDER] is realised by the conflation of CLAUSE and BINDER, and the realisation-rule for CLAUSE requires the feature [as] − an ad hoc feature identifying the word *as* − in the environment BINDER.

In order to prevent *as* from occurring in a [modal] clause, we use a structure-building rule (rule 2g) to prevent BINDER from conflating with IN-DEFINITE, which, as the reader will remember, is a function which realises [modal] .

However, according to the system-network it is possible for a clause to have [substitute noun-clause] requiring *so*, as well as [clause as BINDER] , requiring *as*; these features are clearly not compatible, and we prevent them from occurring together by preventing their realising functions from combining with each other. This is effected by structure-building rule (2i): SUB-STITUTE ≠ BINDER.

The transitivity function of the noun-clause

Each of the features [reaction] , [modal] and [factive] allows a different range of transitivity-functions for the noun-clause. The range for each feature can be seen from the table on pp. 238−239: [reaction] corresponds to construction-set XV, [modal] to XVI through XVIII, and [factive] to XIX through XXI. The grammar reflects these differences in the way that we shall describe in 5.7.2 below: each construction corresponds to a set of features, which are realised, inter alia, by a function ('XV', 'XVI', etc.) conflated with LEX; and this defines a range of verbs or adjectives which may or may not allow the noun-clause to have some particular transitivity function. We can leave the discussion of the way in which this works until 5.7.2.

Extraposition

There is just one relevant fact about extraposition that is peculiar to these constructions: if the matrix-clause is [modal] , and the noun-clause is SUB-JECT, then extraposition is obligatory:

> **That he was overworking* seemed to everybody who knew him,
> It seemed to everybody who knew him *that he was overworking*.

By way of contrast, with the feature [factive] this is not so:

> *That he had been overworking* emerged at the inquest,
> It emerged at the inquest *that he had been overworking*.

Accordingly, the grammar includes a realisation-rule for [modal] which introduces REPORT and conflates it with CLAUSE; and also the following structure-building rule:

(2p)   REPORT ≠ SUBJECT // CLAUSE ≠ LATE.

This makes extraposition obligatory wherever CLAUSE is conflated with both REPORT and SUBJECT.

However, there is an additional qualification of the rule to be covered: that extraposition is obligatory only if the matrix-clause contains no 'complement', which can arise only if it is [attributive]. For instance, if we add *most unlikely* after *seem*, the example given above becomes acceptable:

> *That he was overworking* seemed most unlikely to everybody
> who knew him.

In order to build this qualification into the grammar we add a condition on the rule that introduces REPORT, as realisation of [modal], so that REPORT will be present only if the matrix-clause is not [attributive].

5.5. Fronting and discontinuity

In this section we shall be discussing constructions like the following:

> *Where* do you think *she put it*?
> *She* seems *to be happy*,
> *Rice* is hard *to cook*.

In each of these examples, some item is separated from the rest of the noun-clause, so that the latter is discontinuous. Discontinuity can only be handled by a fairly sophisticated grammar, so the way in which this grammar generates such structures will doubtless be of particular interest to the reader.

The discontinuous constructions that we shall be discussing all involve 'fronting' of one of three kinds: SUBJECT-fronting (4.2.5), COMPLEMENT-fronting (4.2.6) and QUESTION-fronting (4.2.7). However, fronting does not always lead to discontinuity; the reader will recall that in 4.2.5 I extended 'fronting' to cover constructions in which the noun-clause is not SUBJECT, and in which its two parts are in fact immediately next to each other:

> I believe *her to be a competent violinist.*

The grammar covers both kinds of fronting, with and without discontinuity, and we shall include both in the discussion in this section.

We shall take the three main kinds of fronting one at a time, but in a different order from the order we followed in chapter 4:

(1) COMPLEMENT-fronting, as in

> *Rice* is hard *to cook*

(2) SUBJECT-fronting, as in

> *She* seems *to be happy*,
> I believe *her to be a competent violinist.*

(3) QUESTION-fronting, as in

> *Where* do you think *she put it?*

5.5.1. *COMPLEMENT-fronting*

The matrix-clause: features determining structures

If there is COMPLEMENT-fronting, the matrix-clause must have among its features the following: [object-oriented] (32) and [unrestricted-aspect noun-clause] (25). The realisation-rules for the former feature in the environment of the latter include:

> + FRONTED,
> + COMPLEMENT ‖ FRONTED,
> + XII = LEX.

That is, if the matrix-clause has these two features, then its *own* structure must include the function FRONTED, the noun-clause's structure must include COMPLEMENT, and the item that has the latter function must be in the place defined by the former — in other words, COMPLEMENT in the noun-clause's structure must be immediately below FRONTED in the matrix-clause's. (For the meaning of the up-ended 'equals' sign in the realisation-rule, see p. 263.)

In addition to the features just mentioned, the matrix-clause must also be [attributive], because the only 'lexical predicates' that can have the relevant function, XII, are adjectives like *easy* and *difficult* (see 5.7.2 below). This means, among other things, that the noun-clause must have the function SUBJECT. Now there is a conflation-rule,

(4g)   FRONTED = M-SUBJECT // + CLAUSE = SUBJECT,

which makes FRONTED (which must occur in the matrix-clause's structure) be conflated with M-SUBJECT if CLAUSE is conflated with SUBJECT – as it must be, from what we have just said.

There are two further structure-building rules that are also relevant: an addition rule,

(3k)   + PRE-CLAUSE = FRONTED, Q-FRONTED,

and a compatibility-rule,

(2r)   CLAUSE ≠ SUBJECT // CLAUSE ≠ LATE *and* + PRE-CLAUSE.

The first of these adds PRE-CLAUSE to FRONTED, which means that it and any functions conflated with it are functions of the noun-clause, though not in the same bundle of functions as CLAUSE (p. 261); and the second ensures that the clause will be extraposed if the main clause contains PRE-CLAUSE and the noun-clause itself is SUBJECT – as it is in the cases in question.

Taking account of all these rules, then, we can say that if the matrix-clause has the features [object-oriented] and [unrestricted-aspect noun-clause] its own structure will include the following functions:

(a)   M-SUBJECT = FRONTED = PRE-CLAUSE,
(b)   SUBJECT = CLAUSE = LATE,
(c)   XII = LEX.

The order in which these bundles will appear in the structure is entirely predictable from the sequence-rules which refer to M-SUBJECT, to LATE and to ATTRIBUTE (with which LEX is conflated).

The noun-clause: structures determining features

Turning to the noun-clause itself, we can also say that its structure must contain COMPLEMENT, and that this function is positioned with reference to functions in the matrix-clause's structure rather than in the noun-clause's own structure: COMPLEMENT is positioned immediately beneath M-SUBJECT = FRONTED = PRE-CLAUSE in the matrix-clause. Thus the structures of the two clauses in our example must include the following functions (functions that are specified by rules other than the ones that I have mentioned in this discussion are bracketed).

M-SUBJECT	(FINITE)	(ATTRIBUTE)	SUBJECT	
FRONTED	(BE)		CLAUSE	
PRE-CLAUSE			LATE	
COMPLEMENT			(TO)	(PROCESS)
Rice	is	hard	to	cook

There is one other rule to take note of: there is a general convention (p. 263) that any function introduced by means of an up-ended equals sign — as COMPLEMENT is here — must *also* be required by the noun-clause's own features. That is, the noun-clause must have features which would in any case require its structure to contain COMPLEMENT.

Our grammar does not cover clauses that do not contain a noun-clause, such as the noun-clause in the above example, so let us take a rather more complex example instead:

Most people are easy *to persuade that they need a holiday.*

There are two noun-clauses here, one embedded in the other; the one in question is the larger one, which is italicised. The matrix-clause has the features [object-oriented] and [unrestricted-aspect noun-clause], so it automatically follows, from the various rules discussed above, that the noun-clause's structure must contain COMPLEMENT, and that the noun-clause's own features must also require COMPLEMENT. This they do: they include [with processer, clause as participant, active, clause as GOAL, with ADDRESSEE], whose realisation-rules mean that the clause's structure must include, inter alia, ADDRESSEE (not conflated with SUBJECT). The structure-building rule (3f) adds FIRST to ADDRESSEE if it is not conflated with SUBJECT, and (3j) in turn adds COMPLEMENT to FIRST — so that COMPLEMENT is in fact required by the noun-clause's features, as I claimed it was.

The relation between the matrix-clause's features and the noun-clause's features is a very indirect one, as the reader will have realised from the example just given. Perhaps it will be helpful if I summarise the various relations that I have just described:
(a) the matrix-clause has the features [object-oriented] and [unrestricted-aspect noun-clause] ;
(b) therefore the *noun-clause's* structure must contain COMPLEMENT, whose position is identified by the position of M-SUBJECT in the matrix-clause;
(c) therefore the noun-clause's structure must also contain either FIRST or SECOND, since COMPLEMENT is only introduced by a structure-building rule which adds it to either of these functions; in our example it is FIRST that leads to COMPLEMENT;
(d) therefore the noun-clause's structure must include ADDRESSEE, since (according to our grammar) it is only the presence of the latter that allows FIRST to be added, by a structure-building rule;
(e) therefore the noun-clause's features must include [with ADDRESSEE] , since it is only then that its structure will contain ADDRESSEE; moreover, it must also have the feature [active] , since otherwise ADDRESSEE would be conflated with SUBJECT, which would rule out FIRST.

5.5.2. SUBJECT-fronting

SUBJECT-fronting is more complicated than COMPLEMENT-fronting, for three reasons. Firstly, there are five alternative combinations of features that the matrix-clause can have, each of which allows SUBJECT-fronting; whereas only one combination of features was involved in COMPLEMENT-fronting. Secondly, the fronted item is not always in the same place in the matrix-clause's structure: it may be before the main verb, as M-SUBJECT, or after it, as FIRST. And thirdly, SUBJECT-fronting is recursive.

The matrix-clause

The five feature-combinations which allow SUBJECT-fronting are located in systems 23 through 37, though not all the systems in this sub-network are relevant. The relevant ones are repeated on the next page. In table 5.14 are the relevant feature-realisation rules.

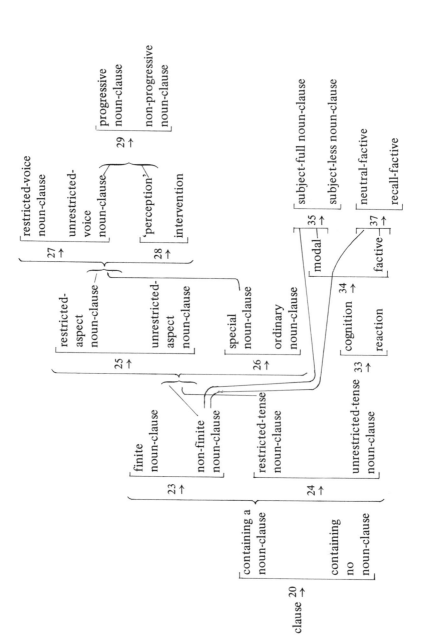

Table 5.14

System	Feature	Realisation
26	ordinary noun-clause	+ FRONTED // [restricted-aspect noun-clause] *and not* [clause as completer]
27	restricted-voice noun-clause	+ FRONTED
29	non-progressive noun-clause	+ FRONTED
30	SUBJECT-fronting	+ FRONTED
33	cognition	+ FRONTED // [non-finite noun-clause] *and not* [subject-less clause] *and not* [recall-factive]

The feature-realisation rules for these features introduce the function FRONTED into the matrix-clause's structure, but no more than that. This function then acts as a 'trigger' for a variety of structure-building rules which fill out the matrix-clause's structure and add M-SUBJECT in the noun-clause's structure.

First of all there are rules which conflate FRONTED with either M-SUBJECT or FIRST:

(4g)   FRONTED = M-SUBJECT // + CLAUSE = SUBJECT,
(3f′)   + FIRST = FRONTED // + CLAUSE ≠ SUBJECT.

That is, if the noun-clause is itself SUBJECT, then FRONTED conflates with M-SUBJECT; otherwise it conflates with FIRST. Compare the following, for instance:

The earth was believed *to be flat*
FRONTED   CLAUSE
M-SUBJECT   SUBJECT

They   believed *the earth   to be flat*
M-SUBJECT   FRONTED CLAUSE
SUBJECT   FIRST

Then there is a rule which adds PRE-CLAUSE to FRONTED:

(3k)   + PRE-CLAUSE = FRONTED, Q-FRONTED.

This shows that FRONTED and CLAUSE are functions of the same item, although they are not conflated.

Thirdly, there is a rule which makes extraposition obligatory if the noun-clause is SUBJECT:

(2r)   CLAUSE ≠ SUBJECT // CLAUSE ≠ LATE *and* + PRE-CLAUSE.

According to this rule, the noun-clause can be extraposed, as it is in the first of the last two examples quoted; so we should expect an expletive *it*, as in 'normal' cases of extraposition. But this is ruled out because rule (4g) above means that M-SUBJECT must be conflated with other functions, and the rule which introduces *it* as realisation of M-SUBJECT stipulates that no other function must be conflated with it.

Fourthly, there are a variety of rules which position the functions with which FRONTED is conflated, notably M-SUBJECT and FIRST. There is no need to say anything more about the rules for M-SUBJECT, so we can concentrate on the rules for FIRST:

(3i)   + POST-VERB = FIRST, SECOND, THIRD, AGENT, LATE,
(1b)   BINDER $\supseteqq$ M-SUBJECT → PROCESS → POST-VERB.

These two rules guarantee that FIRST follows the main verb (PROCESS).

(1c)   FIRST → SECOND → THIRD → LATE.

This rule guarantees that the fronted item precedes the rest of the noun-clause, since this will always have the function SECOND.

And finally, there is a rule which attaches M-SUBJECT below FRONTED except where COMPLEMENT is attached below it:

(3m)   + M-SUBJECT ‖ FRONTED // *not* COMPLEMENT ‖ FRONTED.

The various rules that I have just listed mean that our example sentences include the following structures, with a few more functions added (in brackets) to give the structures more shape.

FRONTED M-SUBJECT PRE-CLAUSE	(FINITE) (BE)	(PROCESS) (PASSIVE)	CLAUSE SUBJECT LATE (GOAL)		
M-SUBJECT			(TO)	(BE)	(ATTRIBUTE)
the earth	*was*	*believed*	*to*	*be*	*flat*

(M-SUBJECT) (SUBJECT (ACTOR)	(FINITE) (PROCESS)	FRONTED FIRST POST-VERB PRE-CLAUSE	CLAUSE (SECOND) (POST-VERB) (GOAL)		
		M-SUBJECT	(TO)	(BE)	(ATTRIBUTE)
They	*believed*	*the earth*	*to*	*be*	*flat*

The noun-clause

The noun-clause must have M-SUBJECT in its structure, and this restricts the features that it can have. However, as with the fronted COMPLEMENT, there is no *direct* relation between the presence of M-SUBJECT and that of any particular features. Instead, the relation is mediated by a structure-building rule:

(31)   + M-SUBJECT // + SUBJECT.

In other words, M-SUBJECT is automatically introduced when SUBJECT is present. As far as the latter is concerned, however, it *is* directly related to features of the clause: if the clause has SUBJECT in its structure then it must have one of three combinations of features, [independent, indicative], [dependent, finite] or [dependent, non-finite, with SUBJECT]. Since SUB-

JECT-fronting only occurs in constructions which demand a non-finite noun-clause, the latter must have the third of these combinations of features.

Recursive SUBJECT-fronting

The features that allow SUBJECT-fronting are selected entirely without reference to the contrast between [dependent] and [independent] and all the other contrasts that decide whether or not the matrix-clause can itself be a noun-clause. Consequently a matrix-clause in which there is SUBJECT-fronting can itself be a noun-clause whose M-SUBJECT is fronted; and since the fronted M-SUBJECT of a noun-clause is also M-SUBJECT in the matrix-clause, it is the same item that is fronted in each case. For instance, consider the following example:

There is likely *to appear to be a kink in the rod*.

The item *there* is at one and the same time M-SUBJECT in three different clauses: in *there to be a kink in the rod*, in *there to appear to be a kink in the rod*, and in *There is likely to appear to be a kink in the rod*.

Our grammar allows for constructions like these — indeed, it would be very hard to exclude them. Matrix-clauses and noun-clauses both select their features from the same network, and there is nothing to prevent a matrix-clause from having the same features as its noun-clause, since the matrix-clause can be [dependent]. In particular, there is nothing to prevent them from both having features which allow SUBJECT-fronting, whether these features are the same or not. For instance, in the following both noun-clauses have the feature [SUBJECT-fronting] (30).

People tend *to manage to get by somehow,*

Whereas in the next example the larger noun-clause has [SUBJECT-fronting] whilst the smaller one has another of the features that allows SUBJECT-fronting, [restricted-voice noun-clause] :

Lawns tend *to need mowing every week*.

How does the grammar generate the structures required in such cases, where one construction involving SUBJECT-fronting contains another? As with the selection of features, there is no problem: the feature-realisation rules and structure-building rules which were listed above automatically generate them.

Let us consider an imaginary example, which contains three clauses, numbered 1, 2 and 3, with 3 embedded as a noun-clause in 2 and 2 in 1. Clauses 1 and 2 both have features which are realised by the presence of FRONTED in their respective structures, and furthermore in both of them the noun-clause has the function SUBJECT. The structure-building rules will automatically conflate FRONTED with M-SUBJECT in both their structures, and will also ensure that M-SUBJECT occurs immediately below FRONTED in either case — that is, that M-SUBJECT occurs in the structure of 2 and 3 below the instances of FRONTED in 1 and 2 respectively. But the M-SUBJECT in 2, with which FRONTED is conflated, is itself positioned below the FRONTED in 1, so the M-SUBJECT of 3, positioned below the FRONTED in 2, must also be below M-SUBJECT in 1.

The following diagram should make these relation clear: if the position of one function is determined by that of another, then the two are linked by an arrow pointing towards the determining function.

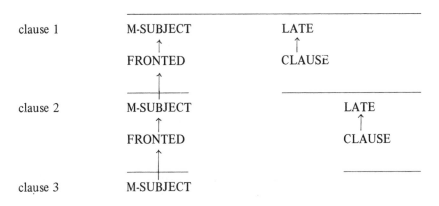

There is one further virtue of our grammar that is worth pointing out: it allows for cases where the fronted M-SUBJECT is the expletive *it*, as in

It seems *to be probable that the cost of living will rise for ever.*

The expletive *it*, it will be recalled, is the manifestation that M-SUBJECT has when it is not conflated with any of the functions SUBJECT, COMPLEMENT or FRONTED, so the fronting of M-SUBJECT must not automatically lead to its being conflated with any of these functions. According to our grammar, it does not.

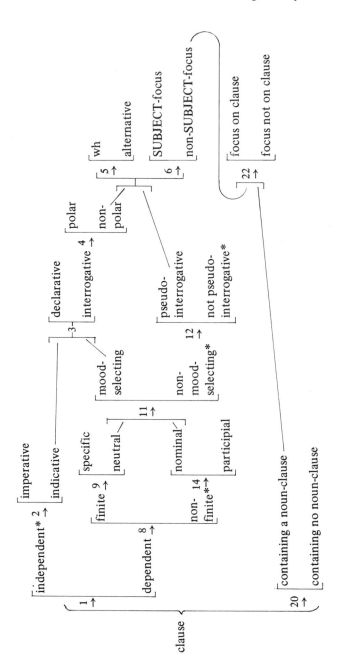

5.5.3. *QUESTION-fronting*

The first two kinds of fronting — SUBJECT-fronting and COMPLEMENT-fronting — are mutually exclusive, but they are entirely independent of QUESTION-fronting: one matrix-clause may involve one of the former as well as the latter, as in

When	does *he*	tend *to get home?*
Q-FRONTED	FRONTED	CLAUSE

This independence is reflected by the fact that the feature which allows QUESTION-fronting is located in a completely different sub-network from the features which allow the other kinds of fronting: in the sub-network which reflects the matrix-clause's mood and dependency, rather than that which reflects its 'construction-set'.

The matrix-clause

There is only one feature that leads to QUESTION-fronting: [focus on clause], in system 22. Nevertheless it will be useful to repeat here a part of the system-network, showing how system 22 relates to other systems. According to this network, [focus on clause] presupposes [containing a noun-clause] and also [non-SUBJECT focus] and [non-polar] or [pseudo-interrogative]. I shall show how [pseudo-interrogative] fits into the grammar later in this sub-section, but for the present we shall pretend that [non-polar] is the only feature that, in the environment of [containing a noun-clause] and [non-SUBJECT focus], allows [focus on clause].

The feature-realisation rules that I shall have to refer to are repeated in table 5.15. A number of structure-building rules will be relevant as well, but I can quote these as they come up for discussion.

The network allows QUESTION-fronting in matrix-clauses that have either of the features [wh] and [alternative], whether they are [independent] or [dependent]. The structures that we shall need to generate for [wh, independent] clauses, like

How do you think *she'll take it?*

are different from those that we shall generate for [wh, dependent] clauses such as

(I was wondering) *how* you thought *she'd take it,*

Table 5.15

System	Feature	Realisation
3	interrogative	+ MOOD-FOCUS // [independent]
		+ BINDER
		+ QUESTION = BINDER } // [dependent]
5	wh	+ QUESTION = MOOD-FOCUS // [independent]
		+ QUESTION // [pseudo-interrogative]
	alternative	+ ALTERNATIVE
6	SUBJECT-focus	QUESTION = SUBJECT // [wh]
		ALTERNATIVE = SUBJECT // [alternative]
	non-SUBJECT focus	QUESTION = COMPLEMENT // [wh] *and not* [focus on clause]
		ALTERNATIVE = COMPLEMENT // [alternative] *and not* [focus on clause]
22	focus on clause	+ Q-FRONTED = QUESTION
		+ PSEUDO-WH = CLAUSE } // [wh]
		ALTERNATIVE = CLAUSE // [alternative]

and also from those needed for [alternative] clauses, [independent] or [dependent] :

> Do you think *she'll do well or badly*?
> (I was wondering) whether you thought *she'd do well or badly*.

I shall discuss these three constructions separately.

[wh, independent] matrix-clauses

As a result of the realisation-rules for [interrogative] and [wh], an [independent] matrix-clause's structure contains QUESTION conflated with MOOD-FOCUS; and MOOD-FOCUS is put at the beginning of the clause by sequence-rule (1d):

$$\text{MOOD-FOCUS} \gtreqqless (\text{PRE-SUBJECT} \to \text{M-SUBJECT}) \to \text{PROCESS.}$$

If the clause also has [focus on clause] among its features, then Q-FRONTED will be added to these two conflated functions, giving a bundle of functions containing QUESTION, MOOD-FOCUS and Q-FRONTED, standing at the beginning of the matrix-clause's structure.

There are two structure-building rules which then contribute to the structure because of the presence of Q-FRONTED:

(3k)   + PRE-CLAUSE = FRONTED, Q-FRONTED,
(3p)   + QUESTION ‖ Q-FRONTED.

The first rule adds PRE-CLAUSE to the bundle of functions already containing Q-FRONTED, showing that these functions belong to the noun-clause, although they are not conflated with CLAUSE. The second rule adds QUESTION below Q-FRONTED, in the structure of the noun-clause: this QUESTION is the function of the QUESTION-fronted item (and ensures that it will have the feature [phrase, questioning], by the realisation-rule for QUESTION). These rules result in structures like the following:

```
MOOD-FOCUS (PRE-SUBJECT) (M-SUBJECT) (PROCESS)        (GOAL)
QUESTION          |              |           |        (CLAUSE)
Q-FRONTED         |              |           |
PRE-CLAUSE        |              |           |
   |              |              |           |           |
 _____            |              |           |        _____
QUESTION          |              |           |   (M-SUBJECT) (PROCESS)
   |              |              |           |        |          |
  Why            do            they        think     she        died
```

We shall discuss later (p. 346) the way in which the presence of QUESTION in the noun-clause's structure is reconciled with the fact that it is not an interrogative clause.

One of the characteristics of QUESTION-fronting is that the noun-clause cannot be un-extraposed SUBJECT:

> *How* does *that she'll come* seem to you most likely?
> *How* does it seem most likely to you *that she'll come*?

The rule which excludes QUESTION-fronting from an unextraposed SUBJECT-clause is

(2r)   CLAUSE ≠ SUBJECT // CLAUSE ≠ LATE and + PRE-CLAUSE.

This is the same rule that makes extraposition obligatory for a SUBJECT-clause if there is SUBJECT- or COMPLEMENT-fronting:

>   *The British to be unfriendly* are said,
>   *The British* are said *to be unfriendly*.

Finally, the reader will have noticed that the realisation-rule for [non-SUBJECT focus] is too specific: it says that what must be conflated with QUESTION or ALTERNATIVE is COMPLEMENT, but in a more complete grammar it will be necessary to allow it to be other functions, such as AD-JUNCT. Not having introduced this function elsewhere, however, I am not in a position to refer to it in this rule.

[wh, dependent] matrix-clauses

The only difference between [dependent] and [independent] wh-interrogative clauses is that QUESTION — which they both have in their structures — is conflated with BINDER in the former whereas it is conflated with MOOD-FOCUS in the latter. In either case it means that QUESTION has to be at the beginning of the clause, only it has to be *absolute* initial when conflated with BINDER. Otherwise there is no difference in the way that structures are built up to allow QUESTION-fronting, so we have [dependent] clauses with structures like the following:

(M-SUBJECT) SUBJECT)	(PRO-CESS)					
		BINDER QUESTION Q-FRONTED PRE-CLAUSE	(M-SUBJECT)	(PROCESS)		(GOAL) (CLAUSE)
		QUESTION				(M-SUBJECT) (PROCESS)
(I	wonder)	why	they	think		she died

[Alternative] matrix-clauses

Having the focus of the question concentrated within the noun-clause is possible not only for wh-interrogative matrix-clauses but also for alternative interrogatives like

> Did they say *that it was a boy or a girl*?

which is, of course, different from

> Did they say *whether it was a boy or a girl*?

In the latter example, the matrix-clause is [interrogative, polar] and the noun-clause is presumably [interrogative, alternative], but in the former it is the matrix-clause itself that is [interrogative, alternative], while the noun-clause is [non-mood-selecting].

The system-network allows for [alternative] interrogative clauses with [focus on clause], but as the reader will have realised such clauses do not involve QUESTION-fronting. We have to discuss them here partly because they are in other ways similar to [wh] interrogatives – in particular in that the construction is recursive, as I shall show below.

The rules for [alternative] interrogative clauses are relatively simple. Being [interrogative], their structures contain either MOOD-FOCUS (if [independent]) or QUESTION conflated with BINDER (if [dependent]); just as with [polar] interrogatives, there are no other feature-realisation rules which conflate more functions with MOOD-FOCUS or QUESTION, so these result respectively in the inversion of M-SUBJECT and FINITE, and in the presence of *whether* or *if*. What distinguishes [alternative] interrogatives from [polar] interrogatives is that the former have ALTERNATIVE in their structure: this is the function of whichever of its ICs specifies the alternatives to be chosen from, coordinated by *or*, such as *a boy or a girl* in the following:

> Was it a boy or a girl?

If the matrix-clause has the feature [focus on clause] as well as the feature [alternative], then the realisation-rule for the former ensures that ALTERNATIVE will be conflated with CLAUSE; and the realisation-rules for ALTERNATIVE will make the noun-clause itself have the feature [alternative] as we shall see below.

The structure of our first example will therefore include the following:

(MOOD-FOCUS)	(M-SUBJECT)	(PROCESS)	(GOAL)
(PRE-SUBJECT)			CLAUSE
			ALTERNATIVE
Did	*they*	*say*	*that it was a boy or a girl?*

The noun-clause

There are two aspects of QUESTION-fronting that we have not yet touched on: the restriction that it is not possible in a 'factive' construction, and the fact that the noun-clause is itself in some respects like an [interrogative] clause. Unexpectedly these two facts turn out to be closely connected in the grammar.

The noun-clause is not [interrogative] — indeed, QUESTION-fronting from an [interrogative] noun-clause is almost never possible, although semantically it may make sense:

> *Where did you ask her whether she put her gloves?*
> *How long did she tell you whether she stayed there or not?*

Nevertheless there are three respects in which the noun-clause is like an [interrogative] clause, and more particularly like a [non-polar] one.

Firstly, one of its ICs either is a 'questioning phrase' (like *which way, how long, who*) or involves a disjunctive coordination (like *a boy or a girl, Fred's or Bill's girl friend*); to simplify the realisation-rules it is convenient to give the function QUESTION to the former and ALTERNATIVE to the latter, and the easiest way to introduce these functions is to say that the noun-clauses containing them have the features [wh] and [alternative] respectively. Thus, in an example like

> *Where did you say she lived?*

the noun-clause has the feature [wh] — although it is not [interrogative] — and its structure includes QUESTION (representing *where*) as realisation of this feature. Similarly, in

> Did you say *that she lived in London or somewhere else?*

the noun-clause is [alternative] , but not [interrogative] , and its structure contains ALTERNATIVE (*in London or somewhere else*) according to the normal realisation-rules for this feature.

Secondly, these functions QUESTION and ALTERNATIVE have to be conflated with other functions — the items that function as QUESTION or ALTERNATIVE also function, at the same time, as SUBJECT or COMPLE-MENT, and as ACTOR, GOAL and so on. The same is of course true of [in-terrogative, non-polar] clauses, and so we can use the same apparatus for conflating QUESTION and ALTERNATIVE with other functions in either case. Exactly what that apparatus will be is still unclear, but it is likely that it will include our system distinguishing cases where QUESTION or ALTERNA-TIVE is conflated with SUBJECT — [SUBJECT-forms] — from cases where it is not — [non-SUBJECT forms] . What is important is that the apparatus will apply equally to [interrogative] clauses and to noun-clauses that are involved in QUES-TION-fronting, so this system in particular will apply to both kinds of clause.

And thirdly, if a noun-clause has QUESTION or ALTERNATIVE in its structure because the question in the matrix-clause is focussed on it, it can have its own 'question' focussed on another noun-clause embedded within it, although it is not itself interrogative. To allow for this, we make such noun-clauses subject to the same system that determines whether the question in an [interrogative] clause is focussed on a noun-clause or not, system 22.

These are the three similarities between [interrogative, non-polar] clauses and noun-clauses that are involved in QUESTION-fronting. The other fact which the grammar has to take account of, as I noted above, is that QUES-TION-fronting is impossible in factive constructions. We can now show how these various facts are incorporated into the grammar.

It will be recalled that the noun-clause in a 'factive' construction must be [mood-selecting], which allows it also to be [declarative] (see p. 321); whereas the noun-clauses in constructions of the kinds which allow QUES-TION-fronting must be [non-mood selecting] . We can take advantage of this difference in order to exclude QUESTION-fronting from factive construc-tions, by making [non-mood selecting] obligatory in the environment of QUESTION-fronting; this will lead to a conflict between the feature required by the factivity of the construction — [mood-selecting] — and the feature re-quired by the QUESTION-fronting — [non-mood selecting] — and this con-flict will be irreconcilable.

Not all clauses that are [non-mood selecting] are involved in QUESTION-fronting, of course, so we distinguish between those that are and those that are not by means of system 12. We call those that are involved in QUES-TION-fronting [pseudo-interrogative] , since they are like [interrogative] clauses without actually being [interrogative]. Then we allow all the systems that apply to [interrogative, non-polar] clauses also to apply to [pseudo-interrogative] clauses, thereby reflecting in a very simple way the similarities between the two kinds of clause.

Finally, how do we formalise the restriction which we stated above, that a noun-clause involved in QUESTION-fronting must be [non-mood selecting]? This too is simply done by the realisation-rules for the feature [focus on clause] which is responsible for all QUESTION-fronting:

$$
\left.\begin{array}{l}
+ \text{Q-FRONTED} = \text{QUESTION} \\
+ \text{PSEUDO-WH} = \text{CLAUSE}
\end{array}\right\} \;//\; [\text{wh}] ,
$$
$$
\text{ALTERNATIVE} = \text{CLAUSE} \;//\; [\text{alternative}] .
$$

These rules ensure that either PSEUDO-WH or ALTERNATIVE will be conflated with CLAUSE, and the realisation-rules for these two functions in turn ensure that the noun-clause will be either [pseudo-interrogative, wh] or [pseudo-interrogative, alternative] — which means that it must also be [non-mood selecting], since this feature is presupposed by [pseudo-interrogative].

Recursive QUESTION-fronting

Our grammar allows for examples like

> *Where* did you say *that she thought she had put it*?

in which an item is QUESTION-fronted out of one noun-clause into the structure of another noun-clause acting as matrix-clause to it, and then out of the latter into its matrix-clause. There is no limit to the number of layers of structure through which the QUESTION-fronting can apply, so the construction is recursive just as SUBJECT-fronting is. This possibility is covered by the fact that system 22, which introduces [clause as focus] and thereby gives rise to QUESTION-fronting, applies to [pseudo-interrogative] noun-clauses as well as to [interrogative, non-polar] clauses.

Let us see how this works out for [wh] interrogative clauses, by considering a hypothetical example where there are three clauses, 1, 2 and 3, with 3 embedded as noun-clause in 2 and 2 in 1. Clause 1 has among its features [interrogative, non-polar, wh, focus on clause], which means that its structure must contain Q-FRONTED conflated with QUESTION, with another instance of QUESTION below Q-FRONTED in the structure of clause 2. Clause 2 in turn has to have the features [non-mood selecting, pseudo-interrogative, wh], because CLAUSE in the structure of 1 is conflated with

PSEUDO-WH; but it also has the feature [focus on clause] which means that
it too has in its structure Q-FRONTED conflated with QUESTION, with a
further QUESTION below Q-FRONTED, this time in the structure of clause
3. The diagram below shows how these functions are related to each other;
once again, the arrows show that the higher function determines the position
of the lower one.

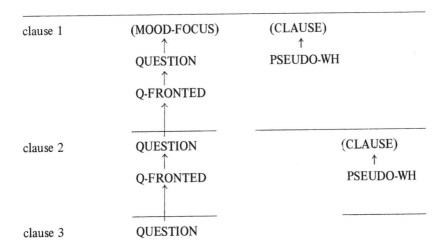

The rules work in the same way, mutatis mutandis, for [alternative]
matrix-clauses: the noun-clauses have to be [alternative] all the way down,
just as the noun-clauses in a [wh] matrix-clause have to be [wh] all the way
down, but the focus of the question does not have to be initial in the matrix-
clause, so there is no discontinuity:

clause 1	(CLAUSE) ALTERNATIVE
clause 2	(CLAUSE) ALTERNATIVE
clause 3	ALTERNATIVE

An example of this kind of construction would be

Did you say *she thought she had put it in the drawer or*
somewhere else?

5.6. The selection of the lexical predicate

The lexical predicate

This section is concerned with the selection of the 'lexical predicate' —
that is, with the way in which the other variables in the matrix-clause restrict
the choice of its 'predicate' (see 4.2.14 and 4.2.15). By 'predicate' I mean
either the item acting as ATTRIBUTE (i.e. the 'predicative complement') or
the one acting as PROCESS (i.e. the main verb); the former if the clause is
[attributive], the latter if it is not. For instance, we can compare the following pair:

It seems likely *that he forgot,*
I believe *that he forgot.*

In the first example it is *likely*, whilst in the second it is *believe*, that is the
lexical predicate in our sense: it is they that reflect the fact that the construction is a 'modal' one, that the noun-clause's tense is not restricted, and so on.

The lexical predicate always has the function LEX, which is introduced by
the realisation-rule for [clause] :

+ LEX = ATTRIBUTE // [attributive]
+ LEX = PROCESS // *otherwise.*

We then use this function as a 'peg' on which to hang the other functions
which help to restrict the classes of items that can act as lexical predicate,
and which we shall be discussing below.

The classes concerned are clearly restricted by the functions which I have
already mentioned: ATTRIBUTE and PROCESS. If LEX is conflated with
PROCESS, the predicate must have the feature [lexical verb] , implying
[word, verb] ; but if LEX is conflated with ATTRIBUTE, then the predicate
has to have [adjectival] , implying [phrase] . These two restrictions are reflected by the realisation-rules for the functions ATTRIBUTE and PROCESS.

Restrictions imposed by the construction-sets

In 4.2.14 I distinguished twenty-one construction-sets which I numbered
I through XXI. Most of them were further sub-divided into construction-sets

which differed from each other specifically in the function of the noun-clause, and these smaller construction-sets I numbered a, b, c and so on.

The main justification for both the more general and the more specific construction-sets is a practical one: it is useful to have a single label for referring to the intersection of a number of different variables, to save having to refer to each of the variables separately. For instance 'XIVb' is the label for any construction in which

(a) the noun-clause is GOAL, but the matrix-clause cannot be passive;
(b) the noun-clause must be [infinitival, with to] ;
(c) the noun-clause may or may not have SUBJECT in its structure;
(d) if SUBJECT is present in the noun-clause's structure, it is not fronted;
(e) COMPLEMENT is not fronted from the noun-clause;
(f) the noun-clause is not introduced by *for* even if SUBJECT is present;
(g) the noun-clause must be [non-past] ;
(h) the noun-clause can be either [perfect] or [non-perfect] ;
(i) the noun-clause can be either [progressive] or [non-progressive] ;
(j) the noun-clause may or may not be [passive] ;

The factors characterising each construction-set are summarised in the table on pp. 330 and 331.

It is hardly necessary to say that the grammar was the basis on which the construction-sets were set up — so much so that the numbering of the construction-sets reflects the progression from the top to the bottom of our system-network. The reader will see how they are related to the system-network if he refers to network A (pp. 244—245): every construction-set is characterised by a different set of features from systems 23 through 37, and conversely, every system from 23 to 37 (with the insignificant exception of 36) helps to distinguish one group of construction-sets from another.

Thus, as far as the grammar is concerned, we can see the major construction-set numbers — i.e. the roman numerals on their own — as convenient labels for combinations of features from systems 23 through 37. For instance, we can see XIV as a label for the following features: [non-finite noun-clause, restricted-tense noun-clause, unrestricted-aspect noun-clause, ordinary noun-clause, engineered event] .

As well as being useful in presenting the grammar, however, the construction-sets have a part to play in the grammar itself: the roman numerals are used as the names of grammatical functions which combine with LEX and which thereby help to 'define the classes of verbs or adjectives that can act as lexical predicate in matrix-clauses that have the corresponding set of features. For instance, the function XIV is introduced by the realisation-rule for [engineered event] , in the environment of [unrestricted-aspect noun-clause] , so that any clause that has these two features, and all the other features which they presuppose, must have a structure containing XIV conflated with LEX.

As with other functions, the roman-numeral functions have realisations, and these are given at the end of the list of function-realisation rules (p. 268). For instance, XVI has the realisation '[A5/6] *or* [V8/9/18/23/24/30/31/32]'. This is to be interpreted as follows: XVI is realised either by one of the features [A5] and [A6], or by one of the features [V8], [V9], [V18] and so on. [A5] is the feature defining the class of adjectival phrases whose head-word is one of the adjectives in class A5, listed in the appendix, and [V8] is the feature defining verb-class V8, also listed in the appendix.

Restrictions imposed by the matrix-clause's transitivity

Completely independently of the features selected from systems 23 through 37, which determine the construction-set the matrix-clause selects from systems 38 through 45, which determine its transitivity and voice – whether or not there is a 'processer' as well as a noun-clause, whether the noun-clause is ACTOR or GOAL, whether the matrix-clause is active or passive, and so on. This set of features also restrict the lexical predicate: for instance, if the clause is ACTOR, then the predicate can be a verb like *amaze* but not a verb like *believe*, whereas if the clause is GOAL the possibilities are reversed.

Once again these restrictions are formalised by means of a range of functions that are conflated with LEX by the realisation-rules for the features concerned. The relevant rules were discussed in 5.2.1 above, so we need do no more here than give an example of the way in which the restrictions are formalised.

If the matrix-clause has the feature [clause as GOAL] – and therefore also [with processer, clause as participant] – then the function GOAL-CLAUSE will be conflated with PROCESS; and therefore, since in these cases LEX must also be conflated with PROCESS, LEX is conflated with GOAL-CLAUSE. This function already excludes many classes of lexical verb, but there are two other functions which may or may not also be conflated with LEX, together with GOAL-CLAUSE: ADDRESSED, realising the feature [with ADDRESSEE], and PASSIVE, realising [passive]. Three different ranges of verbs now have to be specified: those permitted by GOAL-CLAUSE when not conflated with either ADDRESSED or PASSIVE (*want*, but not *repute* or *assure*); those permitted by GOAL-CLAUSE when conflated with PASSIVE but not with ADDRESSED (*repute*, but not *want* or *assure*); and those permitted by GOAL-CLAUSE when conflated with ADDRESSED, with or without PASSIVE (*assure*, but not *want* or *repute*). These restrictions are covered by the realisation-rules for GOAL-CLAUSE and ADDRESSED.

Restrictions imposed by the verb- and adjective-classes

So far we have introduced two kinds of restriction on the classes of items that can have the function LEX: those due to the construction-set represented by the matrix-clause, and those due to its transitivity (with the difference between verbs and adjective-phrases as an instance of the second kind of restriction). Both of these kinds of restriction are formalised by means of functions conflated with LEX. However, there is a third kind of restriction which is not imposed in this way, but simply by the existence or non-existence of an appropriate class of adjectives or verbs.

Before explaining how this kind of restriction arises, let us consider how the first two kinds interact. If the construction-set is XVI, and the matrix-clause has the features [without processer, middle], then LEX will be conflated with PROCESS and also with XVI and INTRANS. PROCESS requires the feature [lexical verb]; XVI requires [A5/6] or [V8/9/18/23/24/30/31/32]; and INTRANS requires [V1/2/3/4/5/6/7/8/9]. Consequently, when these three functions are conflated, the item will have to have features that are permitted by *all* of them, which in effect excludes all features except [V8] and [V9].

The general principle, then, is that the lexical predicate must belong to the *intersection* of the classes permitted by the roman-numeral function and of the classes permitted by the functions that reflect the matrix-clause's transitivity and voice. Now we can explain the restrictions that are due to the verb- and adjective-classes themselves: the intersection of the two ranges of features may be *nil*, since there is *no* class which is compatible with both of two functions that are conflated with LEX. For instance, there is no verb that can have both XIII and INTRANS among its functions: the former function requires one of the features [A1/3] or [V10/16/20/21/22], while the latter requires one of [V1/2 ... /9], so there is no overlap.

What these restrictions mean is that certain – in fact, many – combinations of features which are permitted by the system-network, and which lead to otherwise well-formed structures, are ruled out simply because there is no verb or adjective that could act as lexical predicate. This is perhaps rather a crude way of showing the interdependencies between the systems (23–37) which distinguish construction-sets and those (38–45) which have to do with transitivity and voice; but it is clear how much more complicated the grammar would have been if we had tried to do this in any other way, and it is not clear that this approach has any malignant consequences.

5.7. An example

By way of a conclusion, we shall take just one example, and show what grammatical representation our grammar generates for it, and how this is generated. The example is

Who are all the boys believed to be longing to marry?

This is quite a complicated example, since it involves two noun-clauses, *who ... to marry* and *who ... all the boys ... to be longing to marry*, and the larger of these has two ICs that are fronted from it, one by QUESTION-fronting and the other by SUBJECT-fronting. Moreover, the QUESTION-fronted one is also fronted from the smaller noun-clause.

I shall refer to the three clauses in this example as clauses 1, 2 and 3, with the independent clause as 1 and *who to marry* as 3; and I shall discuss them in that order.

Clause 1

Clause 1 has the following features. For convenience, they are listed to-gether with their realisation-rules:

System	Feature	Realisation
	clause	+ PROCESS + LEX = ATTRIBUTE // [attributive] + LEX = PROCESS // *otherwise*
1	independent	−
2	indicative	+ FINITE + SUBJECT
3	interrogative	+ MOOD-FOCUS // [independent] + BINDER + QUESTION = BINDER } // [dependent]
4	non-polar	−
5	wh	+ QUESTION = MOOD-FOCUS // [independent] + QUESTION // [pseudo-interrogative]
6	non-SUBJECT	QUESTION = COMPLEMENT // [wh] *and not* [focus on clause] ALTERNATIVE = COMPLEMENT // [alternative] *and not* [focus on clause]
7	non-past	−
20	containing a noun-clause	+ CLAUSE // *not* [clause as ACTOR, ACTOR unspecified]

System	Feature	Realisation
22	focus on clause	+ Q-FRONTED = QUESTION ⎫ + PSEUDO-WH = CLAUSE ⎬ // [wh] ALTERNATIVE = CLAUSE // [alternative
23	non-finite noun-clause	–
24	unrestricted-tense noun-clause	–
33	cognition	+ FRONTED // [non-finite noun-clause] *and* *not* [subject-less noun-clause] *and not* [recall- factive]
34	modal	+ REPORT = CLAUSE // *not* [attributive] + TO-FULL = CLAUSE // [non-finite noun- clause] + XVI = LEX // [finite noun-clause]
35	subject-full noun-clause	+ XVII = LEX
36	non-substitute noun- clause	–
38	with processer	+ ACTOR // *not* [actor unspecified]
40	clause as participant	+ GOAL
42	passive	ADDRESSEE = SUBJECT // [with ADDRES- SEE] GOAL = SUBJECT // *otherwise* + PASSIVE // *not* [special passive]
43	actor unspecified	–
44	clause as GOAL	CLAUSE = GOAL + GOAL-CLAUSE = PROCESS
45	without ADDRESSEE	–
46	extraposed	+ LATE = CLAUSE
47	non-perfect	–
48	non-progressive	–

From these realisation-rules we can predict that the structure will include
the following; apart from the conflations shown, we do not yet know anything about the order in which the functions will occur in the structure.

PROCESS = LEX = XVII = GOAL-CLAUSE
FINITE
SUBJECT = GOAL = CLAUSE = PSEUDO-WH = REPORT =
    TO-FULL = LATE
FRONTED
PASSIVE
MOOD-FOCUS = QUESTION = Q-FRONTED

This partial structure is then subject to the following structure-building rules:

Sequence rules

(1a)   TO   →
       PARTICIPLE ⎫
       GERUND   ⎬ = ⎱ (PREPAST → ... BE → PASSIVE = PROCESS)
       FINITE   ⎭

(1b)   BINDER ⊒ M-SUBJECT → PROCESS → POST-VERB

(1d)   MOOD-FOCUS ⊒ (POLARITY → M-SUBJECT) → PROCESS

Compatibility rules

(2e)   POLARITY ≠ PROCESS
(2l)   POST-VERB ≠ QUESTION
(2p)   REPORT ≠ SUBJECT // CLAUSE ≠ LATE
(2r)   CLAUSE ≠ SUBJECT // CLAUSE ≠ LATE *and* + PRE-CLAUSE
(2s)   TO-FULL ≠ SUBJECT // CLAUSE ≠ LATE *and* SUBJECT = GOAL

Addition rules

(3a)   + AFFIX = PAST, PERFECT, PROGRESSIVE, PASSIVE, PARTICIPLE,
       GERUND, FINITE
(3e)   + BE // + PASSIVE ≠ PARTICIPLE
(3i)   + POST-VERB = FIRST, SECOND, THIRD, AGENT, LATE
(3k)   + PRE-CLAUSE = FRONTED, Q-FRONTED
(3l)   + M-SUBJECT // + SUBJECT
(3m)   + M-SUBJECT ‖ FRONTED // *not* COMPLEMENT ‖ FRONTED
(3n)   + PRE-SUBJECT // + MOOD-FOCUS ≠ SUBJECT
(3o)   + FOR-LESS = CLAUSE // + M-SUBJECT ‖ FRONTED *and* CLAUSE = TO-FULL
(3p)   + QUESTION ‖ Q-FRONTED

Conflation rules

(4d)   POLARITY = FINITE
(4g)   FRONTED = M-SUBJECT // + CLAUSE = SUBJECT

These structure-building rules add eleven more functions to the eighteen already specified by the feature-realisation rules, effect a number of conflations, and fix the sequence of the bundles of functions. The complete structure that results from the application of these rules is given below.

1	2	3	4	5
MOOD-FOCUS QUESTION Q-FRONTED PRE-CLAUSE	FINITE AFFIX PRE-SUBJECT BE	FRONTED PRE-CLAUSE M-SUBJECT	PROCESS LEX XVII GOAL-CLAUSE PASSIVE AFFIX	SUBJECT GOAL CLAUSE PSEUDO-WH REPORT TO-FULL LATE POST-VERB FOR-LESS
1′		3′		
QUESTION		M-SUBJECT		

The numbers 1−5 are not part of the structure but simply points to which we can refer below, in order to save repeating the whole structure. We can now move on to the function-realisation rules, repeated below. Instead of listing the functions in alphabetical order, as hitherto, we shall list them according to the bundle in which they occur in this particular structure, which means that a few of them will appear twice (table 5.16).

From these function-realisation rules, we can conclude that the items represented by the five bundles 1−5 must have the features shown below. No features are shown for bundles 1 and 3 because none of the functions concerned have any realisations in that environment, as the reader will see from the realisation-rules quoted. As for bundles 1′ and 3′, we do not show any features for them because they are part of the structure of clause 2, which is not yet complete, so it is too early to decide what features these bundles require. Features with an asterisk are present because of the convention for selecting unmarked features.

1	2	3	4	5
	[be] [finite verb] [present verb] * [non-concordial] *		[en-form] [lexical verb] [V18/24/25/30] [non-finite verb] *	[dependent] [without for] [with to] [pseudo-interrogative] [wh] [non-SUBJECT focus] [non-finite] * [nominal] * [non-mood-selecting] *

Table 5.16

Bundle	Function	Realisation
1	MOOD-FOCUS	–
	PRE-CLAUSE	–
	Q-FRONTED	–
	QUESTION	[phrase, questioning] // = SUBJECT *or* COMPLEMENT, *and not* = PRE-CLAUSE [whether/if] // *not* = SUBJECT *or* COMPLEMENT *or* PRE-CLAUSE
1′	QUESTION	*not yet determined*
2	AFFIX	–
	BE	[be]
	FINITE	[finite verb]
	PRE-SUBJECT	–
3	FRONTED	–
	M-SUBJECT	[it] // *not* = SUBJECT *or* PRE-CLAUSE
	PRE-CLAUSE	–
3′	M-SUBJECT	*not yet determined*
4	AFFIX	–
	GOAL-CLAUSE	[V1/3/4/12/13/ ... /29] // *not* = ADDRESSED *or* PASSIVE [V3/4/12/13 ... /27/30] // = PASSIVE *and not* = ADDRESSED
	LEX	–
	PASSIVE	[en-form]
	PROCESS	[lexical verb]
	XVII	[A6/7] *or* [V9/18/24/25/30]
5	CLAUSE	[dependent] // *not* = SUBSTITUTE *or* BINDER [as] // = BINDER
	FOR-LESS	[without for] // + M-SUBJECT ‖ FRONTED *or not* = SUBJECT
	GOAL	[phrase, nominal] // *not* = CLAUSE
	LATE	[with to] // *not* = FIN-CL *or* INDEFINITE
	POST VERB	–
	PSEUDO-WH	[pseudo-interrogative, wh] [non-SUBJECT focus] // = SUBJECT
	REPORT	–
	SUBJECT	–
	TO-FULL	[with to] *or* [gerundival] // = GERUND-CL *and not* = LATE [with to] // *otherwise*

Clause 2

Clause 2 is the italicized one in

Who are *all the boys* believed *to be longing to marry*?

From our description of clause 1 we know that it occurs at three places in the matrix-clause and that its functions require it to have the following features: [dependent] (1), [wh] (5), [non-SUBJECT focus] (6), [pseudo-interrogative] (12), [with to] (16), [without for] (17). Given these features, it must also have [non-finite] (8), [non-mood selecting] (11), [nominal] (14), [infinitival] (15); thus all of systems 1 through 19 are either predetermined or irrelevant, with two exceptions: system 7 ([past] versus [non-past]) and system 13 ([with SUBJECT] versus [without SUBJECT]).

Moreover, we also know that the structure of clause 2 must accommodate QUESTION and M-SUBJECT. This means that its features must be such that they require its structure to contain these two functions, and in particular that it must have [with SUBJECT], because of M-SUBJECT. So in effect only system 7 out of systems 1 through 19 remains to be selected from.

The features of clause 2, including those that are predetermined by its environment, are the following with realisation-rules.

System	Feature	Realisation
	clause	+ PROCESS + LEX = ATTRIBUTE // [attributive] + LEX = PROCESS // *otherwise*
1	dependent	−
5	wh	+ QUESTION = MOOD-FOCUS // [independent] + QUESTION // [pseudo-interrogative]
6	non-SUBJECT focus	QUESTION = COMPLEMENT // [wh] *and not* [focus on clause] ALTERNATIVE = COMPLEMENT // [alternative] *and not* [focus on clause]
7	non-past	−
8	non-finite	−
11	non-mood selecting	−
12	pseudo-interrogative	−
13	with SUBJECT	+ SUBJECT
14	nominal	−
15	infinitival	−

System	Feature	Realisation
16	with to	+ TO
17	without for	–
20	containing a noun-clause	+ CLAUSE // *not* [clause as ACTOR, ACTOR unspecified]
22	focus on clause	+ Q-FRONTED = QUESTION ⎫ + PSEUDO-WH = CLAUSE ⎬ // [wh] ALTERNATIVE = CLAUSE // [alternative]
23	non-finite noun-clause	–
24	restricted-tense noun-clause	+ NONPAST-CL = CLAUSE + I = LEX // [finite noun-clause]
25	unrestricted-aspect noun-clause	–
26	ordinary noun-clause	+ FRONTED // [restricted-aspect noun-clause] *and not* [clause as completer]
31	engineered event	+ TO-FULL = CLAUSE + FOR-LESS = CLAUSE // [without ADDRESSEE] + SUBJECTLESS = CLAUSE // [transitive] + IX = LEX // [restricted-aspect noun-clause] + XIV = LEX // [unrestricted-aspect noun-clause]
38	with processer	+ ACTOR // *not* [actor unspecified]
40	clause as completer	+ COMPLETER = CLAUSE + INCOMPLETE = PROCESS
41	intransitive	+ INTRANS = PROCESS ACTOR = SUBJECT
46	normal	–
47	non-perfect	–
48	progressive	+ PROGRESSIVE

From these feature-realisation rules we know that clause 2's structure must contain the following bundles of functions, in some order which on the whole is still to be established.

PROCESS = LEX = XIV = INCOMPLETE = INTRANS
QUESTION = Q-FRONTED
TO
CLAUSE = PSEUDO-WH = NONPAST-CL = TO-FULL =
        COMPLETER
ACTOR = SUBJECT
PROGRESSIVE.

Unlike clause 1, however, clause 2's structure is already partially ordered before we enter the structure-building rules: we already know where QUESTION and M-SUBJECT come relative to the rest of the clause (first QUESTION, then M-SUBJECT, then the rest of the clause).

The relevant structure-building rules are the following:

Sequence rules

(1a) TO →
PARTICIPLE
GERUND
FINITE
= (PREPAST ... → PREPROGRESSIVE → PROGRESSIVE = (BE → PASSIVE = PROCESS))

(1b) BINDER ⊒ M-SUBJECT → PROCESS → POST-VERB

(1d) MOOD-FOCUS ⊒ (PRE- SUBJECT → M-SUBJECT) → POST-SUBJECT → PROCESS

Addition rules

(3a) + AFFIX = PAST, PERFECT, PROGRESSIVE, PASSIVE, PARTICIPLE, GERUND, FINITE

(3d) + PREPROGRESSIVE // + PROGRESSIVE ≠ PARTICIPLE

(3h) + THIRD = ATTRIBUTE, COMPLETER

(3i) + POST-VERB = FIRST, SECOND, THIRD, AGENT, LATE

(3k) + PRE- CLAUSE = FRONTED, Q-FRONTED

(3l) + M-SUBJECT // + SUBJECT

(3n') + POST-SUBJECT = MODAL, PREPAST, PREPERFECT, PREPROGRESSIVE, BE

(3p) + QUESTION ‖ Q-FRONTED

Conflation rules

(4f) M-SUBJECT = SUBJECT // SUBJECT ≠ LATE

After these rules have been applied, the structure is fully ordered, and contains six more functions:

6	7	8	9	10	11
QUESTION	M-SUBJECT	TO	PREPROGRESSIVE	PROCESS	CLAUSE
Q-FRONTED	SUBJECT		POST-SUBJECT	LEX	PSEUDO-WH
PRE-CLAUSE	ACTOR			XVI	NONPAST-CL
				INCOMPLETE	TO-FULL
				INTRANS	COMPLETER
				PROGRESSIVE	THIRD
				AFFIX	POST-VERB

6'

QUESTION

Table 5.17

Bundle	Function	Realisation
6	PRE-CLAUSE	–
	Q-FRONTED	–
	QUESTION	[phrase, questioning] // = SUBJECT *or* COMPLEMENT, *and not* = PRE-CLAUSE
		[whether/if] // *not* = SUBJECT *or* COMPLEMENT *or* PRE-CLAUSE
6'	QUESTION	*not yet determined*
7	ACTOR	[phrase, nominal] // *not* = CLAUSE *or* AGENT
	M-SUBJECT	[it] // *not* = SUBJECT *or* PRE-CLAUSE
	SUBJECT	–
8	TO	[to]
9	PREPROGRES- SIVE	[be]
	POST-SUBJECT	–
10	AFFIX	–
	INCOMPLETE	[V12/13/17/37/38/39] // = INTRANS
	INTRANS	[V1/2/ .. /9] // *not* = INCOMPLETE
	LEX	–
	PROCESS	[lexical verb
	PROGRESSIVE	[ing-form]
	XIV	[V1/21] // = GOAL-CLAUSE *and not* = PASSIVE
		[V12/13/15/17/39] // *otherwise*
11	CLAUSE	[dependent] // *not* = SUBSTITUTE *or* BINDER
		[as] // = BINDER
	COMPLETER	–
	NONPAST-CL	[non-past]
	POST-VERB	–
	PSEUDO-WH	[pseudo-interrogative, wh]
		[non-SUBJECT focus] // = SUBJECT
	THIRD	–
	TO-FULL	[with to] *or* [gerundival] // = GERUND-CL *and not* = LATE
		[with to] // *otherwise*

Once again we list the realisation-rules for these functions according to the bundle in which they occur (table 5.17).

If we apply these realisation-rules, and also take account of the conventior for selecting unmarked features, we find that the following features are re-quired.

6	7	8	9	10	11
	[phrase] [nominal]	[to]	[non-finite verb] * [infinitive] * [be]	[ing-form] [lexical verb] [V12/13/17/39]	[dependent] [wh] [non-past] [non-finite] * [non-mood selecting] * [pseudo- interrogative] [nominal] * [with to] [with for] *

Clause 3

To refresh the reader's memory, the third clause is italicized:

Who are all the boys believed to be longing *to marry*?

It is discontinuous because *who* is QUESTION-fronted, and its two parts occur
in places 6 and 11 in clause 2's structure; but to the extent that its features
are determined by its environment, they are restricted by the functions in
bundle 11. Because of these, its features must include the features listed under
11 above, which are all taken from systems 1 through 19. Of these systems,
all but two are in fact predetermined by the environment; the two that are
not are system 6 — [SUBJECT-focus] versus [non-SUBJECT-focus] — and
system 13 — [with SUBJECT] versus [without SUBJECT]. Moreover, the
feature chosen from system 20 is [containing no noun-clause], which means
that all of systems 21 through 46 are excluded, leaving only 47 and 48 to be
selected from.

If we add together the predetermined features and the freely selected ones,
we find that clause 3 has the following features:

System	Feature	Realisation
	clause	+ PROCESS + LEX = ATTRIBUTE // [attributive] + LEX = PROCESS // *otherwise*
1	dependent	—
5	wh	+ QUESTION = MOOD-FOCUS // [independent] + QUESTION // [pseudo-interrogative]
6	non-SUBJECT focus	QUESTION = COMPLEMENT // [wh] *and not* [focus on clause] ALTERNATIVE = COMPLEMENT // [alterna- tive] *and not* [focus on clause]

System	Feature	Realisation
7	non-past	—
8	non-finite	—
11	non-mood selecting	—
12	pseudo-interrogative	—
13	without SUBJECT	—
14	nominal	—
15	infinitival	—
16	with to	+ TO
17	with for	+ BINDER + FOR = BINDER } // [with SUBJECT]
20	containing no noun- clause	—
47	non-perfect	—
48	non-progressive	—

When we apply these feature-realisation rules we find that the structure of clause 3 must contain the following function-bundles:

PROCESS = LEX,
QUESTION,
TO.

There is just one structure-building rule that we can apply to these functions, a sequence-rule:

(1a).   TO   →
         PARTICIPLE }
         GERUND   } . = } (PREPAST ... PROCESS)
         FINITE   }

This puts TO before PROCESS. Since we have already introduced QUESTION because of the features of clause 2, and know that it is beneath Q-FRONTED in clause 2's structure, it follows that it must precede all the other functions in clause 3's structure. Thus the complete structure for clause 3 is

12	13	14
QUESTION	TO	PROCESS LEX

I call this a 'complete structure', and strictly speaking, it *is* complete in the sense that our grammar does not allow us to add anything to it. However, it is clearly far less informative than either of the other structures that I have given, and the reason for this is that most of the systems are ruled out for this clause because it does not contain a noun-clause. In particular, all the 'transitivity'-systems are excluded, which means that we cannot even show that *who* is COMPLEMENT and GOAL as well as QUESTION. This is one of the inevitable prices that we pay for artificially confining the grammar to clauses which contain noun-clauses, so that precisely the simplest kinds of construction are beyond it.

Our grammar, then, does not allow us to give much information about clause 3, and we can regret this. But what is more serious is that, according to the grammar, clause 3 ought to be introduced by *whether* or *if*, rather than by a 'questioning phrase' like *who*: if QUESTION is not conflated with SUBJECT, COMPLEMENT or PRE-CLAUSE, then it is realised by [whether/if]. This means that either I ought to reformulate the grammar to allow *who* as realisation of QUESTION on its own, or I ought to leave this flaw to be corrected when the grammar is expanded to take in simple sentences. I shall take the second alternative.

Apart from *who*, then, the ICs of clause 3 must have the following features because of the functions that they have:

12	13	14
	[to]	[non-finite verb] *
		[infinitive] *
		[lexical verb]

The only function-realisation rules are those for TO and for PROCESS, requiring [to] and [lexical verb] respectively.

We can conclude by bringing all these features and functions together into a single diagram. This diagram represents the description generated by our grammar which fits the sentence

Who are all the boys believed to be longing to marry?

The same description would fit an indefinite number of other sentences, however, such as

What kind of model are modern linguists said to be aiming
to construct?

clause, independent, indicative, interrogative, non-polar, wh, non-SUBJECT focus, non-past, containing a noun-clause, focus on clause, non-finite noun-clause, unrestricted-tense noun-clause, cognition, modal, subject-full noun-clause, non-substitute noun-clause, with processer, clause as participant, passive, actor unspecified, clause as GOAL, without ADDRESSEE, extraposed, non-perfect, non-progressive

MOOD-FOCUS	FINITE	FRONTED	PROCESS	SUBJECT
QUESTION	AFFIX	PRE-CLAUSE	LEX	GOAL
Q-FRONTED	PRE-SUBJECT	M-SUBJECT	XVII	CLAUSE
PRE-CLAUSE	BE		GOAL-CLAUSE	PSEUDO-WH
			PASSIVE	REPORT
	[be]		AFFIX	TO-FULL
	[finite verb]			LATE
	[present verb]		[en-form]	POST-VERB
	[non-concordial]		[lexical verb]	FOR-LESS
			[V18/24/25/30]	
	(*are*)		[non-finite verb]	
			(*believed*)	

clause, dependent, wh, non-SUBJECT focus, non-past, non-finite, non-mood selecting, pseudo-interrogative, with SUBJECT, nominal, infinitival, with to, without for, containing a noun-clause, focus on clause, non-finite noun-clause, restricted-tense noun-clause, unrestricted-aspect noun-clause, ordinary noun-clause, engineered event, with processer, clause as completer, intransitive, normal, non-perfect, progressive

QUESTION	M-SUBJECT	TO	PREPROGRESSIVE	PROCESS	CLAUSE
Q-FRONTED	SUBJECT		POST-SUBJECT	LEX	PSEUDO-WH
PRE-CLAUSE	ACTOR			XIV	NONPAST-CL
				INCOMPLETE	TO-FULL
				INTRANS	COMPLETER
				PROGRESSIVE	THIRD
				AFFIX	POST-VERB
	[phrase]	[to]	[non-finite verb]	[ing-form]	
	[nominal]		[infinitive]	[lexical verb]	
			[be]	[V12/13/17/39]	
	(all the boys)	(to)	(be)	(longing)	

[clause, dependent, wh, non-SUBJECT focus, non-past, non-finite, non-mood selecting, pseudo-interrogative, without SUBJECT, nominal, infinitical, with to, with for, containing no noun-clause, non-perfect, non-progressive

QUESTION	TO	PROCESS
		LEX
	[to]	[non-finite verb]
		[infinitive]
		[lexical verb]
(who)	(to)	(marry)

In order to make it clear that the description strictly speaking includes only the features and the functions, I have bracketed the particular lexical item from our example sentence.

APPENDIX

CLASSES OF VERBS AND ADJECTIVES (see 4.2.15)

I. Adjectives

A1   dangerous, difficult, easy, impossible, possible, safe

A2   bad, good, gratifying, great, hard, interesting, marvellous, nice, pleasant

A3   characteristic, common, essential, indispensable, necessary, normal, typical, usual

A4   exciting, forgivable, odd, regrettable, relevant, significant, tough, tragic

A5   clear, false, obvious, possible, probable, provable, true

A6   certain, likely, sure

A7   bound, meant, supposed

II. Verbs

V1   need, require, want

V2   finish, keep, quit (?)

V3   start, stop

V4   get

V5   begin, cease, commence, continue, recommence, start

V6   come, fail, get, grow, manage, proceed, tend

V7   count, matter, rankle

V8   come (to pass), emerge, eventuate

V9   appear, chance, happen, purport, seem, turn out

V10   bore, cheapen, cheer up, cost, deafen, exhaust, slow down, soothe,
          speed up, sustain, take, tire, wake

V11   alarm, amaze, amuse, anger, annoy, appeal, arouse, astonish, astound,
          attract, awe, baffle, bedevil, befuddle, beguile, bemuse, benefit, be-
          wilder, bolster, boost, bother, calm, charm, cheer, comfort, compli-
          ment, concern, defame, delight, depress, disconcert, discourage, dis-
          grace, discomfort, disgust, dishearten, dishonour, dismay, displease,
          disquiet, dissatisfy, distress, disturb, elate, embarrass, enchant, enrage,
          exasperate, exhilarate, fascinate, fluster, frighten, gall, gladden, grati-
          fy, harm, hearten, help, horrify, humble, humiliate, hurt, insult,
          interest, irritate, madden, mortify, nauseate, nettle, outrage, over-
          awe, overwhelm, pain, please, rankle, relieve, sadden, satisfy, scare,
          shame, sicken, startle, stupefy, suit, surprise, tempt, terrify, torment,
          trouble, unnerve, unsettle, upset, worry

V12   promise

V13   agree, arrange, ask, bear, beg, decide, decree, fear, hope, insist, pray,
          prescribe, promise, propose, stipulate, suggest, wish

V14   command, direct, expect, instruct, order

V15   desire, expect, intend, prefer

V16   advocate, allow, forbid, permit, recommend, schedule

V17   demand, desire, prefer, request, require

V18   hear, see, feel

V19   cause, compel, enable, force, oblige

V20   abhor, admire, avoid, await, bear, cherish, consider, contemplate, countenance, criticize, defend, denounce, deprecate, deride, disavow, discredit, discuss, endorse, endure, enjoy, entail, envisage, eschew, evaluate, examine, forgive, glorify, imagine, justify, miss, neglect, overlook, pardon, postpone, praise, preach, preclude, prefer, prevent, publicize, question, reconsider, relish, repudiate, renounce, resist, ridicule, savour, stand, stop, suggest, survive, try, value, veto, vindicate, visualise, welcome

V21   dislike, dread, hate, like, love, want

V22   deplore, mind, regret, resent

V23   agree, boast, comment, complain, contend, exclaim, explain, hint, hypothesize, intuit, mention, mutter, object, preach, protest, reason, reiterate, remark, reply, say, suggest, teach, testify, theorize, write

V24   allege, announce, assert, assume, believe, certify, claim, conceive, conjecture, consider, decide, declare, deduce, deem, doubt, dream, emphasize, estimate, expect, fancy, feel, figure, guarantee, guess, hold, hope, imagine, imply, indicate, infer, insinuate, insist, intimate, judge, maintain, make out, postulate, predict, presume, proclaim, pronounce, prove, reckon, recollect, report, represent, sense, show, specify, state, submit, suppose, surmise, suspect, swear, think, verify, wager

V25   claim, admit

V26   accept, appreciate, ascertain, confide, disclose, divulge, foresee, gather, learn, neglect, note, own, point out, realise

V27   deny, forget, recall, remember

V28   have

V29   notice, observe, watch

V30   repute, rumour, say, whisper

V31   answer, assure, convince, inform, reassure, show

V32   advise, charge, get, instruct, persuade, prompt, tell, urge, warn

V33   notify, remind, tell

V34   make

V35   help

V36   admonish, appoint, assist, beseech, bestir, bribe, bring, cause, chal-
        lenge, choose, coax, coerce, commission, compel, dare, defy, detail,
        drive, empower, encourage, enjoin, entice, entreat, exhort, force,
        impel, implore, incite, induce, inspire, invite, lead, motivate, pre-
        dispose, stimulate, tempt, train, trouble, trust

V37   let

V38   attempt, condescend, dare, decline, endeavour, forget, hasten, refuse,
        remember, try

V39   ache, aim, aspire, care, consent, dislike, hate, long, lust, plead, strive,
        struggle, thirst, wait, yearn

BIBLIOGRAPHY

Anderson, J. (1969) Adjectives, datives and ergativization. *Foundations of Language* 5, 301–323.

Bazell, C.E. (1962) Meaning and the morpheme. *Word* 18, 132–42.

Catford, J.C. (1965) *A linguistic theory of translation.* London: Oxford University Press.

Chomsky, N. (1957) *Syntactic structures.* The Hague: Mouton.

Chomsky, N. (1967) The formal nature of language. Appendix A in: Lenneberg, E.H., *Biological foundations of language.* New York: Wiley.

Chomsky, N. (1970) Remarks on nominalization. In: Jacobs, R.A. and Rosenbaum, P.S. (eds.), *Readings in English transformational grammar.* London: Ginn.

Dik, S.C. (1968) *Coordination: its implications for the theory of general linguistics.* Amsterdam: North-Holland.

Dixon, R.M.W. (1964) On formal and contextual meaning. *Acta Linguistica Hungarica* XIV, 23–45.

Fillmore, C.J. (1969) The case for case. In: Bach, E. and Harms, R. (eds.), *Universals in linguistic theory.* New York: Holt, Reinhart and Winston.

Greenbaum, S. and Quirk, R. (1970) *Elicitation experiments in English: linguistic studies in use and attitude.* London: Longman.

Halliday, M.A.K. (1961) Categories of the theory of grammar. *Word* 17, 241–92.

Halliday, M.A.K. (1963) Class in relation to the axes of chain and choice in language. *Linguistics* 2, 5–15.

Halliday, M.A.K. (1964) Syntax and the consumer. In: Stuart (ed.), *Monograph Series on Languages and Linguistics, no. 17.* Washington, D.C.: Georgetown Univ. Press.

Halliday, M.A.K. (1966a) Some notes on 'deep' grammar. *Journal of Linguistics* 2, 57–68.

Halliday, M.A.K. (1966b) The concept of rank: a reply. *Journal of Linguistics* 2, 110–8.

Halliday, M.A.K. (1967a) Notes on transitivity and theme in English, Part 1. *Journal of Linguistics* 3, 37–82.

Halliday, M.A.K. (1967b) Notes on transitivity and theme in English, Part 2. *Journal of Linguistics* 3, 199–244.

Halliday, M.A.K. (1968) Notes on transitivity and theme in English, Part 3. *Journal of Linguistics* 4, 179–216.

Halliday, M.A.K. (1969a) Options and functions in the English clause. *Brno Studies in English* 8, 81–88.

Halliday, M.A.K. (1969b) On finiteness and modality in the English verb. Mimeographed.

Halliday, M.A.K. (1971) Clause types and structural function. In: Lyons, J. (ed.), *New horizons in linguistics*. Harmondsworth: Penguin Books.

Halliday, M.A.K., McIntosh, A. and Strevens, P. (1964) *The linguistic sciences and language teaching*. London: Longman.

Hjelmslev, L., translated by F.J.Whitfield (1943/1961) *Prolegomena to a theory of language*. Madison: University of Wisconsin Press.

Hockett, C.F. (1954) Two models of grammatical description. *Word* 10, 210–234.

Hockett, C.F. (1961) Linguistic elements and their relations. *Language* 37, 29–53.

Huddleston, R.D. (1965) Rank and depth. *Language* 41, 574–87.

Huddleston, R.D. (1966) Systemic features and their realisation. University College London: mimeographed.

Huddleston, R.D. (1969) Review of P.S.Rosenbaum, "Predicate complement constructions in English". *Lingua* 23, 241–273.

Huddleston, R.D. (forthcoming) *The sentence in written English: a syntactic study based on an analysis of scientific texts*. London: Cambridge University Press.

Huddleston, R.D., Hudson, R.A., Winter, O.E. and Henrici, A. (1968) *Sentence and clause in scientific English*. University College London: mimeographed.

Huddleston, R.D. and Uren, O. (1969) Declarative, interrogative and imperative in French. *Lingua* 22, 1–26.

Hudson, R.A. (1964) *A grammatical study of Beja*. Unpublished London University Dissertation.

Hudson, R.A. (1967) Constituency in a systemic description of the English clause. *Lingua* 18, 225–250.

Hudson, R.A. (1970) On clauses containing conjoined and plural noun-phrases in English. *Lingua* 24, 205–253.

Kiparsky, P. and Kiparsky, C, (1968) Fact. Mimeographed.

Lamb, S.M. (1964) On alternation, transformation, realisation and stratification. In: Stuart (ed.), *Monograph Series on Languages and Linguistics, no. 17*. Washington, D.C.: Georgetown Univ. Press.

Langendoen, D.T. (1969) *The study of syntax: the generative-transformational approach to the structure of American English*. New York: Holt, Rinehart and Winston.

Leech, G.N. (1966) *English in advertising: a linguistic study of advertising in Great Britain*. London: Longman.

Longacre, R.E. (1964) *Grammar discovery procedures*. The Hague: Mouton.

Lyons, J. (1968) *Introduction to theoretical linguistics*. London: Cambridge University Press.

McCawley, J.D. (1968) Concerning the base component of a transformational grammar. *Foundations of Language* 4, 243–269.

McCawley, J.D. (1969) Tense and time reference in English. Mimeographed.

Matthews, P.H. (1966) The concept of rank in 'Neo-Firthian' grammar. *Journal of Linguistics* 2, 101–109.

Postal, P.M. (1964) *Constituent structure: a study of contemporary models of syntactic description*. The Hague: Mouton.

Postal, P.M. (1969) Review of: A.McIntosh and M.A.K.Halliday, *Patterns of language. Papers in general, descriptive and applied linguistics. Foundations of Language* 5, 409–426.

Robins, R.H. (1959) In defence of WP. *Transactions of the Philological Society*, 116–144. Reprinted in: Robins, R.H. (1970) Diversions of Bloomsbury. Selected writings on linguistics. Amsterdam: North-Holland.

Rosenbaum, P.S. (1967) *The grammar of English predicate complement constructions.* Cambridge, Mass.: M.I.T. Press.

Scott, F.S., Bowley, C.C., Brockett, C.S., Brown, J.G. and Goddard, P.R. (1968) *English grammar: a linguistic study of its classes and structures.* Auckland, N.Z.: Heinemann.

Sinclair, J.McH. (1965) *A course in spoken English. 3: Grammar.* (Prepublication edition). London: Oxford University Press.

Stockwell, R.P., Schachter, P. and Partee, B.H. (1968) *Integration of transformational theories on English syntax.* Los Angeles: U.C.L.A., mimeographed.

GENERAL INDEX

INDEX OF WORDS
(see also the Appendix)

INDEX OF FUNCTIONS

INDEX OF FEATURES